The Chicago Gangster Theory
of Life

V

The Chicago Gangster Theory of Life

Nature's Debt to Society

ANDREW ROSS

VERSO

London · New York

First published by Verso 1994
Paperback edition first published by Verso 1995
Second impression 1996
© Andrew Ross 1994
All rights reserved

Verso
UK: 6 Meard Street, London W1V 3HR
USA: 180 Varick Street, New York, NY 10014-4606

Verso is the imprint of New Left Books

ISBN 0-86091-654-5

British Library Cataloguing in Publication Data
A catalogue record for this book is available from the British Library

Library of Congress Cataloging-in-Publication Data
Ross, Andrew, 1956–
The Chicago gangster theory of life : nature's debt to
society / Andrew Ross.
p.   cm.
Includes bibliographical references and index.
ISBN 0-86091-654-5
1. Environmental policy – Economic aspects.   2. Environmental
policy – Moral and ethical aspects.   I. Title.
HC79.E5R656   1994
333.7 – dc20
94-18514
CIP

Typeset by MHL Typesetting Ltd, Coventry
Printed and bound in Great Britain by
Bookcraft Ltd, Midsomer Norton, Avon

Contents

Acknowledgments

This book is dedicated to the memory and example of Alexander Wilson.

Michael Sprinker was a splendid editor of this manuscript. Mike Davis offered a challenging reading. Colin Robinson was a gracious publisher.

Friends and colleagues were generous to help with and comment on individual chapters: Rosalyn Deutsche, Bill Howarth, Tom Keenan, Philomena Mariani, Dorothy Nelkin, Jeff Nunokawa, Neil Smith, Danny Walkowitz, and Rob Wilson.

Research assistance was provided by the remarkable David Serlin, technical assistance by Alyssa Hepburn and Gina Diaz.

For their hospitality and help in Hawaii, Fiji, and Tahiti, many thanks are due to Wimal Dissayanake, Ed Kamau'oha, Jocelyn Linnekin, Rubina Forrester, Jean-Christophe Bouisson, Sudesh Mishra, Shaista Shameem, Michael Shapiro, and many others at the Polynesian Cultural Center and Brigham Young University in Laie.

For providing the motivation for two of these chapters, my thanks to Kyong Park, Shirin Neshat, and Amerigo Marras, at the Storefront for Art and Architecture.

Some of the material in this book appeared in earlier forms in *Artforum, boundary 2, Social Text*, and *South Atlantic Quarterly*.

Introduction

Why not begin, as ecology has ordained, with a local environment? As a city dweller who does not regard himself as much of a nature-lover, it is important to start with the stores in my neighborhood. Living in Manhattan's SoHo, you quickly become immune to the buzz surrounding the latest fancy amalgam of art, commerce, and fashion to set up shop in the vicinity. For some time now, all new stores are obliged to have some environmentalist component, whether they stock organic products, or whether they harbor an appeal to indigenous ways of life. In SoHo, Gourmet Green is the flavor of every month. It may be body lotion made from babacu palm nut extract, or passionflower massage oil, bio-chic perfumes containing pheromones, shirts with tagua nut buttons, shoes with natural heels, prints from the Andes, seaweed scrub, unbleached cruelty-free garments, petroleum-free lip balm, cotton shower curtains, silk coffee filters, herbal toothpaste, botanical therapy haircare, nontoxic paints and energy-efficient fixtures for the environmental home, CD recordings of future primitive music, opportunities to sponsor a dolphin or a pygmy, or a broad range of foodstuffs from the rainforest harvest gathered by the Amazon rubber tappers.

If Mother Earth shops anywhere, it's here. But she better have good credit — nontoxic things have other ways of burning a hole in your pocket. We now know, however, that the toxic life of most consumer products in the mass market only appears to come cheap. For one thing, their low cost depends upon heavily subsidized energy drawn from nonrenewable resources. As long as the true costs of production are externalized, consumer markets will

1

continue to inflate the price of sustainable commerce while maintaining the depressed cost of the daily poison sold to lower-income consumers. But if socially responsible consumption is to expand beyond gourmet/bohemian markets, for which SoHo is a showpiece, it will require more than the kind of revolution in industrial auditing that takes account of social and environmental costs. Something like the value-driven propaganda campaign of ideas that accompanied the democratization of consumerism in the 1920s will also be necessary. The appeal of this campaign will no longer be to patriotic values — it is the duty of American citizens to consume — as it was in the 1920s. This time, the values will have to appeal to people prepared to see themselves as citizens of the world and as accountable in their daily conduct to fellow citizens in other regions and cultures.

If you believe the advertising campaigns, there would seem to be little resistance to such thinking from the captains of industry. In recent years, the explosion in free-market environmentalism has adopted such appeals as its chief publicity vehicle, with every major corporation transforming its image overnight into that of a gentle green giant, respectfully paying lipservice to the CERES principles of sustainable business (forged after *Exxon Valdez*). However, the effect of this 'greenwashing' is that consumers are barely encouraged to investigate their preferences; they simply become world citizens by proxy if they buy products from a company advertising itself either as a responsible business citizen, or, in the case of pioneer companies like Benetton and Body Shop, as a commercial version of the UN.[1] This is not to say that ecological concerns have not had a significant impact — beyond the realm of public relations — on a broad spectrum of industrial and commercial activity. For example, the boom in environmental services and waste management is one of the largest growth areas within the postindustrial economy. It is not only possible that portions of the Cold War arms treasury will increasingly be converted into cleanup operations, but also likely that a paramilitary environmental-industrial complex with new ties to some transnational security bloc of states will emerge from the primitive military-industrial complex of the Cold War era.

Some would argue that the World Bank already functions in developing countries in ways that facilitate such developments, especially through its green fund, the Global Environmental

Facility, which has proven more powerful as a global policing mechanism (i.e. medium of deregulation) than the UN's Sustainable Development Commission. Indeed, the New World Order imagined on behalf of liberal capitalist societies in the wake of the Cold War has adopted environmentalism as one of its new diplomatic agendas, along with human rights, especially favored as the rationale for the new kinds of UN-sponsored military interventions in the Third World. On the economic front, the Rio accords of 1991 set the official seal of the World Commission on Environment and Development on plans for a global environmental market. Global capitalism is officially supposed to be proceeding under the rubric of 'sustainable development,' a phrase (or a contradiction in terms) that has become the corporate mantra of the 1990s.[2]

In the USA, the local equivalent — a trading market that allows companies that pollute below certain levels to sell pollution credits to dirtier companies — has been legislated under the Clean Air Act of 1990. This introduction of a new property right (the right to pollute, which, like all liberal rights, can be threatened or damaged) is surely one of the most bizarre outcomes of the new antiregulatory thinking, further reinforced by the Progressive Policy Institute's (think-tank of the Democratic Leadership Council) blueprint for the Clinton administration, *Mandate for Change*. A neo-liberal program to make the market work to regulate the market, this document contained a chapter, called 'Greening the Market,' which argued against 'command-and-control regulation' and in favor of introducing market mechanisms into all facets of environmental policy.[3]

Without hastening on their own collapse, capitalism and its liberal political institutions appear to have achieved a leveraged buyout of environmentalism by incorporating significant facets of ecological thought and practice. Environmental concerns have not only come to be represented by a permanent department of corporate operations (almost every large company has its own environmental manager, along with a string of scientists, lawyers and MBAs specializing in environmental areas); they have also became a *condition* for economic growth in certain sectors (in the burgeoning environmental industries), and a persuasive ideology for penetrating unsaturated markets in what Lawrence Summers, the World Bank's chief economist, infamously referred to in a 1991 memorandum as the 'underpolluted' Third World. It remains to be seen whether free-market environmentalism will function in a kind of homeopathic manner, eventually rendering capitalism immune to even the most radical challenges of the ecology movement, and transforming environmentalism into business as usual, or whether it is simply a desperate way of deferring a final series of apocalyptic encounters with a steadily deteriorating natural world in which capitalism limits its own growth by destroying its conditions of production through environmental collapse.[4] What is clear, however, is the increasing split in the ecology movement between those proponents of organizations who firmly support the developments in corporate environmentalism, who blessed the Rio accords and NAFTA, and who have one foot in the door of White House and World Bank policymaking, and those others who have resisted capitulating to the savage compromises demanded as part of the process of empowering environmentalism's ideas.[5] In Germany, the Greens have long been riven by such divisions, now manifestly apparent, and deepening by the day, among the large North American organizations and in the other international NGOs increasingly active within the UN.

Those who continue to think of ecology as a preserve of left-liberal thought and action have been dismayed by these developments. And yet, for the best part of a century before the ecology movement flowered in the early 1970s, it had been generally right-wing, including among its several tendencies fascist groups and movements, who fervently espoused ideas about the conservation of nature, biological holism, nutritional purity, rural simplicity, energy efficiency, scarcity economics, strong regulation of industry, and small-scale living, to name only a few of the agendas associated today with environmentalism. Such movements flourished among Northern European and North American groups (John Birchers, for example) troubled by incipient Aryanism.[6] The history of ideas about nature, and the relationship of human cultures to nature, is so extensive that it would be naive to think that any political tendency could claim ecology for its own, even temporarily. The recent development of corporate environmentalism is proof, if any were needed, that nature is the ultimate people-pleaser, whose name can even be lent to and honored by causes associated with its destruction.

In addition, it would be misleading to suggest that the divisions among environmentalists have developed only as a result of the mercurial rise of free-market environmentalism. Almost since its inception, with Earth Day in 1970, the modern ecology movement has been home to schools and factions quite antagonistic to each other. Except for the name of 'ecology' itself, virtually nothing unites the bioregionalists, Gaians, eco-feminists, eco-Marxists, biocentricists, eco-anarchists, deep ecologists and social ecologists who pursue their ideas and actions in its name.[7] The yawning gulf between eco-humanism and biospheric egalitarianism, for example, is quite broad enough to compass without describing each tributary rift and fissure. It is fair to say that no social movement has had such discordant voices within its ranks, and, one might add, for such good reasons. All the more difficult, then, to reconcile the dominant media image of 'environmentalists' as univocal in their advocacy of this or that course of action. Even within educated public opinion, there is a tendency to accept this image of singular identity on behalf of environmentalism and to ignore the differences that exist between, say, ecologists whose priority is social justice, and those whose priority is to preserve wilderness. The consequences of overlooking these differences are potentially dire, especially in an age that is hosting such a wholesale revival of appeals to the authority of nature and biology. As the language of environmentalism becomes a language of power, if not government itself, nature's laws are invoked once again as the ground of judgment and the basis of policy. Arguments taken from natural science are employed to lend substance to social and cultural policies. Descriptions of the physical world become prescriptions for our daily lives.

The arguments pursued in this book warn against the tendency, surfacing again, and often in the name of environmentalism, to wield biological authority as a model for social well-being. In short, we may soon be engaged yet again in the struggle to prevent nature becoming the referee of our fate. But before I lay out some of these arguments, no doubt with the false clarity that introductions of this sort demand, let me return to the messy field of examples, where things acquire sense, not from logical expectancy, but from the way you walk around them, pick them up, see them from different angles, at odd times of the day, and in varied company.

In one of the fierce heatwaves of the summer of 1993, a new SoHo store opened, next to the First People's Gallery (which represents indigenous artists from the Northwest of the USA and Canada). The store is called 'Evolution' (subtitled 'Natural History in SoHo'), and it sells an assortment of animal skulls and bones, fossils, butterflies, insects in amber, polished minerals, coral, and richly colored sea shells. Here, skulls of lions, hartebeest, skunks, warthogs, husky dogs, water buffalo, coyote, and alligators adorn the walls and fill display cabinets and jars alongside python ribs, shark jaws, squirrel monkey skeletons, ostrich eggs, dinosaur teeth, impala horns, and snapping turtle shells. Interspersed with the animal remains are human skulls and bones — feet, toes, clavicles, femurs, pelvis, fingers and ribs. It wasn't the first store in town with such potentially macabre offerings. 'Maxilla and Mandible,' uptown, near the American Museum of Natural History, has a larger collection that emulates both the museum's system of classification and categorization and its antique decor. A smaller store for offbeat collectors in Little Italy caters more to the well-heeled sicko. The SoHo store took its place on gourmet row, within hailing distance of eco-emporia like Origins, Greenlife, Terra Verde, The Nature Company, and After the Rain, and multipur-pose New Age spaces like the Open Center.

In 'Evolution', nonnatural history had been bleached as clean as the bones, even though, for me at least, random, Poesque resonances still played around their polished, white edges: Jeffrey Dahmer, Deacon Brodie, Emperor Bokassa, Auschwitz, Hannibal Lecter, Michael Jackson's Elephant Man, and Einstein's brain pickled in a jar. The result was high-end kitsch, where the patina of science is presented without apologies, and where, in this case, simple leftovers from life can be taken for art. (By contrast, death kitsch of the sort worn by goths and death-metal fans forsakes the banality of the body to honor the gruesome.) The skulls in this store were not exactly reminders of human mortality, nor were they being sold like religious relics, imbued with the spirit of their former owners. Rather, what this display demonstrated was: (a) the comprehensive levelling of all species hierarchy (something only evolutionary science has been capable of suggesting); and (b) the restoration of hierarchy through aesthetics, whereby the remains of certain charismatic fauna are elevated above others as commodity furniture items (who would prefer the skull of a rabbit to the skull of a hippopotamus?). In this, you could say that the display acknowledged the antihumanist philosophy of modern environmen-talism while recognizing those media tactics whereby public sympathy for endangered species can be mustered according to a celebrity scale of size: the gnat-catcher, the snail darter, the spotted owl, the panda, the African elephant, the dolphin, the whale.

Humans rank low on that scale. As a homeless person once

remarked to a friend of mine, the city authorities would pay more attention to him when he was dead, when they would be obliged at last to find a resting place for him, or his bones at least. In apocalyptic times, however, the disturbance of human bones is the ultimate revelation of unnatural violence. When a disruption of weather patterns produced the epic Mississippi flood of 1993, the most scandalous (and biblical) media coverage was of a cemetery in Hardin, Missouri being washed away by the floodwaters. One of the biggest rescue efforts (to the tune of half a million dollars) was launched, mostly in vain, to retrieve the bones and skulls of the pioneer settlers that had been carried off downstream. Verily the earth did open, and the dead, as it were, came forth from the grave. In this case, the event came to signify the impermanence of human life on the land: one day, no traces will be left. The bones of ancients − Pleistocene Man, the pharaohs, indigenous peoples − have long been attributed an exalted power to denote the endurance of settlement − while the bones of persecuted groups, like Jews and African-Americans, speak of particular histories of dispossession. Dinosaur bones, traditionally, have been our reminder of species extinction. At a time when environmentalism has raised apocalyptic fears about the extinction of all species to new levels, ancestral bones have taken on a significance not tapped by traditional religious cults of human remains. Yet while ecocentric ethicists have famously posed the question 'Do trees or rocks have rights?,' few have sought to assess the rights of bones.[8] Humans, it is often assumed, exercise more than enough anthropocentric arrogance while living. Why extend their privileges into the afterlife? And yet some bones are useful to environmentalists for their instrumental value − burial sites, loosely protected under environmental law, sometimes stave off the developer's bulldozer (in horror movies, the vengeance of disturbed bones is even more spectacular). The ancestral bones of an indigenous people command especial significance. Part of the cultural identity of the indigenous group, community or tribe is bound up with the bones, and is seen to be violated if the bones are disrespected. Indigenous groups whose histories and geographies have been forcibly displaced insist that they are restoring part of their identity by repatriating ancestral bones from museums and universities.

Whether bones have rights or not, most people do worry about their treatment. The most commonly asked questions at the

'Evolution' store relate to whether the bones on sale have been acquired *ethically* (only weirdos want to do business with grave robbers). That human bones, in particular, are on sale, may give an extra frisson to the questioning, but consumers are eco-hip enough to know that they aren't supposed to discriminate among the species, at least not in public. Indeed, consumers in other eco-oriented stores, and increasingly in supermarkets, might be found asking similar questions about the origin, composition, manufacture, and biodegradability of certain products. The more certifiably 'natural' the process and the components, the more valuable a product will be. The irony of this principle should not escape us. Nature, which was once assigned the lowest possible value in the account books of industrialization, is now fetching the highest market prices. Once the source simply of raw materials to be extracted and transformed into commodities, nature is now a valuable origin of exchange value in its own right. In the age of environmental accounting, nature enters the market not just as source of property or mineral value, nor just for its capacity to sustain its soil, water, and air, but also for its own sake, as a desirable signifier with inherent worth and value to consumer markets.

Some proclaim that the only way to save components of the natural world is to assign them a properly high market value, and to enter environmental costs into every form of accounting, from debt-for-nature swaps to pollution credits. Others insist that nature should be beyond the pricing life of markets. This is not simply a debate about wilderness areas, rainforests, or wetlands. It relates, for example, to the commercial encroachment on the human body and to the industrialization of biological processes that forms the basis of biotechnology and genetic medicine. The debate also has a special bearing upon the future of indigenous peoples and Third World cultures that have survived outside, or on the outer margins, of the world economic system. Indeed, one of the origins of the movement in socially responsible business lies in the trading agreements made with rainforest people in the Amazon region in the late 1980s. Initiated by Cultural Survival to cut out intermediaries, rainforest marketing was intended to help local people deal with the modern world as equals. The project brought together tappers, miners and natives in a commercial version of the rainforest alliances for social justice that had been forged in the wake of Chico

Mendes's murder. As co-habitants of the Amazon who had long been antagonistic to each other, the Indians and petty extractors were now seeking common control over the use of their home in the face of vicious exploitation by local ranching and logging elites. Selling their own products directly was an alternative both to the nature preserves created by land-for-debt swaps (and governed by North American conceptions of uninhabited 'wilderness') and to the appropriation of tribal knowledge by the big pharmaceutical companies.[9] Critics of this commercial practice contend that the logic of the market will transform the social relations and destroy the cultural identity of the native peoples. Above all else, their tribal identity should be protected against the depredations of capitalist logic.[10] Without doubt, the protectionist view, which has its native supporters nonetheless, is influenced by centuries of romantic fantasy about the 'virgin' rainforest populated by innocent peoples living in a state of nature. Yet nothing in the supposedly primal rainforest has not been touched by the extensive native use of fire for sustainable agriculture over the centuries. The result is a region, hardly Edenic, and an ecosystem that have been comprehensively reshaped by peoples who have no timeless identities but who have dynamic social histories of their own.

At the risk of generalizing from the specific example of the Amazon, the difference between sustainable harvesting for a market and subsistence agriculture for local needs may be of more symbolic importance to First World romantics than of material significance to native peoples threatened with eviction, poverty and extinction. One need only consider the vast proportion of time and energy devoted by First World environmentalists to native issues in the Third and Fourth World (but only after destruction of the rainforests came to be seen as a threat to the global ecology) as compared to the attention focused upon the environmental racism practised upon targeted populations of color in the West to gauge the powerful sway of neoromanticism over the ecology movement.

Most Fourth World and Third World peoples have highly adaptive social and cultural economies, some of them long used to commercial encounters, even with nonlocal economic systems. So, too, have modernizing elements of Western culture long been used selectively and syncretically for internal ends by both elite and subaltern groups in indigenous societies, sometimes to mount political dissent, sometimes to reinforce communal identity. On the other hand, the cultural survival of indigenous peoples often depends directly upon certain environmental rights enjoyed in traditional habitation of a region. As Ted Benton puts it, 'bereft of access to the conditions of life which sustained them bodily and culturally, the victims of lost environmental rights are prey to catastrophic loss of identity, and to addiction, disease, humiliation and rampant exploitation.'[11] Modernity's tradition of universalized rights, which played such a liberatory role in breaking the parochial hold of feudal communitarianism in early modern Europe, has different, often deleterious, practical effects today upon indigenous populations in Third World countries, and even in the First World. Such considerations go beyond the romantic impulses harbored by First World environmentalists for whom the condition of the 'noble savage' is more a reflection of their own comfortable anxieties about modernity, just as it was in Rousseau's day, than an acknowledgment of the practical choices available to the vast and differentiated spectrum of native peoples in a local–global economy. For such environmentalists, indigenous peoples are often asked to play a role akin to that of charismatic megafauna in the realm of animal rights. Consequently, according specific rights often results in the 'living museums' of nature preserves or the ghettoizing of indigenous reservations that prevent native peoples from engaging modernity as equals. On the other hand, indigenous land claims often appeal to a communal land ethic that is a radical challenge to the individual property ownership system of liberal societies. It would seem, then, that the environmental case for indigenous peoples demands the attention of a discourse of specific rights *in addition* to a discourse of universal rights that guarantees equal autonomy. This is surely one of the lessons of postmodernist thinking that is willing to acknowledge and accommodate the continuance of premodern, customary conceptions of the land.

Does this mean then that the environmental rights of, say, migrant farmworkers, or urban ghetto, barrio, and rural poor in the West are qualitatively less important than those of rainforest people? You don't need to mystify organic village life to recognize that habitats and environments, even the high-density built environments of the city, are an intrinsic component of people's identity. Deterioration of, or dislocation from, such environments can also have catastrophic effects on communities whose sense of coherence is linked to places. Modernity has shortened the average community memory of environments, but it has not entirely transformed us into abstract, rootless individuals. Indeed, most environmental struggles today draw their support from people's willingness to be seen, often for the first time, as members of a particular community threatened by this or that toxic imposition upon their health or well being. The social impetus that generates those forms of support goes much deeper than is suggested by the term 'affinity politics' — penned to describe coalitions formed among an otherwise heterogenous group for a specific, and commonly shared, purpose. What distinguishes such collective impulses from more traditional forms of communitarianism is the leeway to reject 'the community's position' on other issues; supporting opposition to a toxic waste storage depot, on the one hand, for example, and rejecting opposition to an AIDS day care center on the other. Of course, the consequences of this — NIMBYism — are often just as injurious. The toxic waste is sited elsewhere, in a community that is less organized, has less political clout, or is so poor that it needs the blood money: in North America, one need only think of 'sacrifice zones' like Louisiana's 'Cancer Alley,' Navajo lands, or the *maquiladora* border belt.[12]

Advocates of bioregionalism suggest an alternative form of communitarianism geared to the biophysical economy of a geographically bounded region.[13] According to this philosophy, the social life of autonomous communities would be determined by local 'laws' of nature. Everyone would be living within the means of the region, and would be unable to exact an unequal toll upon resources elsewhere. The limits of social and political freedom would be set by the finite limits of the natural economy in the region. In enshrining the principles of small-scale economies, decentralization, and face-to-face democracy of eco-anarchist thinking, bioregionalism looks back to a low-density, rural-tribal past when communities 'coincided' geographically with bioregions defined by watersheds, or microclimates, or biomes. Despite their commitment to ideals of participatory democracy, bioregionalists have been unable to convince many that they will improve upon the repressive history of most autonomous communities, often characterized by the persecution of minorities unprotected by federal statutes, and by parochial hostility to outsiders. Above all, bioregionalism embodies, as a political and cultural policy, fundamentalist strains of biological determinism that run unevenly throughout mainstream environmentalist thought. These strains have an ancient resonance in metaphors comparing social systems to biological or natural forms of organization. The belief that society ought to conform to nature is nothing new. With the rise of modern environmentalism this belief has taken on a new cogency. The model of nature's way, held at bay for much of this century, has been revived with much gusto and quasi-religious fervor in recent years. For some, this revival is welcomed as a counterblast to the destructive arrogance of humanism; for others, the much greater danger is that the authority of nature, and hence of the status quo, will become a despotic vehicle for curtailing rights and liberties.

This book was written with the aim of sorting out some of the arguments on both sides, although, as will quickly become evident, it leans towards the latter. Indeed, one of its origins lay in the perception that environmentalist discourse about scarcity and limitation in the natural world was beginning to reinforce, if not translate into, calls for a reduction in rights and freedoms in our civil society. Over the last two decades in the West, there has been steady right-wing pressure to scale down liberties of the sort that were created on the back of the postwar consumer boom, and that generated a crisis in the authority of the state at the end of the 1960s. The dominant message is 'Expect less,' whether to enforce a Franklinesque frugality or to dampen the passion for public affluence. To cite a single, but symptomatic, example, here is Shelby Steele, African-American neoconservative, explaining in a typically Malthusian way how resource scarcity is structurally at odds with the movement towards minority empowerment through state action:

> In a society of increasingly limited resources, there will never be enough programs to meet the need . . . we black Americans will never be saved or even assisted terribly much by others . . . There will be no end to despair and no lasting solution to any of our problems until we rely on individual effort within the American mainstream — rather than collective action against the mainstream — as our means of advancement.[14]

The rise of modern environmentalism has coincided with the backlash bandwagon that Steele and others are riding, and has reinforced, consciously or not, the coercive spirit of the campaign for supervoluntarism. At other times, the link is more overt; in many parts of the world, for example, women's reproductive choices are coercively restricted in the name of curbing the global population crisis. Many classic environmental writers and theorists have supported the perception that, just as there are limits to economic growth in a material world, there are also limits to the rights and liberties associated with the growth and material abundance that characterize Western consumerism.[15] Reckless squandering of the world's resources is easily equated with a surfeit of freedoms in our dominant cultures. A price has to be paid, a sacrifice made. Living within our means, this narrative goes, requires a drastic lowering, not only of our material expectations, but also of the culture of social growth that has accompanied the rise of materialism in the West and elsewhere. A libertarian culture aimed at a postscarcity world is now perceived by the majority of environmentalists to be hopelessly utopian, impractical, perhaps pernicious. In some neopuritan quarters, it is even seen as a primary cause of the ecological crisis. Asceticism, self-denial and guilt are the order of the day.[16]

These are widely shared sentiments — to our great detriment, as I shall argue. They have entered public opinion variously, but not least through the evangelical spirit that is the apocalyptic house style of so much environmental writing. In so doing, they have provided some fuel for the austerity economics and the austerity culture that has become the operating principle of global capitalism. As I argue in Chapter 2, this austerity climate emerged out of manufactured fiscal crises like that of New York City in 1975 as capital's solution to setting limits to liberal welfare economics, and was subsequently taken up as national policy and by the World Bank as a way of controlling the world debt economy. Contemporaneous with this development was the rise of an environmentalist discourse of limits, in economics and population ecology with the 1972 Club of Rome report *Limits to Growth*, and in more philosophical (including sociobiological) quarters with appeals to the environmental determinism of limits in nature. Perhaps the quintessential example of globalization is the Gaia hypothesis, the advocates of which hold that the ecosystemic operations of Earth as a single planetary organism constitute the ultimate realm of judgment in all matters biological. Far beyond the appeal of humans, Gaia is nonetheless numbering our fate in its balance of accounts.[17] The allure of Gaian thinking, at this point in time, is plain to see. It is a scientific philosophy that offers a premodern paradigm of unity-in-nature that is the exact inverse of liberal humanism, possessive individualism, and mechanistic science. It also represents the ultimate ethical extension of rights to the whole Earth. But conferring rights upon nonhuman subjects and objects is one thing — about which there is a long and informed debate, rooted in the tradition of natural rights, and its extensions. Ceding authority to the voice of the planet is another. There are too many ventriloquists around who will speak in its name for us to feel entirely comfortable with that. Gaians represent very well the tendency that would sacrifice human and social judgments at the altar of some higher, superbiological entity.

Gaia notwithstanding, it would be naive to ignore that the rise of the modern environmentalist movement has been concurrent with the globalization of the economy; both have shared the common discourse of transnational interests. The planetary concerns of ecologists were pursued at the same time as capital's move to break free of the labor-friendly constraints of national Fordism and enter into GATT's capital-friendly global phase of operations. Consequently, the national ideology of affluence, mobilized to create the vast white American middle class of the postwar period in the image of a 'people of plenty,' has been replaced by an austerity regime more endemic to the persistently disenfranchised and impoverished sectors of the population. This class, maligned by ecologists and statisticians the world over for its infamously wasteful style of living, has dwindled under the new dual economy of gourmet store and discount chain classes. As part of capitalist restructuring, this middle class, and cognate strata in other countries, have been disciplined by the politics of scarcity, budgetary constraint, and other austerity policies rationalized by reference to a monstrous national debt.

When the environmentally minded talk about living within our resource budget, when they accept scarcity as a default condition, and when they argue that we have already consumed or physically ruined the future, they are speaking a language strikingly similar to that used to describe the global debt economy. This is one of the reasons that free-market environmentalism has had such a smooth lift-off. By this I do not mean to suggest that environmentalism is an ideological product of the postindustrial capitalist economy. In its radical forms, on the contrary, it is one of the most powerful challenges to fundamental principles of capitalist exploitation. Ideas do not emerge out of a social vacuum, however, and the language employed to present them is the language of the moment, defined as functional by the most dominant economic interests.

Environmentalists are often oblivious to such social milieux in presuming that the biological ethics governing their ideas and prescriptions are governed by (higher) natural, and not social, laws. To the contrary, ideas that draw upon the authority of nature nearly always have their origin in ideas about society. If this book's arguments had to be summed up in one sentence, that would be it. But there is still a great deal of cultural work and persuasion to be done before such an aphorism becomes common sense. Environmentalists need to be convinced that their arguments do not exist outside of the sphere of ideologies that governs our social reality; the way that we think about the natural world has more to do with our social world than anything else. The ecologically impaired need to be persuaded that ecology can be sexy, and not self-denying. Culturalists and social constructionists who believe that the nature/ nurture wars are over need to be persuaded to think again — biologism and social Darwinism have returned with a vengeance, and are a driving force behind the sweeping new world view engineered by biotechnology and genetic medicine. And social philosophers of all stripes need to be prepared to ask why the idea of 'human nature' so doggedly persists in popular consciousness.

Accordingly, this book is a contribution to a long political struggle to which ecology has added a new dimension — the history of strong opposition to those who view social patterns as either rooted in nature or else explained and justified by nature. We are in dialogue with the natural world, it is not our supreme court. There are no 'laws' in nature, only in society, because 'laws' are made only by us and can therefore only be changed by us. Nature, in short, does not always know best. And with the exception of those tiny pockets of wildness that have not been made over by humans, what we know about nature is what we know and think about our own cultures. Those who say otherwise are either living in a very old dream of science, or are desperate enough to want some unanswerable authority in control of their, and our, lives. This is not to deny for one second that natural processes exist, or that they are urgently threatened by the impact of our economic and political institutions. The ecological crisis is real enough; eco-collapse looms at every point on the spectrum from biota loss to freshwater contamination to climatic change. Precisely because this is so, an ecologically sane future will not be achieved without some form of revolution in social and economic justice. More democratic forms of economic life are needed if individual participation in ecologically sound activities is not simply to be dismissed, as it often is by social and socialist ecologists, as voluntarism.

In this respect, we cannot afford to go on acknowledging scarcity and abundance as ultimate criteria of social value. Scarcity is a political tool, skillfully manipulated by the powerful whenever it suits their purpose. It is not a natural condition, as the dismal science of economics has long declared. Contrary to popular belief, capitalism's primary effect is not to create wealth; it creates scarcity, first and foremost. The period, far from over, in which the West pillaged the world's resources, was not a temporary respite from some natural condition of scarcity; it was a period that established and defined scarcity as a condition and effect of unequal social organization, maldistribution, and political injustice. These conditions still exist, and in the case of the worsening North–South imbalance, are more injurious than ever to the social and physical world. You do not have to romanticize tribal life to recognize that basic survival needs — food, water, warmth, and adequate clothing — in many debt-stricken Third World countries are threatened daily in ways that were not apparent in precolonial times. The structural poverty and hunger that has accompanied postcolonial underdevelopment and monocultural farming is not the result of natural scarcity, not at a time when the world's food production is still above the levels for supporting its population.[18] An ecological society, therefore, lies beyond scarcity simply because scarcity ought to be understood as a structural component of unequal development or underdevelopment. Such a society, among other things, is one in which scarcity and abundance no longer make sense. This is why it is still possible, indeed crucial, to speak of postscarcity societies as an ecological goal.

In Judeo-Christian ethics, scarcity, voluntary poverty, and asceticism are prized as virtues. Unquestionably, this tradition has reinforced a fierce evangelical tendency among environmentalists to cast us all as ecological sinners in a fallen world. Even by the standards of material, as opposed to religious, culture, it is no easy task to gauge the empirical evidence for scarcity and abundance. Eighteenth-century European voyagers to the South Seas interpreted the presence of portly islanders as proof of their discovery of an abundant prescarcity society. Today, in the consumerist West, thinness is the sign of abundance, a luxury reserved for the wealthy and powerful; to be overweight is often a sign of poverty.

In liberal, postindustrial societies characterized by patterns of overconsumption and an investment system based on exploitation and production for profit, the argument for scarcity-induced sacrifices often extends, as I earlier described, to the sphere of rights and freedoms. This call for a cutback comes from the left as well as the right: as David Pepper warns us, green socialism, which he advocates, will be 'less prone to totalitarianism than some previous "socialisms," though it will still entail sacrifice of some extant liberal "freedoms" . . . but this may be no bad thing.'[19] Pepper speaks from a socialist tradition that is rightly suspicious of the possessive individualism of the liberal rights tradition. Despite the emancipatory achievements of the bourgeois tradition of universal rights, whose utility was recognized if not condoned by Marx and others, clearly these rights are abstract, and are thus enjoyed by those with the most power to exercise them. Rights and freedoms have to be more fully grounded in conditions of communal and environmental well-being and must be tied to a system of distributive justice in order to be fully shared by all. This state of affairs is not necessarily incompatible with the role of central government that is so shunned by many anarchist-oriented environmentalist groups. More than any other agent, it is the state that has the power to dismantle and reformat the military, economic, and political institutions that stand in the way of social and environmental justice. Besides, the nation state is not what it was; these days, when it acts in its own interest, it can even be a bulwark against the tendencies of global corporations.

On the other hand, the state can still serve as an efficient medium for repressively shaping the moral and cultural climate. In recent years, we have seen the long chill of austerity settle over the region, establishing an air of cultural prohibition that is reinforced daily in a thousand ways by this or that regulatory 'just say no' bulletin. As capital goes through its latest cycle of binge and purge, scarcity, eco-style, has become one of the new discourses of regulation, directed with the force of religious guilt at the level of the individual conscience. The result is an acquittal, on the one hand, of corporate responsibility, and an evasion, on the other, of the hedonism that environmentalist politics so desperately needs for it to be populist and libertarian.

17

Those who wish to distance environmentalism from the radical disposition of the other new social movements often proclaim that its concerns are essentially conservative, and that it is the future-oriented tendencies of free-market libertarianism that are most destructive of the natural world. This emphasis has helped to define ecology's popular character as antiprogressive and antilibertarian.[20] So, too, the extensive interest in traditional nature philosophy, traditional models of kinship, and traditional technologies has reinforced this image of environmentalism's antimodernist world view. The social price of this kind of ecological philosophy may be too high to pay if it involves such inbuilt prejudices against modernity. Australian environmental historian John Young, for example, who dismisses the romantic espousal of preindustrial ideologies and technologies, and acknowledges the need for a culturally appropriate belief system that will define our ecological obligations, argues nonetheless for a renewed faith in kinship of the sort that has guaranteed responsible attitudes towards the environ-ment in the past: we may need, he writes, 'to reevaluate the importance of the family, with its obligations to particular children and particular parents, as likely to provide a more compelling rationale for good environmental management than individualism tempered by an abstract notion of intergenerational responsibi-lity.'[21] Such appeals to traditional family values and patriarchal orders of kinship leave little room for those who believe that a prerequisite for natural diversity is a large measure of social and cultural diversity of the sort that is generally unavailable in a society dominated by traditional family structures. As the mainstream environmental organizations cosy up to the dominant corporate life forms (many such organizations now depend directly upon corpor-ate funding to survive), the struggle to retain ecology as a radical forum for environmental justice will only sharpen and intensify.

Notwithstanding the level at which I have thus far pitched the argument, this book is not a theoretical tract. It is a series of what would probably be called cultural studies in the broad sense. My aim is to show what happens when ideas about nature are put into practice. But those ideas do not only derive from legitimate science, they are also ideas about nature as often understood in popular consciousness — a mixter-maxter of TV nature shows, tabloid superstition, journalistic science reporting, vestigial folk culture, Arcadian romance, weekend hobbyist pantheism, and what-have-you. Each chapter focuses on a set of public, political events, and assembles an analysis that highlights specific ecological issues and questions. The first chapter to be written was a response to the Gulf War of 1991. That war was the first explicitly ecological war, when ecological questions were never far from the forefront of public opinion, from control over oil resources to assessments of the environmental damage caused by military actions. It was also a war of images in which the role of media was hotly debated. What was the relationship between these images and the toll of actual, and potential, destruction that accumulated during and after the war? Did it make any sense to speak about an 'ecology of images' of the sort that was loosely attributed to the role of media in that war?

The bombs that fell on Baghdad and Basra in 1991 led me to write subsequent chapters which examine how ecological arguments drawn from the natural world fare in the world of social and cultural affairs. Those chapters took me all the way to Polynesia, the historical home of ecological romanticism, and back again to New York City, to ponder the bomb that damaged the World Trade Center in 1993. In between was the bombing of Kaho'olawe in Hawaii, and Mururoa in French Polynesia, and Bravo 20 in Nevada, and the mounting collateral damage of the New World Order everywhere. The ravages of militarism are all too apparent in these, some of the most arrogant spectacles of ecological destruction in our time.

The bulk of this book, however, is about less visible forms of damage, because it takes seriously the argument that ideas, even metaphors, have an active, constituent impact upon our environments. How we organize our societies, under the aegis of what kinds of intellectual authority, are crucial ecological matters. Science has increasingly provided that intellectual authority and has helped us diagnose the condition we understand today as the ecological crisis. But science alone cannot provide a coherent and livable philosophy that will explain our social and ecological obligations. Often it is a source of misunderstanding, especially when its accounts of natural life are adopted as a model for social life. Take my title, *The Chicago Gangster Theory of Life*, which is most fully explained in my last chapter. It derives from sociobiologist Stephen Dawkins' book, *The Selfish Gene*, in which he compares the human gene to a 'successful Chicago gangster.' This is the kind of metaphor, typical of sociobiology in general, that projects assumptions about nature back and forth between biology and society in a vicious rhetorical circle. Among other things, what it proposes, in ways that bolster social Darwinism, is that competitiveness in human societies has some kind of natural basis in the genetic structure of life. This is the latest scientific version of the Malthusian theory about competition over scarce resources that has bequeathed such a dismal legacy to evolutionary biology and other powerful sectors of ecological consciousness. Employing much the same principle, anarchists, communitarians, and social democrats have long argued that cooperation, and not competition, is the key tendency of all natural life. Kropotkin's *Mutual Aid*, written after his travels in Northern Asia had shown him examples of cooperation and sociability among animals, is the classic text in this tradition:

> Happily enough, competition is not the rule either in the animal world or in mankind. It is limited among animals to exceptional periods, and natural selection finds better fields for its activity. Better conditions are created by the *elimination of competition* by means of mutual aid and mutual support . . . 'Don't compete — competition is always injurious to the species and you have plenty of resources to avoid it.' That is the *tendency* of nature, not always realized in full, but always present. That is the watchword which comes to us from the bush, the forest, the river, the ocean . . . That is what Nature teaches us.[22]

The Marxist tradition has its own equivalent of this thesis. It proposes 'conflict' as the motor of social progress *because* the dialectic of nature rests upon contending forces.

Competition, cooperation, or conflict — take your pick. Nature can be politically reassuring for anyone who wants it to be. We have known that for a long time. The challenge of ecology in the years ahead is to encourage forms of social thought and action that do not mistake wisdom *about* nature for the wisdom *of* nature.

1

Cultural Preservation in the
Polynesia of the Latter-Day
Saints

Jetlag and cultural studies had placed me in a resort hotel on Fiji's Coral Coast, not far from the verdant Sigatoka Valley, the 'salad bowl' of Viti Levu. That evening in the hotel, which catered to regular Pacific vacationers and to world travellers (backpackers) alike, the big event was a Christmas party (1992), thrown both for the foreign guests and for the staff of this and neighboring hotels. After some ceremonial *kava*-drinking (*yaqona* in Fiji) that was highly convivial and not presented as a spectacle for tourist consumption, the workers were treated to a sumptuous dinner and then joined the guests and other locals for a cabaret-style entertainment entitled 'We Are The World,' performed by ethnic Fijian staff at the hotel. Humorous skits included Japanese, Australian, English, and French tourist stereotypes greeting each other according to their own national-ethnic mode. The main part of the show featured lipsynching impersonations of the rock and pop stars who had contributed to the anthem of 'We Are The World' and who had appeared in its music video version: Stevie Wonder, Michael Jackson, Bruce Springsteen, Huey Lewis, Tina Turner, Bob Dylan, Cindi Lauper, Ray Charles, Whitney Houston, and Kenny Rogers. The Fijian Ray Charles was outstanding.

Perched on a stool at the bar, I fell into conversation with the jolly Australian owner of the hotel, who tried hard to convince me that none of the performers had seen any video images of the stars they were mimicking so competently. As the Fijian Dylan took to the stage to deliver the least accomplished of the evening's performances, my white host cracked some jokes about the novel spectacle of this 'black Bob,' and, on learning that I lived in the USA, launched into an equally offensive account of his one trip to California — the punchline of the story being his attempt to pronounce Yosemite as 'Yo Semite.' Once the stage show was over, the evening divided into three different spectacles. In the entertainment space, a guitar trio informally led the Fijian workers through a long medley of traditional songs, observed by only a few tourists, mostly from the hippy world traveller contingent. Meanwhile, some Fijian hipsters had joined the array of Westerners now flocking to the bar, where a dance floor and ersatz international pop music supplied the invitation to mingle. A third diversion was provided by two young Swedish women, sporting the Heidi hairdo only six weeks after Madonna had pioneered it, who had taken over the pool table and were holding the attention of hard-drinking Indo-Fijian male locals on the nondancing side of the bar. Fitfully intoxicated by each of these scenes, jetlag finally forced me to retire, but not before concluding wanly that this, surely, was 'the world' that the famous music video had been incapable of rhapsodizing, here returning culturally deranged images of itself to the Western eye. What was present here was infinitely more involved than the shiny, happy pluralism dreamt up by Michael Jackson and his videogenic companions.

There were, of course, sober explanations for each of the intersections of social space that evening in Fiji. The unusual combination of metropolitan (predominantly Australian) ownership of the large hotels with the constitutionally ordained ethnic Fijian ownership (83 per cent) of the land upon which the hotels are built; the marginalization, within the tourist industry, of the Indo-Fijians (who are allotted backstage hotel jobs with no face-to-face contact with guests); the space claimed by and devoted to nontourist-oriented traditional culture; the global intimacy with American popular culture; and the mimicry of Western ethnicities. (There certainly was an explanation but there was no excuse for the bad pop music.) While it may have shared many of the standard features of the cultural environment conventionally found in any upmarket Third World tourist destination, this was no generic example of that peculiar new landform that has become one of the primary arenas for intercultural exchange in the postcolonial world. Far from universal, the particular forms of cultural spectacle I encountered in that hotel were fully expressive of local Fijian history and Fijian politics.

Two days before, for example, the *Fiji Times* had carried an editorial responding to Australian Premier Paul Keating's official apology to Australian aboriginal peoples for two centuries of genocide, displacement, and discrimination (a call echoed a year later in Bill Clinton's apology to native Hawaiians). Applauding Keating's sensitivity to indigenous lifeways, the editorial suggested that although only doomsayers would consider traditional culture in Fiji to be under threat, readers might take this opportunity to reaffirm their support for indigenous values. If you want a North American equivalent, imagine the *Wall Street Journal* calling for a reaffirmation of support for corporate capitalism! For, in Fiji, where the Great Council of Chiefs is still unassailably the legislator of the national culture, and where a system of near-apartheid rule, established by military coup, is responsible for governing in the name of indigenous Fijian values, it would be fair to conclude that the traditional lifeways have never been 'lost.' Almost one hundred years of British colonial administration (1874−1970) had created and strengthened the power of the chiefs by creating a state within a state through the system of indirect rule. The colonial decision, taken in 1879, to introduce indentured Indian laborers (rather than draft natives) to work on sugar plantations meant that today's ethnic majority of Indo-Fijians were originally displaced from British India explicitly in order to prevent the erosion of the Fijian way of life, and thus to preserve traditional culture and safeguard native rights. The 1987 military coups, aimed at terminating the development of a multiracial society under the Coalition Party, established a constitutional state wherein a minority (Fijian) population exercised political control over the majority (Indians), all residents are racially classified and cannot cross-vote racially, Christianity is the state religion, racial restrictions apply to land ownership rights, and the inhabitants of traditional cultural environments, like the heavily sanctified rural villages, are accorded all sorts of material and political privileges.[1]

In this milieu, it is fair to say that traditional culture is not only hegemonically enforced against Indo-Fijians subordinated under the apartheid system, it is also a medium for the political control of regional, tribal, and class differences among ethnic Fijians themselves, broadly divided between east and west, and rural-chiefly and urban-commoner. Consequently, comparisons like that of the *Fiji Times* with the example of Australian aboriginal culture, or with the Maori in New Zealand, or with native Hawaiians — all indigenous peoples socially denied to differing degrees within powerful Western nation states — miss the mark. There is a world of difference between the cultural power of 'tradition' in Fiji and in countries where indigenous peoples have either struggled to attain some measure of political autonomy, as in New Zealand, or are still denied elementary forms of self-determination, as in Hawaii and Australia. (To take an example from my end of Europe, the political meaning of a display of Scottish Highland dancing is quite different, for reasons historically rooted in the internally colonized settlement of Britain, from that of rural Morris dancing in England.)

No more useful are comparisons, for reasons of scale, of Fiji with Papua New Guinea, French Polynesia, Vanuatu, the Cook Islands, or Tonga. The particular colonial and postcolonial histories of these states and others in the region have determined that the 'politics of tradition' in the Pacific means something different from island to island, depending on the local conjuncture of political forces. In some cases, 'tradition' is a vehicle for justly reclaiming 'native' rights that were historically denied; in other cases, tradition is invoked unjustly to deny 'local' rights to others. Too many different agendas have been, or are being, pursued in the name of the *preservation* of traditional cultures for kneejerk liberal deference to indigenous values to stand as an adequate response on the part of nonnatives, especially when 'world opinion' can make a great difference to a government's domestic policies. In most cases, anxiety, native and nonnative, about the 'vanishing' of traditional ways of life — a longstanding rhetorical fixture in popular ethnographic consciousness — has a much more complex local significance than the neoromantic rhetoric of extinction and preservation suggests. In places where the creation of 'new traditions' is as common as the preservation of the old, the strategic uses that are made of this anxiety are manifold, and are mined for political gain — by everyone from rebel insurgents to tribal chiefs to development-minded politicians — as regularly today as they were in the precontact period of Pacific life. And when the name of 'tradition' is too rigorously attached to some classifiable view of ethnic identity, then a certain ugly chauvinism is unavoidable.

Fiji is a case in point. Its near-apartheid policies assume the cultural homogeneity of an ethnic group in ancient historical possession of the land, and yet the supremacist identity of 'ethnic Fijian' actually refers to a far from homogenous native population descended from a mélange of Melanesian settlers, Polynesian 'invaders' (Tongans, mostly), and intermarriages with Samoans and Europeans. Less ancient still is the power of the chiefly aristocracy, created in its present form for the purposes of British rule during the nineteenth century. This does not alter the fact that there was widespread sympathy for the Fiji coup among indigenous Pacific Islanders, for whom the reinstatement of the chiefly oligarchy was seen as a triumphant assertion of native claims, and not at all as a defence of class interests or a racist counterrevolution. On a larger geopolitical scale, however, the coup may have proved that indigenous tradition today is as serviceable as ever to the strategic interests of Western powers and transnational corporations seeking to divide and pacify all resistance in the Pacific region. Looking beyond the boundaries of the nation state, few would argue that the emergence, under Timoci Bavadra, of Fiji's multiracial Coalition Party, did not pose a regional challenge to those larger powers who intend to dominate the new 'Pacific century,' and who lent their covert support to the coup. Weaning Fiji, French Polynesia, and Papua New Guinea from the Nuclear-Free and Independent Pacific Movement was a major preoccupation of the nuclear powers in the 1980s. Low-intensity conflict and internal ethnic friction provided effective historically sanctioned means to that end.[2]

The politics of nationalism in the late colonial and postcolonial period has focused special attention on the role of cultural tradition, whether for symbolic reasons or as material underpinnings for economies that have sought to preserve 'a way of life' by resisting integration into capitalist world markets. Nothing is more contested among the thousand-odd Pacific island cultures than 'culture' itself. Indeed, cultural nationalism has often been indistinguishable from political nationalism in the Pacific in ways that are quite striking to Western eyes used either to separating cultural politics from 'real' politics, or to viewing cultural politics in terms of conflicts between abstract representations of social and economic life: individualism/

communitarianism; puritanism/libertarianism; assimilation/multi-culturalism, etc. In the Pacific, culture is not a colorful appendix to power, it is the normative medium of political contests.

In this chapter, my aim is to consider the way in which discourses about cultural preservation that were fundamental to initial European perceptions of Pacific Island life have become a para-mount element of the politics of the region today. Nothing seems to come more naturally than to pit the preservation/destruction of traditional culture (which always includes 'the environment' in the case of indigenous peoples) against voices that argue for develop-ment in the islands. While some overarching synthesis is promised by the language of sustainable development (the new lingua franca of corporate environmentalism), the rich mythology of 'paradise lost' still holds sway over debates about the region's future. More often than not, the conventional binary option in these debates, of tradition versus progress, feeds off a history of thinking shaped by the 'fatal impact' thesis of Western contact by which Pacific peoples were passively doomed to suffer the ravages wrought by an introduced culture based upon exploitative cash and wage econo-mies and driven by the environmentally destructive philosophies of possessive individualism, rationalism, humanism, materialism, and nationalism. Termed thus after the famous book by Alan Moore-head, this apocalyptic thesis was first advanced by explorers like Cook, who regretted their involuntary introduction of European vices into Polynesian paradises, and by philosophers like Diderot who, in responding to the hand-wringing accounts of Cook and others, passionately argued that Europeans should eschew any further contact with these original Edenites in deference to their natural sanctity. Defined from first contact, then, as a philosophical test case of survival or extinction, the Pacific way of life still serves today as a litmus test for Western anxieties about the growth and development of industrialized societies. By the same token, the Western way of life often serves as a negative model in the region, a crazy mirror for native anxieties about the future of a past partly romanticized and partly still lived.

The worst legacy of this dialectic is that it perpetuates the dangerous picture of a death struggle among cultures, in a region of the world that once served as the crucible for evolutionary theory, from the observations of the naturalists who were well accommo-dated on Cook's voyages, to the seminal work, on Fitzroy's voyages,

26

of Darwin himself. Consequently, the entire region became a colorful stage set for biological science to demonstrate its theories of species extinction — cultural and social, as well as natural. Having outlived the worst of social Darwinism, many Pacific Islanders became test subjects for a different kind of survival of the fittest this time around: the side effects of twentieth century weapons of mass extinction. The apocalyptic backdrop served the nuclear powers equally well when they persuaded the islanders that the sacrifice of their environments was for the benefit of all. President de Gaulle introduced the nuclear presence to French Polynesians by announcing in 1956 that their islands would be 'a refuge and a centre of rebirth for our whole civilization.'[3] US Commodore Wyatt told the Bikinians that they were like the children of Israel bound for the Promised Land before requesting that they leave their island 'for the good of mankind and to end all world wars.'[4] In the case of the Rongelapese, the Marshallese and many others, there was no such consultation. Henry Kissinger's comment about the Marshallese spoke for itself: 'There are only 90,000 of them out there. Who gives a damn?' The result — the monitoring of generations of contaminated Islanders — remains one of the most gruesome chapters in science's history of experimentation on living things.

At best, however (if one can follow such obscene examples with a more benign note), the Western—Pacific dialectic is testimony to the long history, on both sides, of mimetic behavior in the postcontact period. This history is best described, not by the all-or-nothing scenarios of 'fatal impact' in which colonial culture uniformly and irresistibly penetrates a defenceless native culture, but by the messy account book of cultural and economic exchange in which the institutions, rituals, and objects of both cultures are selectively appropriated, recontextualized, indigenized, and used for strategic purposes often quite alien to the ideological makeup of these foreign bodies.[5] Cultural contact was (and is) a two-way contest. However unequal the balance of forces, the advantage sometimes lay on the weaker side. In the age of the fledgling 'Pacific Century,' with the US Cold War policy of 'strategic denial' loosening its paranoid grip, and a new hysterical migration of capital and labor criss-crossing the ocean, the new axis is truly global—local. Contrary to the wet dream of the 'Pacific Rim,' constructed by delirious post-Fordist, mega-trend-watching economists, the myriad cultures and statelets in the region have their own micropolitical ways of absorbing and

27

weathering the steady pressure of global forces that cross their beaches.[6]

What first drew me to the stories I will try to tell in this chapter is the knowledge that the Pacific Islands, Polynesia in particular, are the birthplace of modern ecological romanticism. Ever since the first European voyages, Polynesia has served as a paradigm for Western ideas about scarcity and abundance, poverty and affluence, industry and leisure, communalism and anomie. Perceptions of Polynesian life played a crucial role in the formative political and economic philosophy of modern liberal society, and have continued to shape thinking about the place of human societies in the natural world. This paradigm has obtained a new lease on life with the emergence of the ecology movement, in which the traditional culture of Third and Fourth World peoples has become as much a new object lesson for the future of the West as a medium for negotiating the recovery of decimated indigenous peoples the world over. It has also had a visible impact on Pacific life in the growth of an extensive tourist industry that not only depends for its lifeblood upon the Edenic myth of Polynesia, but also functions today as the primary agent of neocolonial development in the region. Now that the contradictions of cloaking First World development in the guise of Fourth Worldist spectacle are all too apparent to even the mass tourist, this industry has found an alternative wardrobe in the emperor's new clothes of eco-tourism.

The stories that follow are presented in the knowledge that I may simply be writing one more chapter in the strange history of the Western obsession with Polynesia. Among other things, I am, after all, yet another prying *tuturani*, to use a Vanuatu term for whites (literally 'stay stay day'; or 'people who appeared one day, and never left') which Scott Malcolmson chooses as a title for his excellent political travelogue of the Pacific.[7] I will press on, anyway, in the hope that since my stories are neither romantic nor apocalyptic, they may help to dissipate the power of the genres that have fuelled this long obsession. In assembling the stories here — under the banner of jetlag and cultural studies, and in sober consciousnes s of the stories told by a long line of other *tuturani* voices: anthropologists, travel writers, beachcombers, colonists, missionaries, explorers, and novelists — my intention is also to outline a political ecology of the many-layered region that is, at this moment in time, at once the American Pacific, the Asian Pacific and the indigenous, interisland Pacific.

As for my own initial attachment to the stories, it may seem odd but not finally absurd to confess that it stems from my experience of having been born and raised as a lowland Scotsman, in the shadow of the Highlands and their inhabitants, which, like Polynesia, is one of the most romanticized spots and peoples in modern Western history, and of having breathed the heady air of cultural nationalism all through my own youth and for many ambivalent years after. At this point in time, there are no justifiable credentials for writing about other cultures, and there is no doubt that it has been one of the most damaging occupations pursued by those who luxuriate in their good intentions, especially Westerners. Intercultural understanding is a flimsy liberal edifice, and attempts at cross-cultural alliance politics are fraught with unequal power plays. The most honest, or least delusory, path is to accept that writing about others (nothing will silence this desire) is usually autobiographical, and to hope that the self-indulgence carries over, *mutatis mutandis*, into some useful region of thought and action for which there are no guaranteed navigational coordinates.

As a footnote to this declaration, I had, at some point in my research, considered writing a comparative study of the romance of the Scot and the romance of the Polynesian. That study will have to wait, and, in any case, it belongs elsewhere if only because the cultural study of Scotland is not quite as central to the history of ecological ideas as the cultural study of Polynesia. Fantasies about the Highland glens do not produce the equation 'scarcity equals affluence,' as they have often done in the South Seas. Had I written that study instead, it would surely have touched upon the colonial meteorological romance of the Scot with the Polynesian, which I will signal here only by citing one of the great weather poems of bi-oceanic literature: Robert Louis Stevenson's ode to Princess Ka'iulani, the half-Scottish heiress apparent to Lili'uokalani's Hawaiian throne, written as she was about to leave Honolulu in 1889, somewhat reluctantly, for a stiff season of Northern schooling in a stiff Northern clime.

> Forth from her land to mine she goes,
> The island maid, the island rose,
> Light of heart and bright of face:
> The daughter of a double race.

Her islands here, in Southern sun,
Shall mourn their Ka'iulani gone,
And I, in her dear banyan shade,
Look vainly for my little maid.

But our Scots Isles far away
Shall glitter with unwonted day,
And cast for once their tempests by
To smile in Ka'iulani's eye.

[Written in April to Ka'iulani, in the April of her age, and at Waikiki, within easy walk of Ka'iulani's banyan. When she comes to my land and her father's, and the rain beats upon the window (as I fear it will) let her look at this page; it will be like a weed gathered and pressed at home, and she will remember her own islands, and the shadow of the mighty tree, and she will hear the peacocks screaming in the dusk and the wind blowing in the palms, and she will think of her father sitting there alone]

Ironically enough, it was Hawaiian weather — a storm on the heights of Waimea on the Big Island — that would precipitate the rheumatic death, some years later, of the last Princess of Hawaii.

The Easter Island Lesson

At some point in youth most of the readers of this book were probably invited to ponder over the 'mystery' of the Easter Island statues. I am sure that some of the fantasies about this 'mystery' varied from culture to culture, even from household to household, but the Ur-narrative, whether it involved visits from extraterrestrials or Thor Heyerdahl's colorful wars of conquest between the 'long ears' and the 'short ears,' was probably the same romance about lost civilizations that I absorbed, and which still holds sway over some part of my barnacled imagination. Only recently have environmental historians given us the straight dope about Easter Island (and many other 'lost civilizations' to boot).

Indeed, environmental collapse has become the favored explanation today for the decline of history's great civilizations; for the Victorians and their high-minded descendants, the explanation was moral decadence. In the first chapter of *A Green History of the World* (a timely addition to the venerable genre of histories of the world), Clive Ponting chooses to tell the Easter Island story as a 'lesson' in how hierarchical societies can turn their limited resource bases into instruments of environmental collapse.[8] The story about Easter Island is one of increasing social stratification in which clan chiefs competed in symbolic self-aggrandizement through the building and erection of the famous stone *moia* and *ahu*, transported around the island on vast tracks of felled tree trunks. The resulting deforestation leached the nutrients from soil that was none too productive to begin with, deprived the islanders of vital technological resources like fishing nets, canoes, and timber huts, and had a corrosive effect on the belief systems. Consequently, the first European visitors in 1722 came upon an environmentally devastated land: its people were in perpetual warfare and sanctioning slavery, their food economy was in a cannibalistic phase, and a cultural amnesia prevailed among them about the origins and meanings of the twenty-foot high statues. Surely, says Ponting, the Easter Islanders must have seen what was happening to the forests and the soils? And yet, far from devising ways of staving off eco-collapse, their leaders, ever covetous of prestige and status, intensified the competition over available timber by carving more and more statues. Perhaps, he concludes, there is a lesson here for us today, facing ecological collapse on a planetary scale, and subject to the short-term ambitions and *folie de grandeur* of our own leaders.

Whatever you think of Ponting's 'lesson,' it is by no means a simple story, based upon — at last — the empirical facts. For one thing, the shift from mystery genre to didactic genre provides no real opportunity to introduce the voices of islanders who are silenced in new ways and cast, yet again, as exemplary types in the latest morality play about the survival of (mostly Western) civilization. Polynesians have been delegated to play such passive roles, in allegory after allegory, ever since first contact. In the latest script, written by Ponting and others, the islanders have been moved from their Edenite role as unconscious heroes in the annals of environmentalism to that of unconscious villains. In other words, it's still all or nothing: harmony or destruction, extinction or survival.

If Ponting's lesson denies the Easter Islanders any active role as conscious, social beings with complex cultural politics, it does at least present a revisionist picture of precontact Pacific life, filled this time by peoples with histories, peoples with politics, and peoples with physical effects upon their habitats. In particular, it links the social ecology of a hierarchical order with destructive environmental practices. In this respect, it has come to challenge other, more familiar stories about peoples without history. Currently, the most friction-laden challenge is to the highly reverent account, favored by many Pacific nationalists, of ecologically wise peoples living in respectful harmony with nature until the arrival of the white man. What is embellished in this account is the picture of a small-scale, sustainable society governed by the encyclopaedic practical wisdom of traditional knowledge and resource management in agriculture, reef use, and agroforestry, all worked communally and with a minimum of self-interest.[9] The technology of environmental management was cultural and religious ritual, translated today into the more modern ethic of 'caring for the land' and respecting its sacred sustenance of all forms of life. Such accounts are often at variance with the historians' picture of island environments radically transformed, degraded, and, at times, exhausted by intensive modes of food production requiring complex, artificial ecosystems. There is barely one inch of land in Oceania, and virtually none of the wilderness prized by First World environmentalists, whose native ecology has not been radically altered by native use of fire, water, and earth in agriculture.

A similar variance is evident if we consider more closely the view that the use of natural resources was environmentally protected and managed by ritual and ceremonial contracts with deities. In socially stratified Hawaii, use of the natural environment was regulated and constrained by chiefly *kapu* (*tapu* throughout Polynesia, or taboo, as European seafarers came to call it), a sacred system of consumption laws which applied to all aspects of the food, labor, and general material economy. It is likely that the sacred preservation of *kapu* often functioned ecologically for the communal good, either to guard against overfishing or overhunting or to conserve species during breeding seasons.[10] But they also served as a means whereby nobility could reserve certain species — sea turtles, for example — for their own consumption at particular times of the year, or to exact labor and tributes from commoners for their chiefly comfort and aggrandizement through warfare. Indeed, the uses made of *kapu* were virtually indissociable from the exercise of power. If ecological conservation was an effect of the *kapu* system, then it was as much a selective byproduct as a communally minded aim of the chiefly control of resources. Consequently, the effect could be reversed if and when the structure of power was redefined, either from above or below.

Transgressive relations of exchange with European visitors, whether symbolic, material, or sexual, were often pursued by commoners (*maka'ainana*) with a view to circumventing the *kapu* system established in the chiefly interest and observed unevenly throughout the Hawaiian social order. *Maka'ainana* circumvention of chiefly power was then explicitly expressed and advanced through trade and commerce with foreigners in ways that threatened the monopoly tendency of the *kapu* system.[11] Concomitantly, the erosion and abandonment of the old religion, as in Hawaii, was finally a recognition that it no longer served the oligarchic interest, and, in the case of the new, centralized Hawaiian monarchy of the Kamehamehas, was an obstruction to their continued succession.[12] In the case of the *maka'ainana*, their trading relations with sailors and, later, whalers initiated a context for the commodification (heavily sexualized in the case of women) of goods and labor that, ultimately, would end in their own proletarianization and the privatization of their commonly worked lands. In the case of the chiefs (*ali'i*), accustomed to creating new *kapu* to enhance their advantage, their exploitation of *maka'ainana* labor in the early nineteenth-century sandalwood trade, conducted with British and Americans looking for a commodity to trade with the Chinese, was not only the last breath of the *kapu* system, but also the most environmentally destructive phase of properly precolonial history. Any candid estimate of the ecological record of prehistoric and precolonial Hawaii, and Polynesia in general, would have to account, then, for the political manipulation of *kapu* by commoners and nobility alike.

While these considerations of class power are often downplayed in nationalist accounts of precontact and postcontact life, indigenous historians have made a strong case that class analysis of this sort is often a Eurocentric misconception of the cultural and religious universe of Polynesian society. They argue that ideas about land tenure were closely tied to chiefly trusteeship or stewardship of resources, and that the social equilibrium (*pono* in Hawaiian) of the culture was bound up in a belief system of reciprocal obligations that cannot simply be dismissed as feudal ideology. Recovering this indigenous world picture involves a serious consideration of the *mo'olelo*, or genealogical oral histories, that have also been over-looked or dismissed by nonnative historians as cosmological fiction.[13] Consequently, among history's most immediate tasks from the native point of view is to distinguish its picture of precontact sustainable societies from the often similar Edenic picture that is the legacy of the European romance with Polynesia — the mythology of paradise found and lost — in which European exploration of these islands was the evidence for Rousseau's theory (published almost twenty years before in 1749 in the *Second Discourse*) of the Noble Savage living in a state of benevolent nature, and thus enjoying an Arcadian relation to a naturally abundant environment.

From documentary evidence in the journals of Cook and Bougainville, cast as records of voyages of scientific exploration and not of imperialist plunder, Polynesia would come to be viewed as a prescarcity society, devoid of the corruptions of civilization like sin and greed and envy, and abundant enough to extend all of the necessities of life — water, food, and women — more or less freely to its foreign visitors. Like the earlier Columbian visitors to the New World, Cook and his fellow voyagers were coming from European lands long degraded by deforestation, overgrazing, and overharvest-ing, and where social organization had generated widespread scarcity and poverty. The discovery of abundance in nature had already been prefigured in Columbus's and others' experiences in the New World, and drew upon fantasies in the West dating back to Greek literature about the repossession of the Isles of the Blest.[14] As it happens, the natural benevolence of the islands had little to do with the survival of the Polynesians. In fact, the voyaging Polynesians had travelled from island settlement to settlement with a survival kit in the form of a basic portmanteau of plants and animals: coconut palm, taro, sweet potato, yam, sugarcane, breadfruit, banana, panadanus, chestnut, arrowroot, weeds, snails, pigs, dogs, chickens and lizards, and occasional stowaway species. The various island landscapes were generically altered, terraformed, and on occasion exhausted over time to accommodate these species and plants. Among other things, this is why they all presented a similar appearance to the Europeans (unlike their social systems).

The men of science on board Cook's and Bougainville's ships did see and occasionally record evidence of treeless islands and other forms of degradation, but chose for the most part to rave about the people of plenty. They were most unfettered in their euphoria about a culture where 'love is the chief occupation.' Cook's naturalist Joseph Banks wrote of their landfall in Tahiti, 'the scene was the truest picture of an Arcadia, of which we were going to be kings.' Of the open sexual mores of the people of Tahiti, Bougainville's naturalist Philbert Commerson had earlier observed, 'They know no god but love.' The tales of native women insisting on fucking sailors for free have haunted the sexual consciousness of Europe ever since. Polynesian women, of course, had specific social and cultural reasons for making love to the Europeans. K.R. Howe suggests that women of low birth were ordered to prostitute themselves for the political advantage of the chiefs; among other things, it placated European firepower.[15] Marshall Sahlins argues, in the case of Hawaii, that the women were acting in accord with the rules of sexual passion (*le'a*) that governed status and advancement in Hawaiian society.[16] Caroline Ralston shows that while the women may have initially acted in a culturally appropriate way, sex quickly became a medium of commercial exchange, as the *ali'i* moved to monopolize all forms of trade with Europeans through the *kapu* system.[17] Whatever the reasons, the fantasy of an unrestricted sexual economy among Polynesians proved crucial to the Enlightenment's ideological reworking of Arcadian myths about man in a state of nature.[18] Concomitantly, it was venereal disease rather than dysentery, measles, and smallpox — the much bigger killers — that proved a source of profound ethical discomfort.

In his classic study of the work of graphic artists on board the great South Seas voyages of discovery, Bernard Smith shows that the dominant rhetoric and iconography used to depict the noble inhabitants of these Isles of the Blest was indeed Greek-Arcadian.[19] A major strain was also Orientalist, evident in the imagery deployed in paintings and drawings of Polynesians in which the conceptual visual model was drawn from the Indian subcontinent. Banks used the term 'Indian' to refer to natives of Tierra del Fuego, Tahitians, Maori and Australian Aborigines alike — a generic usage conventional since Columbus's misconceptions about his geographical location in the Caribbean.[20] Consequently, the uses made of the newest Noble Savage by European political philosophy were redolent of similarly Arcadian interpretations of the 'Indians' of the New World, whose social orders provided much of the substance for the Enlightenment idea of a free commonwealth of political liberties (instated, of course, in republican North America itself). But

Columbus had also demonstrated, not for the last time, that wherever the Noble Savage was, the Savage Beast would surely be nearby, lurking, if nowhere else, in the projective, bullet-chamber fantasies of the European mind. There was no preexisting bestiary of human monsters active in European forecasts about the Pacific, but, like Columbus's division of natives into gentle Tainos and fierce Caribs, Polynesians fell into prescribed antithetical niches in the European fantasy-repertoire. Smith describes well how the 'soft primitivism' ascribed to the noble Tahitians had to be set against the 'hard primitivism' of the repugnant Maori and Aborigines. After the death of Cook and the Maori killings of some of Marion du Fresne's crew, even the Polynesians took on a schizophrenic tendency of being pacific and violent by turns.

No sooner had the metropolitan fashion of natural innocence subsided than the Noble Savage ceded to the poor, benighted child of nature in urgent need of salvation from a missionary sensibility overflowing with cumulative guilt about the expulsion from Eden. From the appearance on the scene of the London Missionary Society in 1797, the agents of progress, improvement, and redemption visited a new set of repressive taboos upon the erstwhile free spirits of the New Cythera. Generations of dreamers from Paul Gauguin to Thor Heyerdahl would report on the missionary's brutal subjugation of native sensuality: no dancing, no wrestling, no singing, no copulating, no tattooing, no drinking. Happiness turned into sadness; eternity interrupted by change; all or nothing.

In this century, the vicious cycle that transforms idyll into purgatory has been as powerful as ever. The most famous case is of course that of Margaret Mead, whose scientific restatement of the Edenic myth of Polynesia in *Coming of Age in Samoa* had a profound effect on cultural mores in the USA. Writing about the effect of her book in 1961, she noted that '[t]hose who saw American society in the 1920s as a rapacious and consuming monster greeted this book as an escape — an escape in spirit that paralleled an escape in body to a South Sea island where love and ease were the order of the day.'[21] In the 1920s, the turbulent movements for sexual freedom at home took inspiration from a book that depicted another society tolerating sexual relations from an early age, and hence as less neurotic in general about its body culture. Driven by a high ethical purpose, Mead argued that Westerners, by contrast, paid too high a price for their 'civilization,' which generated undue 'storm and stress' for their overdisciplined adolescents. Growing up in the happy society of Samoa was 'easy'; there were no suicides, no sexual repression, no obsessions with nuclear familialism, no guilt, no competition, no overpowering emotion, no oppressive hierarchy attached to rank, no rigidity in social convention, no aggression, no Christian sin/guilt, no adolescent deviants, no rapes, and no frigidity. Mead's ethnography of Polynesian free love animated the sexual counterculture of the day, just as the antipsychiatry literature of R.D. Laing, Wilhelm Reich, and Paul Goodman helped to stimulate the sexual liberation movements of the 1960s.

In retrospect, it is all too easy, and embarrassing, to see how Mead's lush romantic ode to the easygoing native reiterated all of the Noble Savage myths. How do we therefore explain its remarkable and sustained credibility as a picture of another culture? First, it offered a properly *scientific* confirmation of what most people still wanted to believe about Polynesia but had relegated to the realm of their own adolescent musings. Second, it was read, as ethnography was then conventionally read, in Mead's own words, with an eye to 'the absoluteness of monographs on primitive societies, valuable precisely because they were the records of an order which would soon vanish but never return.'[22] In other words, idyllic Polynesia, even if it still existed in Mead's snapshot account ('a handful of young girls on a tiny island . . . stand[ing] forever like the lovers on Keats' Grecian urn') was on the verge of disappearing, like all good Golden Ages, and so this scientific record would be all that remained.[23] Thus went the antique rhetoric of the 'vanishing primitive,' which had taken on neo-Darwinian overtones in previous decades as a scientific discourse that actually helped to prepare for the extinction of peoples like the Tierra del Fuegians and Tasmanians at the same time as it denied native peoples a complex life in the present. Sixty years later, it was still necessary to refer to the official power of this rhetoric in order to contest it. In 1988, for example, a bill referred to as the International Cultural Survival Act was introduced before the US House of Representatives; it was intended to protect and promote the survival of indigenous peoples around the world. Representative Benjamin A. Gilman introduced the bill thus:

> Most of us, regardless of our political leanings, assume that indigenous peoples and tribal societies are bound to disappear — destined to the

dustbin of history. Most of us would assume that this process is as lamentable as it is inevitable. Historical processes do not make small traditional societies disappear. Greed and a lack of understanding, however, do.[24]

Five years earlier, in 1983, Derek Freeman had published his controversial rebuttal of Mead's findings in *Margaret Mead and Samoa*. There, Mead's Samoa was put to the sword of science by which it had come of age. Freeman's scientifically researched Samoa was a harsh, conflict-ridden society where the incidence of rape, homicide, suicide, and domestic violence ran as high as anywhere in the West, where competition for rank and status was bitterly aggressive, and where social codes of virginity and monogamy were rigidly enforced.[25] I cite Freeman's book here not to review or enter into the anthropological controversy it generated, but to show how an antithetical Samoa, populated by the Samoan equivalent of gangsters and psychopaths, had to be created, and was in fact solicited, by the generic story that Mead had told about peace and love. Both Mead's and Freeman's accounts were appallingly divorced from the larger social context of a Pacific region undergoing massive social change in the twentieth century.[26]

The consequence, in any case, was that once again Polynesians were being held to ransom at the court of opinion; guilty or not guilty of being perfect; all or nothing. Despite the persistence of old bromides — in 1989, Dan Quayle referred to Samoans as 'happy campers' — urban Samoans have long dedicated themselves to countering the Happy Samoan mythology that has become an element of the 'model minority' of the official demographic designation, Asian/Pacific Islander. The legacy of this countercul-ture in popular music runs from the postpunk band, The Angry Samoans, to the gangsta rapper crew, The Booyah Tribe ('boo-yah' representing the sound of a gangsta weapon being fired), whose members grew up in the street gang culture that now links urban Samoan populations in Los Angeles, Honolulu, and Auckland.

It is just as common to find the cycle of idyll and purgatory in the same narrative about Polynesia. Take Thor Heyerdahl's account of his first visit to the Pacific on field research in the late 1930s, where he hatched the theories of Polynesian migration made popular later by *The Kon-Tiki Expedition*, *Aku-Aku*, and *American Indians in the Pacific*. *Fatu-Hiva: Back to Nature*, the account of the trip he and his wife Liv made to the Marquesan island of Fatu-Hiva was rewritten, translated into English, and published for the still-booming hippy market in 1974:

> Back to nature? Farewell to civilization? It is one thing to dream of it and another to do it. I tried it. Tried to return to nature. Crushed my watch between two stones and let my hair and beard grow wild. Climbed the palms for food. Cut all the chains that bound me to the modern world. I tried to enter the wilderness empty handed and barefoot, as man at one with nature . . . I ran away from bureaucracy, technology, and the grip of twentieth-century civilization. My only garment, if any at all, was a flowery loin-cloth, and my home was of plaited yellow bamboo. I drew no salary, for I had no expenses; my world was free for birds and beasts and barefoot men to help themselves to what they needed, one day at a time.[27]

The narrative records that for the better part of a year, these paradise hunters lived like king and queen of a South Sea island, where abundant nature produces all year round: 'Adam and Eve, when God drove them out of the garden of Eden, must have felt the very opposite of us when we started our walk into the lush valley of Omoa at sunrise next morning' (*FH*, p. 49). Not to be denied any element of the fantasy, they take up residence on the old royal terrace in the valley, unearthing the royal household implements and the king's old stone chair. (The cover of the book sports a photograph of Heyerdahl wearing royal headgear: 'Feeling like a king, I could actually put an ancient Marquesan crown on my head for the occasion. Or was I the first hippy?') Trouble in paradise quickly and inevitably makes its appearance, in the form of disease, 'taboo,' and disaffection with the return to nature. There is nowhere for modern man to escape, Thor and Liv conclude; nature lies 'within,' but at least they now have some idea of what man has traded in for civilization. They head back to Europe on the brink of a world war, but not before Thor has accumulated all of the clues that will inspire him to solve 'the riddle' of the origins of the Polynesians by locating their provenance in Central America; clues in the stone statues redolent of Inca sculpture, in the oral tales of the origin journeys of Tiki from the East, in the physiognomy of the indigenous people, and in the ubiquity in Polynesia of South American plants like the sweet potato, the maho hibiscus, and the pineapple. And not before other lessons are learned about environmental degradation on a visit to a treeless island, Motane, which serves Heyerdahl as an allegorical landscape for prefiguring his later archaeological investigations on Easter Island, or for ominous predictions about the fate of the planet: 'Motane is not the only place on our blue planet where man, eager for improvement, is turning back the biological clock' (*FH*, p. 218).

Not for the first time, the Polynesians who appear in Heyerdahl's book serve mostly as raw evidence for speculating about the racial — Aryan? Arabic-Semitic? Malay? — and geographical — Indonesia? Egypt? South America? — origins of their ancestors. Not for the last time, their habitat, when it is not 'nature on the seventh day,' serves as a preachy example of human disregard for the natural world. True to the twin genres of the book, escapist-adventure and mystery-archaeological, everything authentically Polynesian is either vanishing or has already vanished; Tei Tetua, a central figure in the book, is the 'last Polynesian known to have participated personally in cannibal ceremonies'; on a later visit Heyerdahl recalls he 'could not find on Tahiti a single Polynesian of guaranteed pure stock for blood-group studies' (*FH*, p. 185). Heyerdahl's Fatu-Hivans are still part-time children of the sun, but they have long internalized the white man's disease, preferring, for example, to live under corrugated iron roofs rather than palm thatches because these habitats are signs that say 'we are no longer savages.' The foreign paradise hunters are the ones who will build the thatched bamboo huts in urban centers like Papeete and make precontact architecture fashionable again.

More than any other writers in this century, Mead and Heyerdahl have shaped popular consciousness about Polynesia, and have done so in the name of science. Both had 'agendas' for which Polynesia would be a test case. Mead was looking for a negative instance to disprove the school of biological determinism. Her study of Samoa challenged universalist theories about adolescence and upheld the culturalist view that social environments were paramount in shaping human behavior. Her parable of a sensuous paradise spoke directly to the modernist taste, at home, for primitivism. Heyerdahl was looking for a spectacular single explanation for settling the 200-year-old debate among scholars of Oceania about the origins of the Polynesian settlers.[28] As it happens, his own obsessive quest to put an end to all of these origin debates ran concurrently with other campaigns for final racialist solutions. He records, for example, that Professor Günther, Hitler's chief anthropologist at the Völkerkunde Museum, convinced that the Polynesians were Aryans, would later ask Heyerdahl to bring him skulls from the Marquesas to prove Günther's thesis (*FH*, p. 99).

However well intentioned, both Mead and Heyerdahl were riding out the last phase of ideas generated by the discourse of 'civilization,' with its roots in cultural imperialism and its scientific complement in Herbert Spencer's social Darwinist creed. As a culturalist, Mead may have been committed to the relativist imagery of the 'family of man,' and opposed to the neo-Darwinian emphasis upon the superiority of the fittest, but her study was nonetheless framed by the reverse rhetoric of what a more advanced society could learn from an undeveloped one. For Heyerdahl, the conversation was even more one-way; moreover, it was framed by the racialist legacy of nineteenth-century attempts to Aryanize the Polynesians that succeeded eighteenth-century attempts to Hellenize and Orientalize them. Like many before them, Mead and Heyerdahl saw a *career opportunity* in the Polynesians. In every other respect, they did their utmost to ignore or disdain their proximity to other Westerners — the presence of the US Pacific fleet in Samoa, white, and mixed-race residents of the islands, beachcombers, and, most abject of all in the eyes of the anthropologist, the growing company of tourists. Yet the influence of their books arguably has had its greatest impact on the Pacific tourist industry. For it is in the burgeoning culture of island tourism that all of the great thematic mythologies of Polynesiana have been resurrected and retrofitted — Mead's idyll of the carefree life, where worry is taboo, and Heyerdahl's search for first peoples, the *purest* race, before the rot of civilization. Both themes are powerful, compensatory elements for Western skepticism and guilt about the ultimate social value of limitless development. As such, they are the bestselling stories that help to regulate the international division of leisure for the global tourist industry. Over the period of time in which mass tourism has developed in the Pacific, anthropologists have ceased to be interested in these stories, and consider tourist manifestations of them, as always, to be apart from their own, less vulgar, concerns. And yet, just as they shared more than they cared to recognize with the detested missionaries who preceded them, anthropologists have a good deal in common with the tourist.

Indeed, anthropologists' temporary stay of residence in foreign cultures, with superior means, limited access, and varying degrees of interpretive competence barely distinguishes them from that of the independent tourist.[29]

Whether you are an anthropologist who goes to work, or a tourist who goes to play (or a cultural studies scholar who is supposed to do both), it is difficult for anyone who has ever landed at a Polynesian airport not to be conscious of the history evoked by the vigorous welcoming reception of music, flowers, and broad smiles. What is being repeated a hundred times a week at these airports is the benign story of cultural contact — a story in which the friendly islanders hail the incoming ships, all the way from Captain Cook's *Resolution* to Delta's flight 2203 from St. Louis. In Hawaii, this is especially ironic given that the Hawaiians not only welcomed Captain Cook as Lono the returning god of cosmic reproduction, but also killed him as the god who would have to die in order to reproduce the social belief system. That is, if you believe this story — it's more likely that Hawaiians could quite easily tell the difference between a god and an undernourished Englishman.[30] Even today, however, you can be sure that the famous *aloha* welcome is not extended to all and sundry. On two of the many occasions I have landed at Honolulu International Airport, I was followed and rigorously questioned by drug enforcement agents, unwilling to believe much of what I said about my identity. No less difficult was the task of assuring friends and academic colleagues that my research trips to Polynesian tourist resorts were the object of serious scholarship!

Postmodern anthropology has long since ditched many of the scientific assumptions associated with the classical practice of ethnography and ethnographic writing. Anthropologists have become less functionalist, more committed to learning from native voices and participating in social change. In that same space of time, the stationary pictures of prelapsarian societies that were once the staple of classical anthropology have become the primary commodity of the tourist trade. In fact, it is invariably the mass tourist who is now invited to play the role of the classical ethnographer, encouraged by the guide books to venture beyond the Kon-Tiki stage shows and strike out for the highlands or the interior in search of authentic village life. 'It still exists, but may be gone by the time your next vacation rolls around, so rent that car now . . .' This is tourism's own version of ethnography's vanishing object. And like the ethnographer's snapshot of the last days of a dying race, tourism's invitation harbors the sharpest of contradictions, since it is often seen as destroying the natural beauty and authentic culture it has to preserve as its prime commodity. See paradise before it's gone, announces the very industry associated with the destruction of paradise. But is the lesson of Waikiki the same as the lesson of Easter Island?

No Business Like Tour Business

Nowhere, one would think, are the contradictions shared by both the anthropologist and the tourist more visible than in the 'cultural parks' of ethnographic tourism, that sector of the industry which brings the tourist into contact with performances of traditional cultures, as distinct from other tourist categories: cultural tourism (based on the idea of the picturesque or landscape appreciation), ethnic tourism (based on contact with preindustrial folk cultures), historical tourism (museums and monuments), recreational tourism (sun, sports, and romance), sex tourism (sex), environmental tourism (remote destination areas), religious tourism (pilgrimages), or archaeological tourism (ruins). Cultural theme parks or centers — 'living museums' of traditional culture without any actual resident inhabitants — are the primary spectacle of ethnographic tourism.[31] In staging what Dean McCannell calls the 'performative primitive,' their 'cannibal economics' demands that the ex-primitive pretends to shun money, property, and all of the returns of modernity in exchange for a living wage.[32] The historical lineage of the indigenous exhibit, however, lies in the great imperial exposi-tions and world's fairs, where 'the native village' was a showcase for the colonial powers to display their territorial possessions and subjects to visitors.[33]

Over the course of two years in 1992–93, I paid several trips to one of the best known ethnic theme parks — the Polynesian Cultural Center (PCC), located on the north shore of Oahu, just around the coast from Sunset Beach, the wet dream of world surfing culture, and a good forty miles from Waikiki, the grand signifier of mass recreational tourism in the world today. The PCC, which was thirty years old in 1993, is the most successful and profitable cultural park in the world, with over a million visitors a year. It has served as a model for many similar commercial ventures in the business of ethnographic tourism — in Fiji, Bangkok, Seoul, Cairo, Jakarta, Manila, Ponape, and China — and as an inspiration for indigenous tourism developments — the Northwestern Alaska Native Association's decision, for example, to construct model Inuit dwellings and performance spaces for tourist visits.

The PCC is located in the Mormon community of Laie; it is owned and managed by the Church of Jesus Christ of the Latter-Day Saints, and is staffed, for the most part, by students at the adjoining campus of the Brigham Young University (BYU), who work part-time there to fulfill their scholarship arrangements at the college. About 30 per cent of the students at BYU are from the Pacific Islands (of that percentage, the return rate home is about 20 per cent), over 40 per cent from the Hawaiian islands. Up to 85 per cent work in the PCC as entertainers and performers in the seven reconstructed Polynesian villages that fill the forty-acre landscape of the park, representing Hawaii, Tonga, Fiji, Samoa, Tahiti, Maori New Zealand, and the Marquesas. Each model village is presided over by a chief, often real chiefs and talking chiefs from the islands exercising full chiefly privileges both within the Laie community and back home, although US labor laws restrict them from treating employees in too chiefly a fashion. In the period of time during which I made my visits, the villages became 'islands,' and, to appease chiefly pride, village chiefs became island managers in control of their own budgets. Tourists, mostly in organized groups bussed in from Waikiki, visit each of the villages in turn, and are treated to performances of song and dance and demonstrations of material culture, such as tapa clothmaking from tree bark, plaiting, fishing techniques, or food preparation. The chiefs and staff are available to talk to tourists who have more exacting questions to ask about nonmaterial aspects of the culture and customs. A large gift shop sells Polynesian tourist art. The tourists' day at the center is capped off by a lavish *luau* and a showstopping Broadway-style evening extravaganza called 'This is Polynesia,' performed in a vast open-air theater.

The time period represented in the villages is assumed to be precontact, although the traditional cultures are presented as if they were timeless, continuous with the past and the present. In the brochure's words, these are 'the islands as you always imagined they would be.' There is no attempt to disabuse tourists of the idea that the villages represent existing lifeways today on islands that most will never visit, although a casual conversation with any of the performers or guides will reveal how little the students know, and how much they have learnt only recently about their traditional cultures in order to perform their roles. A great deal of scholarly attention has been devoted to ensuring the detailed architectural, ecological, and artifactual authenticity in the villages. This task is overseen by an environmental historian from Easter Island, Sergio Rapu, the director of the Institute for Polynesian Studies at BYU and Director of Cultural Development at the PCC. Rapu and his research staff also tend to act as cultural brokers between Polynesian specialists on the faculty of the BYU campus and the business-minded administrators of the PCC.

The origins of the PCC lay in three early developments: (1) the profitable custom, from the late 1940s, of staging a monthly *hukilau* (communal fishing practice) — plus *luau* — for visitors to the Laie community; (2) the need for a communal house for Maori saints doing temple work in Laie — the idea that they could entertain for their keep was suggested by a Mormon (LDS) elder who had seen Boy Scouts perform American Indian dances in Colorado; and (3) the desire on the part of scholars at the BYU's Polynesian Institute to combat the 'inauthenticity' that had crept into tourist presentations of Polynesian culture. In 1963, the PCC's adventure in balancing the authentic face of Polynesia with entertainment codes and talent imported directly from Hollywood officially got under way, just as the decades-long *hapa haole* craze in Hollywood and Tin Pan Alley for *hula* and Hawaiian music was petering out. Hooked into the Oahu tourist circuit through tourbus 'packaging,' the PCC turned a profit in 1967, and never looked back until the tourist recessions of the early 1990s. In replacing the locally managed *hukilau*, the PCC returned the Laie community to a condition of economic dependence upon Salt Lake City, since it duplicated the function of an earlier sugar plantation founded by the first Mormon missionaries to supply Utah.[34] Partly as a consequence of insensitive *haole* (white foreigner) management appointed by Salt Lake City, labor problems have been persistent at the PCC since its inception, resulting in at least one strike by Fijians in 1974, and a successful suit brought against the PCC by the National Labor Relations Board. For almost a decade the Internal Revenue Service unsuccessfully challenged the tax-exempt status that the Center enjoyed as an educational center in the business of cultural enrichment rather than commercial gain. In 1992, a local circuit court judge ruled against the PCC's tax-exempt status. Over the years, the PCC has garnered the reputation of being a minimum wage employer, exploiting the availability of a labor force of students with low financial demands.[35]

Until 1975, the adminstration of the PCC was almost wholly *haole*, and generated a good deal of resentment among islanders in the community and at the university. Indeed, Laie is probably the only citadel of Mormonism where antiwhite sentiment and impiety for the Utah Way runs deep enough to be a vocal element of the institutional culture. A 1993 April Fool's issue of the BYU campus newspaper *Ke Alaka'i* — dated April 1, 2013 — ran a feature on the addition to the PCC of Haole Suburbs as another model village, featuring identical tract houses. Performances included 'walking like a haole,' 'using a remote control,' and 'dancing out of rhythm,' while the food offerings included macaroni and cheese, and peanut butter and jelly sandwiches.

As a tourist development and source of community revenue, however, the Center stands as a remarkable achievement, with a minimum of social and environmental impact on the town of Laie itself, since tourists make the return trip to Honolulu immediately their visit to the park is over. The mission statement of the PCC pledges its efforts to 'preserve and portray the cultures, arts, and crafts of Polynesia.' Its practical purpose is to help provide a college education for Pacific Islanders, one that includes learning some of their own traditional culture, which, for many of these urban students, means encountering 'rural' customs for the first time. No one would deny that the Center is also seen as a missionary tool, not only for potential conversions among tourists, but also for spreading goodwill in Hawaii and throughout Polynesia on behalf of the Mormon Church. It is likely, however, that many visitors leave the park without having ascertained its relationship to the Church. In any case, the park includes a reconstruction of a missionary home in the Mission Village as an entrée for the curious visitor, and student workers, many of them former missionaries and practised proselytizers, often communicate their dependence on the benevolence of the Church. The more curious can take a guided tour to the Temple in Laie, an architectural curio to say the least. At least one scholarly reader of the PCC, Terry Webb, has found a distinct Mormon narrative in the structure of the tourist visit to the PCC villages. The

Marquesan village, at the far end of the park in the middle of the village track, was originally conceived as a monument to a dead Polynesian culture. In passing through the somber Marquesan *tohua*, preceded and succeeded by the other dynamic Polynesian exhibits, the visitor was following a narrative familiar to Mormon history, which details the rise, fall, and restoration of ancient civilizations. What is thereby emphasized, according to Webb, is the fragility of Polynesian culture, whose preservation is ensured by the activities of the LDS.[36]

While the presentations at the PCC make little attempt to portray the social history of Polynesia, especially as it pertains to plantation colonialism and other modes of underdevelopment, there are moments when the pressure of this history is unavoidable, and is best defused through comedy. One such moment occurs in the act of Sielu Avea, who delivers the following scripted monologue (with some improvised variants) to visitors to the Samoan village during a coconut husking demonstration. It is a classic example of staged ex-primitivism:

I know you've spent a lot of money to come here to look for us, so here we are. I am from New York. Seriously, friends, welcome to Samoa, you know when you come to our village of Samoa, when you visit our islands, you have to say *talofa*, you can't say *aloha*. I want everyone to say *tálófa* [audience says *tálófa*]. Terrific! [sardonically] We, Samoans, are the happy people. Friends, welcome to our cooking place, it's called the pizza hut. [laughter] In Samoa, remember this area belongs to the men. In Samoa, the men do all the cooking for the family, ladies don't cook. That's why I ran away, and came here to get more education. Someday, I'll go back, and change it — I'll take a microwave oven. [A demonstration of firemaking follows, involving rubbing sticks together] You flick your bics, we rub our sticks . . . You wanna see flames, give me five dollars, and some gasoline. On rainy days, we don't cook, we go to McDonalds. [laughter] Seriously, folks, to cook we always use the coconut milk. To get the milk, we need a ripe coconut. This one is ripe, you can tell by its color, it always turns brown, it turns brown like me. This one is ripe, and it tells me that some of you are not ripe yet. [overzealous laughter] That's a joke. We also use this object. Now this is what we call *mele'i*. Say it. [audience complies] In English 'sharp stick.' Say it. [audience says 'sharp stick'] We're gonna use the stick for husking the coconut. [demonstrates in three steps] I was doing that in slow motion for your convenience. In Samoa, this is one of the competitive sports among young men and women. Record for the men — three seconds. Ladies — two days. If you let the ladies cook, we'd never eat, then we'd all go to McDonalds. Now we have to learn how to crack the coconuts. To crack it you have to start at the face — this line is the softest spot, which you have to hit with a hard object. You can use hammers, knives, screwdrivers, dynamite. In Samoa we use our foreheads. You don't believe it, do you? [advances threateningly on audience member] Close your eyes! A lady from Canada came here last week and told me that she put a coconut on the ground and ran it over with a lawnmower. A young man from Texas put on his .45 and shot the thing between the eyes, while his mother-in-law was holding the coconut. Please don't do that. In our islands, this is what we use, a rock — all you do is hit across the line — if it doesn't come out in two pieces please don't blame me. I am a pure Samoan, this is a Hawaiian coconut, made in Taiwan. [successfully divides the coconut, macho style, audience responds] Thank you, believe it or not. That's the end of our demonstration, folks, if you have any questions, take them with you.

This kind of jaunty deflationary talk undercuts the pious devotion to authenticity required by the PCC's mission. It is the only such scripted moment in the entire day's presentation, although the generally easygoing attitude (the happy, carefree native) is encouraged to some degree in all host—guest relations at the Center. It is significant that these few relatively politicized comments about modernization, gendered division of labor, skin privilege, and touristic colonialism are presented in the form of what we might call Samoan Borcht Belt shtick. (Clowning has its own rich social history in Samoa and throughout Polynesia.)[37] Sielu, a mathematics graduate, is one of the most popular items at the park, and you can hear him do similar, if slightly more risqué, standup routines at the downtown Waikiki Comedy Club. He has not only entered island entertainment history by appearing in a regular spot with Don Ho at the Polynesian Palace, but has also been a guest on the 'Oprah Winfrey Show' and acted in 'Murder, She Wrote,' accumulating so much local *mana* that he alone of the PCC staff is permitted to wear tattoos and improvise with his script. Sielu also enjoys the privileges of partial Samoan hegemony in the community and at the PCC,[38] the Samoans being the dominant Polynesian group with the most secure identity, and perhaps thus in the indulgent position of being able to poke fun at themselves. In the menu of ethnic differences officially presented within the PCC, the Samoan comic represents the type of the happy Samoans — alongside the superstititous/ religious Hawaiians, warlike Maori, melancholy Marquesans, friendly Tongans, romantic Tahitians, and scary Fijians.

The inclusion in the PCC of Fiji, much of whose ethnic population is Melanesian, was once hotly debated, and is still resented by some, as I discovered in some conversations with older, often openly racist, staff workers.[39] It was not until 1954 that Mormon missionaries began to work in Melanesia, when 'President McKay was satisfied by anthropologists at the National Museum in Suva that Melanesians were in no way related to African negroes,' and not until 1958 that Fijians who had 'a considerable admixture of Polynesian blood' were allowed to be ordained.[40] In reinforcing the Melanesian/Polynesian division, the Mormons were reproducing typically Western prejudices that have generally favored Polynesians and given short shrift to Melanesians, from the time of the first European voyages. The very term 'Melanesian' carries negative connotations throughout Western literature. Eminent anthropologists are in no way exempt. A typical example is the opening line of Raymond Firth's classic *We, The Tikopia*: 'We were surrounded by crowds of naked, chattering youngsters with their pleasant light and brown velvet skins and straight hair, so different from the Melanesians we had left behind.'[41] Epeli Hauofa, the Tongan anthropologist, has challenged this picture of Oceania constructed by over a century of Western anthropological writers who have continued the European business of romanticizing Polynesians and their regal chiefs, and denigrating Melanesians and their swaggering, entrepreneurial 'big men.' Melanesians, Hauofa writes, 'fight, compete, trade, pay bride prices, engage in rituals, invent cargo cults, copulate and sorcerize each other,' but they do not 'love and laugh and moralize and philosophize like the Polynesians.'[42]

Inscribed in the park's geography is the PCC's demarcation of distinct cultural identities among the Polynesians themselves. The visitor is invited to be an ethnographic investigator, to learn something about the customs that differentiate one island people from another. The net effect is to reinforce what some scholars think of as a specifically 'Western' idea of ethnicity, which stresses a rigid view of cultural identity by emphasizing the homogeneity of a local culture transmitted without variation down through history.[43] In most respects, this view of identity is a direct result of the colonial history of the Pacific Islands. Colonies were carved out and bilaterally isolated by the economic, political and cultural demands of the respective colonizers, while the intensive Christianization of the Pacific radically transformed every indigenous island culture in ways largely determined by the dominant missionary orders. Only in recent years have the nationalist movements, united by common anticolonial goals and the desire for a nuclear-free region, encouraged the acceptance of a pan-Pacific identity, transcending Western-induced differences among island peoples.

The historical evidence of widespread intercultural and inter-island exchanges and borrowings and appropriations in the precolonial Pacific have helped to challenge further the power established by this Western paradigm of ethnicity. At the same time, the paradigm of cultural essentialism has also helped to reinforce primordialist views of native custom promoted in the postcolonial period by Westernized national elites seeking a socially cohesive identity for their newly independent states. Nationalist intelligentsia and politicians tend to celebrate the purity and continuity of indigenous custom ('traditional' is often quite different from 'indigenous'), even as they incorporate as traditional those creolized elements of the culture that are a normative and probably permanent result of centuries of colonial activity, not all of it by Europeans. In this respect, the decolonizing elites do what Pacific politicians have always done — interpret the past and its customary practices in such a way as to legitimize their own power, whether they are speaking from the margin, as in Hawaii or New Zealand, or from the center, as in Fiji or Vanuatu. As in most other regions of the postcolonial world, the various cultural revivals associated with the Pacific nationalist movements have made ethnic (clan or tribal) identity a strong feature of the new regimes. In the same period of time, of course, the development of Pacific tourism has fuelled the debate in ways that cannot always be confined to the national situation. The global tourist industry's demand that Pacific peoples reify their traditional cultures in order to survive in a modern cash economy has added a new dimension to the representation of local cultural renaissances. In some respects, tourism has helped to preserve and revive aspects of traditional cultures, but in ways that many nationalists condemn as inauthentic and as a continuation of colonialism by other means.

I will return to these debates later. I mention them here not to establish that the PCC is some kind of manageable textual microcosm of the current state of Pacific Island cultural politics, or that it invites a 'reading' that sees its structure accordingly. Nothing so tidy is attempted here. Tourist sites like the PCC are not simply ideological documents to be deciphered, quotation by quotation, layer by layer. In addition to being the product of multiple institutional histories, philosophical and political, they are also an economic presence in the daily lives of workers and host communities, and a major environmental presence on the land. I do want to acknowledge, however, the extent to which the functioning of a site like the PCC is highly informed by exactly those debates about cultural identity that have occupied nationalist intellectuals, high chiefs, anthropologists, postcolonial administrators, and the like, and that these debates are often played out in various ways in day-to-day disputes about the running of the park. The testimony lies as much in the stories told by staff and workers on site as it does in the PCC's official tourist descriptions or in the research conducted by its associated Mormon scholars.

In the interviews I conducted as part of a bargain-basement ethnography of the park, my impression was that the Polynesians who work there were comfortably ambivalent about the overlap between: (a) their given performing identities as Tongans, Samoans, Hawaiians, etc.; (b) the faux identities that they often take on as performers − Tongans playing the part of Marquesans, because of the shortage of Marquesan students, Samoans playing Hawaiians just for the hell of it, and Filipinos playing the role of Polynesians in the night show, because sometimes any brown body will do on stage (Maori, a little too *haole* in appearance and accent, are something of a problem); (c) the identities that they negotiate within their own not always customary communities in Laie and as part of the pan-Pacific community on campus; and (d) the overriding identity that they observe as Mormons (the majority are). In conversation, I found that one Samoan, for example, described herself and indeed all Samoans as 'hammy' and 'happy-go-lucky,' and thus naturally suited for reasons of social and cultural homogeneity to the comic role typified by Sielu − 'we enjoy being exploited,' she said to me, while at the same time acknowledging the vulnerability of this position. Later on, she acknowledged that her own history and family network is completely pan-Pacific, the result of intermarriage, extensive migration, and intercultural influence. Outside of the uneven pressure of the patriarchal *matai* system of village life, what was truly Samoan for her was as much an academic question as it was a lived practice, and this did not trouble her at all. A similar ambivalence seemed to apply to her Mormon identity, as with others I interviewed; there are elements of the Lamanite-Hebraic identity ascribed to Polynesians that would be officially acknowledged at the level of LDS church ritual and yet are ignored and even ridiculed at a lay level of daily life. In particular, a high degree of doubt was cast on the Mormon theory of the migration from South America of the Polynesian peoples. In general, Polynesian Mormons are officially supposed to be honored within the church, but most feel that they are actually subject to discrimination. To be a truly traditional Polynesian, after all, would mean not being a Mormon.

If anything, the picture of ethnic pluralism that emerged from my conversations with administrators and staff at the PCC has more to do with the way in which Polynesians there negotiate daily a whole range of different identities than with the rather stationary picture presented by the PCC's mandate to preserve the vanishing traditions of each island culture. The same could be said of the park's primary form of address to tourists, primarily North American or Japanese — these are all one people, but they have and always have had different ways of doing things — an accentuated version of what passes for the official North American version of multicultural pluralism — we are all Americans but . . . [fill in the blanks] — that has become the state religion of Hawaii. In general, the class profile followed by the PCC performances is *ali'i* — no one demonstrates how to cook a dog for dinner — and the selection of students is often based on aesthetic discrimination, which is to say that the lighter-skinned and most handsome are favored (in keeping with the prejudices of island nobility who often kept their daughters out of the sun). No exhibit at the PCC dwells on pre-Christian rituals of human sacrifice, infanticide, headhunting, cannibalism, or widow-strangling, and, in deference to Mormon morality, there is virtually no exploitation of longstanding conventional fantasies about sex and gore in Pacific island life.

It would be easy to go on cataloging all of the representational shortcomings and discrepancies of the park and bewailing the idealized version of traditional Polynesian culture swallowed by a million visitors a year. Critics of Disney theme parks have made a fine, if tedious, art of this kind of exposé. Its many critics, including Hawaiian nationalists, have a low opinion of the PCC, generally citing it as a debased example of the commercialization of Polynesian culture, the more so since its activities are legitimized by the scholarly stamp of Dr. Rapu and his research team, while underwritten by an unlikely coordination of the interests of the tourist industry and those of the Mormon Church. Scholarly critics of the PCC often treat the park as if it truly were a pedagogical medium, exhorting its administrators to provide more authenticity so that students and tourists alike will learn more from their respective performances and visits. Indeed, all the staff I talked to voiced such sentiments themselves, in the course of lambasting the overly commercial elements of the PCC.[44]

However important as responses to the general activities of the PCC, these criticisms tell us very little about the popularity of the park as a genre of tourist culture. Although the term 'theme park' is taboo in Laie, the PCC obviously belongs to the broad spectrum of constructed tourist environments that can be grouped under this rubric. The spectrum runs from in-your-face kitsch to antiartifice sanctuary; not just Knott's Berry Farm, PTL's Heritage USA, and Dollywood, but also the landscapes of world's fairs, outdoor folk museums, heritage parks, conservation areas, land trusts, zoological parks, safari parks, wilderness parks, and UNESCO's world heritage sites and biosphere reserves — all with different generic tales to tell about the social and natural ecology of the regional histories and geographies that they evoke. As Alexander Wilson has argued, in a generous critique of these bounded landscapes, each of these sites appeals in some way, not just to nostalgia for human settlements that are no longer possible, but also to genuine popular anxiety about the future of human settlements in our technologically saturated world. Most parks, he points out, employ history as a retreat from some unsavory present, but they also speak critically to people's sense of communitarian deficiency in the present.[45] In North America, in particular, the theme park's model vision of the self-sufficient utopian community has a profound resonance in the Republic's and in Native American history. To complain that the sanitized stories told there are meretricious is like complaining that soap operas give an improbable picture of most people's daily lives.[46]

Each site along this spectrum responds to the conventions of its genre and is the result of a set of contractual expectations negotiated with its likely visitors. Predominant generic principles may include artistic kitsch, historical authenticity, picturesque solitude, or even biotic co-evolutionism. In this respect, the park genres are little different from any other genre of popular culture bound by a conventional contract with its audience. With the exception of resentful intellectuals, few go to the Disney parks without prior Disney competence. To a greater extent than with soap operas, however, one could say that tourist parks are also material environments, and that their physical and social existence has a powerful environmental impact on the land, whether conservationist, as in the case of wilderness areas, or destructive, as in the case of Disneyworld, which has damaged the Floridian acquifer, destroyed the surrounding wetlands, and drastically altered the ecosystem of central Florida.

It has also been argued by postmodern geographers and architectural theorists that the theme park is now the favored model for urban development. For the critics represented in Michael Sorkin's collection, *Variations on a Theme Park*, the theme park — an urban form that merely simulates urbanism — has encouraged the kind of architecture that appears to draw authoritatively upon reconstructed historic period forms. The corrosive power of these simulations has spread beyond their enclosed environments, and is becoming omnipresent in our cities where, thanks to 'creative geography,' we are always somewhere that is merely like somewhere else — 'We no longer visit theme parks, they visit us.'[47] For Sorkin and his contributors, the theme park utopia, and all it represents, is the exact opposite of a critical utopia that negates the status quo. Worst of all, it is a primary symptom of the decline of democratic public realm and the galloping commodification of all public space.

By now, it is easy to itemize the standard elements of this narrative of decline.[48] The good old days are always just ending or have always just disappeared; popular culture is usually to blame; all that is to be salvaged is a more authentic, virile past; and the only agent to be found in the narrative is Capital itself, inexorably adept in its capacity to evade regulation, and creatively destructive in the promotion of built environments sympathetic to its own interests. Such a narrative is useful up to a point, but in the absence of other stories, it has the effect of further empowering what is already empowered, dispossessing people of whatever agency they thought they had, and generally reinforcing the conditions it seeks to oppose. Worst of all, with regard to the case in point, it assumes that tourists are mindless cretins whose consumerism entirely defines the limits of their responses to tourism.

Visitors to Disneyland or Disneyworld do not believe that they have visited the past or the future, any more than visitors to the PCC conclude that they have visited Polynesia. The reasons for visiting these sites are multiple, as are the uses made of visits to all such places that express, on our behalf, a popular relation to environments, past, present, and future. This is as true of the ethnographic tourist industry in the Third World as of the heritage industry in the First World where there is scarcely a sizeable town that does not boast a handful of nostalgia centers, usually for rural days of yore, but increasingly for early industrial sites and places of labor.[49] We tend to know a lot about tourism, but relatively little about what tourists do with it or use it for. Despite tourism being the single largest item in world trade at 8 per cent (and growing 23 per cent faster than the global economy as a whole), the world's biggest mover of populations in peacetime, the biggest employer outside the military, the modern medium of neocolonial relations between First and Third Worlds, the uneasy passport to development for many countries, and one of the most important media of intercultural knowledge today, relatively few studies in the vast literature on tourism itself examine what tourists actually do with this intercultural knowledge. Exit questionnaires of the sort that I consulted at the PCC cover a broad range of comments, from the informants who enjoyed nothing better than the jokes of the 'funny Samoan,' to those who were bewildered by the PCC because 'there was nothing to compare it to,' and those who found it 'extremely enlightening to learn that they were not a primitive people.' More casual conversations I had with tourists on the site revealed visitors who knew an immense amount about Polynesia — tourists who make a point of learning almost as much about the history of their favorite tourist destination as of their own culture.

Among the student workers with whom I spoke, some acknowledged the learning opportunities afforded by working in the park, some complained about the low wages, and others confessed that they would do anything to get a degree from an American university. After all, the PCC-BYU complex plays a vital role in the university education of thousands of Pacific Islanders and in the economy of the islands (where an average wage is $300 a year), since some part of its revenue is channelled back there through students' wages, and a percentage of the graduates return to staff, among other things, the tourist industries of their own islands.[50] More often than not, these students return home with songs and dances that have already circulated around the islands through the clearing house of the PCC. John Jonasson, former Minister for Foreign Affairs in the Cook Islands (a Polynesian group not represented at the PCC), and now Professor of Political Science at BYU, recounted how he and a troupe had performed a Cook Island dance in Tahiti that he had subsequently seen presented as Tahitian at the PCC, and would no doubt make its way back into the islands as Tahitian. On the other hand, the PCC is also a nursery for Western entertainment talent, sending students into show business, and has played its own role in the history of commercial popular culture. As a Hollywood outpost, it played host to scenes from the Elvis Presley film, *Paradise Hawaiian-Style*. It was a Mormon in Laie who invented the steel guitar.

Everyone I interviewed had a tale or two to tell about the (in)authenticity of some detail in the park. After a while, I realized that the stories were really about something other than authenticity. Historically, the PCC has been shaped by the often competing interests of three institutions – LDS, BYU, and the industry-minded administration of the PCC. Every aspect of its construction and administration has been fraught by internal politics from its inception, usually revolving around the conflict between money-making and educational incentives, set against the doctrinal backdrop of the LDS. Consequently, the daily debates among staff about the authenticity of details at the PCC – from the placing of a banyan tree to the length of a dancer's skirt – are actually a highly charged arena for winning points or concessions in the ongoing bargaining war among these three institutions. Theology, academic scholarship, and commerce, each vying for control over the right to preserve Polynesian culture. Throw in the chiefs, genealogically perfect, and scornful of challenges to their cultural authority, especially from the PhDs, and you have stories that the PCC itself cannot tell, and lessons that do not always speak for themselves.

The Lesson of Waikiki

Visitors to the PCC are also visitors to a Hawaii that is often termed the species extinction capital of the world. Seventy-five per cent of all land and plant extinctions in the USA have occurred there; 50 per cent of native insects are gone; half of nonmigrant birds are extinct, and half of those remaining are on the federal endangered list, 30 per cent of which is accounted for by Hawaii alone. All of this in an island ecology that is unique because of its specific biotic history and geographical remoteness. With everything from volcanic coastal formations to high alpine deserts, the Hawaiian islands still boast the highest number of endemic species — 90 per cent — in a biogeography that harbored no hostile, pestiferous, or competing species until it was settled by Polynesians and then by Anglo-Americans. Colonized by waif dispersal — with each new colonizer species arriving every 20,000 years or so — and creatively filled by adaptive radiation — whereby open and uncontested habitats offer diverse ecological opportunities for founder species — the Hawaiian landscape became a rare site of evolutionary biology, even by the standards of island biogeography. Its biotic diversity lends itself still to the Edenic narrative, while setting the scene for the postlapsarian sadness that pervades the melancholic romance of Hawaii.

In the last couple of decades, the romantic ecological myth of prehistoric Hawaii — of Polynesians living in respectful harmony with nature — has been challenged by archaeologists at the same time as it has been revived in other, militant forms by native nationalists. In common with the Easter Island story, the picture of precontact Hawaii that emerges from nonnative scholars is that of an advanced Stone Age society that was as much a transformer and destroyer as it was a steward of physical environments. As in other Polynesian habitats, the ancient dry forests of the lowlands and coastal wetlands were destroyed to facilitate the cultivation of plants and garden trees — bananas, taro, coconuts and breadfruit — and suffered desertification from overgrazing.[51] The cleared forests were replaced by fire-maintained fern-grassland savannahs, with infertile and eroded soils underneath. Predators introduced by the colonizers took their toll on flora and fauna, while an extensive spectrum of flightless birds were wiped out by human predation. These developments did not occur because humans, as a species, are naturally destructive. In the case of Hawaii, they were the result of a particular social ecology.

Patrick Kirch has noted that the Hawaiians displayed a considerable divergence both from the ancestral models of other Polynesian societies and from the transformation of the island environment.[52]

This divergence was evident not only in an elaborate sociopolitical structure — a rigorous class system of up to four rank echelons, wherein the chiefs' monopoly of power increasingly cut across lines of kinship — but also in the development of intensive modes of food production that depended upon the creation of artificial ecosystems — from the cultivation of vast fishponds for fish husbandry, to massive valley irrigation systems, and large-scale dryland field systems. Kirch argues that both of these developments were linked, the expansive productive economy responding to the political economy. On the one hand, there developed a class system whereby ruling chiefs (*ali'i nui*), alone among the Polynesian societies, attained the status of gods on earth, controlled the pie-shaped land units (*ahupua'a*) that were the basis of self-contained polities, and ensured their monopoly over land, labor and resources by *kapu* or by the *makahiki* system for collecting commoners' tributes. On the other hand, there developed an intensive system of high yield, or surplus, food production that responded to the consumption demands of the ruling class households or to the political designs of the chiefs, either for waging war against rivals, or for self-glorification in the construction of *heiaus*. At the time of contact, Kirch estimates that a population plateau had been reached, either because the carrying capacity of the land was overextended, or because the demands of the nonproducer elite were taking their toll on the tribute-bearing commoners, or because chiefly competition had led to endemic warfare.[53]

The story told by nationalists is quite different. According to David Stannard, population levels were rising at time of contact, and food was in such abundance that it drew the attention of Cook and other commentators. Others, like Haunani-Kay Trask, emphasize the nonfeudal 'interdependence' of the relationship between *maka'ainana* and 'their *ali'i* caretakers,' resulting in a wise and beneficent society that viewed and protected the natural environment as a family member.[54] Environmental damage, from this point of view, was primarily a postcontact development, and took on its first mature form only in the near-feudal economy of the sugar and pineapple plantations.

Either way (elements of both stories are probably true), the toll was evident — lowland forests universally clearcut, with considerable loss of topsoils, valley slopes terraced, watersheds radically transformed through irrigation systems, reef flats converted to fishponds, and many species of birds (geese, ibises, rails, owls, hawks, eagles, ravens, and songbirds) slaughtered for food and ornamentation to the point of wholesale extinction. These patterns of environmental degradation on the part of Polynesians were magnified a hundredfold in the postcontact period. The practise of relocating water serviced the plantation system, and, more recently, the tourist and condo developments. Biotic loss was accelerated by the pell-mell introduction of pestiferous species. The rainforests were devastated by Hawaii's contribution to the China sandalwood trade in the early nineteenth century, a trade that stretched the chiefly tax collection system to the point of slave labor when *ali'i* decreed the *maka'ainana* delivery of wood to meet their hunger for Western luxury items (local legend has it that commoners tore the sandalwood out by the roots to put an end to the trade). Masquerading as the liberation of the *maka'ainana*, the Great Mahele of the late 1840s (the land redistribution Act that instituted Western privatization of land tenure and left commoners with about 1 per cent of the available land) provided the impetus for clearing upland forests on land authorized for sale to foreigners who instituted capitalist plantation agriculture. The forests that survived the ravages of feral livestock underwent another trial at the hands of a maverick botanist, Harold Lloyd Lyon, hired by the sugar planters in the early twentieth century to prevent any further dieoff. Lyon harbored a theory about the *decadence* of Hawaiian flora:

> It has been recognized by all students of the Hawaiian flora that the indigenous trees and shrubs which constitute the rain forests on our watersheds are in a very delicate state of health, and that the slightest interference from man or his domestic animals so disturbs their balance that a rapid deterioration sets in which soon terminates in the death of the majority of native plants.[55]

Lyon held not only that the forests were destined to wither away in toxic volcanic soil, but also that he was destined to replace them, with simplified fig tree forests — a theory which thankfully failed when put to a sample test.[56] Finally, when the plantation system gave way to tourism as the mainstay of the economy, land speculation, hotel development, and golf course construction took an ever-increasing toll on the remaining lowland forests, on coastal ecosystems, and on botanical diversity generally.

Lyon's theories of forest conservation — any human contact will put an end to the old forests — surely owed more than a little to the lens of decadence through which native Hawaiian culture had come to be viewed in the decades before and after the overthrow of the Hawaiian monarchy by US forces in 1893. Those who utilized the rhetoric of the dying race could always find philosophical and scientific support to maintain their vital interests. On the one hand, there was the creed of social Darwinism that 'explained' the selective perishability of life, especially among indigenous island peoples, and, on the other hand, there was the egalitarian righteousness of a republicanism that had condemned to history the aboriginal legitimacy of aristocratic rule. A similar attitude prevailed on the mainland with respect to the American Indian, whose image in eighteenth- and nineteenth-century popular culture was that of the vanishing, melancholic remnant of a doomed aristocratic order.[57] This rhetoric would be turned around in the name of Hawaiian nationalism, which bore its first full flower during the reign of Kalakaua, the 'merrie monarch.' His call to 'increase the race' was a direct response to the broad perception that by the late nineteenth century, the Hawaiians themselves had become an endangered species. It has been estimated that their numbers had fallen from a precontact population of as much as 800,000 to 40,000 in a little over a century.[58]

One hundred years later, the demographic increase in the native Hawaiian population is higher than any other group on these multicultural islands, and likely to go higher if the blood quantum is redefined to include anyone with a drop of Hawaiian blood. There is nothing more hip (and profitable) than traditional Hawaiian culture, which has enjoyed a major renaissance in the realms of sports, performance arts, agriculture, language, material crafts, and spirituality. And yet Hawaiians themselves, like other US indigenous groups, remain, for most part, an underclass, suffering high unemployment, catastrophic health problems, low educational attainment, disproportionate incarceration in prison and military service, employment ghettoization, high crime and suicide rates, and increasing outmigration.

One of the stories about the 'survival' of the Hawaiians is about history made under conditions entirely not of their choosing. It is a narrative of their forced integration into the world system of capitalism, and therefore focuses exclusively on the peripheral dependency of the islands upon external, metropolitan influence for over three centuries — first the fishing fleet captains, the fur traders, and whalers, then the sandalwood merchants, the missionaries, and the sugar and pineapple planters, and now the land developers, the airlines, and the transnational tourism conglomerates that bring six million visitors a year. Consequently, all internal developments in the islands are seen as a result of the inexorable influence of metropolitan capital in every phase of Hawaii's peripheral history — its indigenous people a servant class still, working as domestics in the Waikiki hotels or as drivers of the tour buses — even as Hawaii's own multinational corporations (direct descendants, in some cases, of the original missionary families) have extended their neocolonial activities all over the Pacific in the last thirty years.[59] The result of this kind of analysis — guided by dependency or world systems theory — is often to deny any degree of autonomy to indigenous cultures, and to ignore the ways in which specific groups make use of external influence to transform internal social relations.[60] Domestic class and gender conflicts are downplayed, and a picture of the culture as static and weak is assumed, and for which museum-style preservation is the only possible response to the destructive commodity-logic of external penetration.

That precolonial Hawaiian culture was flexible and dynamic in its social structure accounted, among other things, for the capacity of Kamehameha to form a monarchic dynasty, and for the *ali'i nui* to monopolize their power and wealth through foreign trade. The same could be said for the ability of commoners, especially women, to challenge the *kapu* system and use small trade and sexual relations with sailors to circumvent the power of *ali'i*. The lack of highly prescriptive kinship rules meant that the status of *kama'aina* (child of the land) could be conferred on nonnatives for reasons of right action. Marshall Sahlins has argued that Hawaiian social structure was so open to expedient negotiation that Cook's crew and subsequent Europeans could be quickly incorporated under the category of *kama'aina*, or what, today, the Hawaiian Visitors Bureau calls 'Hawaiians by heart.' The disastrous consequence, however, was that 'the foreigners had no obligation to act like natives, and they had less appealing categories to put the natives in.'[61] Just as in other parts of Polynesia, native hospitality was perceived as an invitation for outsiders to exploit and plunder, but it was also a byword for the social flexibility of the native culture, wherein 'new traditions' can easily be formed to accommodate both the modern and the customary. Consequently, today Hawaii is probably the most multicultural polity in the world. This is the direct result of a history of imported plantation labor (the heavy ethnic stratification of the plantation system still lingers on), but it is also a testament to the continued dynamism of a local culture for which the *aloha* spirit is not entirely a creation of the Hawaiian Visitors Bureau, and for which the extended family structure of *'ohana* is not merely the name of the cartel of banks serviced by cash machines installed in Honolulu supermarkets. Nor was traditional Hawaiian society so weak that it simply collapsed on contact with a cash and wage economy, or with institutions of private property. In fact, the communal mode of production of the *maka'ainana* has long outlived the hierarchical mode of production controlled by the *ali'i*. Exchange-in-kind and subsistence farming persisted in rural areas like Hana, East Moloka'i, Wai'anae, Waimanalo, Keanae, and Kahalu'u well into the 1970s.[62] So, too, *haole* planters found native Hawaiians to be so resistant to plantation labor that workers had to be imported from China, Japan, the Philippines, and many parts of Europe and South America.

Similar stories could be told of native resistance to Calvinism, whose congregationalist power receded radically when the chiefly hierarchy (the missionaries' main vehicle) disintegrated, or of the insurgent opposition to the overthrow of the monarchy in the 1890s, or, indeed, of the remarkable resurgence of the sovereignty movement over the last twenty years.[63] Radical Hawaiian writers associated with the Bamboo Ridge movement have also contributed to a cultural renaissance in the region during the last two decades, joining other Pacific authors like Subramani, Albert Wendt, Epeli Hauofa, Keri Hulme, Patricia Grace, and Vilson Hereniko, in reimagining the past, present, and future of the islands from a local point of view.[64]

These are the stories that attribute to people a sense of historical agency and resistance, even under the worst conditions, while those about the relentless destruction of their culture resign them to exactly the passive fate visualized only in the most powerful, near-genocidal fantasies. Faced with a choice, however, the cultural politics of most nationalist movements (and Hawaii is no exception) often favors the latter kind of story because it provides the most powerful anticolonial narrative, and the most likely to achieve results. The ensuing *Kulturkampf* turns upon the political act of reviving and reclaiming precontact cultural forms that have been lost or threatened to the point of extinction. Acknowledging hybrid elements of the *hapa haole* cultural history, or the development of a distinctive, multiethnic *local* culture, in the postcontact period is seen as a luxury, a concession, even an impediment, at a time when the struggle for self-determination demands more clearcut symbolism, drawn from a more 'glorious' past, untarnished by nonindigenous traces. The ancestral past, with all of its pure cultural trappings, is the key to the decolonization of the mind. This is the basic formula of cultural nationalism, or as historian Lilikala Kame'eleihiwa puts it:

> The Hawaiian stands firmly in the present, with his back to the future, and his eyes fixed upon the past, seeking historical answers for present day dilemmas. Such an orientation is to the Hawaiian an eminently practical one, for the future is always unknown whereas the past is rich in glory and knowledge.[65]

Does it matter whether or not the glory was mostly enjoyed by the indigenous aristocracy? Only if the nationalism seeks to live solely by the sword of the past. In the case of Hawaiian nationalism, the most serious of the sovereignty groups have long since begun to legislate their way into the future.

In 1993, the sovereignty movement reached a symbolic climax, seizing on the centenary of the US overthrow of the Hawaiian monarchy to push home autonomous claims for self-government, for reparations from the USA, and for reclaiming the native land base, carved out of the 1.4 million acres (originally 2.4m) historically entrusted to the Hawaiian people. Much of this land has either been withdrawn or appropriated for military bases or is currently leased out to nonnatives by the state of Hawaii. The activist wing of the movement originated in organized protests (*Hui Alaloa*) against commercial development in rural areas on Moloka'i in the early 1970s, and took a strong oppositional stand against the US Navy's bombing of the island of Kaho'olawe. As part of the massive military appropriation of Hawaiian land that followed the Japanese attack on Pearl Harbor, CINCPAC's (US Pacific Command) 25-year desecration of the island provided a highly visible example of US contempt for land held sacred by indigenous activists. In the course of the struggle to gain religious, cultural, educational, and scientific access to Kaho'olawe, activists came to forge the principles of protection, stewardship, consecration, and revitalization of the land that have become the cornerstone of the movement philosophy of *aloha 'aina* (love of the land). Consequently, the fight to reclaim Kaho'olawe became the Wounded Knee of the Hawaiian movement, providing its own martyr to the cause, George Helm, who was presumed drowned in 1977 in the island's waters, and ultimately shifting the focus of the movement from cultural symbols and practises towards the economic need for a land base (ironically, the activist group PKO — Protect Kaho'olawe Ohana — has since taken the position that Kaho'olawe is all the land base that native Hawaiians require).

The bombing was finally stopped in 1990, and the Kaho'olawe Island Conveyance Commission recommendation to define the island as a cultural reserve was sent to Congress in April 1993. Later that year, Congress approved the Defense Appropriations Act, setting aside $400m for the Navy to clean up and restore the island's flora and fauna before turning it over to the state. As the move to reclaim the land base quickens, the option has been raised of returning all the ceded lands appropriated during World War II for military reservations, air stations and missile ranges. Such claims were driven home by the convening of a People's International Tribunal, *Ka Ho'okolokolonui Kanaka Maoli*, in August 1993, to adjudicate the record of US crimes (political, economic, ethnocidal, and ecocidal) against the native Hawaiian people (*Kanaka Maoli*). The work of the Tribunal was conducted with an internationalist eye on the UN's new Draft Declaration on the Rights of Indigenous Peoples and was aimed, in part, at reestablishing Hawaii's claim as a nonself-governing territory eligible for decolonization under Article 73 of the UN Charter.

The drive for self-government can be found among a broad spectrum of over forty different organizations, grouped under the consortium, *Hui Na'auao*, and spearheaded by the largest sovereignty group, *Ka Lahui Hawaii*. Initially, the sovereignty movement was largely modelled after Black, Chicano, and Native American nationalist movements of the 1970s. *Ka Lahui*'s political goals are currently focused on the attainment of 'nation-within-a-nation' status, similar to the relationship between over 370 American Indian treatied nations and the federal government.[66] Like many American

Indian communities, those Hawaiians who will be eligible, by ancestral demonstration of indigenous birthright, and who will choose to live on the land base 'must abide by the rules of occupance and cultural identification.'[67] But the Hawaiian movement has just as much in common with other Pacific nationalist movements in their struggle for decolonization, not least in the shared opposition to military occupation and nuclear use of native lands. It has also generated a militant renaissance of interest in traditional culture: hula, surfing, outrigger canoe racing, myths and genealogies, featherwork, lei-making, taro planting, poetry, music, nature spirituality, and the production of intellectuals in the tradition of *kahuna* scholar-priests.[68]

On the prevailing political issue of land rights, a land preservation ethic (*malama 'aina* − reciprocal care for the land) emerged, charged with the full sacred significance of the ancient nature religion at the same time as it was shaped by a political recognition of the need for a land base. The reassertion of this land ethic played a major role in the struggle against environmental abuse by developers, while it also encouraged a full-blown cult of nature. Thus, Richard De Leon, one of the activists on the first PKO access to liberate Kaho'olawe from its military occupation, described the assistance rendered by natural elements on the devastated island:

Special things happened on Kaho'olawe. Clouds would come from Haleakala to shade us as we worked; water would drip from cut kiawe branches; sudden gentle rains would bless the *'aina*. And after we finished clearing a house site, a strong wind blew right through the clearing, as if to say '*Mahalo* for clearing my view. I can see my island once again.'[69]

De Leon's comments were typical of the pantheistic sentiments projected onto Kaho'olawe by activists in their bid to redeem the devastated island from the US war machine and convert it into a spiritual haven, or place of refuge (*pu'uhonua*). The resurgence of this nature atavism has lent a certain righteousness to nationalist claims that cannot easily be overridden by the cost-benefit analyses conventionally applied to environmental impasses over proposed development projects. The ecological philosophy of *aloha 'aina* and *malama 'aina* has been a crucial vehicle for the recovery of traditional land, water, gathering, and access rights according to customary law. *Aloha Aina*, first adopted by the modern movement by Helm in 1976, had also been employed as a titular term by a group of royalists at the turn of the century. While its antiquity as a lived practice among Hawaiians, especially *ali'i*, has been questioned, *aloha 'aina*, along with its more active ethic *malama 'aina*, has emerged as an appropriate political and cultural response to the state's blatant misuse of native lands, held in trust but mostly withheld from Hawaiian families, except under the notorious leasing operations of the Hawaiian Home Lands Commission.

As in other Pacific movements, the cultural revival of indigenous customs has also been analyzed by nonnative islanders and anthropologists alike as a creative construction of urban intellectuals' ideas about rural, subsistence life. All over the Pacific, indigenous elites' assertion of tradition and custom, reconstructed from oral sources, archaeological remains, and historical documents, often presents an idealized version of the precontact past in order to promote unity among peoples whose ancestors were often warring antagonists, divided by clan and language into mutually exclusive communities, or whose ancestral chiefs employed an equally selective representation of the past (by constructing their own genealogies, for example) to consolidate and extend their power.[70] Tradition, thus understood as the polar opposite of Western ways, and consciously presented as a customary unity (*kastom* in Vanuatu, *la coutume* in Kanaky, *Maoritanga* in Aotearoa, *fa'aSamoa* in Samoa, *Vakaitaukei* in Fiji, *Fakatonga* in Tonga) the better to oppose colonialism, often includes cultural forms that developed during the colonial period, or as a result of entanglement with colonialism. Material objects and ritual practises with a 100-year history are endowed with antiquity and employed as counterweights to Western forms. As a result, traditional culture today is more 'traditional' than it ever was.

For example, the historical theory of a unified Maori culture — *Maoritanga* — with a common point of migration/settlement in the Great Fleet was initially conceived as part of the Pakeha policy of assimilation, whereas the pan-tribalist solidarity of *Maoritanga* is embraced today by Maori nationalists for antiassimilationist reasons.[71] The history of many postcolonial nation states shows that indigenous elites who come to power in the name of unified tradition and custom are often structurally compelled to suppress internal cultural diversity and innovation in the continuing name of anticolonial solidarity. In the Pacific, claims based on indigenous birthright and attachment to customary tradition have been employed to establish the sovereignty of peoples long denied their 'native' right to self-determination, but they have also been used to deny 'local' rights to more recent immigrant minorities, or interracial islanders who do not meet the requirements of the blood quantum. Fiji is the best-known example, but even in Hawaii, where Asian-American communities exercise a large degree of commercial and political power, the descendants of imported laborers from China, Japan, and the Philippines have some reason to be wary of nationalist arguments that position them as junior partners of *haole* colonialism and challenge their legitimacy because they lack ancient ties to the land.

Anthropologists and other scholars who point to the innovative or dynamic quality of cultural nationalists' use of tradition are often seen as complicit with the continued denigration of indigenous peoples.[72] European colonial cultures had a relatively free ride from their intelligentsia when it came to authenticating and glorifying their own traditions or claims to antiquity, while the anticolonial movements have run into more friction with scholars. Sympathetic scholars who nonetheless write about the 'invention of tradition,' and especially white postmodernists who eschew any notion of cultural authenticity or ethnographic authority, are often asked to be silent or to suspend their critical voices in the name of liberal guilt or political expediency. Anthropologists are sometimes restricted in their access to countries if their research is likely to throw any doubt on the customary authority of ruling elites. It is not enough to point out that cultural invention, or innovation, is a daily activity, practiced in all societies at all times by those promoting change or pursuing political advancement. Nor is it enough to demystify Western ideas about authenticity and native Otherness. Authenticity itself may be just another Western invention, but it is one of the most effective bases for getting native claims legally recognized, reviewed, and settled. Some recognition of the strategic value of appeals to cultural authenticity must be acknowledged without jeopardizing the grounds upon which their legitimacy is based. Situations where scholarship is likely to play an influential role in forging the politics of the postcolonial state are hardly the time and place for scholars to take to the high ground; scholarship, after all, has always been employed for political ends, and there is every likelihood that the critiques of 'tradition' by anthropologists and archaeologists will be used to weaken native claims. In Hawaii, as in many instances touching upon sacred American Indian sites, archaeologists and anthropologists are habitually contracted by state and federal authorities to adjudicate the (in)authenticity of native sites that may stand in the way of development. On the other hand, the checkered political history of postcolonial states shows that, in the long run, self-censorship is not always the best course to adopt. Active, critical voices, whether they are raised on the inside or the outside, are needed at all points of the process. Support for anticolonial efforts should include respectful support for discouraging indigenous elites from assuming a repressive solidarity on the basis of appeals to tradition and custom.

Of course, it is one thing to criticize an appeal to tradition, it is another thing to *feel* that appeal and therefore to recognize the powerful aura with which a set of material objects, clothes, words, legends, battles, songs, dances and performances can become infused in an anticolonial situation. Only those who have been involved with a cultural nationalist tendency will know fully what that feels like. For outsiders, cultural nationalism will likely be irrational, backward, evangelically misguided. For secular adherents, the passions of nationalism can be as logical as the air they breathe, and all the more righteous if the symbols of passion have been reclaimed from the oppressors. My experience in growing up with the anticolonial use of Scottish 'traditions' is my own ambivalent witness to the charismatic appeal of this process. The tartanry of Scottish cultural nationalism today is not quite the 'barbaric' peasant tartanry that was banned by an Act of the Westminster parliament in 1746, the year after the Jacobite uprisings; nor is it quite the pseudo-aristocratic tartanry that was exempted from the ban and coopted as military fashion in the famous Highland regiments formed by the English to police the Highlands and to fight colonial wars the world over. Nationalist use of tartanry is wielded in the full knowledge of that history of suppression and cooptation, but its symbolism also transcends history altogether, since the claims of nationalism are required to be rooted in distant antiquity. It matters little that the idea of tartanry as ancient and venerable was largely an innovation of anglicized Lowlanders and Englishmen obsessed with a Northern version of the cult of the Noble Savage.[73] In Scotland, the ludicrous restoration and preservation of the ancestral culture of Celtic clan chiefs bestowed legitimacy on modern aristocrats who faithfully served Westminster and Holyrood, but it also came to provide a symbolically empowered base for the intelligentsia to recruit elite factions, including many aristocrats, within the burgeoning nationalist cause. So, too, it has proven to be a powerful populist vehicle in the struggle for hearts and minds.

A similar pattern could be found all over the Pacific, where colonial rule often involved coopting the instruments and agents of customary power,[74] a process that included the creation and empowerment of chiefly cohorts hitherto alien to the social order. In the heat of the anticolonial struggles and thereafter, it mattered little that the nationalist-approved customs were often hybrid byproducts of colonialism, or that chiefs, for example, appeared in Melanesia where they had no prior history.[75] Under the aegis of what passes for tradition, perhaps only native languages remain truly indigenous, and most have been greatly affected by non-Oceanic linguistic influences; in many instances, moreover, it is pidgin English that is the language of nationalist resistance, seen as traditional although it is hardly indigenous. What matters most is the political meaning that can be invested in cultural forms, whether in the indigenization of colonial power, or in the cargo-cultish transformation of foreign institutions. In either case, both the colonizer and the anticolonialist have had their uses for the discourse of the 'preservation' of traditional culture. For those non-Westernized commoners who are likely still to be living out rather than celebrating indigenous practises, the outcome of this discourse of preservation does not usually lend itself to more democratic forms of self-determination; it tends to sustain, if not reinvent, tribal and patriarchal forms of hierarchy. The long-term problem, then, may not lie with postmodernist ethnography, much of which is all too willing to be silenced on political issues, but rather with those voices and discourses, both native and nonnative, whose interests are best served by promoting the preservation of traditional cultures.

Epeli Hauofa, for example, sees a continuity between the recent concern for preservation, funded largely by international organizations, and the nineteenth-century discourses and practises of 'improvement' employed by scholars, missionaries, and colonial administrators to save native peoples from extinction. What is at stake today, he asks, in this discourse of preservation that is shared across a spectrum that includes the transnational tourist industry and often radical environmental groups?

> I do not see why the cultures of ex-colonial peoples should be singled out for preservation, or for that matter, for much concern about their survival. Those industrial countries that have dominated the Pacific Islands for the last two hundred years have not displayed much concern with the preservation of their own cultures as such; in fact, their position of dominance has been achieved through constant, ruthless changes in their traditions; the whole idea of growth and development means continuous change of technologies and value systems. In view of this, one cannot help but suspect that underlying the seemingly humane concern about the preservation of the traditions of the islands of the South Pacific, and indeed of the Third World in general, are some rather insidious motives including keeping sections of communities contented with their relative poverty and oppression.[76]

Nor does Hauofa spare the Pacific Way propagated by postcolonial elites who are culturally homogenous across the Pacific, for it is they who are the 'main beneficiaries' of the new regional economy of Oceania, driven by development policy-makers in Wellington and Canberra, and shaped by controlling transnationals into a distinctive unit of the global economy. Different but related questions could be asked of these elites who use the 'preservation' of tradition, especially the aristocratic leadership tradition, to suppress internal diversity and legitimize their power through appeals to custom and Christianity. Preserving tradition from the outside can freeze a culture in place and thereby reinforce its underdevelopment. Preserving tradition from the inside can deprive subaltern groups of a usable history in which their challenges to the native elites are progressive precisely because they are challenges to tradition. Alternately, the peasantry have their own economic reasons for clinging to traditions that are often quite different from the 'tradition' of the privileged. As Hauofa puts it elsewhere:

> the problem is not so much a cultural one of stubborn adherence to outmoded traditions as it is an economic matter. The poor adhere to their traditions because they have been consistently denied any real benefits from their labor. Their adherence to their traditions is a matter of necessity, of economic security.[77]

I have focused on the topic of 'preservation' because it lies at the heart of current ecological debates about traditional or indigenous cultures. Right now, indigenous peoples are fixed in the limelight of global environmentalists' concerns. Among other things, this is one way of displacing attention from the fact that many of the frontline victims of environmental violence live in our own inner cities or in unspectacular rural communities. So, too, Third World peoples have learned that they stand a better chance of having their claims heard by environmental groups if they present themselves as Fourth Worlders, which is what the global tourist industry, for different reasons, encourages them to do. (Ironically, this recalls a pernicious history, in Western nation states, of treating indigenous peoples and indeed communities of color as if they were 'closer to nature' and therefore just above wildlife on the great chain of being.) And, as for *echt* Fourth Worlders, increasingly under pressure to preserve their 'authenticity,' the injunction, from concerned First Worlders, is often to shut out the modern world, eschew all trade with cash economies, and shun all postneolithic technologies (a kinder, gentler form of underdevelopment?). The pattern here is simply to *reverse* the order of precedence that used to govern neo-Darwinian thinking about the survival of cultures. In the new version, the less developed cultures are the ecologically fittest, and hence all other occupants of the great chain of being (now more like the food chain), but especially First Worlders, have a significant investment in the preservation of these traditional cultures.

This reversal is proof of the continuing power exercised by the romantic model of traditional subsistence living. To the secular or the environmentalist eye, the economy of a traditional society may look like a sustainable, static equilibrium of needs and production. And yet the role played by divine energies, shaped, channelled, and mediated by elite groups, makes it a moving, dynamic equilibrium, serviceable to ruling-class interests from moment to moment. That this equilibrium could be held intact by religious ideology even in the face of wholesale environmental exhaustion — the 'lesson' of Easter Island — is testimony to the fact that a society bound together by a nature philosophy holds no guarantee of ecological well-being if it is governed by a pyramidal social hierarchy that depends upon selective access to natural resources to maintain its power.

Surely we need to recognize when calls for the preservation of traditional culture do not see the forest for the trees. Such calls often celebrate the perennial wisdom of nature, and assume that it taught its best precepts in the presence of a stable social order, without a history, without a politics, and without any internal challenges to its hierarchical rule. Change, according to this perspective, only came from the outside, and it was all destructive. Anthropology has long since moved beyond this primitivist view towards a more dynamic analysis of social processes, but the romantic primitivism it helped to create still governs popular consciousness. Most of all, primitivism plays an important role in the contradictory formation that is modern First World environmentalism. We don't always have to ask the following question, but it is a useful one to keep in mind. Who were the 'first ecologists'? The 'Indians' of European romantic myth then and now, or a society, *that has not yet appeared*, traditional or otherwise, in which the conscious organization of political, economic and cultural life is directed towards maximizing the diversity of natural life by minimizing social inequality?

Zion in the Pacific

There is at least one institution in my story with its own unique version of cultural preservation. If there was one place in the late nineteenth century where Hawaiians were reproducing at prodigious rates, where ancestral ways were being restored, where elements of the extended family (*'ohana*) had been rejuvenated, and where the traditional agricultural commons looked as if it was being worked, it was the Mormon community of Laie itself, where the LDS had purchased the entire wedge-shaped *ahupua'a* that had been the Hawaiian land unit before the Great Mahele. King Kalakaua and Queen Kapiolani, who came to visit in 1874 and thereafter, were so impressed by the colony's Hawaiianness that Kapiolani is reported to have considered Mormon baptism, and Queen Lili'uokalani, Kalakaua's successor, did actually join the Church in 1916, citing the affinity between LDS doctrines and the old *aloha* ways (she saw fit to join a number of churches, but by the end of the century Hawaiian membership in Mormon and Catholic churches had, in any case, outstripped the pioneer Calvinist missions).[78] To begin to account for the historically favorable reputation, in Hawaii, of the Laie community − the home of the PCC, and the flagship community for the vast network of Mormons in Polynesia today −

it is enough to recall that, from the first, the LDS took the side of the native backlash to a missionary presence that had forcibly purged the local culture of many of its customary ways. In general, the Mormons profited from the benign comparison with the other Christian evangelists who had preceded them in the Pacific, like the high-minded Congregationalists of New England or the lower middle class 'godly mechanics' of the London Missionary Society, bent on self-improvement in their fierce missions to eradicate the depraved ways of benighted islanders.[79]

But it is equally important to see Mormonism as a variant of US colonialism in the Pacific region, America's 'ocean of destiny' as proclaimed by Theodore Roosevelt, and treated as such by the US military presence for much of this century. The early history of the specifically 'American religion' of Mormonism can be seen as a concentrated version of American expansionist desires in the Western territories, and eventually in the Pacific region. Thus, the great Mormon trek to Utah has come to be seen as part of an epic chapter in nation-building, at the same time, ironically, as the Mormons themselves were being persecuted from state to state, even unto Oceania, for their fierce communitarianism. Classically dissenting in the tradition of the great American jeremiad, Joseph Smith and his followers cooked up a pungent belief stew of charismatic theocracy and weird doctrinal arcana which increasingly contrasted with the corporate blandness of other churches, even those quintessentially American sects like the Jehovah's Witnesses, Seventh Day Adventists, Christian Scientists and Pentecostalists which were all born, like Mormonism, on waves of revivalist enthusiasm.[80] Among the many revivalist movements in the 'burned-over region' of upstate New York which were candidates for the role of redeeming the nation from its postrevolutionary excesses and restoring the true gospel religion, the Mormons alone survived and made the passage from sect to institution. Indeed, Mormonism alone was strong enough and nationalistic enough to pursue its own policy of manifest destiny doctrine in the mid-to-late nineteenth century, transforming its postmillennialist covenant into a coherent belief-system about pre-Columbian history in the Americas, while channelling its missionary fervor into an effective machine for converting heathen souls in the Pacific where LDS missions were often the first 'official' American residential presence in a region of the world more heavily missionized than any other.[81]

Dedicated to restoring a primitive, patriarchal Church, degenerated after centuries of Christian diversions, Mormonism is a highly domestic American religion, with a revelatory story to tell about pre-Columbian American geography and ethnology. According to aspects of Mormon doctrine that most concern Polynesia, a group of Israelites led by the prophet Lehi (from the tribe of Manasseh) escaped the Babylonian captivity and sailed the seas to settle in Central America, where their Hebraic civilization flourished for a thousand years until destroyed in a great civil war between Nephite and Lamanite factions in 400 AD. The descendants of the backslidden Lamanite victors — marked for their sins by darkened skin — make up the native peoples of the Americas. Like Heyerdahl, the Mormons maintain that Polynesia was settled not only from South East Asia, but also from Central America. They were led there, in a mixed company of Nephites and Lamanites, by one Hagoth in 55 BC (Alma 63: 5−10), considered by some Mormon genealogists to have been Hawaii-Loa, the founding ancestral figure who figures in many Hawaiian genealogical chants.[82] In Mormon doctrine, Polynesians are therefore descended from the House of Israel, and their traditional religion is a remnant of the primitive and true Church of Christ (the Hawaiian worship of Kane, Ku, and Lono being a trinitarian vestige, for example). Accordingly, many narratives of Christian typology — about Creation or the Flood — have been found in the primitive religions of Polynesia; the Hawaiian ritual of the coming of Lono is also an ancestral memory of Christ's visit to Israelite America (Quetzalcoatl, the white-skinned god), which temporarily united the feuding factions of Nephi and Laman, and his promise to return. So too, Mormon historians have found resonances of the great transoceanic voyages in the *Popul Vuh*, the sacred book of the Quiche-Maya of Guatemala, and accounts of the history of neo-Israelite settlers like the Ulmecs and Nahuas in the Aztec works of Ixtlilxochitl that appear to parallel the *Book of Mormon* itself.[83]

In a religion that has always interpreted skin color as significant, Polynesians, like other indigenous peoples of the Americas, bear the troubled mark of the Lamanite for their ancestral strayings from the gospel religion, and yet they are supposed to enjoy an honored, covenanted identity within a church especially committed to their redemption. Consequently, they will revert to their ancient historical identity and become 'properly' Caucasian again as the latter days come around, or, as the *Book of Mormon* used to put it: 'their scales of darkness shall begin to fall from their eyes; and many generations shall not pass away among them, save they shall be a white and delightsome people' (2 Nephi 30: 5−6) − the 'white' having been changed to 'pure' in the 1981 edition. R. Lanier Britsch, the official historian of the LDS presence in the Pacific, acknowledges that it is not clear exactly when this aspect of doctrinal belief was accepted by Church elders, but that certainly the first missionary saints in Hawaii in 1851 were telling their would-be converts about their privileged 'birthright as children of Abraham and Lehi.'[84]

It was not the first time that Christian missionaries in the New World, especially those obsessed with ancient Israelite religion, had offered this identity to native peoples. The story was nothing other than an expedient medium for accelerating the initial snailpace rate of conversion, but this particular theory of Polynesian origins was hardly exceptional in the flood of origin speculation that was projected onto Polynesia in the mid-nineteenth century. Indeed, Samuel Marsden, the first Protestant missionary to visit New Zealand, wrote of the Maori, in 1830, that they were 'sprung from some dispersed Jews, at some period or another, and have by some means got into the island from Asia . . . They have like the Jews a great natural turn for traffic; they will buy and sell anything they have got.'[85] Certainly, the theory of the Israelite origins of American Indians was accepted as a literal belief by many Americans in the early nineteenth century, and Joseph Smith, author of the *Book of Mormon* in the early 1830s, was no exception. One of the bestselling books of 1833, Josiah Priest's *American Antiquities and Discoveries in the West*, forcefully argued that the American Indians were remnants of the lost Israelite tribes.[86] Ellis, like others, seriously considered the evidence that Polynesians were of the same race as Native Americans. While no longer a mainstream Christian belief, these theories are a cornerstone of Mormon doctrine still, and underpin much of LDS's own discourse about the preservation of traditional culture. The Mormon mission to preserve remnants of the House of Israel has made their syncretic blend of prophetic and primitive Christianity work particularly well on Native American reservations and in the Pacific Islands where the population density of converts is highest − over 300,000 − and where extravagant temples (by Pacific standards at least) can be found in Tonga, Samoa, Tahiti,

Hawaii, and New Zealand. Combined with the LDS mission to baptize and record the genealogy of all humans, living and dead, this has made Mormon religious ideology a conservationist one — as distinct, say, from the Protestant ethic that was commonly allied with cognate liberal ideologies of enlightenment progress, self-improvement and social engineering.

Generally speaking, Mormons were perceived in the Pacific as whites with a difference (they were accorded a similar reception among American Indians in the West), sympathetic to local cultures, levying no taxes, favoring in-kind economics, teaching and not preaching by example, appointing lay natives to high church offices, in favor of communalism and large families, patriarchal authority, and the old ancestral ways that had been banned by Congregationalist missionaries. The Mormons even had their own taboos — no coffee, tea, liquor, or tobacco. So, too, the native interest in genealogy, memorialized in oral chants, was courted by a church with a huge institutional stake in this very subject. To the great delight of Mormons, some Polynesian genealogies go back almost as far as Adam. In return, LDS elders claim to help Hawaiians with land claims that require genealogical proof. This was religious neocolonialism that always sanctioned the native way, and profited, in native eyes, from ignoring the Western way. To this day, the Mormon promise of a land ecologically renewed and returned to its pristine state (with the reestablishment of the tent of Zion in Jackson County, Missouri, home of Eden) has a powerful appeal when indigenized in some version of reclaiming the land and the old ways.

The contradictions involved in the Mormon way can be highlighted by briefly describing the career of Walter Murray Gibson, an adventurer so obsessed, early and late, with the establishment of a personal empire in the Pacific, that he sought out first the Mormon Church and then the Hawaiian monarchy as accomplices in his designs. Mindful of the federal military siege of the Salt Lake City saints in 1857, and cognizant of the rumor (partly generated by Gibson himself in Washington) that the Mormons were about to be run out of the USA, Gibson wrote to draw Brigham Young into his ambitious plans:

It has been in my heart many years, to propose to you . . . emigration to the islands of Oceania . . . I have spent many years among the 'isles that

76

wait' for the Lord; and while I lay in a dungeon in the island of Java [imprisoned by the Dutch for intervening in their colonial affairs], a voice said to me; 'You shall show the way to a people, who shall build up a kingdom in these isles, whose lines of power shall run around the earth.'[87]

The imperialistic tone of the letter speaks for itself, and must have spoken equally to Young's own vision of a world religion, since, in no time at all, Gibson was sent on an official LDS Pacific mission to Malaysia and to the emperor of Japan. In fact, he never made it beyond the Hawaiian Islands, where he assumed leadership of mission affairs on the island of Lanai, considering the settlement there to be 'but the baby of [his] kingdom.'[88] There is still a good deal of legendary speculation about the 'excesses' of Gibson's personal jurisdiction over a mission that was in serious decline by the time of his arrival in 1861. He would eventually be excommunicated in 1864 for playing king and dictator beyond the dictates of Salt Lake City, and for 'additions' to Mormon doctrine that amounted to an overly zealous interpretation of the LDS policy of incorporating local cultural patterns. It is alleged that he titled himself High Priest of Melchizedek (a heady doctrinal innovation) and encouraged his acceptance as a Hawaiian high chief, that he partially revived the *kapu* system, introduced all manner of native Hawaiian rituals, including dances by unMormon-like 'priestesses of the temple,' into LDS religious ceremonies, and personally profited from selling Church-owned land to members.[89] It sounds as if Gibson had a high old time on Lanai, and that he saw his early career as a Mormon as an expedient vehicle for imperial schemes he would go on to pursue with Hawaiian royalty like Kalakaua, and with *haole* sugar kings like Claus Spreckels. On the other hand, the occurrences in Lanai were very much in tune with the waves of religious reversion that had accompanied native Hawaiian opposition to the missionary presence. By mid-century there were many recorded instances of anti-*haole* revivalist movements preaching new religions which incorporated ancestral gods like Pele and Lono, and secret societies that mingled Masonry with native religion. Syncretic religion was a primary medium of resistance to the ongoing expropriation of land and proscription of native culture by the missionary families.[90]

Gibson's 'privateering' aside, however, the ease with which his ideas about colonial expansion agreed with Mormon missionizing is quite representative of the premises shared between would-be redeemers of the failing native cultures of the Pacific, and the paternalistic developers of their natural resources. In a set of lectures he gave on arriving in Honolulu, Gibson outlined his own views on economic development, comparing the Western presence in Polynesia with his own experience of Malaysia:

> Prosperity on earth, as well as hope of heaven, is to be best developed in the production of needed staples for the world's use, rather than in a loafing life on barren coral reefs, and eking out a low grade, vegetating existence on poi and pandanus. The Polynesians are dying out on such a diet − and wasting away also − owing to some civilized virus in their blood, and the lack of all national hope in their hearts; but the Malaysians are increasing on rice, sago, and plentiful meat and fruits, which increase is also owing greatly to organized labor in plantations and mines and furthermore because they have some congenial native governments and a national hope that the white man has not yet been strong enough to destroy with his false ethnological views and ill-adopted contrivances of governmental and even of social order.[91]

Convinced, from his own bitter experience with European colonials, that 'it is impossible that a mission that seeks to plant a miniature European form of religion in Malaysia can succeed,' he expounded his theory that empire must be built from within and below, not imposed from without, as the New England missionaries had done in Hawaii. One of Gibson's examples of pernicious development[92] was the use of 'tropical labor' in the cotton and rice fields in the Southern states of the USA, and he would later support nationalist policies about the immigration into Hawaii of Polynesian rather than Asian labor. The tendency of LDS policy in these matters was much the same. Indeed, the mission's move from Lanai to Laie on Oahu was partly precipitated by the need for a profitable cash crop − sugarcane − that could fill the coffers in Salt Lake City. The evolution of 'tithing-in-kind' all over Oceania meant that where cash was short, free labor, in addition to compulsory missionary labor, could be mobilized to build schools, chapels, temples, and even the PCC in Laie (a much more profitable venture than the sugar plantation had been).

It could be argued, then, that Gibson's colonial adventurism highlighted the cognate desires of the LDS. But his next and most famous career as the pronationalist Prime Minister of Hawaii also showed how a nativist policy of the sort advocated by LDS elders could engender powerful political consequences if pushed far enough. In the pages of his Hawaiian-language newspaper *Nuhou*, Gibson took a strong stand against the Puritanization of the islands, while inveighing at every opportunity against the activities of the business-planter-missionary elite. In recommending women's suffrage, championing indigenous foods and medicines, advocating Polynesian immigration to 'increase the race,' opposing the proto-annexationist cession of Pearl Harbor to the USA, and allying himself with Kalakaua, Gibson had won such widespread native support that he was elected to the premiership in a landslide in 1882. From this office, he pursued his design for an Oceanic empire by persuading Kalakaua to become primate of a Polynesian League composed of Pacific Islands unclaimed by European powers. Gibson's 1883 Hawaiian version of the Monroe Doctrine, pledged to defend 'the inalienable rights of the several native communities of Polynesia' against foreign interference, met with a hostile reception from the USA, and an ill-fated military expedition to intervene in the race for Samoa between the USA, UK, and Germany resulted in a series of *coups d'état* in Honolulu, the signing of the 'bayonet constitution' that eviscerated the powers of the monarchy, and the expulsion of Gibson from Hawaii by the forces of the planter elite. The resulting overthrow of the monarchy and the act of annexation may have occurred in any event, as an inevitable stage of American regional expansion and integration into the world capitalist system. But the phase of nationalist fervor that Gibson lived through and, in part, superintended, had a considerable impact: it not only transformed the autonomous planter bourgeoisie into a class that had to collaborate with Hawaiians (in order to rule) and with mainland interests (in order to trade), but it also inspired the first renaissance of Hawaiian customs at the court of the 'merrie monarch' and created a powerful legacy of anticolonial sentiment that successive generations of the sovereignty movements have drawn upon. The other side of the coin is that, as with any nationalist movement, the revival of interest in indigenous custom and history served to sharpen people's perspectives about desired forms of government. The fall of the nationalist monarchy also witnessed the advent of a democratic base that would eventually bring non-Polynesian immigrants — Chinese, Japanese, Filipino — out of the plantations and directly into the upper echelons of the polity.

While the LDS were not offically aligned with the nationalist cause, their own interests have often coincided with native movements in Hawaii and generally throughout the Pacific. Just as often as it was used to affirm the ancestral ways, Mormon doctrine was used by native dissidents to mount internal challenges to the chiefly system. Not too many chiefs cared for a religion that did not exalt their own positions, which deferred to Salt Lake City chiefs, and which provided an alternative history for their people. In providing an explanation of how Polynesians would be redeemed and saved, LDS doctrine attracted subalterns looking for a future beyond the chiefly celebration of the glorious past. In her study of Tongan Mormonism, Tamar Gordon argues that the Mormons' blend of (dynamic) prophetic and (static) primitive religion offers a double identity that is useful to many Polynesians — on the one hand, a vehicle of modernization, the way forward, a doctrine with a future that is lacking in traditional religion; and on the other, a vehicle for cultural preservation, maintained through the primitive Lamanite identity.[93] It is without too much hypocrisy, then, that the LDS, alone of the Christian churches actively indigenizing their Pacific missions in the age of cultural nationalism, can say that it has always been in the business of cultural preservation.

Hagoth's Star Trek

The PCC is a striking example, however, of how selective the LDS's cultural preservation has been. Preserving a shoreline is one thing, preserving a culture another; the case is always made in the name of certain interests, and with certain aims. At one point in the early 1980s, there were plans at the PCC to construct a sister park called Gateway to Asia. The decision was made instead to build an IMAX film theater which would feature a narrative film about the nomadic history of the Polynesians, eventually entitled 'Polynesian Odyssey.' IMAX, the latest spectacular development in high fidelity motion picture technology, had been my reason (as an IMAX fan) for going to the PCC in the first place. As one of the participants in the 1990

Honolulu International Film Festival, I had been invited to a premiere showing which included a special guest tour of the PCC. On viewing the film I was struck by some of its religious narratives, and I was intrigued by the contradictory presence of this massive high-tech film complex on a site dedicated to theatrical ex-primitivism. IMAX cinemas are usually located in sites of cultural and scientific interest: usually scientific museums — Canadian Museum of Civilization, Tycho Brahe Planetarium, La Géode in Paris, Hong Kong Space Museum, Osaka Science Center, NASA, EPCOT, American Museum of Natural History in New York City — but also in places of natural sublimity — Niagara Falls, Great Barrier Reef, Grand Canyon, Coomera, Puebla. An increasingly essential element of the construction of such sites, IMAX has rapidly become part of the history of the use of photography in the institutional preservation of nature — the surveillance, production, control (and extermination) of nature.

From the late nineteenth century, the camera has been present to record and preserve the dying moments of wildlife and native peoples alike, whether as an accompaniment or successor to the safari gun or the developer's bulldozer or the F-111 fighter bomber or the Star Wars satellite.[94] There is a persistently uneasy but intimate relationship between the research and development of film technology for military purposes, on the one hand, and its civilian use as a means of photographically preserving that which is often directly threatened by the activities of military industrialism on the other. The wide gauge 70mm film used for IMAX is indeed a spinoff from US Air Force reconnaissance technology, while its Xenon-lit projector is based on NASA designs for floodlighting rocket launching pads. Paul Virilio has described how this 'cinema of the future' counteracts the vertigo-inducing IMAX approach shots and helicopter sequences by replicating the action of the inertia powerhouse — that unit of military technology which corrects the trajectory of pilotless bombers and missiles. The effect of IMAX's famous airborne sequences is to simulate weightlessness and free fall at the same time; for many spectators, this also induces motion sickness. Through these viscerally affective stimuli, IMAX has dramatically expanded the capacity of cinema technology to represent, simulate, and colonize space — and not just earthly space, since IMAX has been the camera of choice in recent space missions.

With the exception of a live Rolling Stones concert film (arguably a contribution to the 'preservation of nature' or, at least, an endangered species), IMAX film production has been confined mostly to the genres of nature docudrama and science exploration, whether in remote geographies (Antarctica, space missions), or the habitats of charismatic species (beavers, mountain gorillas, whales), or awesome natural events (Pacific Rim volcanoes). In these immensely popular films, spectators are afforded superhuman visitation rights to places and at speeds hitherto only enjoyed by cartoon or comic strip characters. Consequently, the spectacle-centered focus of the IMAX format demands that the natural world be experienced as a world of extremities and special effects; there is no kitchen-sink drama there, and the epic quality of the film resides in the spatial scale of its affect, rather than in the temporal dimension of the narrative. This is not uncommon in other film genres, for which the narrative is a conventional vehicle for the main commodity of the spectacle. More than a film genre, however, IMAX is an entire cinematic technology with a costly filmmaking apparatus that requires its own massively expensive theater (the PCC's modest theater cost $11m), and, until recently, an institutional home in one of the temples of modern scientific tourism. Calculating that this technology, with its giant simulation theaters, will be the key to drawing home video audiences back into the theaters, the big corporate players — Iwerks Entertainment, IMAX, and Showscan — are currently battling for big screen monopoly of this special attraction cinema. Heir to the nineteenth-century spectacle technologies like the Diorama, Cosmorama, Octorama, Diaphorama, and Panorama, IMAX's modern form owes as much to the supersensory space rides and voyages at Disneyworld as it does to the history of nature documentary. Indeed, increasingly few tourist sites fail to provide visitors with a film or slide presentation as preparation for or accompaniment to the main attraction. Companies like IMAX and Iwerks are convinced that the main attraction of the future will soon be their own multimedia theaters, featuring virtual reality, simulation rides, and interactive large-screen pictures.

Like any other cinematic technology, IMAX is also, in Christian Metz's words, a 'mental machinery,' related in various ways to a particular ideological moment that could be termed globalist. The planetary perspective afforded by a technology like IMAX is fully elaborated in Graeme Turnbull's *Blue Planet* (subtitled *A Portrait of Earth*), filmed by astronauts on NASA's space shuttle missions. The spectator is invited to embark on a 'Mission to Planet Earth,' and from an orbital perspective, an environmental survey of the planet's trouble spots is conducted; rainforest fires, silt and topsoil flow into the Gulf of Mexico and the Yellow Sea, desertification in the Sahel, smog in Southern California, severe weather formation, earth crust movement. Unlike the narrative technologies of Hollywood cinema, the epic perspective here is neither directly nationalist nor neocolonialist, but is intended to be planetary in terms of a scale and ideological point of view appropriate to its subject matter. *Blue Planet* is by no means a great film, but its significance in the history of film technology may come to match that of *Birth of a Nation*, *Ivan the Terrible*, or *Lawrence of Arabia*.

The PCC's *Polynesian Odyssey* (directed by Keith Merrill) is a film that many of Laie's Polynesian scholars to whom I talked openly described as embarrassing, and it is shown in a theater that has not had the dramatically profitable success originally hoped for. It is, however, a remarkable expression of LDS policy concerning the use of high technology as a missionary medium. Unlike most IMAX films, *Polynesian Odyssey* does attempt an epic treatment of history by recreating fictional scenarios from the nomadic chronicle of Polynesian wanderings across the 'common highway' of the Pacific. The film is billed as 'the greatest story *never* told,' a reference to the fact that Polynesians' own accounts of the great ancestral voyages were typically discounted as fantasy by white Westerners. The film's scenarios depict the voyagers setting off from the East Coast of South America as well as from the West Coast of Asia, a boar hunt on Samoa, a wedding on Tahiti, tribal warfare on Hawaii, and European contact; all are interlaced with heavy doses of spiritual reflection. At times, the narration lays it on thick: 'Who were they, these first courageous Vikings of the sunrise? . . . Who were these strangers . . . by what power did they move upon these waters? . . . Our beginnings are lost in time . . . Our odyssey is an epic of departures and arrivals, our journey is but a shadow of eternity and endless progression . . .' The PCC film is about spiritual causality and divine stewardship over the peoples and lands of the earth.

By contrast, many visitors to Oahu may also see another IMAX film that frequently shows in the Waikiki theater (Hawaii is the IMAX capital of the world, and recently hosted the annual IMAX

Film Festival). Entitled *Hawaii: Born in Paradise*, made by radical documentary-maker Robert Hillman and written by Olivia Crawford, this film tells stories about the ecological history of Hawaii that, by contrast with *Polynesian Odyssey*, revolve around physical causality and human stewardship. In this film, shown in the Waikiki tourist bubble that boasts one of the highest population densities in the world, humans barely figure at all, except as part of some informal eco police corps, helping to pollinate plants in remote spots, fencing off rainforest areas for conservation, and scientifically surveying the underwater volcanic formation of new islands in the Hawaiian chain. In the long historical span of evolutionary biology on the islands, human agency is reduced in scope to a brief cycle of coming and going, while the prevailing ethic espoused by the film is the need for preservation for the future. As you leave the cinema to join the tourist throng on Kalakaua Avenue, street vendors are hawking the cheapest T-shirts to be found on the islands — most carry ecological messages about protecting and preserving the environment!

The PCC 'epic' is tailored to the biblical model of dramatizing the covenanted spirit of a wandering people, a theme that is echoed in almost all of the films (over 25,000) officially produced by LDS's formidable media apparatus. When it comes to high-tech telecommunications, LDS is a media monopolist, and not just in the business of televangelism. Bonneville International, the Church's broadcast arm, is a communications conglomerate which owns TV and radio stations, a growing number of satellite/cable and telecom systems, huge chunks of stock in major newspapers, and a satellite system that links the world's largest private closed-circuit TV network outside of AP and CNN, connecting over five million Mormons worldwide in sixty countries. LDS's archaic theological image is additionally underpinned by an immense capital investment in high technology, which includes the Eyering Research Center, for developing sophisticated missile guidance systems, and a string of companies working for NASA and the US military sector. This has become the Mormon Way — a primitive superstructure, appropriate to a church whose theocratic doctrine and antediluvian morality are still like those of a seventeenth-century revivalist sect, combined with a sophisticated infrastructure, embracing the most advanced machinery of technological modernity.

Notwithstanding the LDS's own success in the business of

religious tourism — there are twice as many tourists to Temple Square as to Yellowstone Park, and over six million visitors to Mormon visitor centers around the world — the high-tech primordialism favored by the corporate culture of the Church joins hands with the luxury-class primordialism of the PCC that is the major commodity of the Pacific tourist industry. In Hawaii, the ads for the PCC in Japanese specifically focus on the IMAX theater as a major attraction. Generally, they link the ancient Polynesian technology of colonization — the double-hulled canoe — with IMAX's space-age theater in a way that evokes the famous shot match at the beginning of *2001: A Space Odyssey* between a spinning bone and a nuclear weapon in orbit. This split image not only speaks well to the Mormon taste for science fiction,[95] it also evokes the significance, for Polynesians, of the *Hokule'a*, the famous double-hulled canoe built in the late 1970s to disprove the random-voyaging theories and to authenticate the Polynesians' legendary navigational accuracy, and which has played a central role in the renaissance of pan-Pacific consciousness ever since.[96] In a touch that would appeal to Mormon SF sensibility, the crew of the space shuttle Columbia shared radio communication with the *Hokule'a* crew during their respective 'voyages of discovery' in July 1992. After its first voyage in 1979, Herb Kane, the boat's designer, had called it 'the spaceship of our ancestors.'

The juxtaposition in the PCC ad captures very well the basic conditions of ethnographic tourism — a highly developed infrastructure, which holds frozen in place as its core a primitivist superstructure. As I have pointed out, this image also speaks eloquently of the spectacle's Mormon sponsors, pioneers in the use of new technologies to colonize the past. Picture, in your mind's eye (as far as I know, there are no images in the public domain) the Granite Mountain record vault in Cottonwood Canyon, twenty miles from Salt Lake City, where, in vast subterranean caverns, the LDS is building a database of genealogical records for all humans in history. Here, the dream of universal conversion is being pursued, night and day, as the saints do their temple work, busily baptizing the dead by proxy. The aim of this database is to be word perfect (to cite the name of Provo, Utah's famous word processing program). The Granite Mountain archive, far and away the most extensive on record, will be used for all sorts of purposes: it is increasingly consulted, for example, in the age of genetic medicine to ascertain hereditary lines of disease. In this story, it figures as a high-tech version of the oral genealogies that structured traditional cultures, biblical and Polynesian alike. As such, it is an answer to Brigham Young's call: 'We will not wait for the Millennium ... We will commence as soon as we have a temple, and work for the salvation of our forefathers; we will get their genealogies as far as we can. By and by, we shall get them perfect.'[97]

Under the Banyan Tree

There is considerable irony in the idea that the 'human zoos' and 'living museums' of Third World tourism are today one of the guarantees of cultural preservation. Indigenous opponents of hotel culture's encroachment, like Sione Tupouniua, have pointed out that tourism is structurally doomed 'to destroy what it wishes to see preserved.'[98] Others, like Masiofo Fetaui, cast their warnings in full recognition of the economic potential harbored by the preservation of Pacific cultures: 'destroy it − and you have destroyed your main asset which can never be created again.'[99] Accepting the existing reality of tourism, some proponents of indigenous values have insisted that the industry take responsibility for preserving customs wherever they are marketed for commercial ends. In Hawaii, for example, George Kanahele, a leading intellectual in the cultural renaissance movement, has worked with the state to introduce Hawaiian values and customs into hotels, arguing that the 'Hawaiianness' of the tourist destination is a major factor in its profitability. Managers of hotels may yet be obliged to undergo a course and pass an exam in Hawaiian culture and history; it will be much more difficult, of course, to equalize host−guest relations according to traditional modes of Polynesian hospitality.[100] Some forms of indigenous tourism, like those conducted by the Kuna of Panama's San Blas Islands, the Eskimo of the Bering Straits, or the Cuyabeno in Ecuador, have become socially appropriate and self-sustaining.[101] Some ethnic groups, as in Indonesian Toraja, have used ethnographic tourism as a self-managed economic base for negotiating a more legitimate space for themselves within the nation state; in effect, tourism has transformed Torajans from an oppressed minority into a national asset.[102]

In the USA, tourism is often cited as instrumental in saving and preserving the Indian arts and crafts of the Southwest. And yet the act of preservation, especially when it becomes official, tends to legislate what kind of culture an indigenous people can produce. A case in point is the Indian Arts and Crafts Act, passed into US law in 1990. The bill, drafted to protect the tourist boom in Southwestern indigenous artmaking, makes it a crime punishable by a fine of up to a million dollars or fifteen years in federal prison for nonNative Americans to present art that is recognizably Native American. A Native American is defined as at least one quarter Indian as certified by the nineteenth-century blood quantum. As Ward Churchill has pointed out, the blood quantum can be viewed retrospectively as a strategy of statistical extermination: at the rate of intermarriage, it was perceived that Native Americans would soon be defined out of legal existence. Just as the blood quantum criterion prescribed what an Indian was (a criterion rejected by many who refuse tribal enrollment, and irrelevant to many others whose tribes are denied federal recognition), so the 1990 Act, enforced by looking for signs of 'Indianness' in art, more or less prescribes what American Indian art should be — not Jimmie Durham, or Edgar Heap O Birds, but 'the Carlos Castaneda-oriented canvases' of the Bradley Group, and the sentimental, pastel designs that characterize Southwest motel room art.[103] Making radical art that challenges expectations of 'traditional' culture, from outsiders and insiders alike, is rarely perceived as 'native' art; it is not Indian, or Hawaiian, or Aborigine art, although it may be made by Indians, Hawaiians, and Aborigines. Consequently, the political power harbored by native art is restricted to an 'authentic' image of the traditional culture, a ghettoized form of cultural expression that is aesthetically forbidden to comment on the modern world and modern politics. Self-determination by this route comes at the cost of excluding oneself from modernity and becoming politically, if not culturally, confined to an artistic ghetto.

Dean McCannell has distinguished between what he calls constructed ethnicity — the path chosen by anticolonial indigenous leaders to make their claims — and reconstructed ethnicity — the process by which tourism promotes the 'restoration, preservation, and fictional recreation of ethnic attributes,' creating a museum-like commodity out of ethnic identity.[104] The tourist mode of representation is continuous with a long and pernicious history of *exhibiting* native peoples as living rarities which Barbara Kirshenblatt-Gimblett dates to the presentation of Eskimos in the streets of Bristol in 1501, and has continued through centuries of street fairs, freak shows, circuses, and world's fairs.[105] In accordance with the favored trope of salvage ethnography, the same peoples have often been 'vanishing' for the last two centuries, theatrically exhibited as the 'last' of their dying race. The contradictions of this kind of performance art have begun to permeate those Pacific island cultures, with restricted resource bases, export cash crops that are subject to heavy competition on world markets, and a long history of exporting unskilled labor, for whom tourism therefore offers an attractive source of foreign exchange, and an ecological mode of development which is potentially friendly to traditional lifeways.

However, when a country decides to become involved in tourism, it invariably enters into a global system of neocolonial structures of economic and political exchange in which it has little control over the definition of its self-image.[106] Just as the vast bulk of services purchased by tourists are owned by metropolitan interests, and are located in the export enclave of the local tourist bubble, so too, the power to represent the local culture is no less external than it was under colonial administration. Much of the problem lies in the dual demand of the modern tourist trade, similar in many ways to the LDS paradigm of high-tech primordialism. On the one hand, the demand for a modernized infrastructure, i.e. luxury accommodation and Western-style amenities, and on the other hand, for a pre- modern superstructure, i.e. the spectacles of reconstructed ethnicity which are the star attraction of the visit.[107] The expensive infra- structure takes a heavy social and environmental toll, and what are often emphasized and reinforced in the superstructure are the most hierarchical and exotic features of a culture's traditional social organization (those most Other to the liberal, democratic societies of Western tourists' experience). This situation could be interpreted as a classic example of cultural underdevelopment, where foreign capital profits from the recreation and the freezing in place of a particular set of traditional features and precapitalist values that then come to define the ethnic identity of an otherwise modernizing culture. Consequently, tourist development in the Third World has proven to be an exemplary form of postcolonial capitalist development, guaranteeing colonial-type modes of surplus extraction through a culture industry that markets the spectacle of undeveloped precontact life. The emergence of multinational corporations within the tourist industry has not changed this model, as it has done in other areas of core—periphery relations, where modernization has become a goal of capital rather than an obstruction to metropolitan interests that had been hitherto suppressed. Indeed, dependent development — the modified neocolonial principle of the new world economic order — is the very essence of the Third World tourist destination.

Of course, it will be said that the model is only a model, and the spectacle is only a spectacle, reflecting only the desire of capital and not the complex presence of its wage-based cash economy in the skin and bones of societies that are still, to some extent, semisubsistent and based on exchange-in-kind. But the tourist spectacle is not just part of an industry product, it has also become some part of indigenous custom itself, even as it is perceived as a degraded version of the 'authentic' custom that will be practised elsewhere, beyond the tourist eye, but in no less conventionalized a setting (everyone who worked at the PCC expressed concern about the educational quality of the performances, while lamenting their entertainment quality). Dances like the tourist *hula*, or even the many forms of *hapa haole hula*, are decidedly not the 'real thing,' but they have nonetheless come to figure in Hawaiian culture as, in this instance, the *hula waikiki* — a default version of the *hula* for Western eyes, with a historical continuity from the nineteenth-century *hula 'aunana* accompanied by Western musical instruments. Most tourists will see it as 'merely' entertainment, others will see it as 'inauthentic,' and, not content with the 'more authentic' performances at places like the PCC, will seek out performances of *hula kahiko* (traditional *hula*, accompanied by chants) for the real thing.[108]

As an element of people's daily working lives, the tourist performance of native culture is as much an interpretation of Western aesthetic codes as it is an expression of traditional values. Tourist art and performance is, after all, a genre unto itself, and a mode of cross-cultural communication, not unlike pidgin or creole languages.[109] There is nothing new about performing and interpreting 'culture' in this manner for foreign eyes, and Polynesians, in particular, have always made an art out of pageantry performed for others, even for other islanders in the precontact period. Stephen Greenblatt recounts how, on Columbus's first encounter with the natives of Trinidad, he tried to attract their attention by having a tambourine brought up on deck and some young men perform a dance. The Indians fired arrows back at the crew, interpreting the dancing as a sign of war, rather than a show of goodwill.[110] Such failures to communicate culturally are two-way affairs, and both cultures, indigenous and Western, have made creative use of each others' rituals and artifacts, but the process of exchange and sharing has primarily been an unequal one. So while indigenous performers long since learned to present cultural versions which accommodate Western fantasies of primitivism, most tourists do little different today from the official business of Columbus and his cognates — possessing through witnessing and recording (this time with cameras).

Native contempt for tourists is a very particular cultural sentiment, but it is widely shared:

> As our people in Fiji go about their daily tasks of serving the visitors we see an endless succession of the same little old ladies, with the same blue hair rinses, spending the same life insurance money and speaking in the same accents of the same things which have penetrated their similar perceptions. And what of the little old ladies? As they climb in and out of their same cars, their same planes, their same hotel beds, as they eat the same foods, drink the same drinks, and buy the same souvenirs is it to be wondered that many cannot tell from one day to the next which country it is that they are presently visiting? These people travel the world like registered parcels, blindly unaware of the local population, their aspirations, problems and tragedies. Instead of promoting mutual understanding, they promote mutual contempt.[111]

Anyone who lives in an area of tourist interest, even in the First World, will recognize the sentiment (my own Manhattan neighborhood of SoHo, deluged weekly by upscale 'Eurotrash' tourists who want to see bohemian artist-types in a setting where they can still buy stylish clothes and eat increasingly expensive food). But Third World tourism, as is often pointed out, is more than an industrial product or lifestyle trade commodity pursued by an ambient tourist population; it has the effect of transforming social relations in quite drastic ways, and of making natives into 'peasants in paradise.' The most widespread symptoms of these changes include mass movements of population from rural villages to towns and tourist complexes, the rise of prostitution, alcoholism, and proletarianization of craft labor, the growth of racial stratification in the tourist division of labor, feudal conditions of hotel workers, housed in neighboring worker ghettos, master—servant guest/host relations; artificially high cost of living; widespread eviction from housing and land by tourist developers; denial of access to beaches; exploitation of native traditions of hospitality; and degradation of the local environment and religious sites. No surprise that tourists are often the target of aggression, thieving and, most recently, 'terrorism.'

Even for the most ingenuous tourist, there comes a point when the contradiction between the theater of precapitalist Pacific values and the ideology of large-scale tourist development is too sharp to ignore. This perception, combined with widespread criticism of the destructive environmental impact of tourist development, has compelled the industry to think about its own 'sustainability.' Increasingly, eco-tourism offers a leading model for an industry moving away from mass tourism in search of specialized niche markets: adventure tourism, nature tourism, cultural tourism, space tourism (recently announced by Japan's Shmuzu corporation). In 1992, the Travel Industry Association of America published a report on eco-tourism in which the president, Edward Book, announced that 'the travel industry must become more green because the environment is our chief product, our livelihood.'[112] The Pacific Asia Travel Association and the Center for Responsible Tourism have issued guidelines and statements of ethics about low bio-impact tourism. The term 'eco-tourism' was coined by Mexican bureaucrat Hector Ceballos-Lascurian in 1983, when his organization PRONATURA lobbied against developers for the conservation of wetlands in Northern Yucatan on the grounds that tourism in the region was largely made up of North American birdwatchers. These tourists, he argued, would be able to play a role in the local economy, providing jobs while preserving the environment through their presence.[113]

Eco-tourism, then, is more than nature-based tourism for profit; by definition, the proceeds from eco-tourism are used for conservation, and are of local benefit to host communities. This model speaks to the new post-Rio demand that conservation has to be seen to pay its way, while responding to the industry's search for responsible tourist developments to appease the conscience of its increasingly conscientious clients. Working with NGOs like the Nature Conservancy or the World Wildlife Fund for Nature, tourist developers often base their projects on American conservation ideology about 'parks' and 'wilderness areas' that are relatively unpopulated. As Konai Helu-Thaman has pointed out, there is not one inch of 'wilderness' in the Pacific Islands, only environments that have been preserved by sustainable use.[114] The American model had its origin in John Muir's Yosemite, created by excluding the Miwok Indians, followed by the eviction of the Ute and Navajo Indians from Bryce and Zion. The legacy continues in places like the Kidepo National Park in Uganda, where the Ik are alienated from their traditional hunting grounds, and in environmentalists' projections of the concept of primal or virgin rainforest onto regions like the Amazon with a long history of sustainable use by indigenous inhabitants.[115] If eco-tourism pursues the wilderness model, creating depopulated nature preserves for wealthy foreign tourists, then it will replace the old ethnographic model of peoples without history with a new tourist model of lands without people. Rather than watch eco-tourism desocialize their lands, Helu-Thaman and other Pacific Islanders advocate using the environmentalist values of the host culture as the basis for developments that will be of social and ecological benefit. Club Med from the bottom up.

At the end of 1992, I paid a visit to French Polynesia, source of *le mythe polynésien* upon which the no-cash economy of the Club Med is based, and where the French government had finally suspended nuclear testing after thirty years of vainglorious military preening and colonial high-handedness with the natives. Dicing with nuclear death and contamination may have been a stiff price to pay for the artificially inflated import tax economy that accompanied Tahiti's atomic rent, but there is a good deal of irony attached, in any case, to the presence of such advanced technologies of extinction among peoples who are historically supposed to symbolize the last thing in low-tech subsistence living. For as long as the half-life (24,000 years) of plutonium remains a threat to natural life, Moruroa, the French test site, like the Marshall Islands, Bikini, and Enewetok (US), Christmas Island and Maralinga in Australia (UK), and those regions of Siberia, Tibet, and Mongolia selected for testing by the Soviets and Chinese, will stand as vile monuments to the contempt visited upon indigenous peoples in the period of nuclear colonialism. The location of such sites in indigenous peoples' backyards was surely the cruellest tribute to the neo-Darwinian law of ethnocentric dominance, whereby indigenous cultures were deemed least fit to survive, and therefore most fit to host these genocidal technologies.

The end of the Cold War, and, ostensibly, of testing, marks the beginning of the period of nuclear waste disposal, rejected by NIMBYist Westerners, and dumped on Pacific sites like Johnston Island.

Alternately dubbed the happiest and the most miserable people on earth (*Touche pas à mon Gauguin!*), the *ma'ohi* of French Polynesia are now officially compelled to look beyond the protective colonial mask that provides them with the appearance, but not the economic base, of a thriving Third World society. With Cold War testing over, the move from class tourism to mass tourism, or at least to a diverse range of specialized tourism, is seen as the most likely and least environmentally destructive avenue of development. The Tahitians I spoke to are not thrilled at the prospect of an invasion of Long Islanders but, if confined to limited zones of development, tourism allows them to live off the valuable cultural asset of the *mythe polynésien*, saving them from the most un-Polynesian fate of Taylorization in industrialized workplaces, while diffusing the urbanized concentrations of *bidonville* communities that had sprung up around the nuclear industry. The relatively benign presentation to tourists of Polynesia as a traditional Fourth World culture may yet be a small price to pay for evading further proletarianization in the microelectronics net of the Pacific Rim. The Kon-Tiki stage routines can be corny stuff, but, among other things, they reinforce many Polynesians' own view that the Western way of life is so insane that it requires such thin fantasies as escapist relief from its brutal work regimes. All the more reason, they say, to pursue an alternative path of development. In this respect, countries of the Pacific region may be able to modernize, not by leapfrogging over the industrial phase of development, but by exploiting the utopian fantasies of the West while internally creating 'new traditions' of social and cultural life in ways at which Polynesians have always excelled. Cultural innovation of this sort is doubtless a heresy to the doctrine of authentic cultural preservation that is fiercely espoused by advocates of the Pacific Way, but it shows how creatively native idioms interact with and reissue signals from 'outside.'

In Papeete, I talked at length to leaders of a new organization (*Te Niu Nu Ananahi*) pledged to the 'construction of tomorrow's Polynesia.' After a march to protest chronic corruption among the ruling elite (dictatorship was a term used to describe the ambitions of Gaston Flosse, the current president), the protagonists spoke of their nonpartisan agenda for the moral, cultural and socioeconomic development of the region. The values they named were as much those of the French Enlightenment as they were recognizably Polynesian (since Polynesia is now 95 per cent Christian, this 'tradition' obviously includes Western Christian values). Most conspicuous was the absence of primordialist appeals to tribal or ethnic value systems. The Polynesian tradition in effect here was that of inclusion; the founding articles of *Te Niu Nu Ananahi* are addressed to 'polynésiens et polynésiennes de souche, d'adoption et de coeur.' Given the options, here then was one progressive model for renovating local cultural traditions in the crucible of a multiethnic society.

By contrast, I was reminded of an interview I had conducted with Cy Bridges, chief of the Hawaiian village at the PCC, and leader of a well-reputed *hula halau*. Bridges himself is a renowned genealogist and singer of chants whose style is unique to his family — one of his forefathers was court chanter to Kalakaua. As such, he is a passionate defender of traditional aristocratic rights, expressing pride in the PCC's performances of 'real culture' that are reserved for visits from island nobility and royalty, and more than a little scorn for the theatrical faux-court that is elected every year during Aloha Week to preside over festivals like the Merrie Monarch. When I asked him about the claims of the sovereignty movement, he acknowledged that he had many relatives active in the movement, but that the thing he himself cared most about was getting reparations, not from the US government, but from the Kameha-meha family. Kamehameha was the warrior who, with the aid of Anglo-American firepower, subdued and united all of the Hawaiian island clans under one monarchy at the end of the eighteenth century. Bridges' high-ranking family was reduced to the status of royal attendants as a result; hence his longstanding genealogical bitterness. In moments like these, a white postmodernist considers at least three responses: one either remembers what the Socialist International is supposed to be about, or else one marvels at the boundless capacity to make politics out of a usable past, or else one shows respect for the traditional authority of another culture. For me, these responses did not rank necessarily in that order, but all three were registered nonetheless.

Even among island *ali'i*, Bridges' views would probably have been extreme, and yet they struck me with the force of a culture shock that was strangely familiar. Goodness knows, I had heard enough tales in Scotland of longstanding clan feuds, ancient deeds of betrayal, aristocratic claims gathering dust, and titled lives and fortunes ruined by the treachery of one knave or another. I had even met one or two pretenders to this or that title, swelling theatrically with genealogical rancor, all the while exploiting the vestigial cult of the Stuarts on the fringes of the sovereignty movement. Bridges' resentment was surely of a different order. Hadn't the Kamehameha dynasty's centralization of power led directly to the discarding of the old religion, and hadn't their pacts with foreign powers and worship of European ways hurried on the death of Hawaiian sovereignty? Consequently, the continuing status of the nobility in island society had come to stand in symbolically for the lost sovereignty of the Hawaiian people. Respect for their voices is not simply a reflex act of class deference, it is also charged with the nostalgia for past glories that is essential to the 'imagined community' of a Hawaiian nation. On the other hand, the haughty resonance of *ali'i* privilege is just as likely to alienate those not in the elite vanguard of the nationalist ranks, while touching off the anxieties of sympathetic, nonnative *kama'aina* who are generally not considered to be 'Polynesians by heart' by the leaders of the movement.

Similar fears have accompanied the rise of nationalism wherever 'blood' is a criterion of inclusion, and wherever the hereditary power of precolonial aristocratic privilege is utilized as an anticolonial weapon, however symbolic. The history of the Pacific Islands is not simply the history of colonial penetration, it is also the history of the power politics played by island aristocracies. In the postcontact period, chiefly interests were often advanced by exploiting the prestige of Western contacts, not only with state representatives like Cook, but also with traders, beachcombers, and missionaries. European commerce, firepower, and religion were all expediently utilized in the chiefly contests for control of island affairs, and were increasingly useful in administering and maximizing the free labor of commoners released from military service. European contact was as much a political opportunity for dynasties like the Kamehamehas, the Pomares of Tahiti, and the Taufa'ahau of Tonga as it was a 'fatal impact' upon fragile and helpless island societies.[116] No doubt this was part of Bridges' point, but there was no reason to believe that Kamehameha's rivals would have been in a position to behave differently.

Revisionist accounts of the realpolitik of Polynesian chiefdoms resonate with some of the practices of the genealogical chiefs of traditional Scottish Highland society. Indeed, it is not unlikely that attitudes towards the feudal structure of the Scottish Highland clan system served as one of the models for European perceptions of the social and cultural organization of Polynesian societies in the eighteenth century. Nineteenth-century theorists of Polynesian origins like Abraham Fornander, William Ellis, Percy Smith, and, later, E.S.C. Handy also derived the islanders' hierarchical orders from cultures all over Asia and the Middle East: Brahmin, Dravidian, Malaysian, Timorese, Sumatran, Chinese, Aryan, Persian, Egyptian, Babylonian, and what-have-you. These perceptions about European feudalism or Oriental despotism were, and still are, falsely projected onto historical descriptions of precolonial Pacific life, but it is no great leap forward in understanding to replace them with pictures of a harmonious social order from which power relations are absent. Not long after I spoke to Bridges, I attended the annual Hawaiian Scottish Festival in the grounds of Honolulu's Bishop Museum, endowed by Bernice Pauahi Bishop, the last direct descendant of Kamehameha, and home to an institute of archaeology and anthropology which has been the major center for anthropological and archaeological studies of the Pacific Islands. Here was all the paraphernalia of Scottish tourist culture abroad: the pipe bands, the country dancing, the caber-tossing, the souvenirs of Nessie, the saltire brooches and key rings, the *skhean dhu*, the castle calendars, the folk tales (with some Arthuriana, and even Churchilliana thrown in for good measure!), a troupe of medievalists called the Society for Creative Anachronism, and the booths for the various clan societies promoting their own missionary forms of genealogical conversion: 'Let me trace your name for you . . . we'll soon find out where you belong.' The festival was the work of the Hawaiian Scottish Association, organized to promote Scottish culture, and in a typical Polynesian touch, appealing to 'those of Scottish blood and those Scottish by heart.' All genealogical primers on sale, of course, direct the reader to the Mormon archives in Salt Lake City, the nearest thing to an ultimate authority on such matters.

There could be no end of ambivalence about the expression of ethnicity on display here, especially if one knew the reasons that this mixter-maxter of archaic Caledoniana has come to signify Scottishness in the international marketplace of cultural representation — reasons specific to tourist commerce, to the diasporic history of Scottish emigration, and to the romantic primordialism of nationalism. But there was also a local flavor to this Highland gathering amid the palm trees. The Hawaiian cultural renaissance of the last two decades had surely played its part in focusing all islanders' attitudes upon their own ethnic heritage and identity. The Scots, a distinct subculture among *haoles* on account of their accents and dialects, were no exception. An oral history of Scots on the islands had indeed been conducted recently by members of the Caledonian Society. The range of Scottish influence had been widespread and powerful, from intermarriage with the royal family to the occupational stratum of Big Island sugar plantation managers (*luna*) which they monopolized. There was little documentation, however, about the Robinson family, who, since 1864, have owned the island of Niihau, where traditional Hawaiian culture has been preserved in all of the forms thought requisite to the enforcement of its preservation. Three hundred tenants live out the old ways on this, the only island population to vote against statehood in 1959. Tourist visits are restricted to an hour or so, and no islander is allowed to leave and return, lest they are contaminated by modernity. The Hawaiian Family Robinson — first family in the business of cultural preservation.

The same day as the Scottish Festival, in Halawa Valley, native Hawaiian activists were celebrating a year of keeping vigil for their *kupuna* ancestors at a women's *heiau* (*hale o papa*), which lay directly in the path of freeway construction. It had been alleged that archaeological studies conducted by the Bishop Museum had tried to downplay the significance of the site; the whistleblower, staff historian Barry Nakamura, had been fired for criticizing the museum. As a result of the controversy, the freeway is being rerouted to avoid the *heiau*, but it will not be the last indigenous challenge to the work of construction. Indeed, US constitutional law is increasingly being challenged as activists, spurred on by the triumph of Kaho'olawe, seek, under Hawaiian law, to gain access for religious and cultural purposes to all undeveloped lands on the islands. While they claim access according to customary law as native Hawaiians, the objective of their cultural politics is not to reassert native animism but to confront and contest developers who do not consult *kama'aina* as to the history and future use of the land.

At stake, then, in these confrontations, is not simply the revival of customary ways or the protection of burial and religious sites; the contest is over the dominant definition of land use on the islands according to the ethics of either possessive individualism or communal access.[117] Hawaiian appeals to *malama 'aina* entail a fundamental ecological struggle over the first principles of land use. This is not an argument about fencing off wilderness or conservation areas of the sort fiercely pursued by many mainland environmentalist organizations. The aim is not to keep humans out, or, as has historically been the case with conservation areas, to keep undesirable humans out. On the contrary, the argument is about the social reoccupation of space according to principles of sustainability. Nor does it really matter whether the medium of the argument — *aloha 'aina* or *malama 'aina* — was chosen more for its appeal to the current moral power of environmentalism than for its centrality to ancient Hawaiian culture, when land was not viewed as an alienable possession. The point is not to establish another Niihau Island, but to create a lived relation to the land that promises to be neither dominating nor destructive.

In the wake of Bill Clinton's official November 1993 apology to Native Hawaiians (Senate Joint Resolution 19), some form of self-government is likely to be established soon. A Council of Elders met in March 1994 on Maui to discuss plans for a provisional government. Hawaiians are poised to reclaim a substantial part of their island homelands, much of it from military occupation. What happens then will be a test of a cultural politics which has embraced an ancient land ethic in the belly of one of modernity's peripheral centers. From now on, the pursuit of 'Paradise Now' will have to be based on a pragmatic assessment of modernity if only because symbolic and sentimental claims are easily bought off with token offerings. And some part of that assessment will involve deciding what to do with the power accumulated through precarious appeals to blood and nature.

2

Bombing the Big Apple

We are accustomed to think of the islands of Polynesia as isolated ecosystems. Not so with a dense metropolis like New York City. Yet urban ecologists have left us with an influential picture of the city as a functional organism in its own right, regulated by supposedly natural laws that govern the interaction of space and population, and relatively immune both to external economic and political pressures and to community resistance to such pressures. This picture has not gone unopposed. As the campaign for greener cities gathers momentum, we will need to challenge it even further, for it not only draws upon a history of paternalizing ideas about the social benefits to citizens of nature, but also encourages us to see the city as an evolutionary unit, and therefore as the inevitable result of conditions of growth and progress. The story about urban development that I will pursue in this chapter intends to show how innocent and misleading these ideas about organic growth are. It takes as its origin an act of violence — the World Trade Center bombing of 1993. The lacerated social fabric left by this event was an opportunity to reexamine the evidence.

The Art of Land

If you stand in the public plaza of the World Financial Center, the commercial heart of New York's Battery Park City, you will be able to read some celebratory lines of poetry about the city by Walt Whitman and Frank O'Hara chosen by artist Siah Armajani and mounted in bold letters on the balustrade overlooking the Hudson

River. Armajani's balustrade was part of a three-way collaboration with fellow artist Scott Burton and architect Cesar Pelli, one of the public art projects commissioned for the luxury residential and commercial development that rose on the southwestern tip of Manhattan during the heady office-building and land speculative boom of the 1980s. Since Armajani's public art habitually incorporates lines from more classic American writers like Frost, Emerson, Melville, and Whitman, the inclusion of the maverick O'Hara was odd, but not inappropriate in this context. Whatever the reasons for the choice, let it be said that Whitman and O'Hara shared not a few things, homosexuality among them, and that they are rare among American writers for having shunned the antiurban attitude that runs mainstream through the national culture, and is often embraced most fully, to this day, by intellectuals who live in cities and who write about them. This distinctively Jeffersonian tradition is rooted in a constant pastoral craving, and is expressed in a distaste for the urbanization which has, so the story goes, progressively degraded the cultural and political ideals of the republic. The metropolis, from this view, accommodates the spiritual wastelands of high commerce and high society, boasts a gigantist environment that visibly houses barbaric disparities between wealth and poverty, and fosters a desperate culture of anonymity governed by unstable moral codes. A countervariation on this view is the famous Steinberg cartoon of the '*New Yorker*'s view of the world.' Few politicians working a national audience will fail to exploit either the hypermetropolitanism exemplified by the cartoon, or the more widespread antiurban sentiments, tinged with racial prejudice, since they are an essential ingredient of a prevalent populism. Few writers on the middlebrow bestseller lists will fail to appeal to the desire for a human-scale community of participation that is almost by definition impossible in a large city, and few city mayors will fail to utilize the negative image of their own city on the brink of collapse in appeals for federal aid.

While antiurbanism is a low-intensity fixture of American intellectual life, it periodically swells up in the form of back-to-nature movements. In many cases, these can be tied directly to the economic cycles of investment and disinvestment in city centers, or, more accurately, central business districts (CBDs). The exact nature of that causal tie is notoriously difficult to pin down. Are ideas about the environment simply the result of the prevailing economic use of the environment, or do they have a relatively independent life of their own? Suffice it to say that partisan advocacy of the social values of nature has helped to mediate the periodic phases of suburban decentralization and urban recentralization at least since Frederick Olmstead designed the first garden city suburb in Riverside, Illinois in 1869. The ensuing call for civic improvement which culminated in the City Beautiful movement at the tail end of the century borrowed some of its impetus from a back-to-nature movement among intellectuals, and was accompanied by a fierce philosophy of environmental salvation armed with evangelizing ideas about the physical and moral decay of the urban poor. The later move to suburbanization after the center city deconcentration of the 1920s not only satisfied real-estate speculation surrounding the consumer-ist promise of the single-family home. It was also sanctioned in part by the antiurban ideas of the new planning elites, exemplified in the group of architects and planners — among them, Lewis Mumford, Stuart Chase, Benton MacKay, Clarence Perry, Henry Wright, Clarence Stein, and Frederick Ackerman — who formed the Regional Planning Association of America (RPA) in 1923, and who heavily influenced the financial barons, bankers, and developers on the board of the First Regional Plan of 1929, initiating the movement towards the deindustrialization of Manhattan which is all but complete today. So, too, the romantic pastoralism of the 1960s counterculture's occupation of rural communes was not simply a protest against the bulldozer mentality of postwar urban renewal; its demonization of city life also reverberated with the rhythms of 'white flight,' while it echoed, however dissonantly, the fiscal call to desocialize the city issued by corporate America after the ghetto rebellions and the feeble response to them of the War on Poverty.

To some degree an extension of countercultural romanticism, the advent of the environmentalist movement has provided the loudest forum for antiurbanism in recent years. At its worst, antiurban environmentalism is burdened by a rural nostalgia that barely submerges its racism. It perpetuates the monstrous image of the city as a greedy parasite, an overpopulated and dangerously polluted concrete jungle which has long transcended its appropriate biologi-cal limits, and is profoundly at odds with the better-behaved side of human nature — the city as infernal machine, squandering energy and resources, assimilating and circulating poisons of every stripe. Among other things, the espousal and promotion of these hideous

101

images often has the effect of further ostracizing a large portion of residents in cities, who, for historical reasons that include class and racial exclusion, have limited access to the trees, rivers, mountains and wildlife which are the celebrity actors of the environmentalist movements. On the other hand, the circulation of ecological ideas has brought a new dimension to radical and reformist thinking about the future of cities, where most of the world's population now lives (over 80 per cent in Western countries) and will do so in even greater numbers in the future, especially in the megaurban centers that will each be home (and already are in the case of Tokyo-Yokohama) to some 25 to 30 million inhabitants in the next quarter century. Viewed as a physically sustainable ecosystem, a megalopolis of such scale makes virtually no sense; it necessarily subsists on surplus resources from elsewhere. And yet, as a medium for instituting far-reaching changes in energy use, efficient transportation stock, resource preservation, pollution reduction, and waste disposal, the influence of the large cities is unsurpassed in its power. Much attention is paid to model cities like Curitiba in Brazil, where significant changes in transportation systems, waste management, and urban planning have translated into visible advances not only in environmental quality but also in social and economic justice. The movement towards the 'green city' — embracing everything from auto-free environments to rooftop agriculture — is already well under way,[1] while environmentalism, if only because its effects theoretically involve all classes, has become one of the leading activist mainstays against runaway land speculation and unilateral commercial development in physically degraded parts of the city.

But there exists no single blueprint for a green city that in itself would guarantee more, rather than less, social justice. If the development of the green city turns out to be like other historical phases of urban development, then we can expect it to be uneven, generating new forms of privilege and exclusion just as it appears to resolve older social problems. Many North Americans, for example, have come to see the location of manufacturing offshore as a blessing in disguise, ushering in the cleaner environment of the postindustrial city at home. This parochial view requires us to overlook the new manufacturing sites in the Third World where lack of environmental regulation is an open invitation to toxic mayhem. And as for the well-being of the urban workforce (in New York, unemployment figures are still extremely volatile), postindustrial restructuring has meant that the substitution of low-wage, service sector employment for stable, union-wage manufacturing jobs has been accompanied by a drastic reduction of social services once considered integral to the postwar compact between capital and labor. In New York City, the creation of a vast homeless population, the resurgent armies of unemployed, the recent 'discovery' of the informal sweatshop economy, eluding the city's health codes and offering labor at Third World wages, are nothing short of an environmental scandal.

Proponents of the campaigns against environmental racism (focusing primarily on inner city biohazards) have begun to change the pastoral face of green politics, but many components of urban life are not yet configured in the public mind as 'green' issues: adequate housing and health care, access to basic services and inexpensive education, the right to a healthy workplace, freedom from police surveillance and harassment, participation in neighbor- hood self-management, the right to the city both inside and outside racially segregated enclaves, and so on.[2] And yet surely these are all aspects of how people relate to each other within their social and physical environments — a minimal definition of human ecology. Clearly, we need to integrate these issues with concerns about the health of air, water, and soil which are more conventionally seen as environmental problems. It is important to accept that much more is encompassed by the green city than what a recent book (*Green Cities*) emphasizes: 'There is a very strong need for green. It may be a very deep emotion; the need for something green and wild or a place to go for sanctuary or solitude — a place to experience wilderness in the city.'[3] As it happens, parks, gardens and other green places in the city are usually intensely socialized sites, as attested by their multifarious use or by a history of conflict over past uses (the parks movement of the nineteenth century was an overt move to assert social control over the urban working class).[4] In every respect, they are quite removed from what the wilderness school of environ- mentalism understands as 'wilderness' — a place where the sublimity of an unpeopled landscape (its indigenous inhabitants having long since been evicted) erases all of the legacies of social difference borne by visiting nature trekkers, and allows them to transcend those social identities that are judged to be restrictive and irrelevant in the face of unmediated Nature. Indeed, the idea that green space in itself can play a curative role in the lives of deprived urban dwellers harkens back to the nineteenth-century improvement philosophy that set the fashion for creating the great urban parks. The nineteenth-century park was intended to educate civic taste and to elevate (and control) the moral character of the poor and indigent. Green space, in this definition of nature, evoked a neoclassical order of enlightened rationality, progress, and improvement.

For the wilderness ecologist today, green space is a different order of communion; redolent of romantic spirit, yes, but governed by a different kind of moral order. Today, communion involves a thoroughly secular understanding of biological processes that communers are told they must observe if species like our own are to survive. Nature still knows best, not because it is there to be emulated, as an object of enlightenment, but because its knowledge has nothing much to do with human beings, or simply because it is in human nature to have contact with the natural world. Most recently, sociobiologists like Edward O. Wilson have argued that city dwellers in particular suffer physically from emotional deprivation when their circumstances prevent access to open, green spaces; Wilson suggests that humans have a genetic disposition − termed 'biophilia' − which requires them to be close to nature.[5]

These latter ideas about nature are relatively new, and may yet have a significant impact upon the development of ecologically based approaches to the built environment of cities. But urban history shows that ideas about nature have long played a major role, not all of it creditable, in guiding the growth of cities and controlling their populations, whether in the minds of the philanthropic improvers of the nineteenth century, the professional planners of the twentieth, or today's increasingly ecology-minded architects and preservationists.[6] In the course of this chapter, I will discuss the considerable influence that such ideas have had when applied to an environment that is often held to be the very opposite of 'natural.'

For the time being, let us return briefly to Whitman and O'Hara, whose respective praise of the city has been commandeered in the name of Battery Park City. Here are the lines from Whitman, a world-class loafer, who loved throngs of people, because, as he told us, he was large, and contained multitudes. 'City of the world (for all races are here, all the hands of the earth make contributions here): City of the Sea! City of wharves and stores − city of tall facades of marble and iron: Proud and passionate city − meddlesome, mad, extravagant city!' His lines are a swelling, overwrought tribute to a still peripheral but already arrogant port city in the mid-nineteenth century. And then there is O'Hara a century later, a restless camp in an imperial city now more dizzy with world subcultures than in Whitman's time. In contrast to Whitman's grandiloquent populist hymn, O'Hara's lines, alluding by juxtaposition to the bard's own 'Leaves of Grass,' strike a defensive note. 'One need never leave the confines of New York to get all the greenery one wishes — I can't even enjoy a blade of grass unless I know there's a subway handy or a record store or some other sign that people do not totally regret life.' While sniffily conceited in its own mock-serious fashion, O'Hara is really saying that New York won't win any prizes for being a green city, at least not in the conventional sense. What greenery means, for O'Hara, has to be integrated into the buzzing, social world of daily life in a commercial city — not the solitary contemplation of nature, but the social ecology of the metropolis in all of its apparently disorganized complexity, of which botanical life is a part. O'Hara's green is on a more human scale and more accessible than the sanctuary of the wilderness advocate or the grand vista of park and civic monument of the City Beautiful. But the tone is still defensive.

Regardless of why these particular quotations were chosen, they might be read as comments on their location. Whitman's larger-than-life rhetoric gestures toward the extravagant monuments of global trade that rise up immediately behind the atrium of the World Financial Center. O'Hara's ambivalent homage to commerce and nature speaks to the developers' presentation of Battery Park City (BPC) as a collective effort on the part of landscape designers, architects, public artists, and private planners, whose end result embraces the needs of finance capital, residential privacy, aesthetic utility, and waterfront public access, and whose fusion of greenery and concrete has become a compelling model for developing the entire waterfront of Manhattan's West Side. Neither poet, of course, would be comfortable in this location. A roughneck like Whitman might well be taken for a homeless person, and driven off the property at dusk. And O'Hara, for all his cosmopolitan ease and affection for luxury, would find little satisfaction in the sleek corporate atrium of the World Financial Center's Winter Garden, where nonindigenous flora (palm trees) set a scene for stores like Bally of Switzerland and yuppie grazing areas like restaurant Sfuzzi.

Yet the use of art in New York City as an avant garde for the long

front of realtor development and gentrification, whether to glamorize 'undesirable' areas, or create cultural districts as zones of
attraction for middle-class investors, or embellish patrician plans for
macrodevelopment, is well documented.[7] Indeed, this process is so
well known that some of the artists involved in the BPC projects
sought justification for their collaboration on a luxury housing/
commercial development in the fact that BPC, built on landfill
where New York's thriving port used to be, had displaced no
residents and had tried to compensate for its final exclusion of low-
and moderate-income housing (a provision of earlier plans) by
funnelling some of its real-estate tax revenues into public housing
development in Harlem and the South Bronx. In this context,
O'Hara's defensiveness makes even more sense; luxury developments like BPC are now planned architecturally to incorporate
elements — artwork, parkland — that appear to defer to demands
for public space. BPC's natural successor on the West Side, the
Hudson River Park Conservancy, goes by an eco-sounding name
that masks what many believe to be its real purpose: the revival of
the Westway highway project defeated by environmentalists in the
1980s.

A substantial portion of the ninety-two acres of BPC's landfill
foundation comes from the jumbo hole excavated in the late 1960s
for the adjacent World Trade Center (WTC). Much more than
BPC, the WTC, from its inception, has provided the most visible
evidence of the charades of city planning. It is to this controversial
building, perilously anchored in the seventy feet of silt and subsoil
above the bedrock spine of 'Manhattan schist' (unlike the CBD of
Midtown, where the bedrock is only seven feet below the surface,
most of Wall Street rests on nothing very solid) that I now turn to tell
a story about the politics of social ecology of downtown Manhattan,
where I live and work.

Sick Building

The car-bombing of the World Trade Center on March 26, 1993,
contributed only a few lasting images to the media memory banks.
Even after the instant NBC telefilm, 'Terror in the Towers,' much
was left to the imagination of those who remembered *Towering Inferno*
and other popular classics of the 1970s disaster film genre. The stock

images, replayed again and again, were of the stricken building disgorging workers caked in soot and partially asphyxiated — coughing, spitting, gasping and reaching for oxygen masks from Red Cross and ambulance attendants. These were people who had the look of victims of some environmental disaster. Something convinced me that it wasn't really the bombing but the building itself that had been an ecological catastrophe of vast proportions, and that there was a story to tell.

First of all, the bombing proved what public critics had always alleged — that the Twin Towers were a potential death trap. Watching a small construction fire in the early 1970s send smoke curling up emergency stairwells for fifty stories, Amy Herz Juviler, an Assistant Attorney General at the time, had questioned the Fire Department 'at the request of the Attorney General, and the Fire Department assured [her] that this was not the world's safest building . . . Those stairwells, not some but all of them, were flues. There was no break to keep the smoke out.' The picture painted by the Fire Department was so bleak that the issue was dropped: 'We chose not to further alarm our people . . . In the case of a real fire like "The Towering Inferno" we knew there was no escape.'[8]

This incident was only one in the long history of failed attempts to bring the building under city fire codes from which its owner, the Port of New York Authority, is exempt. As early as February 1971, after thirty fires in the first fourteen months of construction, fire officials had been vocal in publicly challenging the safety of the building. Over the years, the frequency of bomb threats and fires, many of them the work of arsonists, elicited no end of anxiety from employees and neighborhood residents. Furthermore, an extensive 1985 report by an antiterrorist task force had warned the Port Authority that the garage was vulnerable to a bomb attack resulting in the shutdown of key safety systems, and should be closed to the public. The recommendations of the report, which included new electronic backup systems above ground level, stepped-up contingency and evacuation plans, and more efficient measures to vent smoke, were mostly ignored.

The result was a not very smart building. In the 1993 bombing, its computerized command and generator backup facilities were easily neutralized, knocking out all power and communications, leaving smoke to rise freely in a stack effect which placed the building's occupants, some of them negotiating 100 floors of stairwells, in extreme peril. For the employees, the building, which, like most high-rise, sealed office towers, is an environmentally 'sick' building with concentrated indoor air pollution, became a 'bad' building. It proved incapable of protecting its occupants, let alone monitoring their location, and probably endangered their lives further because of its architectural form, its height, its sealed air systems, and its prison-size windows — a structural demand of Minoru Yamasaki's tubelike construction which requires maximum stress support from the outer metal sheath. It was widely reported that workers were reluctant to return to this carceral building which had entrapped and almost entombed them like a malevolent, high-tech gothic house. Corporations were easier to convince, since many were offered the package of tax abatements and rent waivers that has become a customary method of retaining business in the city. In the wake of the bombing, security at the WTC and most other government and corporate buildings has been stepped up tenfold, increasing the degree of high-tech employee surveillance to penitentiary-like levels.

The WTC quickly became a visible target for critics on account of its excessive energy use, especially during the oil crisis of 1973, the year the buildings were officially dedicated. Designed with an HVAC system which depended upon unlimited cheap energy resources, it almost immediately became a symbol of energy waste, with its perpetually lit towers serving as arrogant beacons of corporate indulgence at public expense. Architecture critic Ada Louise Huxtable morbidly pronounced that environmentalism would be the nemesis of these megalomaniac 'General Motors Gothic' style buildings: 'Survival, not vanity, is the issue.'[9] The buildings became an easy target of the growing high-rise revolt that fed off public resentment at the microclimates, the 'visual pollution,' and the blockage of light and air created by skyscrapers (the WTC generated winds of up to sixty mph through the gap between the twin towers). That the electricity powering the buildings could service the sizable upstate city of Schenectady was a fact that quickly passed into city folklore. During the period of its closure in 1993, the unlit tower was an eerie void in the city's skyline, like a shrouded capitalist temple, or a military stealth fortress. After all, the night-time lighting of office towers is not simply a necessity for the cleaning labor force (predominantly low-wage immigrant labor), but also a crucial element of citizen consent for these corporate factories which, unlike the older manufacturing buildings, house workers for only a small portion of the week. The radiant presence of the glittering, translucent 'cathedrals of commerce' (to use a term first applied by a clergyman to Cass Gilbert's Woolworth Building) is supposed to reassure us of their reliability and persuade us that their solidity will not melt into air.

But the WTC, whatever its internal flaws and arrogant aspect, has never been a building development unto itself. Its history is a vivid record of the ecology of urban redevelopment in Lower Manhattan's CBD. First mooted in 1946, the plans for a WTC were concretely conceived in the heyday of late 1950s urban renewal by Governor Nelson Rockefeller and the baronial heads of the Downtown Lower Manhattan Association (DLMA) as a kind of corporate United Nations. It was intended not only to 'add luster and prestige to the whole metropolitan region' (in the words of the chairman of the City Planning Commission), but also to 'provide a sound foundation for the expansion of lower Manhattan as the dominant center of finance, world trade, and shipping' at a time when midtown Manhattan was drawing business away from the Wall Street area.[10] Built against strong local opposition, not least from those it would physically displace — primarily the merchants and 30,000 employees of an electronics district of over 300 stores and 1,000 other businesses — the WTC had such an initially devastating effect on the commercial real-estate market that it had a hard time finding tenants. Even though New York State took over a substantial acreage of office space, the rent-up was so slow that an acceptable occupancy rate was not reached until 1983, the year that the building broke even for the first time. The WTC was built and is maintained by the independent public agency of the Port of New York Authority, a bistate authority founded in 1921 to coordinate transportation and terminal facilities as a way of reducing competition for shipping between New York and New Jersey. The authority is endowed with extraordinary government powers to issue bonds, to borrow money at low, tax-exempt interest rates, to condemn private land through powers of eminent domain, and to invest and construct wherever it sees fit. Like other government corporations, its activities are largely immune from public accountability. It has been long been criticized (by early business groups like the Committee for a Reasonable World Trade Center, in conflict in the late 1960s with the equally suspect Business and Labor

Committee for Immediate Construction of the World Trade Center) as a public agency devoted primarily to creating private profit, its showpiece a glorified high-rise office center for private sector customers with minimal connections to world trade.

Financed by a combination of long-term consolidated bonds, medium-term bank loans, and short-term consolidated notes, the WTC's tax-exempt status granted a prolonged windfall to the original thirteen-bank lending syndicate (ten DLMA members among them),[11] while some portion of its operating costs were supported by user fee capital drawn from bridge and tunnel commuters who derived little if any benefit from its existence as a service and processing center for corporate capital. In a 1981 audit report, the New York State Comptroller concluded that the WTC had failed to create a 'conceptual community' of clients involved in world trade and was functioning like any other real-estate operation. The report recommended sale of the building to the benefit of the city, which could collect more realistic real-estate taxes from private owners.[12] Today, for example, the beneficiaries of luxury housing and Grade-A office space in the WTC and BPC currently enjoy tax exemptions, between the two complexes, of well over $200m a year. On the day of the building's dedication in 1973, Theodore Kheel, labor mediator and persistent critic of the Port Authority, had called for the WTC to 'be sold to private enterprise at the earliest possible date,' citing its operation as 'socialism at its worst,' because it competed unfairly with private development, attracting tenants with its low rental rates and other incentives.[13]

Kheel's argument against 'socialism at its worst' repays some analysis if only because it provides a valuable insight into the well-honed process by which the state traditionally subsidizes private profit with public money. In a May 1969 article in *New York* magazine, Kheel wrote:

> The World Trade Center is rising despite the fact that private builders have demonstrated a unique capacity to build office buildings in Manhattan without government assistance. The real needs of the people in the Port District which private industry cannot satisfy include housing, education, community services, medical care, park lands, environmental protection, and, of course, transportation . . .[14]

For Kheel there is no debate about what private industry can and cannot be expected to provide. The result is the status quo in a capitalist state — the process of silent partnership by which the state subsidizes private appropriation of profits by providing some minimum of the social needs of workers and by providing massive infrastructural subsidies: highways, transportation, parks.

The danger posed by the WTC to the likes of Kheel is that the state's subsidy of private interests might be a little too visible, threatening this silent partnership between the interests of private profit and public provision of services and infrastructures. State appropriation of land usually involves the developer in certain social obligations; in the case of the WTC, the development deal obliged the Port Authority to assume responsibility for a commuter railway system (Hudson and Manhattan Railroad — now PATH) so unprofitable that no private entrepreneur would touch it. State agencies like the Port Authority, the BPC, and the Urban Development Corporation (responsible now for 42nd Street and the Hudson River Park Conservancy) function like corporations with no stockholders. They are a precarious though tactical solution to the problems created by an all-too-public intervention in the business of helping private industry, an intervention that requires some form of accountability from elected officials. The WTC, after all, was intended to rejuvenate a whole area of the city, and would come to play a major role in the economic restructuring of Manhattan's CBD. But a large-scale process of this sort would surely require cooperation between the interests of real estate, private business, the large finance bankers, and monopolistic interests in the urban planning sector of city government. What better solution than the Port Authority, a body that has the supergovernment authority to coordinate, if not satisfy, each of these interests? In the wake of legislation like the 1949 Housing Act, which gave the green light to the huge federally funded redevelopment that came to be known as urban renewal, the costs of the social needs outlined by Kheel were increasingly assumed by the state as a direct subsidy to private capital. Kheel does not object to this arrangement, even though he might have argued that the state's obligation to socialize land-use in order to reproduce a labor force for private capital would ultimately conflict with land speculators' need to profit from real estate (too much low-income housing for workers destroys the housing market). In any event, he need hardly have worried. As a stimulant to downtown growth, the WTC proved to be an efficient catalyst for a boom in luxury housing that satisfied the speculators at the same time as it met the needs of corporate employers looking for a high-income professional work-force that would reoccupy the downtown area. The face of urban 'revitalization' took on a decidedly upper-middle-class appearance, while whole sectors of the urban population were delivered into the harsh austerity regime of 'planned shrinkage' of collective services in the wake of the mid-1970s fiscal crises.

The state played its role in subsidizing the new revitalization by granting tax abatements and low-interest bond monies to business, a role that proved much cheaper and less visibly interventionist to the public than either the huge federal grants for urban renewal projects or the task of socializing the older, working-class city had been. As collective services were slashed and the infrastructure deteriorated in the Reagan—Koch years, the state's chief social appeal was reduced to the job of self-legitimation in the eyes of white citizens and taxpayers, usually in the areas of law and order. The recent moral panic about crime, violence and gun control in the nation's cities provided an opportunity to pursue the state's self-legitimation into 'minority' communities (now a majority in many cities), where, for example, the perverse bogeyman of 'black-on-black violence' (any more perverse than white-on-white violence?) was exploited to divide community sentiment and resistance.

The WTC thus straddled two postwar periods of uneven development aimed at renovating the center city, and became a reviled symbol of each in turn. The first phase had been the period of 'urban renewal' (nicknamed 'negro removal') precipitated by a pro-growth coalition of business, real estate, and political interests seeking to stabilize CBD land values and racial homogeneity in the face of suburban flight. The infamous disruption of communities, displacement of 'near-downtown' populations (up to 250,000 families each year, nationally), and devastation of old buildings were all part of the costly burden borne by mostly minority and working-poor center city residents during the decades of 'slum clearance' and their replacement with middle- to high-income housing. The ghetto rebellions of the 1960s are widely acknowledged to have been, in part, a response to these massive projects which notoriously destroyed more low-income housing than they built, and exacerbated racial tensions by evicting and displacing populations, and breaking up communities without consent from those affected.[15]

The large-scale development of the WTC was an especially

arrogant example of the giantism of urban renewal and its record of
evictions and displacements. But the Twin Towers would also come
to be associated with a second, later phase of elite recentralization —
the new physical transformations described alternately as gentrification and revitalization — and thus with the new 'global city' of
finance capital and its two-tier post-Fordist service sector/pro-
fessional economy. Planned explicitly to be the world's tallest
building (subsequently superseded by Chicago's Sears Tower), and
serving, as critic Michael Sorkin pointed out, as a duplicate tribute
to consumer replicability,[16] the towers occupied the highest point on
a city skyline imagined as a corporate graph with peaks and troughs.
The building was central to the transformation of New York from
the nation's largest and most diverse manufacturing town (the city
lost 600,000 manufacturing jobs between 1966 and 1976) into a
central node of the global capital network of credit finance, where
the nerve center of international banking ceaselessly swaps and
circulates 'fictitious capital,' employing hundreds of thousands in
the labor of paper entrepreneurialism. For New Yorkers, the towers,
even more than the adjacent BPC, symbolized the ascendant
corporate city of the 1980s 'decade of greed.' Pre-yuppie New
Yorkers waxed nostalgic for the old 'good city' of the postwar
period, committed to the education, health, and shelter of its
citizens, and reviled the new 'bad city': socially polarized as never
before in its disparity between conspicuous wealth and conspicuous
poverty; briskly indifferent to the basic necessities of large sectors of
its population, housed or homeless; and primarily attentive to the
retention of business at all costs, through establishment of subsidy-
driven business improvement districts or other forms of economic
incentive.

The idea of the WTC was initially sold to the public as a necessary
bid to keep America's Number One port ahead of its competition,
and to the business community as a way of centralizing companies
with ties to world trade. By the 1980s, however, the Port's primacy
in ocean shipping was over. Indeed, the Port, the very *raison d'être* of
New York, had been all but removed, physically, to New Jersey, as
part of the plan to free up land for more lucrative office space. So,
too, the WTC housed many tenants with a quite remote relationship
to world trade, unless one counts international clients or overseas
offices as legitimate criteria.[17] But the building had done its work
nonetheless, helping to reinvent a downtown that would lure

professionals and their consumption dollars back from the suburbs, providing them with the gentrified housing and cultural amenities that gave corporate employees the symbolic credibility they required from a Manhattan address in the 1980s. So, too, Manhattan became the primary center of 'world trade' originally envisaged by the DLMA in their planning for the WTC. By the end of the decade, New York had taken on the broad dimensions of the dual city of post-Fordism, where a high-salaried professional managerial class occupied the residential city of Manhattan, while pockets of the Third World migrant underclass coexisted with the slow decay of the older industrial city in the outer boroughs. The internationalization of the economy had produced a new kind of global city, where, as Saskia Sassen has argued, a finance economy with its extensive service-sector support economy coexists with a proliferating informal economy, sweatshops and all, and a spiralling criminal economy specializing in narcotraffic.[18] After the crash of 1987, the bankruptcy of this economy became all too apparent. In the early 1990s downtown office vacancy rate was running at between 25 and 40 per cent, a scandalous number of New Yorkers were unemployed (400,000 jobs were lost after the crash), and those who had a job often worked at Third World wages.[19]

Design by Nature?

Whether you see it as a miracle or a scandal, the new global city did not come about 'naturally,' as if it were the latest evolutionary form of urban development on the planet. New York could have looked a lot different. And yet, the idea of *the city* has been so central to the linear narrative of 'civilization' that urban growth, or urbanization (customarily used to describe a less agreeable process), is often conceived in evolutionary terms, either analogous to biological processes or as organic development of an advanced social and political community. For example, the latest candidates for advanced evolutionary types are the multiple para-urban cores known as 'edge cities' — creatures, in the words of their craven booster Joel Garreau, still in 'their nymphal, if not larval, forms,' but inhabiting the very latest 'unknown and uncharted frontier' which promises to resolve the enduring contradictions between a pastoral and a business civilization.[20] Even those with reason to be skeptical of organicist descriptions of urban growth still have recourse to the language of evolutionary biology. Mike Davis, for example, describes the projected 'metrogalaxy of $22-24$ million people in Southern and Baja California in 2019' as a 'new evolutionary form . . . We are not talking about larger specimens of an old, familiar type, but an absolutely original, and unexpected, phyla of social life.'[21] Neo-Marxist and Marxist theorists like Manuel Castells and David Harvey, who see cities, historically, as efficient instruments of capitalist accumulation, organized to produce maximum economic surplus value, sometimes appeal to the Marxist version of evolutionism in seeing each stage of urban organization as inevitably determined by successive modes of production. Nonetheless, they are surely right to criticize the more functionalist version of the evolutionary growth of cities, which sees urban organization as a formal, unified response to technological progress, that 'blind and ineluctable force' which mediates between Man and Nature.[22]

I have noted earlier that ideas about biology and nature are an integral part of the history of discussing and planning the shape of cities. Darwinian ideas about environmental selection were habitually applied to the tenement slum cities of the nineteenth century — only the best will survive — while calls for environmental reform appealed to ideas about physical degeneration and biological unfitness among urban slum dwellers. The tenement city was believed to produce a de-evolved physical type, whose degraded capacity to reproduce the species threatened the health of the entire Republic. Of course, much of this public commentary was thinly disguised racist sentiment directed at the immigrant communities rapidly establishing themselves in the tenement slums of American cities. Jacob Riis, a Danish immigrant, encapsulated the dual mood of reformism and racism in his important work of photojournalism, *How the Other Half Lives* (1890). Riis, as Peter Hall notes, detailed the wretched conditions of slum life at the same time as he race-baited the ever-spreading immigrant population in the Victorian 'city of dreadful night.'[23] Plans for civic improvement were undertaken, American style, in the philanthropic spirit of private volunteer groups devoted to the task of bringing physical and moral hygiene into the blighted areas. Eventually, a more centralized system of regulation was instituted to reduce the duplication of work by the myriad of charitable agencies; state intervention emerged in the

1920s in the shape of the new planning fraternity, with their city surveys and zoning powers.

Perhaps the most representative figure of this tradition of environmental reform was Patrick Geddes, the polymath Scottish anarchist whose Carlylean energy impelled him from his early career as a biologist into historic prominence as the father of urban planning, and as a pioneer of ecological principles in civil engineering. The author of many publications on botany, biology and evolution, his Darwinism was opposed to the Malthusian and Spencerian tradition of *laissez-faire* competition and survival, and more influenced by the anarchist principles of cooperation through love and association (his bestselling books on sex, *The Evolution of Sex* [1889] and *Sex* [1914], argued that survival was a result of adaptation of the sexes). His most sustained volume of writings, *Cities in Evolution* (1915) demonstrates well his idiosyncratic interpretation of the Victorian relationship between civic improvement and evolutionary progress. Geddes' dictates about the environmental need for bioregional planning, and his emphasis upon the new, clean 'geotechnic' technologies were favorably adopted by Lewis Mumford and other members of the RPA. They also shared his enthusiasm for the small, self-governing anarchist commonwealths of Ebenezer Howard's garden city, a vision that would come to be rudely caricatured by the reality of North American suburbanization. Steeped in the life sciences, the biological analogy was never far from Geddes' mind. Musing over a population map of London, he wrote:

> This octopus of London, polypus rather, is something curious exceedingly, a vast irregular growth without previous parallel in the world of life — perhaps likest to the spreadings of a great coral reef. Onward it grows, thinly at first, the pale tints spreading further and faster than the others, but the deeper tints of thicker population at every point steadily following on. Within lies a dark and crowded area; of which, however, the daily pulsating centre calls on us to seek some fresh comparison to higher than coralline life.[24]

Extolling the praise of planned urban evolution, he later comments: 'Towns must now cease to spread like expanding ink-stains and grease spots; once in true development, they will repeat the starlike opening of the flower, with green leaves set in alteration with its golden rays.'[25] Such analogies were not simply a consequence of Geddes' flowery prose style. They were based on an enduring trust in the cognate effects of the sciences of evolution, whether biological, ethical, or geotechnical. In his mind, the built environment, even in high-density urban areas, could surely be as rational and progressive as biology had proven the natural world to be.

A less activist preoccupation with botany touched the scholarly concerns of the influential Chicago School of urban sociologists in the 1920s. Robert Park, Ernest Burgess, and Roderick McKenzie found in plant ecology an explanatory system for making sense of North American cities like Chicago in a state of immense flux due to immigration and the ceaseless turnover and reallocation of land. Just as plant ecologists saw a habitat being occupied by different species competitively vying for dominant control over the use of resources, while subdominants adapted to the remaining space, Park, Burgess, and McKenzie saw the functional behavior of urban communities expressed in the same way in the spatial pattern of the city. In the competitive struggle for territorial control of space, dominance progressively diminished with distance from the center city, famously pictured by Burgess as an area of concentric zones. Each zone expands into and invades its neighboring, outer zone in a way similar to the principles of plant invasion-succession, the principles in the urban case being determined by food supply and production and distribution of commodities. According to Burgess, the structural growth of a city was not unlike a beech or pine forest in which the climax or equilibrium state is reached after a series of successive invasions and displacements has established one dominant type of ecological organization which can withstand the impact of other invasive forms. In the case of the city, the invasive element could take many forms; a new mode of transportation, the erection of a major building, introduction of new types of industry, or changes in the economic base. Its most disagreeable manifestation, however, seems to come in the form of 'foreign races and other undesirable invaders' who 'take up residence near the business center of the community or at other points of high mobility and low resistance.'[26]

Here, as elsewhere in *The City*, the Chicago School's famous collection of essays, the biological analogy is infused with assumptions about the pathology of the racial and class composition of neighborhoods and their populations. Each area constitutes, in

Park's term, a 'moral region,' where the 'social contagion' of the environment means that 'the poor, the vicious, and the delinquent, crushed together in an unhealthful and contagious immediacy, breed in and in, soul and body . . .' Inhabitants of these moral regions thereby become 'peculiarly fit for the environment in which they are condemned to exist.'[27] While 'zones of deterioration' encompass the poor and diseased, the Latin Quarter houses 'creative and rebellious spirits,' the 'Black Belt' has 'its free and disorderly life,' and the various immigrant colonies like the (Jewish) Ghetto, Little Sicily, Greektown, and Chinatown combine 'old world heritages with American adaptions.' Second-generation settlement has already demonstrated a creative adaptation analogous to plant life. As for the occupational selection of the immigrants − 'as Irish policemen, Greek ice-cream parlors, Chinese laundries, Negro porters, Belgian janitors, etc.' − McKenzie attributes this division of labor more to 'racial temperament' than to 'old world economic background.'[28] At every turn, the differentiation of space, labor, and economy is afforded a naturalistic explanation, whether by appeal to the organic metaphor, or to pseudo-scientific shibboleths about racial essences.

At other times, the Chicago analysts resurrect a much older analogy between the city and the human body, gussied up now in the new scientific lingo, when they invite us to think of urban growth as 'a resultant of organization and disorganization analogous to the anabolic and katabolic processes of metabolism in the body.' McKenzie goes on to argue that the principle of 'mobility,' 'the best index of the state of metabolism of the city,' is 'the pulse of the community,' because its concentration, in zones of deterioration where stimulation, 'as in the relentless pursuit of pleasure,' is greatest, is just 'like the pulse of the human body.'[29] The city here is no longer like a pine forest, but like an aroused human body.

In reading these influential essays, it is difficult to avoid concluding that it is the very idea of ecology itself, in all of its biological variants, that has become contagiously pervasive in every other turn of phrase. Far from restricting themselves to a strict scientific analogy with plant ecology, these urban sociologists employed a language that is overrun with invasive outgrowths of biological metaphor. The models chosen by the Chicago scholars to explain the bewildering spatial order of the city take on a reproductive life of their own. That a 'teeming' immigrant city would require an analogy with competing species of plant life to explain its behavior says as much about the racial presumptions of Park and his colleagues as it does about the supposed objectivity of the life sciences, teeming with its own sociobiological metaphors. Add to this the appeal, to Park and his associates, of social Darwinism in the work of sociologists like William Graham Sumner, and you have all the ingredients of a Chicago gangster theory of urban life, whereby the city expresses the state of human nature by inviting elites to fight among themselves (and against everyone else) for the use of available space.

The staying power of the bio-organic approach to urban ecology has been remarkable. While the strict spatial determinism of Burgess's zone model no longer holds sway (notwithstanding Mike Davis's semi-parodic attempt to revamp Burgess in his physical mapping of LA's 'ecology of fear'), and while plant ecology has given way to population ecology as the explanatory model of choice for the school of human ecology fathered by Amos Hawley, the conceptual vocabulary of invasion-succession and equilibrium (or contamination and contagion from epidemiology) is still prevalent in urban studies. To cite one recent example, Rodrick Wallace, of the New York Psychiatric Institute, argues the case, in a series of articles, for a 'synergic' link between 'contagious housing decay,' the epidemiological spread of HIV infection, and the 'planned shrinkage' of city services. In his analysis, HIV infection follows the path of housing destruction 'from a geographically contained center in the South Central Bronx to a virtually borough-wide phenomenon.' As the spread of AIDS, dubiously described by Wallace as a 'contagious plague,' furthers the process of housing abandonment and destruction through fire, 'a nonlinear ecosystem coupling between AIDS, contagious urban decay, and population shift' is established: 'Daily encounters with large numbers of people dying of plague might become insupportable, driving the still-healthy in desperation to seek housing as yet "uncontaminated" by overt symptoms of disease.'[30] It is easy to see how the presence of HIV infection as an element of Wallace's ecosystem actually reinforces the language of contagion and virulence customarily applied to housing desertification and structural fire incidence.[31] The result is to view these processes as having a momentum and a logic of their own, and to see their effects as a natural, rather than a social, consequence of certain conditions. Viewing municipal services such as fire prevention as a form of 'immunization' against the contagion doesn't help matters. In a more recent article, however, co-written with Deborah Wallace, the intentionality of these effects is attributed more directly to the social agency of 'planned shrinkage,' described there as 'a virulent and systematic program of malfeasance, misfeasance, and nonfeasance conducted by agencies of government for the political purpose of a self-absorbed and unstable ruling oligarchy.'[32]

In his book, *The Ecology of Housing Destruction*, Peter Salins defends the use of terms like 'epidemic' to describe patterns of abandon-ment, arson, and destruction of housing stock; the damage, he writes, 'spreads in contiguous waves from the original epicenters of devastation, in a pattern quite analogous to the spread of contagious diseases.'[33] What is new, he argues, is the phenomenon of 'a rapidly moving slum that razes buildings and neighborhoods in its path.' This frightening new Pacman is the ecological result of interplay between mutually reinforcing patterns of behavior: ill-conceived public sector policies (rent regulation, public assistance), profit-oriented realtors (are there any other kind?), and self-interested (antilandlord) housing tenants. It is not long before Salins resorts to blaming the victims, since the path of this monster is the same as that inundated by 'an advancing tide of welfare families that generally ripples outward in concentric circles from the original poverty epicenters.'[34] The root cause of this 'terminal urban cancer' — perhaps 'the final spasm of a dying city' — is rent stabilization, welfare dependency, and antilandlord bias. The housing map Salins draws in his more recent *Scarcity by Design* is one where government action is always 'a cure worse than the disease,' and where tenants' self-protection is merely a symptom of 'New Yorkers' eternal desire to get more than they pay for.'[35]

The point to be made here is that urban commentators today, both liberal and conservative, are utilizing the same language of contagion and disease that was prevalent in nineteenth-century discourses about inner-city immigrants. In attributing guilt to these citizens by association with disease, the socially and spatially marginalized are thereby still being held responsible in some way for the conditions of their living environment. In the intervening century, the *scientific* language of urban ecology has lent credibility to all of this nonsense about contagion, epidemics, incubation, contamination, and immunization against pestilence. The result is to naturalize, at every step of the way, phenomena that are entirely social in origin.

Here, for example, is the basic ur-narrative of community change according to the urban ecosystems theory. When a community's environmental substratum is unstable and when immunity to external pressure is weak, it is gripped and progressively devastated by an invasive, malady-like condition, the path of which may be scientifically measured and charted, while its origin is deemed to be the mechanistic result of interplay between components of the urban ecosystem. The language used to couch this explanation is further 'biologized' when public health deficiencies are cited as a critical component of the urban system in decay. The presence of 'real' disease in population ecology seems to have a multiplication effect upon the rhetoric of sickness loosely employed by many scholars in urban studies. Systems theory, above all, provides the most extended basis for comparing a biotic to an urban environment. It provides a language which casts the 'metabolism' of the urban system as subject to control mechanisms, defined as negative feedback (disease and low mortality, for example) which moves a system toward equilibrium, or positive feedback (prolonged economic growth, advanced technology, for example) which moves the system beyond its natural limits and into a state of collapse.[36]

The primary weakness of these explanatory models of organic behavior is that they are incapable of describing the powerful pressure from corporate and government agents in shaping urban development. The effects of the silent partnership between public authority and private developers cannot be easily incorporated into this kind of functionalist model. Nor can pressure from below, on the part of organized community politics. Critics of urban ecology have pointed to its failure to incorporate a theory of the state, or capital accumulation, or, to use Henri Lefebvre's term, of the 'production of space' that is necessary to the advanced capitalist state. From a classical Marxist perspective, the very existence of the city can be viewed as a historical effect of the division of labor and the uneven development of capital formation. From the same viewpoint, suburbanization may be viewed as an effect of the cycles of overinvestment and disinvestment in the center city, rather than as some natural outgrowth of the overconcentrated metropolis. Highly evolved capitalist uses of social engineering are responsible for the bulk of urban redevelopment, including huge projects of the sort undertaken in the name of urban renewal and urban revitalization. Consequently, there are no internal, 'organic' laws of competition over space and location that can adequately account for the nexus of funding and planning at city and federal levels which ensures state aid for the private appropriation of profit. Finally, and perhaps most important, resistance to the urban developments that result from this partnership is widespread and uneven. Such resistance needs to be taken into account in any estimate of the shape of the city if we are to see cities as the outcomes of complex social struggle over contested terrain rather than as organically evolved sociophysical entities.

Austerity Culture

In the instance of New York, with a history of, and a reputation for, progressive government, the test case for the theoretical inadequacies of urban ecology remains the fiscal crisis of the mid-1970s, when the corporate elite staged a coup against the city's own welfare state and established virtually sovereign powers over its fiscal affairs. The popular (conservative) wisdom that emerged from the fiscal crisis and which prevails to this day is that the city cannot live beyond its means by catering to all of the special interests of its broad spectrum of residents. The other popular (liberal) version is that a clique of powerful and venal bankers, with the aid of corrupt city officials, calls all the shots in town. Each version evokes an image of the city as an insular, economic entity, dissociated from the federal state apparatus — an image, in other words, of the city as an economic ecosystem unto itself.

It is fair to say that there is some historical basis for this understanding of the American city. Historically, the official links between central and municipal government have been relatively weak, and were really only established in the Depression year of 1932, when the appeal for federal aid from the first Conference of Mayors saw the origin of large-scale federal responses to the call to 'save the cities': Franklin Roosevelt's National Resources Planning Board was one such response.[37] The subsequent decades of often heavy federal funding for urban development came at a time when manufacturing was at its height, employing a huge urban labor force. Into the breach jumped the state, providing housing, education, and services to maintain productivity and keep down labor costs. The city became a managerial conduit for relieving private industry of the social costs associated with the Fordist compact between capital and labor. State intervention was an essential part of the growth of the private monopoly sector during this period of virtually full employment. As the cost of socialization rose, and consumerism raised popular levels of materialist desire, the expectations of the citizenry grew. Government instituted War on Poverty programs in response to the militancy of student protesters and groups marginalized by poverty and by color which found expression in the ghetto rebellions of the 1960s. By the early 1970s, the social programs generated by the War on Poverty were actually beginning to reach residents of areas hit hardest by urban renewal if only because the funds were being administered and dispensed by reformist federal agencies directly through citizens groups and participating community organizations rather than through the more conservative centers of local government. When the fiscal crisis hit, it came in the wake of the local stress caused by the Nixon administration's draconian cutback in federal programs (federal housing programs were suspended almost immediately after Nixon took office), and the global economic shockwaves generated by the oil embargo of 1973.

In a famous structural analysis from 1973, James O'Connor argues that fiscal crises are a result of the contradiction generated by the three orders of public socialization of capital: (a) social investment capital — the public funding of projects whose profits are privatized; (b) social consumption capital — the subsidizing of housing, health care, education, and transportation for workers; and (c) social expenses capital — required to keep the peace and legitimize the liberal state. Ultimately, the state's expenditures on expanding services far outstrip the state's revenues, as the rate of profit becomes untenably low.[38] O'Connor's structural version of the crisis was theorized at the national level, and so its effects would be unevenly demonstrated in each of the 200 American cities that announced a fiscal crisis (only Cleveland, among the major cities, actually declared bankruptcy — voluntarily in its case). In the case of New York, we are confronted with a city whose official self-image is one of progressive leadership elected periodically by reformist movements triumphing against a corrupt party machine put in place by nineteenth-century entrepreneurs. In reality, the 'reform' movements were often created by businessmen to break up working-class political blocs organized through the machine. Nonetheless, the liberal ideology of the reform tradition meant that city government, in the postwar period, had to legitimize itself by responding to progressive calls for better housing, better medical treatment, higher levels of public assistance, day care, job training, and tuition-free public education at CUNY colleges. While unionized municipal employment trebled, wage employment in the private sector plummeted as the city lost 50 per cent of its manufacturing jobs between 1950 and 1975. The fiscal crisis, and the austerity measures imposed in its wake by the banking elite were a visible attempt to discipline and punish the city for the 'profligate' ways that had earned it a progressive − i.e. 'tax and spend' − reputation.

In fact, New York differed little from other cities in its public expenditure. What made it different (aside from its location at the center of TV news production) was its historic concentration of financial houses and corporate headquarters, and therefore its potential for being transformed into a global corporate center. This transformation would boost land value a hundredfold by converting low-rent industrial space into high-rent office space. The banks themselves had profited royally from New York's expanding welfare state by providing decades of high-interest loans to bale out a city dependent on a shrinking tax base due to industrial disinvestment, the taxpayer revolt, and the limits of regressive tax revenues. By the mid-1970s, the banks, reflecting the shift to offshore production away from metropolitan urban cores, had begun to stake their fortunes on the internationalization of the finance economy. Consequently, they were were no longer dependent on city securities, and so the old social contract between capital and labor had become obstructive, rather than enabling, of their interests. Having profited from overinvestment in the city, the major investment houses like Chase Manhattan, Citibank, Merrill Lynch, Morgan, Manufacturers Hanover, Chemical, and Bankers Trust quickly began to divest by shifting the burden of buying City notes onto smaller investors. At the same time, the bankers sought a more attractive investment climate for international finance capital by dismantling the social contract: they demanded from City Hall a moratorium on capital expenditures, massive layoffs of municipal employees, wage freezes, cutbacks in programs, an end to education subsidies (free CUNY tuition) and CUNY building programs, cuts in public transit, and a harsh review of the city's tax and debt structures. As Eric Lichten shows in his detailed account of the crisis, one of the major points of contention between the banks and the city revolved around who would have the first lien on the city's revenues in the event of a bankruptcy. The ever militant unions or the bankers and their major clients? Initially, the first lien was not guaranteed to holders of City notes, but rather to workers and to urban poor dependent on city revenues.[39] It was only after the banks had used the credit market to pressure City Hall into unconditional surrender that the investors got their first lien.

In the interim, President Ford had refused to bail out the city (FORD TO CITY: DROP DEAD was the infamous *Daily News* headline), and the finance community had succeeded in establishing autonomous governance over the city's austerity boards, first the Financial Community Liaison Group, then the Municipal Assistance Corporation (MAC), and, eventually, the Emergency Financial Control Board (EFCB), in what amounted to an oligarchic grab of the power to direct the city's fiscal affairs. Very soon, city policy was being set directly by the EFCB, which imposed massive austerity measures upon all public sectors. The EFCB either bypassed City Hall or forced it at financial gunpoint to comply with the freezes, cutbacks, and eliminations. Eventually, it was the municipal employee unions, not the banks, that bailed out the city when union pension funds were used to bankroll the budget by investing them in MAC bonds. Whatever adversarial role the unions might still have played in city politics was seriously undermined by this act, since, as Lichten argues, the size of the union investments in the city were so large as to be threatened by any future labor conflict.[40] Not only had the labor movement been disciplined, by massive cuts, for its history of successes in the city; its primary instruments of class struggle had been turned upon itself by the investment debacle.

The fiscal crisis of 1975 was not without its antecedents. William Tabb has diagnosed a familiar cycle in New York's history in which the financial elites charge City Hall with mismanagement through public 'overspending' and subsequently exploit the ensuing crisis as a vehicle to restructure the city physically and to accelerate their own profits. This history includes the Federalists' revenge against the Tammany reformists in the early nineteenth century, and the assumption of direct control by business elites on at least two previous occasions: in the 1880s — when the Committee of Seventy 'rescued' New York from Boss Tweed's excesses — and the 1930s — when the Municipal Economy Commission usurped the powers of the Walker administration. Tabb argues that this cycle of corruption and putative reform masks the systematic process by which a new elite of ascendant economic interests (only publicly visible during crises) seeks to establish fiscal policies and guarantees of government compliance that will protect and further its special interests.[41]

But the 1975 crisis had an impact that went far beyond New York City's limits. The retrenchment and planned shrinkage of services and programs in New York was subsequently proposed as the model for a national policy by Felix Rohatyn, the neoliberal financier who emerged as the MAC's kingpin savior of the city. The austerity policies imposed upon New York, resulting in the calculated abandonment (this is the basic social effect of 'planned shrinkage') of large sectors of the city and its less wealthy residents, ultimately became the prototype for the new federal politics aimed at slashing the USA's version of a welfare state and privatizing services that would subsequently have to be bought rather than publicly provided. So too, the generous tax abatement packages thrown into the lap of corporations and international investors by the city were only an appetizer for the deregula-tionist, supply-side, monetarist policies preferred by the more radically redistributive Reaganomics. Democrat and Republican administrations at the city, state, and federal level have all come to accept the imperative of austerity culture, with its efficiency gospel of budget-balancing, as a logic that is determined by clearly defined limitations on resources.

It would be more accurate, however, to call this a proscarcity politics, since the austerity measures are aimed as much at aggressively breaking labor's social contract and redistributing wealth upwards than at fiscally adjusting to deteriorating economic conditions. Indeed, the creation of scarcity through redefining the budgetary limits of an economy has become the favored strategy of class politics in the new post-Fordist climate. As a result, scarcity, for the lower tier of the dual economy, was clearly tied to abundance for the upper tier throughout the Reagan—Bush years. The monstrous national deficit run up during those years was interpreted as a symptom of affluence and economic growth in the corporate sector until, under Clinton, it was progressively redefined as an economic problem and as a rationale for his austerity politics of 'national sacrifice' shared by all classes. The neoliberal presidential campaign run by Clinton did not seek to challenge the political religion of the austerity state that has by now come to be seen as part of daily 'common sense' rather than as a naked strategy of the corporate class. Clintonian neoliberalism could no longer present a postscarcity future for anyone, it could only promise to equalize the presumed effects of scarcity for everyone.

Austerity economics also became the name of the game in global politics, especially in the policies of the World Bank and the International Monetary Fund, which demand austerity measures (i.e. an investment climate favorable to international business) as a condition for lending to countries economically tied down by debt financing. What material scarcity really means in a global economy governed by credit and reliant on debt-financing markets is anybody's guess and thus the prerogative of the most powerful to define. Just as in a fiscal crisis, when someone in authority decides when and where a crisis condition exists, so, too, with the designation of scarcity. Environmentalism, to which pundits often appeal for an analysis of material scarcity, will no longer provide a straight answer. Whatever use environmentalism has served as a discourse for explaining some of the North/South disparity between scarcity and abundance is now being undermined and assimilated into corporate logic by the post-Rio move to create a world environmental market in the form of free-market solutions to the problem of absorbing, distributing, and exploiting environmental costs. Between the World Bank-administered Global Environmental Facility, set up as a green fund for development, and the work of the Rio Summit's Business Council on Sustainable Development, a global market has emerged to rationalize everything from debt-for-nature swaps to the expedient bartering of individual states' environmental regulations, all in the interests of smoothing the flow of international finance. Far from self-regulating, this free market is governed by a cost-benefit budgetary model, but is nonetheless presented as the best that economists have to offer in the way of a 'natural' solution to the crisis of nature.

Austerity politics and budget consciousness are the governors of dogma currently linking the business of balancing the budget at City Hall or on Capitol Hill and to managing the international debt map at the World Bank. Doubts about the legitimacy of capitalism (how can the richest country in the world not afford to . . .?) can be deferred by technocratic appeals to the limitations imposed by budgetary constraints (now that the diversionary Reagan–Bush strategy of militaristic adventures is less available). The crisis managers present these economies, urban or global, as if they were self-contained ecosystems with their own natural limits to growth. In a 'global city' like New York, where so much of the recent growth and development has been tied to the fortunes of foreign investment and international finance, it would seem that there is less and less justification for viewing the urban unit in this self-contained manner. On the other hand, as Alberta Sbragia has shown, by 1985, 85 per cent of the municipal bonds – the biggest source of urban funds outside of regressive taxation – were being sold not to banks but to individual investors in the household sector. Foreign capital, not subject to US tax laws, does not need the tax shelter of these bonds, and commercial banks and finance houses have accelerated their disinvestment in city securities begun in advance of the fiscal crisis. State spending on capital improvements has been aimed solely at subsidizing the downtown renaissance of real estate/finance capital, and so changes in federal income tax now have a greater potential effect on individual investments in city bonds.[42]

One might conclude from Sbragia's evidence that the map of federal/state/city linkages has changed considerably and tendentially in the period since the fiscal crisis. And yet, these changes are not in the direction of long-term stability. On the contrary, they only demonstrate the fickle and volatile nature of the linkages between the city and the state, ever susceptible to the short-term restructuring that is increasingly necessary to extract maximum land value and to guarantee an economy of flexible accumulation. The City Hall budget which represents the municipal economy is not a relatively fixed continuum, but a variable outcome of shifting patterns of investment and disinvestment on the part of public as well as private institutions. Thus to see a budget and what it represents as an organic system of parts which naturally hangs together is as misleading as to see the global city as a natural, evolutionary product of urban growth.

The Body Politic

What is the relationship, if any, between the the natural ecology of the city's islands and waterways and the social ecology of a metropolis like New York? A conventional environmentalist description might treat the city and its population as a unified organism occupying a single land niche with a limited carrying capacity. In his foreword to *The New York Environment Book*, prepared by the Natural Resources Defense Council in 1990, novelist Kurt Vonnegut gives us a classic example of this view when he praises the book for dissecting New York as if it were indeed one vast organism: examining 'the physiology of the enormous creature millions of us inhabit, for better or worse, as though we were tiny, unthinking parasites,' the book, he says, describes 'the disgusting bodily functions of the drinking, eating, sweating, belching, wind-breaking, hugely excreting host animal, older than the city of Leningrad, incidentally, on which our health depends.'[43] The book does indeed provide an exhaustive assessment of New York's environmental scorecard — in the areas of sewage treatment, air and water pollution, waste disposal, toxic contamination, and overdevelopment — while arguing that the city's public authorities are failing in their duty to safeguard natural resources and protect the health of its citizens. It could be said that this failure persists, despite the relative energy efficiency of cities in general, and New York City in particular, on account of the well-insulated, compacted nature of its built environment (New Yorkers consume energy for heat and electricity at less than half the national average, although they pay dearly for what they get), its extensive mass transit facilities (78 per cent of Manhattan households don't have cars, 56 per cent in Brooklyn, 61 per cent in the Bronx), the loss of its polluting manufacturing base, and its celebrated drinking water supply. Thankfully, the kind of analysis presented in the book avoids the voluntarism that preaches the sole responsibility of individuals either as private consumers or public citizens. Instead, it assigns accountability for the environmental record largely to the city's appointed public officials.

Since the federal government is only now getting back into the business of environmental regulation after twelve Reagan—Bush years of inaction, this appeal to municipal authority would seem to make sense, and yet it calls into question the rationality of seeing the city as an isolated ecosystem, least of all as a coherent body politic unto itself. Stories like the saga of the *Mobro*, the wandering Islip garbage barge from the mid-1980s, and the more recent moratorium on buying cheap electricity from the ecologically disastrous James Bay hydroelectric development in upper Quebec are only two of the more public reminders that the environmental economy of the city involves locations, populations, and most of all, markets (the *Mobro*'s odyssey had nothing to do with the shortage of landfill space, and everything to do with the vagaries of the waste market) far outside of its metropolitan limits. Local successes at evicting environmental hazards within city limits often amount to displacing the problem elsewhere, to less regulated regions of the country, or south of the border to the toxic belt of Mexico's *maquiladoras*. Cities within the USA compete with each other on their environmental records, but if the outcome is simply to turn Northern Mexico into a toxic, industrial wasteland, then acting locally is not cognate with thinking globally.

Nor is it sufficient to see the city as a bioregional unit of such concentrated density that it exacts an impossible toll on the resource base it occupies or draws upon. If there ever existed a natural limit or balance to the city, a scale of urban activity and growth appropriate to the physical resources of its natural location, then that moment was over in a millisecond. Any serious movement to depopulate high-density cities would have a disastrous effect on rural areas and wildlife habitats. In addition, the antagonism between town and country that was so important to Marx's own ideas about economic history (in *The German Ideology* and other texts, Marx saw this antagonism as the 'foundation' of the division of labor and class distinctions)[44] makes increasingly less sense in a megalopolis where the vagaries of international capital have such a profound effect on the movement of populations and the transformations of built environment.

On the other hand, there are good reasons for acknowledging the coherence of the metropolitan landform. The economic key to urban history lies in the division of labor that allowed the first citizens of ancient civilizations to occupy centers of religious and political administration separate from rural production. Later, just to confine the narrative to European examples, the process of capital formation produced the mercantile city-states of the Middle Ages, the centers of manufacturing and consumption of the early and late industrial period, and the sites of information economy in the postindustrial period. In each of these phases, the city has been a geographically concentrated instrument for the process of maximum surplus extraction, its officials entrusted with the task of managing that process.

The political and cultural history of urban civilization, especially in its anarchist version, is somewhat different, emphasizing the growth of a common *civitas* which transcends the tribal and ethnic parochialism of village culture, but it tells a similar story about the concentrated locality of the urban unit. Free citizens with rights of participation and self-government create a face-to-face communitarian body politic based on rational political decision-making rather than on laws of kinship, blood, and custom, or on privileges of property and commodity. Murray Bookchin describes this 'ethical union of people' as a utopian eco-community, which existed at various historical moments in contradistinction to the purely economic existence of the city as a market or center of production and consumption. The emphasis on civic participation as the central principle of social ecology in the city is viewed by Bookchin as 'the social counterpart of biological mutualism.' Citizenship, in all of its obligations, is viewed as 'the social counterpart of biotic involvement in shaping the form of a natural ecocommunity.'[45] The golden moments of Bookchin's eco-community all lie in the past, enjoyed by the great citizenry of the Athenian polis, the medieval confederated municipalities, the Paris Commune, New England town halls, and the Spanish anarchist communes. Compared with these city republics of yore, today's megalopolis is an 'anticity,' perverted by the cancerous rise of urbanization, while its body politic, the creature of propertied oligarchies and state bureaucracies, is a corruption of the ideal of humanist citizenship which once existed in balance with the 'first nature' of the physical world. For Bookchin, the idea of a liberating urban civilization, inevitably in decline as urbanization rose, is still retrievable, but only in the recreation of small decentralized communities linked by the principle of municipal confederationism.

Like most of the discourses linked to the 'decline of the public sphere,' Bookchin's jeremiad rests upon rosy and undoubtedly mythical assumptions about a state of affairs (minus the state) that once was and is no more. Unruffled by contemporary critiques of Enlightenment universalism that would cast suspicion upon his humanism, Bookchin insists that the idea of *civitas* is still a viable political objective, and worth fighting for. In this respect, he never falls prey to the antiurban demonizing that has often been a wearisome component of the environmentalist tradition. Despite Bookchin's pessimism, I would argue that the survival of the urban idea is pervasive in many sectors of city life today, and certainly would describe many of the forms of community and neighborhood-based activism which are the legacy of the urban movements of the early 1970s, in housing, education, utilities, recreational facilities, health care, etc. On a daily basis, most people continue to think of themselves as living in neighborhoods and not in one vast megalopolis; as participants in the ethnic group politics which is still an integral part of New York's urban culture; and as more involved, if not empowered, in city politics than at the level of regional or federal politics. As for the political apparatus of the city, there is a real need for City Hall to legitimize itself as accountable to voices outside of the business sector, a process that involves its officials and agencies to some extent in community politics. Among other things, this is why the city's financial elites prefer to legislate their planning initiatives through commissions and public corporations rather than through publicly elected representatives.

The city, the subnational state, and the federal state are not vertically aligned, each acting smoothly in the interests of the more powerful body in the food chain. Nor are they horizontally linked to the interests of capital in anything like the same way. City politicians and, increasingly under transnationalism, state politicians act in their own interests, to protect their own sovereignty, and so they are often in conflict with each other and with the interests of capital. In terms of democratic process, wherever officials need to be reelected, and consent is required, then competing agendas come into existence, and the playing field is potentially socialized. To the extent that the state retains its function of socializing urban life, environmental protection has become a leading issue, if only because of its perceived importance to the quality of life of upper-middle-class residents. On the other hand, the placing of garbage incinerators and sewage and toxic waste treatment facilities in low-income neighborhoods, not to mention the geography of New York's infamous 'lead belt' (running through South Bronx/Harlem/Bushwick/Bedford-Stuyvesant), all tell a familiar story about the class and racial composition of those front-line victims most likely to suffer birth defects and neurological damage from exposure to environmental hazards.

Nor has grassroots politics in the city rolled over and surrendered in the face of urban renewal and gentrification. The established power of the urban social movements of the 1960s and 1970s lives on: community organizing among citizens of color and gays, squatter movements, urban trade unionism, spontaneous 'riots.' In addition, new and powerful forms of urban activism have emerged in the last decade to address the geographical crises of homelessness, AIDS (increasingly a geographically specific epidemic), police brutality, overdevelopment, and queerbashing. Numerous coalitions created under the aegis of community environmentalism have become a normative feature of the political landscape. Not least of all, the desocialization of the city's infrastructure has also given rise to hip hop, the most creative counterculture to come out of the urban scene since jazz, and the most politically incisive by far. It is impossible to give an account of hip hop's history without seeing the backdrop of urban decomposition against which its stories, mythical, realist and vernacular, have been told. Politics, history and culture *are* being made, as always, under conditions not of our choosing.

Who Ya Gonna Call?

An equally important part of the city's composition is the rich popular mythography that surrounds New York and defines the image of the city in popular culture and urban folklore. No tourist who buys an 'I Love New York' souvenir is blithely unaware of the rotten core of the Big Apple. Ever since the onset of the austerity culture and the slashing of services, a large part of the city's image has been negative. How could it be otherwise when the popular media informs us that entire borough neighborhoods are terrorized (not by occupying police forces but) by the militarized gangster cadres of the criminal economy, when public education is in utter shambles, and when the state of the public health system is visibly defined by the city's map of AIDS and high infant mortality rates, and by its vast homeless population. Blaming the victim, hyping the psychopathology of crime, and bemoaning the inefficiency and graft of public officials have become the number one focus of the city's popular media organs in TV and print, largely responsible for the image of a lawless, uncivil society at the heart of a virtually unliveable city.

These same media periodically nominate extraordinary individuals to fill the moral vacuum created by the abdication of the state in providing services. When they are not ostentatious investors and developers like Felix Rohatyn or Donald Trump, they are comic book superheroes. This is why the *Batman* and the *Ghostbusters* films were Gotham's answer, however incongruous, to LA's *Blade Runner*. Consider *Ghostbusters*, released in 1984, at a time when the radical privatization of services had begun to take its toll on the city's quality of public life. A research program on paranormal phenomena is terminated by the university, and its participants are forced to enter the private sector, setting up their own paramilitary 'ghostbusting' service in a now derelict fire station in a neighborhood described as a 'demilitarized zone.' Their success is sustained by a proliferation of ghost visitations in the form of psychic slime connected to the worship of a Sumerian god (the first urban deity?) whose demonic possession of residents seems only to add to the population of mentally ill already on the city streets after two decades of deinstitutionalization. An activist bureaucrat from the Environmental Protection Agency — the film's baddie — takes a hard line against the Ghostbusters' psychic waste facility and precipitates an environmental disaster of 'biblical proportions.' A desperate mayor looks to the Ghostbusters for a service the city cannot provide. The city is saved at some cost to its infrastructure, for which, we learn in the film's sequel, the intrepid busters are sued ungratefully by every state, county, and city agency in New York.

In *Ghostbusters II*, the slime, associated this time with worship of a medieval European tyrant eager to obtain his green card, penetrates the city through a defunct subway service — the old pneumatic transit lines — causing mayhem and bad vibes among the population on account of its chemical psychoreactivity. The mayor sees this as normative behavior: 'Being miserable and treating other people like dirt is every New Yorker's god-given right.' After an inspirational conversation with the mayoral ghost of the great liberal city of yore, Fiorello LaGuardia, he again acknowledges the failure of the public services to deal with the crisis by calling on the Ghostbusters. The Ghostbusters themselves are immensely popular with residents of the city: 'Sometimes, shit happens, someone has to deal with it, and who you gonna call?' It is clear that the city's failure is synonymous with the Ghostbusters' efficiency in dealing with the urban decay represented by the slime and the ghosts. Here, the private initiative of the subcontractor merges smoothly with the populist call for community empowerment or self-government. With all the funkyass discipline of New Jack Swing, Bobby Brown puts it this way in 'On Our Own' from the sequel's soundtrack: 'Well I guess we're gonna have to take control. If it's up to us, we've got to take it home.'

The *Batman* films offer a similar mythography of the city's landscape where crime, runaway development, environmental abuse, and decaying public services are omnipresent features of the Gotham scene. (The original set design, by Anton Furst, was supposed to be a standard SF near-future, except that it was an alternate New York, developed as if there had been no zoning laws or building regulation — skyscrapers are not then cut back, they almost form a high-rise vault over the city.) The villains in these films are associated with toxic and genetic mutation, accidents involving chemical waste in the case of the Joker, and acculturation to the sewage system in the case of the Penguin, himself the mutant result of 'miscegenation' between a circus freakshow and the daughter of an old aristocratic family. Max Schreck, the capitalist slimeball whose sham populist philanthropy is in class conflict with Bruce Wayne's old blue-blood morality, is exposed as a public utilities profiteer, a slumlord owner of half the 'fire-traps' in the city, and a major industrial polluter of toxic wastes. Looking for a mayoral candidate to further his interests, he endorses the Penguin, underworld crime boss, whose campaign platform is to 'stop global warming, start global cooling now.' Catwoman, the alternative, feminist vigilante, courted as an ally by all of the above, is the only one who ends the film with respect. But by that point she is as homeless as an alleycat.

Integral to the stories told by these films about authority, law, and order in the city — Who Ya Gonna Call? — are moral landscapes dense with biohazards and environmental jeopardy. On the other side of authority lies a city teeming with biological perils. Surely no other city has had such a fantastic bestiary of historical residents — from alligators to ninja turtles — in its sewage tunnels. Linked, from the mid-nineteenth century on, to the alien presence of immigrant populations busily breeding mutant Americans, the rich zoological life of the underworld has continued to be a source of representation for threats to the urban racial order. Occasionally, the sewers give rise to vigilante heroes like the Teenage Mutant Ninja Turtles, those obnoxious, pizza-guzzling frat boys in the guise of turtles who, belatedly in common with the whole generation of postwar comic superheroes, mutated through contact with radioactive waste.

The representation of the urban vigilante, in particular, took on a special cultural significance in the 1980s, when the rule of deregulation and privatization created an ideological demand for strong, masculine revenge figures who would take on crime where government authority was seen to be impotent. In public life, this was the decade of Bernhard Goetz, the New York 'subway vigilante,' NSA operative Ollie North, Rambo, the MIA-obsessive, and the supervoluntarism encouraged by Reagan and Bush. In comic books, the superhero vigilante tradition was resurrected bigtime, most famously in Frank Miller's *The Dark Knight Returns* (1986), the first of the superhero 'adult comics,' and the prototype for Tim Burton's blockbuster film. Miller's ageing Batman was hardly the archetypal 'liberal who's been mugged,' but he was conscious of the political disrepute that had befallen the vigilante tradition, not least because the civil rights movement had exposed its full history of racist practises. In Alan Moore's *Watchmen* (1987), government reform had banned the costumed superhero vigilantes, while right-wing opinion was trying to revive them from retirement; the exception, of course, is goody two-shoes Superman, who, in Miller's novel, is working for the State Department, never tiring of defending property values and dispensing two-bit charity. In the darker world of the Batman genre, where white justice must sometimes go hooded, the streets are always awash with racially mutant criminals and always need to be cleaned up. In the postliberal Gotham of the 1980s, where all public institutions are seen to have failed, the mantle of action falls again on the revenge-oriented Batman, guided by the rationality that he learned from his parents' death: 'the world only makes sense if you force it to.' Symptomatically, the narrative of Burton's film is motivated by an opening scene in which a 'decent' white, Rockwellian family cannot hail a cab in Gotham streets. As some kind of indication of the state of urban decay, this scene all too visibly flirts with the knowledge that it is black males, no matter how bourgeois in appearance, who have trouble hailing cabs in New York City.[46]

Individualistic solutions to crime problems are the very stuff of pop culture, but these films were a source of raw ideological footage for the Reagan—Bush redefinition of control and authority over urban affairs, shifting what remained of the public focus on the War on Poverty back to wars on drugs, crime, and the welfare state. While oppositional New York films like *Do the Right Thing* and *Brother from Another Planet* and many of the films of the black renaissance of the 1990s start out by expecting nothing from the centers of public authority, films like the *Batman* and *Ghostbusters* movies assumed from the first that the problem of control and authority is paramount — Who Ya Gonna Call? (For Public Enemy, of course, the answer is '911 is a Joke'.)

Perhaps this is hardly surprising in a town with a tradition of such strong topdown rule. The paternalist, if not overtly patrician, component of this undemocratic tradition surfaces in caricature in some of the comic-book supervillains who ride roughshod over citizens' livelihood and welfare. And yet, any serious history of New York's urban development over the past century, like Robert Fitch's recent *The Assassination of New York*, demonstrates how monstrously the city has been used as a profitable resource (and permanently shaped as a result) by the designs of a relatively small number of individual financial barons, and, above all, by the Rockefeller family. The fortunes and dynastic obsessions of that family have had a staggering impact upon the physical appearance and political economy of the city in the time between their leasing the land for the Rockefeller Center from Columbia University in 1928 to their sale of the Center to Japanese investors in 1988. As Fitch puts it:

> the family's whole involvement in planning the city is the result of a series of astonishing accidents, blunders, awesome miscalculations. New York turned into a gigantic tar baby for the Rockefellers. So tightly were they bound to the terms of the Columbia ground lease and to the blighted neighborhood of west midtown, they found they could only tear themselves loose by completely reconfiguring Manhattan — and in the process, tearing apart the delicate web which joined the city's small interdependent manufacturers.[47]

The Rockefellers and their like are long accustomed to speaking in the name of their patrician 'responsibility' for the city, but that responsibility is understood to have clear limits: it rarely extends beyond the bailiwick of the real-estate economy and the investors and corporate clients to whom they are exclusively responsible. In moments of crisis, then, like the fiscal emergency of the mid-1970s, the 'function' of the city is put up for redefinition. What is the city supposed to do for its residents? What are its responsibilities, its duties, its goals? Who Ya Gonna Call? This is more or less what Manuel Castells calls 'the urban question' (in contrast to the presumptive 'urban problem'). The answer to the urban question — what is a city for? — is almost never taken to be the domain of the private sector. Despite its centrality to the process of private accumulation, the 'city' is wholly designated as the sphere of public responsibility. In fact, the corporate world has the biggest invest-ment in the urban question, and yet it structurally shields itself from answering that question. Given their druthers, the elites would rather hear us talk about urban problems.

In public language, 'urban problems' has become a codeword for race, when it does not refer to the crisis of services like housing, transportation, welfare, health care, and education. In the new austerity state, urban decay is either supposed to signify the limits of the welfare state, and the failure of public authority to pay its way, or the capacity of the poor to destroy their own neighborhoods assigned by banks and speculators to undergo the vicious cycle of devaluation and gentrification. Wherever it was not conceived as a permanent ghetto formation, this process of 'self-destruction' proved no obstacle to the forces of profit and speculation; indeed, it was the very engine of gentrification, aided and abetted by an image industry devoted to rendering urban decay fashionable. (The aestheticization of poverty is surely one of the more astonishing stories to tell about the economy of the postmodern city. Walking around a neighborhood like SoHo, the central display window for downtown redevelopment, it is still tempting to believe that the omnipresent graffiti and peeling walls were hurriedly applied for the 'inner city' location look coveted by advertising agencies and fashion photographers in the 1980s.)

With the abdication of the state's interest in creating a progressive 'open city,' New York's mythography no longer includes a set of future images which looks beyond a city in decomposition. But aside from *Escape from New York*, the original 'new dark future' film in 1980, New York has not been cinema's idea of a future city, let alone the site of a futuristic city, for many decades. *Escape from New York* established a carceral image of Manhattan which has persisted in various forms; it has passed into the political unconscious of corporate architecture's security-conscious version of fortress building, and was issued with a new wake-up call in the wake of the WTC bombing. Not infrequently these days, the imagined form of a medieval walled city swims into focus as the city planning commissions consider the numerous plans for commercial and residential developments of New York's waterfront, the location of the city's few pockets of remaining industry. (Since the entire coastline of New York City amounts to 578 relatively undeveloped miles — twice as large as the waterfronts of Baltimore, Boston, Oakland, Philadelphia, San Diego, Toronto and San Francisco *combined* — these waterfronts are already a major social and ecological battleground.)[48]

The apocalyptic picture of a 'city under siege' is now activated during each new crisis — Washington Heights, Crown Heights, the Gulf War (when urban mythology, among other things, had Abu Abbas running a terrorist cell on 14th Street), 1993's 'storm of the century,' and the Muslim fundamentalist threat in the wake of the WTC and bridge-and-tunnel bombings, with the enemy laying siege from the vantage point of Jersey City, and potential Trojan Horses in every vehicle with Jersey license plates. What Mike Davis calls the 'ecology of fear' in his recent remapping of Los Angeles has one of its most visible correlates in the concrete fortification of the island city-state of Manhattan. Indeed, as he points out, the gigantist, dystopian built environment of *Blade Runner* speaks more to the modernist vision of a 'Monster Manhattan' with its soaring gothic skyline than to the 'great unbroken plains' of LA's bungalows and ranch-style homes.[49] So, too, the alternate zones of segregated security space and community imprisonment that dot Davis's map of LA can be found more readily in the geography of Manhattan, magnified by the vertical scale of the segregating high-rise barriers, and in those parts of Queens and Brooklyn that hosted the 1980s expansion of the CBD. Buckminster Fuller's memorable geodesic dome over midtown Manhattan in 1960 was proposed as a witty hymn to technological utopianism. Today, it is a sinister message from the last days of innocence, reminding us more of a massive detention camp than of a climate-controlled environment from the world of *The Jetsons*.

A conversation I recently overheard in the swimming pool of a Waikiki hotel between two white tourists from New York City illustrates the role of humor in constructing the city. They were complaining about the omnipresence of hookers at the nearest intersection. Having paid through the nose for a vacation in paradise as part of their escape from New York, they did not relish finding what they called a 'bad neighborhood' on the doorstep of their hotel. The way they saw it, they could have that experience in New York on any day of the week. I smiled sympathetically, knowing they were only half joking, while appreciating that at least they weren't revelling in Japan-bashing, a favorite American tourist indulgence in Hawaii. For some time now, such portable jokes about the degenerating morality and crumbling infrastructure of city life have been an element of local pride for New Yorkers. Humor of this sort serves to normalize perceptions of urban deterioration while, at the same time, it reinforces the *esprit de corps* of residents required to think of themselves as survivors rather than citizens with rights to their own city. Counteracting the sentiments of those who remember an older New York of safe streets and supportive government, this kind of humor flattens out history. This is the way the city is and has always been; like it or leave it. The survivalist component of this humor has a long history in the working-class experience and memory of immigrant and minority communities. Its recent appropriation by yuppie attempts to glamorize the physical dangers of residency has resulted in the preferred cliché of New York City's boosters — despite everything, it is still the most exciting city in the world. This is a strange kind of citizen mentality, reinforcing, as it does, the fashionable simile that likens New York to a war-torn Third World city.

By far and away the favored referent for the yuppie chroniclers, however, is that of the 'urban pioneer.' Commentators like Neil Smith have analyzed the class and racial overtones of the 'frontier spirit' that accompanied gentrification in the 1980s, when young professionals moving into newly chic downtown housing stock were emulating a process rendered fashionable by SoHo artists who had seen themselves as the original 'urban pioneers,' displacing the 'urban natives.'[50] The yuppie aesthetic which includes a street-level high of 'living on the edge' also heralded the return of social Darwinism to the mainstream of urban culture. Urban space had to be fought over to be reoccupied. Blocks had to be made secure. Suburban life had dulled middle-class fantasies of city street life and the professional—managerial class was now reentering the fray.

140

What Louis Wirth, in a famous essay from the late Chicago School called 'Urbanism as a Way of Life,' once wrote about urbanites in general seemed more appropriate in the 1980s to yuppies alone: 'The close living together and working together of individuals who have no sentimental and emotional ties foster a spirit of competition, aggrandizement, and mutual exploitation.'[51] For Wirth, following the ideas of Georg Simmel, the pecuniary nexus of the city had replaced personal relations as a criterion of value with predatory relations or, more generally, relations of utility. In common with the Chicago ecologists, the yuppie version of the urban jungle included different species within the city fighting for domination within a neighborhood, or, as a 1980s yuppie bumper sticker put it, 'Whoever dies with the most toys wins.'

The Great SoHo Freakout of 1993

For a quick taste of the rhetoric of the frontier, consider some of the chapter titles of Jim Stratton's *Pioneering in the Urban Wilderness*, a 1977 book which chronicled and celebrated artist loft renovations in downtown Manhattan: 'Drawing the Wagons Into a Circle,' 'Demolition of the Habitat,' 'Unfriendly Indians,' 'Hiring a Guide,' and 'Clearing the Clearing.' Stratton's titles were an ironic foretaste of the yuppie invasion that was beginning to encroach upon the artist communities. Stratton begins his book with an ecological swipe at 300 years of wasteful housing development:

> In the beginning there were only tepees. But from the moment the earliest settlers learned they could profit by evicting the present tenants and replacing the old housing stock with log cabins, the New World was locked on a course of Out with the Old, Up with the New. It was, in fact, not until the Raze and Raise philosophy ran into economic trouble in the late 1960s that it fell out of its state of grace in America. The high cost of waste was already forcing a move toward recycling in other disciplines, but it was the shortage of money and the high cost of construction that finally urged some similar sense of conservation in the housing industry. Enter the artist.[52]

The story, so often told, of the establishment of the SoHo art community and the preservation of its factory loft buildings appeals to environmental correctness on two counts. First, they saw the loft renovation movement as an act of resistance against the gigantist plans of the urban renewers; in the case of SoHo, resistance to New York University's bulldozers to the north, and to the Lower Manhattan plan of the DLMA for a crosstown expressway through Broome Street which would seal off the corporate enclave to the south, all the way down to Battery Park. Second, they hailed structural conversion of the lofts as an exemplary act of recycling old buildings, and saving neighborhoods from abandonment and destruction. After the modernist bulldozer, the postmodern retrofit. From a sociological perspective, the organized struggle of artists for legal recognition and protection of their interests and the subsequent development of the community as an art haven was an unanticipated triumph of collective social action in the city. Not only did it appear to fly in the face of the developers' plans, it also seemed to confute the old rules of competition over land-use value that had influenced the spatial determinism of the Chicago School. Loft conversion was an example of human ecology in the city, where collective social action can outbid the market and create an alternative philosophy of residential development which is nondestructive and community-oriented.[53]

That, at least, is the exemplary narrative handed down and absorbed into the epic folklore of the district. With bourgeois values and prices prevailing everywhere today in SoHo, this narrative's heroic luster is wearing a little thin, and it is a matter of debate whether the creation of SoHo ever was a spontaneous artists' initiative, or whether its epic origins lay in some steep barometric trough of the investment climate that rendered land values so dormant that only the presence of a culture industry could stimulate renewed development.[54] The domestic cult of industrialism spawned by the renovation of old manufacturing space provided the necessary cultural veneer to glamorize these new residential milieux. Artists, as always, were the shock troops for a postindustrial sensibility that had to inhabit the actual corpse of industrial modernism in order to prove that its range of associations had been superseded by something new. (In the same way, the built body had pumped itself into fashionable prominence only when muscles were no longer the sign of manual labor.) In addition, the presence of artists generated a whole new industry in itself, what Sharon Zukin calls the 'artistic mode of production' with its own service-sector economy, and two-tier labor pools.

Today, despite the recession, and the movement of the epicenters of artistic life to European cities like Cologne and Milan, the interests of the 'art world' industry are still quite fully identified with this tightly zoned area of downtown Manhattan. Here, the interests of real estate, tourism, and the gourmet retail trade feed off the ever-bounteous platter of symbolic capital served up by Art's self-generating veneer. 'Artistic license' goes a long way in the space of a few short blocks. As a result, SoHo, like the CBDs of Wall Street and Midtown, is both of the city and not of it. Unlike the CBDs, SoHo's privileged air of exemption is seen to be earned by serving some god other than Mammon. The tax abatements and the state support extended to the community in a variety of ways clearly subsidize the 'business' of art, boosting land values in much the same way as collectors and philanthropists use the arts as a medium for speculation and tax shelters.

The story of SoHo's sense of exceptionalism, however, is not simply about the social ecology of real-estate investment. It has as much to do with the political ecology of communitarianism. In the late spring of 1993, zealous opposition on the part of residents, gallery owners, and merchants to the proposed siting of an AIDS treatment facility in SoHo caused one almighty row within the community and its environs. The fiercely divisive row lingered on, generating repercussions that go far beyond the neighborhood. Notwithstanding the city's 'fair share' policy of equitably distributing social service facilities, both 'beneficial' and 'burdensome,' SoHo hosts virtually no such sites, while its own population has one of the highest rates of HIV infection in the city. Accordingly, the local Community Board welcomed a proposal by Housing Works, an outgrowth of ACT-UP, and a nonprofit provider of services for formerly homeless with HIV/AIDS (and, frequently, with histories of chronic substance use and/or mental illness), for a day treatment center for their recently housed clients. Not even Housing Works, accustomed to fierce resistance from the conservative block associations and volunteer committees that periodically spring up to represent the 'voice of the community,' expected the resulting storm of opposition from a community with a reputation for liberally supporting social work — mostly elsewhere. The SoHo Alliance, with a long activist experience of successfully protecting the neighborhood against speculative development from outsiders — a reactive rather than a proactive history, in other words — initiated a campaign of misinformation about the proposed center, whipping up a phobic squall of hysteria among residents and businesspeople. Most of the resulting fantasies were drawn, chapter and verse, from some tabloid bible of white middle-class urban dread. One such fantasy circulating at the time conjured up the image of junkies lurching out of the facility and stabbing the babies of the neighborhood with HIV-infected needles.

Reading the letters of NIMBYist opposition sent to city and state officials (viewed and extracted here as a matter of public record) was particularly harrowing since at the time I was living on the block of the proposed Greene Street site, and since I discovered, in the process, how many of my neighbors were bigots. Read as an ethnographic archive, the letters, which mostly followed the lead of SoHo Alliance's misinformation, were nonetheless an evocative document of a community's self-image of its social environment. Most of the letters appeal in some way to the exceptionalism of SoHo, to its social 'fragility,' to its history as a pristine haven of 'decency' in an 'unliveable city'; 'a uniquely stable community,' 'a true middle class family oriented community,' 'one of the city's few neighborhood successes . . . vibrant, appealing and largely crime-free,' plagued most recently by 'aggressive beggars' and now threatened by the Housing Works facility with 'the transportation of hundreds of drug abusers and their inevitable retinue of dealers and violent types' followed by 'the muggings and the burglaries and weapons and shootings and people living in doorways . . . all the hell that comes with it.' From the evidence of the letters, most of their authors must have believed they were living in Mister Rogers' Neighborhood, and here indeed is the kind of plea Mister Rogers himself might make: 'Please don't chase us out of our neighborhood. Let us live in peace.' Others were more apocalyptic: 'It won't be long before every resident who can leave SoHo, will leave SoHo. Every gallery. Every boutique. It will be just another place to buy drugs and get high.' Brokers wrote, attesting to the 'negative fallout' on loft prices. Gallery owners wrote, worried about the impact on visiting European art collectors who are not used to 'problems relating to drugs, homelessness, and mentally ill individuals.' Aesthetes wrote, wringing their hands about the effect on 'the most noteworthy street in SoHo for cast-iron architecture' (wot! more urine-induced rust?). Law-and-order types wrote, demanding to see the criminal records of Housing Works' clients. Someone in my neighboring building wrote, inveighing against casual shoppers on the street that delimits the southern boundary of SoHo: 'Canal Street lures thousands of walking scum every day,' and suggested that the city help to 'purge' the neighborhood of their presence rather than 'import more customers' for the 'pornographers and brothels.' Family values ran high throughout, as did cheesy appeals to the vulnerability of children. Even the letters in support of the site imagined the neighborhood as a model community, exposure to whose values would surely benefit the facility's clients. Aside from the strong racist and classist undercurrents, the authors of the letters seem to feel that they were being punished in some way, not only for being 'good liberal people,' but for living in a 'good, liberal community.' As one overwrought caller to Housing Works put it: 'Why are you making me look like a bigot?' Is this the true psychology of the liberal conscience or what? Inevitably, or so it seemed, one prominent opponent proposed a therapeutic support group for liberals like himself who had contested the site.

For those seriously interested in advancing AIDS care in the neighborhood (including those SoHo residents, gallery owners, and merchants who subsequently formed the advocacy coalition SoHo for AIDS Care to contest the dominant sentiment), the relevance of this brouhaha to the art world might have been limited had the principle of artists' communitarianism not been invoked so often by the victorious opponents of the site as a rule of exclusion and discrimination. Much cited was a letter (a historical document in its own right) from gallerist Tony Shafrazi, who had profited from dealing in the work of Keith Haring, the most prominent artist to have died of AIDS and to have dealt with the disease in his art. In this letter, 'the SoHo community' was glorified in the usual fashion as a national treasure, 'contributing immeasurably to the economic, cultural and intellectual life of New York and the United States,' now threatened by the alien presence of people 'who have absolutely nothing to do with the world of art and culture . . . [and whose] presence would devastate this model community which needs to reserve its hard-won victories against crime and urban blight.'

Such a view was, of course, simply an extension of formalist theories of art and culture, theories now put into practice in the name of the 'artists' community' — a safe haven from the corrosive worldliness of the 'bad city.' But no small irony lies behind Shafrazi's and others' evocation of this idea of community. After all, the earliest artist residents in this area had started a cooperative movement (spearheaded by the Fluxus artist, George Maciunas's idea of the Fluxhouse) aimed at establishing a utopian community, self-owned and organized along anarchist principles of self-determination. This idea of community is still prized above all in that tradition of political ecology committed to the values of urbane tolerance, civility, and radical democracy. The phobic self-image released like a toxic cloud over the proposed AIDS treatment site in 1993 was so far removed from these values that one was left wondering whether there is anything in the social practice of modern communitarianism to distinguish SoHo today from Simi Valley, the suburban community that hosted the initial Rodney King trial and became a symbol of white flight and white fear in Southern California.

One of the differences between SoHo and Simi Valley is the ideology of vanguardist art that suffuses the Manhattan neighborhood with its legacy. Art did make a difference, but only in ways that sharpened the intolerance. The SoHo Alliance (and its ad hoc pressure group, the SoHo Community Coalition) which opposed the AIDS treatment site is the successor to the original cooperative South Houston Artists' Association and the SoHo Artist Tenant Association, which waged successful zoning battles with city commissions and bureaucracy, and which formed Artists Against the Expressway and other activist coalitions. Residential legalization in 1970 was achieved partly through using the argument that artists were engaged in 'light manufacturing.' It was no small irony that, over twenty years later, the city's Building Commission, under strong pressure from the SoHo Alliance, reversed an earlier oral decision and ruled that a 'manufacturing' district like SoHo required the Housing Works project to adapt to special zoning codes for health facilities, thereby rendering the Greene Street site impractical (the zoning laws are intended to protect clients' health from the noxious side-effects of manufacturing).

The other, more alarming, anachronism at work in the whole affair was that the images of HIV/AIDS most 'acceptable' to the opponents of the Greene Street site were clearly those of white gay male artists, once associated with the dominant media image of the disease, but now outnumbered by the clients of color and/or drug users that AIDS organizations like Housing Works primarily serve today. As one letter writer, among many, put it, this facility 'does not service our community; it does not service any artists with AIDS.' Some shred of humanitarianism could be salvaged from this objection: artists were at least committed to looking after their own. But the underlying fantasy of this and similar comments was about drawing the wagons into a circle, and in this respect it drew upon the formalist notion of art as a principle of order in a contagiously disordered world. If only the disease had been confined to artists, if only it were an artist's disease, then art could have contained the disease, just as art, in its modernist version, contains the world through its formal ordering and by keeping its contagious element at bay.

In retrospect, this modernist ideology of art had played no small part in the whole idea of an artists' community in SoHo. The rhetoric of immunity and contagion that was central to modernist purity surfaced with a vengeance within a community, well served by its history of self-protection and preservation (with the help of the Friends of Cast Iron) to discriminate and exclude the wrong kind of outsider. The result was a kind of communitarianism that gives citizenship a bad name. As a case study, it proves how powerful and conservative the consciousness of preservation can be in shaping the social ecology of urban life. In the case of SoHo, a specific (modernist) ideology of art — the worship of pure, quarantine space — contributed in no small measure. A disease — HIV/AIDS — and a social condition — poverty/homelessness — fed the phobias that often give a biological gloss to discourses about the built environment. The actual presence of a disease (not a heroic artist's disease but the poverty-struck disease of the Other) reinforced the pathology of exclusion, and magnified the publicly aired fantasies about the 'the decline and ruination of SoHo' into something approaching the Fall of Byzantium.

Urban Jihad

Whether it was the result of a heroic struggle on the part of artists, or yet another functional example of urban 'invasion-succession,'[55] or the solution to a temporary lull in some investment cycle, the SoHo building conversion/recycling movement and its allied 'art effect' proved to be one of the catalysts for the reentry and residential occupation of downtown Manhattan by high-salaried professionals employed in the new global finance economy. Plans for the reorganization of downtown had appealed to the latest booster vision of New York as a global city, indeed *the* global city. Despite, or because of, the internationalization of the economy and the dispersal of production from core sites, there had emerged a need for global cities to be seen, in Saskia Sassen's words, as 'highly concentrated command points.' Contrary to forecasts, early and late, that the postindustrial information society would decentralize business practises, Sassen argues that the need for a whole range of technical support — maintenance, reprogramming, repair, and backup — services have tended to concentrate, in key centralized locations, the corporate use of those advanced communication technologies that have enabled the spatial dispersal of flexible, specialized production.[56] The management of the new finance economy requires a large network of ancillary services — accounting, financial analysis, management consulting, international legal advice, business law, advertising — in addition to low-wage administrative and word processing services. This ancillary network also supports financial subcontractors, commercial houses, investment banking and markets that are subsidiary to the large international operations but use their global capability. According to Sassen, global cities like New York, London, and Tokyo have become advanced production sites of financial 'products' in their own right. The result, unforeseen by postindustrial boosters like Daniel Bell, is a dense agglomeration in the old city centers of face-to-face business activity that often depends on access to insider information. More predictable has been the rapid decline of union shops and the proliferation of an informal sweatshop economy, employing immigrant or part-time female labor in the food, garment, retail, and textile sectors, where zoning rules, tax and insurance regulations, safety standards, child labor, and minimum wage laws are all routinely violated. The more enlightened, socially just information order once imagined by Daniel Bell and others may exist to some degree in the professional—managerial enclaves, but it is structurally dependent today on the primitive labor regimes of minimally educated immigrant minorities in the dense metropolitan centers.

It is a matter of debate whether the image of New York as a global city has been borne out. Even those companies that stand to benefit most from the condition of the global city have been leaving town steadily over the last decade and a half. The devastating aftermath of the 1987 crash has left a tell-tale story, on the ground, of the overbuilt, overinflated, and overextended infrastructure constructed around the heady discourses of the global information society. At this point in time, it is unclear whether much of the 25 million square feet of additional office space built in the 1980s, and now lying empty, will ever be used, at least as offices. The more permanent outcome of the 1980s economy is the number of new immigrants who now populate the city's outer boroughs. Beginning in the late 1970s, huge amounts of foreign investment poured into the USA, partly to debt-finance Reagan's military buildup, partly to secure access to a large, unified consumer market, unprotected by national trade policies. The USA became the world's largest debtor nation, its regional economies unable any longer to respond to the lead of US capital and the US state. Correspondingly, the new global economy's international division of labor generated vast migration streams, many of whom came to New York City from Asia, the Caribbean, the Middle East, and Latin America to work in the informal and the service-sector economy. Combining the labor streams with refugees from wars and disasters, the World Bank estimated that the South—North flow across national borders in 1992 amounted to 100 million people.[57]

The city of global finance had become home to the cultures of the globe in ways that were quite different from patterns of immigration and acculturation in the earlier monopoly capitalist era of the Golden Door. While the rate of immigration came nowhere near to the figures achieved at the turn of the century, the new immigration produced multicultural communities which, unlike the previous wave of mostly European immigrants, had no common Western traditions. What ramifications did these developments have for the political and cultural coherence of the US state? No event could have provided more of a public focus for this question than the bombing of the World Trade Center, the subsequent bomb plot, and the conspiracy trials of the suspected ring of bombers. The nets of intrigue and conspiracy publicly projected onto these suspects multiplied and mutated like a nuclear chain reaction in the months following the WTC bombing and the later suspected plot to blow up the UN, the Federal Building, and the Port Authority's Hudson River tunnels. When the long list of likely sponsoring 'terrorist states' and 'organizations' had run its course in the media — Iran, Iraq, Syria, Libya, Sudan, Pakistan, Nicaragua, the Serbs, the

Croats, Hezbollah, Hamas, the Colombian drug cartels (the late Pablo Escobar wrote to the US Ambassador, 'They can take me off the list, because if I had done it, I would be saying why and I would be saying what I want'), the Senderoso Luminoso, the IRA — one thing was clear. The suspects were very much in residence, which is to say that, far from being 'hitmen' dispatched from overseas, they had roots and family in the new immigrant communities ringing the metropolitan area. Many of the suspects were also products of the aftermath of the Cold War, recruited and trained under US auspices for the largest covert war of the Reagan years — the Afghan *jihad* that was the ideological equivalent of the Spanish Civil War for many of the international volunteers who flocked to Peshawar for the cause in the 1980s. American Muslim radicals who had gone to fight with the Afghan *mujahideen*, with the aid of billions of dollars in CIA money and weapons, were now bringing the *jihad* home. Nothing, not even evidence of a monstrous international terrorist network, could have presented more of a nightmare, or a godsend, to the national security bloodhounds. Like the domestic omnipresence of 'red spies' at the height of Cold War paranoia — they could be your neighbors — the new terrorist was no longer recognizably alien, at least not for those accustomed, in their communities, to the presence of Muslims, members of the fastest growing religion in the USA.

Before discussing the political ecology of the trials themselves, it is worth dispelling some of the amnesia surrounding the history of domestic bombings in New York. Indeed, this was not the first time that the WTC had been bombed. During construction in 1970, a propane blast, heralded by a prior bomb warning, injured six workers on March 16. Nine weeks later, a bomb destroyed the on-site offices of the general contractor. The first blast came ten days after the famous Greenwich Village townhouse explosion, which had killed fugitive members of SDS's Weathermen faction, engaged in a bombmaking party that went wrong. Four days later, bombs exploded in the midtown office buildings of Socony Mobile, IBM, and GTE. Scores of anonymous bomb threats followed: 590 over a 36-hour period. Threats and evacuations became routine in the city's business sectors. Mayor Lindsay appealed for civil calm. The City Council President warned of an informal coalition of armed terrorist cells operating under the Maoist principles of urban guerrilla warfare; the Young Lords, the Black Panthers, and the

Weathermen being most prominent. Governor Rockefeller demanded a review of the state's dynamite laws. Explosions daily rocked almost every city in the country. Other public experts tried to link the nationwide bombings to a high-level 'war council' at the Weathermen convention in Flint, Michigan, some months before. Meanwhile, Rap Brown, on trial in Cambridge, Maryland, was being pursued by right-wing bombers, one of whom assassinated his SNCC colleague Ralph Featherston. Also bombed was the Manhattan home of State Supreme Court Justice John Murtaugh, presiding over the pretrial of thirteen Panthers accused of conspiracy to bomb public places. Not long before, an East Village 'ring' was arrested after a bombing spree that included targets such as RCA, GM, Chase Manhattan, Marine Midland, Grace Trust, United Fruit Company, Criminal Court Building, and the Armed Forces Induction Center.

Compared to the two-year bombing season of 1969—70, the bomb hysteria that prevailed in the aftermath of the WTC blast was like a holiday firecracker. But consider the difference in the political ramifications of the two moments. After the midtown corporate bombings of March 1970, UPI received a letter claiming responsibility by the Revolutionary Force 9, and designating the targeted corporations as 'enemies of all life' for their profiteering from Department of Defense contracts, not only in Vietnam

> but also from American imperialism in all of the Third World. They profit from racist oppression of black, Puerto Rican and other minority colonies outside Amerika, from the suffering and death of men in the Amerika army, from sexism, from the exploitation and degradation of employees forced into lives of anti-human work, from the pollution and destruction of our environment.

The letter's critique of the 'industries of death' continued, with attacks on the American way of life that 'sucks up 60% of the world's resources — for 16% of the planet's population [sic] — and then wastes them in compulsive consumerism and planned obsolescence,' and ends with a plea for the justice that comes with revolutionary action. This was an exemplary late New Left appeal, at the height of its Third Worldist rhetoric. Compare it with the letter received in the wake of the WTC bombing from a group calling itself the Liberation Army Fifth Battalion. The letter lambasted US policies in the Middle East and appealed to public guilt:

> The American people must know that their civilians who got killed are not better than those who are getting killed by the American weapons and support . . . The American people are responsible for the actions of their government and they must question all of the crimes that their government is committing against other people.

The first letter is aimed at specific corporate targets, and at the collusion of business and political elites. It takes issue with official policies from a domestic or internal standpoint. The second letter is more indiscriminately addressed to the American people as a whole, and its criticism of the American way of life is clearly posed from an external position. Media commentary on the New Left bombings reflected the sense of a family quarrel; generational differences about US policy were being expressed by the sons and daughters of America's white elite, and this view extended as far as white radical chic could be stretched in espousing minority causes like the Panthers and the Young Lords. By contrast, media commentary on the 'Islamic' bombings initially treated the affair as a foreign threat, for the most part, with coverage of Islamic affairs making the usual distinction drawn between the traditional kinds of Islamic states — friends of the West, basically, like Saudi Arabia — and the new, radical Islamic states like Iran by whom the USA is still demonized as the Great Satan. In addition, distinctions were drawn between the older generation of fundamentalists from the Muslim Brotherhood (founded in Egypt in 1928 by Hassan al-Banna), and the younger, more 'impatient' extremists, among whom is counted Sheik Abdel Rahman, Jersey City's exiled leader of Egypt's Islamic Group (Gama'a al-Islamiya), and Gulbuddin Hekmatyar, the leader of Hezb-i-Islami in Afghanistan, along with the Sudanese Hassan al-Turabi, the Tunisian exile Rashid Ghanoushi, and the Algerian head of the Islamic Salvation Front, Abassi Madani. This media coverage had little to do with the actual Islamic world — a billion diverse people living in diverse kinds of societies, from theocratic kingdoms to secular democracies. Rather than informing Westerners about the complex struggles (between secular and religious movements) within the Islamic world itself, it was purely a reflection of Western interests in defining that world. This tendency did not go unnoticed in the public media, and was vigorously resisted by defense lawyers involved in the trials. To cite only one example, William Kunstler, as active in the defense of the suspects as he was at the time of the 1970 bombings in the trials of the Chicago Seven, Rap Brown, and others, protested at the principle of guilt by association applied to suspects who happened to attend the same Jersey City mosque: this scurrilous logic, he said, was 'like trying to connect two people because they both went to St. Patrick's Cathedral.'[58]

In August, the government finally indicted Sheik Abdel Rahman and fifteen others under a seditious conspiracy act with a broad latitude to link together a series of events from the assassination of Meir Kahane in 1989 to the 1993 plots. Under this rarely used law, the suspects were charged with 'conspiring to overthrow, put down, or destroy by force the Government' by 'levying a war of urban terrorism against the United States.' Since the law measured guilt simply by the evidence of plotting rather than by any attempt to carry out an insurrection, it was judged by many to come close to threatening freedom of speech and belief. Ronald Kuby, Kunstler's associate, argued that the government had created a 'vast mythical Islamic conspiracy' in order to cover up its own bungling, or its active instigation, of the WTC bombing itself through the activities of inside informant Emad Salem. Journalists like Robert Friedman asked more pointed questions about the extensive cover-up of the roles played in the whole history of events from Afghanistan to the bombings by 'bungling FBI agents, Mossad moles, and CIA officials as zealous as the sheik's holy warriors.'[59]

Despite the possibility of disclosures embarrassing to the state's security agencies (none of which surfaced during the WTC trial), the pre-judicial publicity generated by the press and the state in the months leading up to the trials not only succeeded in fixing a high ratio of guilt upon the suspects but also created a national climate of suspicion regarding all Middle Eastern immigrants, especially Muslims from Arab countries. Armed terrorist cells were plotting away again in the heartlands! Anti-immigrant sentiment rose precipitously in the months following the trial; resident aliens were encouraged by the White House to seek citizenship to ease hostilities.

Pat philosophizing about the post-Cold War order placed the WTC incident in the context of pat theories about the resurgence of premodern conflicts, often in the most bizarre ways. Novelist Robert Stone's *New York Times* op-ed article, published five days after the bombing and entitled 'New Barbarians,' was an embarrassingly typical example:

> [A]s America's influence contracts, the world returns to old romances. In Europe, blood and soil are back. In what is sometimes still called the third world, religion flourishes. In our radical interpretation of democracy, our rejection of elites, our well-nigh demagogic respect for the opinions of the unlearned, we are alone . . . Entire populations are on the move. The migration of the world's poor has been compared to the barbarian migrations of the fifth century A.D. Borders are porous; in jet planes and on rafts, desperate people cross oceans. Literally and figuratively, our cities have no walls. We have lived for a long time like ancient Rome, relying on far-flung power for defense. To a degree we have claimed exemption from the forces of history. Now, late in 'our' century, history is presenting old, half-forgotten bills.[60]

In truth, it is Stone's own prose here that claims exemption from the forces of history, spinning analogies on the world like some deranged Rumpelstiltskin from a faery turret's windows. Anticipating the sack of New York, Stone imagines the new barbarians' revenge on America as 'the home of the unadorned Economic Man,' which he finds personified in the rational reductionism of the Twin Towers architecture. Economic man is nothing if not adorned in the global city that drew the new migration streams into its labor pool. As for the barbarians, you can almost sense, in Stone's Roman analogy, the ideological relief at the revival of the old apparition of 'orientalism.' After a century of crude attempts to scare up the socialist specter of collective man, the West here returns to its more dependable, and racially evocative, non-Western enemy. Suddenly, 'ancient' conflicts are considered more legitimate and therefore more dangerous than modern, capitalist ones. This scenario was repeated by many a policy hack in the early 1990s, following the lead of academics like Samuel Huntington who pontificated about the essential clash between the civilizations of Islam and the West.

Stone's article lent its voice to the tide of commentary defining the shape of a post-Cold War order in which 'Muslim fundamentalists' are increasingly depicted as the world's Number One enemy of democratic life. It hardly goes without saying that two years before, in the Persian Gulf, the Western allies fought a war to liberate a Muslim nation that is more 'fundamentalist' than virtually any other, and yet the term 'Muslim fundamentalist' has come to enjoy a diabolic life in public consciousness as a byword for all things deemed alien to decency and reason. In the flak surrounding the WTC trials, the relationship of Sheik Abdel Rahman's circle to the activities of US-sponsored fundamentalists like Gulbuddin Hekmat-yar and Abdur Rafool Sayyaf in Afghanistan was widely noted, further complicating the equation of the 'Muslim fundamentalist' with the State Department's own selective definition of 'terrorist.' In general, however, this relationship was suppressed, and given a wide berth by commentators analyzing the trials. Clearly, 'Muslim fundamentalists' had been serviceable to US interests abroad as subversives at large, most notably as a thorn in the flesh of secular Arab nationalists, even, and especially, when they vigorously mouthed anti-Americanism, as Hekmatyar and his fanatical CIA-bankrolled followers had done all through the 1980s. The World Trade Center trials marked the first phase of the domestic version of this new Orientalist narrative. Despite all the public attempts to dissociate the alleged activities of the suspects from the life of the majority of American Muslims and from Arab-Americans, secular and Christian as well as Muslim, many used the WTC and conspiracy trials to reinforce the image of this emergent post-Soviet threat as the new 'enemy within.'

Forty years before, Ethel and Julius Rosenberg, Communist 'enemies within,' were put to death after a trial that served to define the present and future state of the Cold War. Leaving aside the issue of the Rosenbergs' alleged involvement in espionage, few would deny that the Rosenberg trial was used, expediently, to justify the establishment of a national security state that, to this day, has denied its citizenry access to information not only about public affairs but also about the surveillance of their private activities. The Rosenberg trial was not, of course, simply a political trial, required in order to demonize the designs of the Soviet Union and to crack down on the domestic left. It was also a case allegedly involving technology transfer, the very essence of industrial espionage, and the engine of economic warfare. The primary effect of the trial may have been more economic than political. In many ways, the anxieties it generated about atomic warfare served as the *raison d'être* for the permanent arms economy which has underpinned US policy, both foreign and domestic, ever since. (President Clinton's first projected military budget was higher in constant dollars than average spending during the Cold War, confirming that the defense industry is still the most efficient way of providing a 100 per cent public subsidy for researching and developing new technologies for American corporations.) Just as important, however, the Rosenberg trial was arguably the first public postwar event to trouble popular faith in the fledgling national security apparatus. Today, it is second nature among most Americans to distrust the intelligence activities of institutions like the FBI, the CIA, and the NSA. Elites from the White House down undoubtedly selected the Rosenbergs to serve as punitive examples, but the trial ultimately came to function as a publicly tolerated 'limit' to the state's repressive activities, a limit set largely as a result of the continuing attachment of the American left to the Rosenberg case. Today, as the extent of the AEC and DOD's insolent atomic experimentation with US and Pacific Islander subjects is being officially disclosed, the treatment of the Rosenbergs will increasingly be seen on a continuum with such activities, as one more act of state terrorism upon its own citizens in the Atomic Age.

What will continue to make the trial exceptional, however, is the role it played in the history of the American left. Today, it poses some difficult questions indeed. At the time, anti-Communist liberals referred to the trial as the end of an age of innocence (code for Stalinism) for the left. Forty years after, we might be tempted to think of the 'innocence' of the Rosenberg moment in much larger historical terms, not restricted to leftist circles alone. To begin with, the broad left rallied in support of the Rosenbergs in ways it could not and would not during the World Trade Center affair. Some might have sympathized with the anti-imperialist rhetoric imputed to the 'Liberation Army Fifth Battalion,' but the ultimately religious basis of such appeals made little headway with those committed to Third Worldist struggles for modern, secular states, threatened daily by fundamentalist movements all over the world. There was no end of ambivalence among those who suspected a frame-up and were prepared to put the FBI under immediate suspicion, and who, at the same time, thoroughly abhorred the letter and spirit of fundamentalist practices. This ambivalence has a deeper historical dimension, however.

At the dawn of the Cold War, the dominant contest in political ideology was over the soul and shape of modernity itself — what was it going to look like? Fritz Lang's Metropolis? Auschwitz? Levittown? Disneyland? a kibbutz? or a communist youth summer camp in the Catskills? Today, we cannot take modernity for granted in quite the same way. The rise of Muslim fundamentalism is taken to be a symptom of the resurgence of ethnic particularism, tribalistic nationalism, and religious chauvinism in a world that was supposed to have been claimed in advance by secular modernity. Because they all took modernity itself for granted, none of modernity's ideologies — neither liberalism, nor Marxism, nor propertarianism, nor free-market libertarianism — foresaw a future in which religio-moral conviction would be playing such a major role in our political culture, locally and globally. The future was not supposed to play host to such 'regressive' tendencies. Modernity was supposed to have subsumed cultural and religious differences in the name of the universality of rights and the righteousness of reason. By 1993, it was assumed, Satan would surely have been consigned to the flames of history, and yet right now his is the name on many tongues, Muslim and Christian, in the USA and abroad.

Again, forty years ago, the social milieu of the Rosenberg trial was marked by demands made upon first- and second-generation immigrants — assimilation, patriotism, consumerism. The Rosen-bergs themselves had lived among Popular Front Communists who claimed direct descent from Jefferson and Lincoln, and whose strategic patriotism was trumpeted by their friends and supporters as loudly as it was called into doubt by the government's case against them. By contrast, the backdrop to the WTC trial was the mode of material existence among the new postcolonial migrant communi-ties, for whom the melting pot had long been rejected as an ideology of the past. Indeed, it is on the basis of their experience and history that cultural *difference* has been proposed, if far from accepted, as an integral part of a new kind of democratic state. Tolerance of cultural differences within such communities is the challenge for liberal pluralism today, not the old demand for cultural assimilation. As always, the challenges for radicals are based on enfranchisement and empowerment, and are rooted in a full understanding of institutio-nal racism as a complex, and evolved set of beliefs and practices. Forty years ago, the assimilationist North American state used the Rosenberg trial to define its boundaries. From a less paranoid view, that trial marked one of the limits to state power — in other words, it wouldn't happen again, at least not in quite the same way. Official suspicion of Jewish 'fifth-columnist' loyalties (like those imputed to the Rosenbergs) has abated somewhat as the likely recipient of these loyalties shifted over the years from the international socialist cause to the US-friendly state of Israel. As Jewish-American identity has become less alien, largely because of international political interests, the case of the Muslim-American has become more visible, and more complex. If only because of Western interests in the Islamic world, there has been considerable pressure to avoid another kind of cultural Cold War in which Westerners nurse their images of some stereotypical Muslim enemy, as hot-tempered and fanatical as the Soviet version was cold-blooded and self-denying. There is little evidence that American citizens learned anything lasting about Islam or the Arab peoples from the extensive media commentary during the Gulf War, and, given the grisly fate of the Bosnian Muslims, there appears to be little political will in Washington to address the human rights of an oil-less people of Islam. The trials of the alleged bombers and conspirators were set up not only as tests of legal justice; they were also bound to turn into tests of cultural justice.

The real resident alien in the trials, however, was the World Trade Center itself. Its construction had been central to attempts to transform the infrastructure of the global economy, but the story of that construction involved a good deal of violence within the city that would not ordinarily be termed 'urban terrorism.' The WTC stands on ground with a rich history, next to what used to be one of the world's great ports. The economy it came to symbolize has drawn in a labor pool from all over the world, to work at wages much lower than the skilled blue-collar workers that had been displaced during thirty years of the Clearances into the harsh geography of unemployment. Today, it is surrounded by acres of vacant office space, occupying floor after floor of near empty buildings. The area does not look like a bombed-out neighborhood but that is what it is. As for the answer to the question, 'Who bombed the Big Apple?,' it lay, as I have tried to suggest, as much with the history of the WTC's planners as it did with the trial of the building's alleged bombers.

3

The Ecology of Images

The bombing of the World Trade Center was on a continuum with the bombs that heralded the New World Order in Baghdad two years before. In many ways, they belonged to the same narrative about the shape of politics after the Cold War. And yet these respective acts of violence are officially separated by the different classes of meaning attached to 'terrorism' and to 'war.' This separation has long been challenged as an example of political expediency in recognizing friends and vilifying enemies. Among other things, this chapter considers something different — ecological grounds for challenging the separation.

The Gnat's Eyelash

Many commentators on the Gulf War of 1991 have argued, in retrospect, that it was a new kind of war. For some, it was the first postmodern 'hyperwar' (the Pentagon's own term) strategically engaged as much in the electromagnetic environment of video, radar and computer screens as on the geophysical terrain of Kuwait and Iraq. The levels of automation involved in the Allied coordination of satellite surveillance, war gaming, telepilotry, remote digital guidance, and massive near-instant destruction of the enemy completely tipped the balance between the war of representations and the reality of war as a brutal physical encounter.[1] Others argued, from a moral rather than a technological point of view, that the Gulf War was not a war at all, but a slaughter, in which the noncombat aerial bombardment and the turkey-shoot kill ratio of almost a quarter of a million Iraqis to a few hundred Allied casualties (many as a result of friendly fire) made a nonsense out of any rules of military engagement that had historically applied to warfare in the past.[2] Still others suggested that the Gulf War was less of a military engagement than it was a test of opinion management conducted by the corporate state upon the vast media population addressed by television during the crisis. The defeat of Iraq was nothing compared to the feat of public consensus-making attempted with government (dis)information fed through commercial media channels.[3]

While I would not dispute any of these arguments, my additional claim here for the originality of the Gulf War is that it was the first *explicitly* ecological war in modern history. In this war, ecological concerns were a preeminent feature from first to last, from the OPEC oil-pricing imbroglio that impelled Saddam Hussein to invade Kuwait, to the use of the environment as a weapon by both sides, to the monumental ecological consequences, for refugee populations and for the physical environment, of the destructive forces unleashed during the forty-three days of combat. For the first time, informed international opinion about these environmental disasters dwarfed and outlasted the sentiments aroused by the political and economic ramifications of the war. Not surprisingly, this focus helped to shape the sizeable antiwar movement that sprang up to protest the war, from high-school walkouts to mass demonstrations all across the world. Within two weeks of the onset of the Allied blitzkrieg, a massive protest march in Washington DC was led, appropriately, to Capitol Hill by a Greenpeace world balloon hoisted on high.

If nothing else, the leading role of Greenpeace was an acknowledgment that a new ecological dimension had been conclusively added to the struggle against militarism. The Old Left had mustered primarily economic arguments against wars in the earlier part of the century — wars were fought for profitable control over colonies or to enrich munitions industries. This analysis extended into the peacetime of the Cold War when a permanent war economy served to stabilize and regulate the recurrent crisis tendencies of overproduction and underconsumption in the world capitalist system. In the movement against the war in Southeast Asia, the New Left brought a social and cultural critique — sweetly encapsulated in the slogan 'Make love not war' — to bear upon the institutions of militarism that had reached deep into the behavioral structure of society. Appealing to the *alternative* ideas and values of the counterculture and the antinuclear peace movement, this critique found its dominant media profile captured in the image of a student placing a flower in the barrel of a National Guardsman's rifle during a Washington mobilization. In the volume of ecological analysis generated before, during and after its official life as a 'limited' engagement, the Gulf War contributed a new *scientific* dimension to the economic, social, and cultural analyses of the peace movements.

It is probably fair to speculate that sectors of the public learned more about the environmental effects of modern warfare than they did about the recent history of the Middle East, or 'the world of Islam,' or about the political bases of the New World Order.[4] This is ironic, given that the predominant use of science in the war itself was for destructive purposes. As a Greenpeace report on the war put it: 'It is an eerie statement to say that scientific advances provided more accurate information on how many smart bombs were needed to destroy a bridge in Baghdad, than on how many human casualties there would be.'[5] The public debate about environmental degradation countered a virtual blackout of information on the subject mandated by a White House gag order that applied during the war to the Interagency Task Force of US scientists from the Centers for Disease Control, the Environmental Protection Agency, and other federal organizations. The Department of Energy forbade its scientists to discuss their research with the press, and, in the months following the war, the National Oceanic and Atmospheric Administration, constantly monitoring the region through its satellites, consistently downplayed the height of the smoke plumes and the extent of airborne pollution generated by the Kuwaiti oil-well fires. The US authorities who suppressed this information were nonetheless in full possession, from the Fall of 1990, of the results of studies (commissioned from the Sandia National Laboratory in Albuquerque among others) of the potential scale of ecological damage, from the torching of Kuwait's oil wells to the massive movement of refugees. The Department of Defense's veil of secrecy about biological and industrial warfare was only briefly pierced in November 1993 when the cumulative evidence of tens of thousands of Gulf veterans suffering from 'Gulf War syndrome' prompted the first sign of official attention to the effects of the war's biohazards and industrial pollutants upon its combatants.

Given the tight lid of secrecy around this kind of information, it is surely a testament to the communicability of the ecological crisis in the Gulf that it impinged on public consciousness to such a degree. Awareness of this public concern may have affected the subsequent UN decisions to intervene, in the name of humanitarianism, in Somalia and on behalf of the Kurds in Northern Iraq, but not in areas like Bosnia-Herzegovina or Haiti. While the Gulf War may not have generated the fully disastrous effects forecast by the most apocalyptic scientific assessments, both sides dramatically violated every international 'law' or protocol, discussed at Geneva or the Hague, pertaining to environmental warfare. In the absence of TV footage of human casualties, rigorously censored by the state and the military, our screens were awash with images of environmental atrocities. In the alternative media, which performed admirably from first to last, ecological analysis provided front-page copy and front-line ammunition for opposition to the war.

At the same time as it raised concerns about militarism's threat to physical environments, the intense spectacularization of the Gulf War through TV fuelled a growing debate about the current shape and future of media ecology. As we are repeatedly told by industry boosters, we are about to enter an age of superinformation, with 500 TV channels dancing on the horizon, and a vast array of new communication networks linking up by the day. What seemed like the massive coordination of disparate media channels to sell the Gulf War to the public surprised even the most hardened critics of the corporate state's media monopolies, who were more than a little taken aback when the evidence for their longheld conspiracy theories so visibly surfaced on the screen, day after day! General Norman Schwarzkopf had boasted of his strategists' planning: 'We had a completely robust strategic air campaign that was very executable right down to a gnat's eyelash.' For the spectators of the Gulf War's blood sports, he could just as easily have been describing a political ad campaign, or a football game plan. Indeed, the general's wartime statements drew directly upon the hardball media vernacular characteristic of campaign managers and football coaches alike. Employing the precision metaphor of the 'gnat's eyelash' prized by technically minded tacticians, Schwarzkopf offered a folksy version of the kind of macho linguistics that diminishes the enemy (in this case to the size of a gnat on a lion's back). But the gnat was also the press (with no teeth), the diminutive force of its eyelash being an estimation of how little independent power was allocated to the media in the Schwarzkopf game plan for a war that was itself all but over in the blink of a gnat's eye.

The Target-Rich Environment

At least two urgent needs emerged from the war in the Gulf. First of all, the US Congress needs to sit down and draft a constitutional amendment to ensure the separation of press and state. That would probably require a much better Congress than any money can buy, but it might help to protect against the collapse, all too clear from the first hour of Gulf War combat, of the distance conventionally observed between the corporate media and the corporate state, respectively engaged in the ratings war over images and the strategic war over oil resources. John Holliman, one of two CNN reporters in the Baghdad Hilton during the initial aerial bombardment, set the tone for the TV war spectacle to follow when he referred admiringly to the 'beautiful red and orange bombs' and 'beautiful tracer fire' in the night sky. The technically sweet aesthetics of the TV war, which many people compared to a Nintendo game, was the culmination of what other critics have increasingly come to call the military-industrial-media complex, concentrated in the hands of fewer and fewer conglomerate owners, with vested interests in each sector of production. Consequently, the TV ratings war became an integral part of many viewers' experience of the minute-by-minute progress of military operations in the Gulf. Everyone became an instant media critic. Many even became Baudrillardians without knowing it, repelled by everyone else's (and never their own) fascination with the simulacra of war cooked up by the Pentagon and the networks (a simulated aerial view of Baghdad from an F-111 pilot's perspective — who would *not* want to see that?). Baudrillard himself, ever the unhappy lover of simulacra, wrote a rather facile book entitled *The Gulf War Didn't Happen*. Members of the Center for Defense Information, a group of disaffected Pentagon ex-employees, quickly confirmed what many of us suspected: that, in view of a job well done by the TV networks, the Pentagon decided not to release their own independent footage and propaganda in the USA. To top it all, antiwar protesters (including myself) marched this time, not to the Pentagon, but to the TV network buildings in midtown Manhattan. This made sense — the protest was intended to prick the professional conscience of the news fraternity — but it also pointed to a failure of systemic analysis. Denied access to the corporate workings of military industrialism, activists feel that they still have at least one foot in the door of media making, but the 'linkage' suggested by the phrase 'military-industrial-media complex' was often forgotten in the rush to paint media professionals as craven or war-mongering.

When all is said and done, media professionals, like any other professional cohort, act to advance their own interests, and hence will boost the power of the media whenever possible. The Gulf War was an opportunity for the major networks to train the spotlight upon themselves. It was a moment when reporters like Christiane Amanpour, Arthur Kent, Wolf Blitzer, Bob Simon, Peter Arnett, and others achieved no small measure of fame for their services. It was also a moment when CNN finally came to maturity as a global network, expunging the word 'foreign' from all broadcasts: at one point, Saddam Hussein reported that 'we are getting our news from CNN just like everyone else.' At the same time, a vast majority of journalists were individually outraged by the controlled access and censorship mechanisms imposed upon them by the Pentagon's reporter pool system, but no major US media organization was involved in any of the three lawsuits that unsuccessfully challenged press restrictions.[6] The Pentagon gamble, however, was that the controlled war spectacle would be enough of a boost to the cause of TV — the golden apple being the live war broadcast — for criticism from the ranks of the press to be isolated, and mostly symbolic. For the most part, the gamble paid off. While the TV anchors were drawing the heat from antiwar protesters, the defense contractors and the generals were laughing all the way to the bank.

Not that criticism of the media's role in the war was not justified, especially when it was directed at the TV war's exploitation of popular xenophobia. But we cannot forget that the nightly firework display in the Gulf skies and the spectacle of laser-guided glider bombs and Tomahawk missiles piloted by Digital Scene Matching Area Correlation technologies were also an explicitly seductive advertisement for the power of the media commodity itself. Aside from the fact that TV networks like NBC are owned by parent companies that are major defense contractors in their own right, what is the relationship between this economy of the media spectacle and the economy of war and oil consumption that provided the political context for the war? In a war openly fought for control over dwindling oil resources (the model, now, for the twenty-first-century eco-wars for which dystopian science fiction has so long prepared us), the Gulf footage also served to advertise another helping of high militarist economics, sustained by the uninterrupted flow of cheap fossil fuels. Donella Meadows, co-author of the seminal 1974 study *Limits to Growth*, pointed out in a Dartmouth College teach-in that there is only one activity in our society for which alternative energy could not provide a substitute for oil — war itself, especially war on the scale of rapid mobilization demanded by the Gulf War. The war, then, was fought, as Grace Paley commented, to ensure the future of war.[7] Is this the future, also, of green militarism? In *Fires of Kuwait*, an IMAX film about the effort to extinguish the oil-well fires, a Hungarian firefighting team retrofits a Soviet tank by mounting it with jet engines from a MIG fighter, engineered to blast out water with high velocity. It may have been a counterspectacle to the damage caused by bombing during the war, but it was also an ironic twist on the practise of turning swords into ploughshares.

Just as the media industry acts in its own interest, so, too, we were confronted with the evidence in the Gulf of the war industry acting in its own interest. The Gulf War proved that these two sets of industrial interests are intimately related. Perhaps the most telling Pentagon images in this respect were those shot on January 26 by a camera mounted on a GBU-15 glide bomb en route to destroying the Sea Island terminal's pumping mechanism for the Mina al-Ahmadi oil-tank farm, which controlled the flow of hundreds of millions of gallons of Kuwaiti oil spilling into the Gulf waters. Schwarzkopf claimed, quite erroneously, that the attack reduced the flow to a 'trickle.' In fact, the flow continued almost unabated until the middle of March, totalling up to six million barrels of crude.[8]

What was crucial about the Pentagon footage was the visual perspective of the US Navy as 'Captain Planet,' waging war against Saddam's 'environmental terrorism' in what must surely also rank as the first photo opportunity for politically correct militarism. The prelude to this bizarre footage was best summed up in the previous day's three-inch-high headlines in the scab edition of the New York's strike-bound *Daily News*: SADDAM ATTACKS EARTH! — a headline worth an appearance in any bad SF movie.

The oil spill itself became one of the chief stories of the war. Fed from various tributaries, including the initial refinery fires reported at the al-Khafji oil storage facility, and the repeated US bombing of oil tankers, final estimates of the spill put it as high as 11 million barrels. Exact information was scarce, however, primarily because of the military ban on publicizing LandSat images, which, among other things, would have revealed the widespread airborne pollution generated by Allied bombing of refineries, tankers, and other oil facilities in the period before Iraq blew up the Kuwaiti oil wells. Consequently, media treatment of the spill was quite fantasmatic, varying dramatically in the assessments of its size and of the flushout cycle of the Persian Gulf (anything from two to two hundred years). In the absence of any footage of enemy casualties themselves, the slowly spreading oil slick in the Gulf waters quickly came to embody, for Western audiences, many of the diabolic features attached to the pseudo-biological 'Arab threat.' The meaning of the slick no longer lay simply within the traditional iconography of corporate oil-spill images, incomplete without stock footage of an oil-drenched seabird. The new image-arsenal of 'environmental terrorism' gave this oil slick layers of additional meaning. When it was not a 'military obstacle' or 'logistics problem,' in Pentagon parlance, the slick was yet another mess for the West to fix with its wondrous technology. Most pernicious of all, however, the slick came to personify (oily) Arab treachery, whether it signified the dark, inscrutable evil of Saddam Hussein or the sinister, inexorable spread of Arab nationalism and/or Islam. The more prosaic story is that the largest oil spill in history contaminated 400 miles of shoreline, habitat, among other things, to two million migratory wading birds. In contrast to the Prince William cleanup after the *Exxon Valdez* spill, Saudi and Kuwaiti ecologists decided to leave much of the damage to beaches, mud flats, seagrasses and algae to heal naturally, while the international community, with the egregious exception of the USA, footed what remained of the marine cleanup bill.

If the oil slick became the leading ecological actor during the war itself, the spectacle of the 700 burning Kuwaiti oil wells played the starring role in the media war's denouement. This sooty spectacle satisfied a Western and, I suppose, specifically Christian desire for images of hellfire appropriate to wartime, images that were widespread in the wake of bombing raids on Baghdad and Basra, but denied us by military censorship. The fires also provided a lasting reminder of Saddam's appalling scorched-earth policy, which had included the sack and pillage of Kuwait City, the destruction of Kuwait's beaches by construction of an intertidal defense system and veritable plantations of antipersonnel mines, and the devastation of the desert ecology by the building of fortifications and vast oil trenches. Jassim Mohammad al-Hassan, a Kuwaiti ecologist who wrote a detailed study of the environmental effects of the Iraqi invasion, suggested that the extensive Western speculation about impending ecological disaster for the Gulf and for the world as a whole helped to strengthen Saddam's resolve to wage environmental warfare.[9]

Whether this speculation was accurate or not, evidence of worldwide effects accumulated during the year following the war, long after the midday blackout of Kuwait City skies presented a foreboding spectacle summoned up from the darker side of science fiction. *Atlantis* space-shuttle astronauts noted the mantle of dust and smoke partially obscuring their views of the earth, and acid rain and sooty fallout were detected by the Mauna Loa observatory in Hawaii. On a more speculative front, a cyclone hit Bangladesh in April, massive floods ravaged Central and Eastern China, affecting 200 million people, countries in the region had their coldest summer on record, while the Middle East went on to endure bizarre winter weather featuring blizzards, torrential rain and persistent snowfall.

It is not so easy to separate these presumed effects of the Kuwaiti fires from the culture of 'strange weather' around the world that has become a staple genre of environmental commentary in recent years. What one can say is that these effects joined the earlier forecasting of large, apocalyptic events (monsoon failure, equatorial holes in the ozone layer, permanent climatic change) in claiming the media headlines. What went unreported, for the most part, was the environmental damage that was less spectacular, or else casually accepted as part of war's normative effects. A good deal of this neglect stemmed from the popular conception that there is no life in a desert, and thus there is no desert ecology to devastate. (Indeed, in their letters from the Gulf, soldiers repeatedly spoke about the ugliness and barrenness of the desert, and their longing for the green landscapes of their homes in the temperate West.) Consequently, there was little coverage of the desert 'moonscape' created by B-52 carpetbombing (only 7 per cent of the Allied ordnance was smart bombs), or of the devastation begun with the installation of the two armies — the garbage, sewage, and toxic waste created by two vast alien populations totaling over two million in a desert whose ecosystem is in many ways more delicate than that of the Gulf waters. Off-road vehicles and massive troop movements did extensive damage to the desert pavement, layered with pebbles and stones lodged over centuries, held in place by a crust of living microorganisms, and socialized by the larger ecology of plants and reptiles, birds and rodents. With the stability of this floor disturbed, sandstorms generated drifts that covered roads and unexploded ordnance, altering the landscape quite radically. The vast oil lakes, which long outlasted the extinction of the oil-well fires, lured whole populations of confused, migrating birds to an oily demise, while the lakes' contents seeped into desert bedrock and the Gulf waters. Equally underreported was the war's devastating impact upon civilian populations in the aftermath of the systematic destruction from the air of the water and sewerage infrastructure of Iraq (including the targeted bombing of over forty biochemical and nuclear facilities). Thousands died daily from malnutrition and disease in the subsequent year, half the country's livestock perished; some estimates concluded that up to six million civilians were either killed, wounded, rendered homeless, or turned into refugees.[10]

These are stories that were not adequately told, either because of Pentagon censorship, media burnout, or, quite simply, because they require more than a sound-bite analysis and a set of atrocity images. Nothing else could compete, in media terms, with the twin spectacles of the oil spill and the burning oil wells. Consequently, the stories that did get told featured the US military (the biggest single polluter in its own country, generating a ton of toxic waste every minute in peacetime) in the Captain Planet role of combating environmental damage. Here, surely, was one of the war's more obscene aspects – the bestowing of ecological sanctity upon a military institution that makes a mockery of public review of the toxic effects of its weapon testing (especially nuclear) and production of war matériel in the USA, while national environmental laws are considered nonbinding in overseas territories. In fact, the Bush administration's wartime decision to exempt military observance of the 1970 National Environmental Policy Act was implemented in only one instance, and circumvented in many others, precisely because it was feared that a general exemption would invite too much public criticism.

In the long run, the most injurious effect of war coverage is that it displaces attention away from the daily economy of military activity in peacetime. Barry Commoner once suggested that if we took the trillion annual dollars squandered on world military expenditure, we could feed, clothe, and educate the world's population, and build a postgreenhouse economy freed from dependence on fossil fuels. As a cost-benefit analysis, this is ecologically persuasive. But such an analysis assumes that these disparate areas of social and economic life are not already linked in the first place — in other words, that institutional militarism, structural poverty, undereducation, and capital-intensive, hard energy production are not fundamentally linked in the world system of power relations. It is this kind of statistical calculation that generates the illusory promise of something like the 'peace dividend' in the wake of de-escalation of the Cold War. And yet, all too quickly, we find that 'scarcity' of some sort curiously prevents the reallocation to social programs of the vast economic resources devoted to the military, while noting that, in spite of this scarcity, there is always money to fight wars. It is not, then, simply a case of moving resources from one sector to another. Institutional militarism is much more than an obscene budgetary appropriation from the federal tax base. It is a highly complex embodiment of social, political, and cultural conditions of power, each with its own complex history. Militarism can no more be reduced to the testosterone factor — it's a male thing — than it can be reduced to the specific economic need of capitalist production for market stability. If militarism is an ecological threat, the root problem lies: (a) in the social ecology of its own institutions, more profoundly undemocratic in their entire power structure than any comparably hierarchical, or authoritarian, political body: and (b) in the long, cumulative history of militarism's hegemonic coordination of other institutions in society. All wars after the Gulf now demand urgent ecological analysis, not just because their consequences are physically damaging, and may imperil the survival of species on the planet — but also because they are rooted in a social ecology of domination that continues to sustain the power of some humans at the cost of the majority of others.

Credible Forms of Lust

If we are to communicate critiques of this sort publicly, then some better understanding is required of the role currently played by media images that are considered to be ecologically meaningful. We need more acute attention to cultural studies of ecology. Unlike other social movements relating to civil rights, women's rights, and lesbian and gay rights, the ecology movement has not generated its own tradition of cultural criticism in the last two decades. This can partly be explained by the ceding of authority to science in most matters ecological, but it is also due to the persistent notion that the environment does not have a human face. After all, the object of green criticism is not to uncover forgotten histories, or to open up a space for unheard voices. The earth does not speak back in quite the same way as women, people of color, or lesbians and gay men.

Among other things, the Gulf War led me to discover that theoretical discussion of ecological issues in media studies was very thin on the ground. One of the few related discussions I seized upon was Susan Sontag's book *On Photography* (1977), at the end of which she called, somewhat metaphorically, for an 'ecology of images':

> Images are more real than anyone could have supposed. And just because they are an unlimited resource, one that cannot be exhausted by consumerist waste, there is all the more reason to apply the conservationist remedy. If there can be a better way for the real world to include the one of images, it will require an ecology not only of real things but of images as well.[11]

A decade earlier, in her book *Against Interpretation* (1966), Sontag had made a similar kind of call for an 'erotics of art.' This call was answered loudly and clearly in literary and cultural criticism during the subsequent two decades; the kind of criticism that has focused on the libidinal, or psychosexual relationship between images, language, and human desire. By contrast, there has been precious little in the way of a response to Sontag's call for an 'ecology of images.' It is unfortunate but perhaps instructive that we may have needed images from war to provide the impetus for belatedly responding to Sontag's call, and for seriously debating the consequences for cultural studies of an 'ecology of images.' Four years into a decade that deserves an adequate green cultural criticism, nothing seems more central than to debate the ecological role and character of images — not only their use in telling ecological stories but also the ecology of the image industry itself, considered in all its aspects of production, distribution and consumption.

170

My comments on this neglected debate will perforce be speculative and exploratory. I take my starting point from the divisions
traditionally used to differentiate film criticism into two schools of
thought. On the one hand, there emerged the 'images of women'
film criticism, the images seen as either positive or negative
according to a content analysis. On the other hand, what came to be
known as film theory developed, devoted, among other things, to
analyzing how the 'film form' of narrative logic embodied the social
history and technological development of the film industry as a
whole. In a similar way, one might distinguish analysis of 'images of
ecology,' whether positive or negative, from discussion of the
'ecology of images' which might describe the economy of their
production and circulation.

To begin with what looks like the easier category, what are
'images of ecology'? Aside from the long history of 'images of
nature' in the genres of nature and wildlife photography, films, and
documentaries, there has appeared over the twenty-four year
existence of the ecology movement a genre of image in which the
natural environment figures quite distinctively as a narrative
element, usually endangered and in some advanced state of
degradation but also often in a state of repair, reconstruction, or
even in pristine good health. In recent years, we have become
accustomed to seeing images of a dying planet, variously exhibited
in grisly poses of ecological depletion and circulated by all sectors of
the image industry, often in spots reserved for the exploitation fare
of genocidal atrocities. The clichés of the standard environmental
image are well known to us all: on the one hand, belching
smokestacks, seabirds mired in petrochemical sludge, fish floating
belly-up, traffic jams in Los Angeles and Mexico City, and clearcut
forests; on the other hand, the redeeming repertoire of pastoral
imagery, pristine, green, and unspoiled by human habitation,
crowned by the ultimate global spectacle, the fragile, vulnerable ball
of spaceship earth. These images, which call attention to the actually
existing state of the environment, are intended to have different
meanings from the more traditional genres of nature images like
landscape painting or picturesque photography (notwithstanding
the obvious caveat that 'Nature' itself has played host, historically,
to a whole spectrum of social meanings). In this respect, then — the
conditions under which images of nature have come to communicate
specifically ecological messages — we can speak of the advent of

171

'images of ecology' in recent years. I use this phrase also to acknowledge that the term 'ecology' itself has a much broader, public meaning today than its traditional definition within the natural sciences as the study of the relationship between species and habitat.

I will have more to say about images of ecology, because we cannot assume that we have a self-apparent understanding of the power of these images. In other words, I don't mean to suggest that it is, in a sense, the more *vulgar* of the discussions I will be pursuing here and that, having briefly pinned it down, we can move on to higher things. For the time being, however, I will devote some space to the question of whether images can have an ecology in their own right, if only because it is a less widely recognized idea in the first place. To do so, we must consider the social and industrial organization of images – the processes by which they are produced, distributed, and used in modern electronic culture – and ask if there are ecological arguments to be made about those processes, or whether their relation to ecological processes is simply metaphorical.

Sontag's discussion of photographic images is, again, my starting point. In *On Photography*, a book about the 'ethics of seeing' the world through the voracious filter of image consumption, she argues that the world is consumed and used up by our appetite for images. In Sontag's view, the world has been reduced to a set of potential photographs; its events are valued for their photographic interest, and large sectors of its population have become 'tourists of reality' as a result. While she sees the act of the photographer as 'essentially an act of non-intervention,' (*OP*, p.11) the knowledge that an audience gains through images is always gained cheaply; it is always knowledge at 'bargain prices' (*OP*, p.24). Sontag is careful to avoid the jeremiac tones of those who have historically lamented the popularity of the image over reality, but there is no mistaking the repulsion that wells up beneath her fascination with modern image addiction. 'Industrial societies,' she writes, 'turn their citizens into image-junkies: it is the most irresistible form of mental pollution' (*OP*, p.24). Surely Sontag has in mind here a Judeo-Christian meaning of 'pollution,' as applied to the *moral* equilibrium of the mind-body and marked by the perversion of that balance. She is clearly invoking the older, moral stigma of spiritual pollution to describe what she sees as our overconsumption of images and the consequent depreciation of the world's reality resources. There remains a persistent distaste in her comments. Later in the book, the same charge returns, this time couched in metaphors that anticipate her later preoccupation with sickness:

> The possession of a camera can inspire something akin to lust. And like all credible forms of lust, it cannot be satisfied; first, because the possibilities of photography are infinite, and, second, because the project is finally self-devouring. The attempts by photographers to bolster up a depleted sense of reality contribute to the depletion. Our oppressive sense of the transience of everything is more acute since cameras gave us the means to 'fix' the fleeting moment. We consume images at an ever faster rate, and, as Balzac suspected cameras used up layers of the body, images consume reality. Cameras are the antidote and the disease, a means of appropriating reality and a means of making it obsolete. (*OP*, p.179)

When Sontag speaks of photography as a 'credible form of lust' (just exactly what an 'incredible' form of lust might be is left for the reader to toy with), an addictive pleasure for which we will ultimately have to pay the consequences, she seems to want to convey a strongly moral or religious sense of retribution, reinforced here by the description of visual technologies as both 'the antidote and the disease.'[12]

Let us try to place Sontag's remarks about image addiction in the context of ecological arguments about the historical role of science and technology in the degradation of the natural world. In this light, camera technology can perhaps be seen as an embodiment of what ecological writers mean by the colonization or domination of nature, a historical tendency that now threatens the physical world with an immediacy that is all the more ironically apparent to us through those very 'images of ecology' that have become standard media atrocity fare in recent years. If Sontag's arguments can be read as taking this thesis one step further, into the realm of the epistemology of images, then we might summarize her discussion of the capacity of images to 'deplete' reality in the following way. The production and consumption of images is a central element in our relationship to our social habitat. Just as the technological overproduction and overconsumption of raw materials can wastefully exhaust the capacity of an ecosystem to sustain itself, so too a similar tendency in image production and image consumption diminishes our capacity to sustain a healthy balance of life in the social world of our culture. There comes a point, if you like, when one image too many tips that balance between reality and simulations. This way of drawing out a working analogy from Sontag's comments may be rather crude, but it seems fair; and I have put it in these terms because they highlight more clearly the question that troubles me about this argument.

Can we talk about technologies of cultural production and cultural consumption in terms that so clearly parallel the way in which ecologists have talked about the effect of similar technological or industrial processes upon a natural ecosystem? Does the recycling, say, of images and narratives — arguably the ground rhythm of most cultural production — have anything like the same ecological meaning as the recycling of newspaper or aluminium cans? Yes and no. To be sure, there are already many common elements on both sides of the analogy, not least of which is the material organization of technologies within the film and image industry, and I will have more to say about that topic presently. But the differences are crucial to consider, for the very reasons that culturalists have had to perpetually resist the reductionist claims of strict determinists of every stripe. Just as it is important for ecologists to think about technologies as fully *cultural* processes, embodying ideas and values and not restricted by definition to hardware development and economic growth, so too, culturalists ought to be able to think of cultural products as meaningful in ways related to, but not determined by, the industrial processes that created them. The advantage, then, of the analogy that I have sketched above is that it invites cultural critics to think more about how culture is produced and consumed in potentially wasteful ways. The danger of the analogy is that it is also an invitation to forget what we think we know, say, about the versatility of the images themselves — how they are received and used for all sorts of purposes, not the least of which, in the present case, are how images of ecology can be used to activate popular support for the repair of our local and global ecologies.

Sontag's analysis leaves little room for this kind of speculation. In addition, her remarks subscribe to the school of silly thought that rails against image overload in our modern information society. Information glut has become a favored object of attack from commentators on the right and the left, besieged, apparently, by the cacophony of voices, publications, images, and technologies that have voraciously swallowed up their mythical 'public sphere' and are aggressively trying to communicate with us all at once. Even on the level of the quantitative argument, I have never been happy with this response since I have always assumed that most people in this world would rather have a surfeit of information (whatever that means) than a dearth. For the genuinely information-poor, there is nothing more crass than the commentator who complains that he or she has 150 TV channels and not one is worth watching. Information, of course, is not the same thing as intelligence or knowledge; its quantity tells us no more about its reception than a quantitative estimate of the number of proliferating TV channels or the number of viewing hours clocked up by the average couch potato can tell us about the uses made of those television images selected by any particular viewer. *That*, after all, is supposed to be the job of cultural studies, which assumes that competent viewers of images have their own, highly organized ways of making sense of the range of images available to them. No more useful is the response of postmodernist theorists like Baudrillard or Jameson who see the helpless victims of information overload as schizoid or paranoid casualties of forces beyond their control. As for the repeated warnings about the predominance of images in our politics and our everyday lives, most of these alarm signals issue from within the 'media' themselves — media owners, media professionals, media critics — that is, from groups who have a vested interest in seeing the image business as all-powerful.

The most useful critiques of media culture remain those that focus on the economic organization of information technologies, on the ever new and profitable ways of restricting access to information and making it an increasingly scarce commodity. Contrary to the image-glut school of thought, which leads the moral crusade against the overavailability of information, getting access to information today is just as uneven and as expensive as ever; this is as true in the tradable global market, where information is a primary commodity, as it is in the home, where it is increasingly difficult, for example, to receive a decent TV signal without paying through the nose for cable. The rhetoric of information abundance, in this respect, is difficult to distinguish from the rhetoric of scarcity.

The AntiReality Principle

For an analysis of the process of creating image scarcity, one need look no further than the economic organization of the film industry in the age of the megahit. In Hollywood, the medium-priced picture is disappearing fast as the film industry is increasingly organized around two markets: the blockbuster market ($15 to $100 million for production, up to $10 million for wide release, and up to $50 million for global advertising and distribution), and the much cheaper, direct-to-video/cable market. In the blockbuster market especially, the familiar industrial process of recycling and recombining images, narratives, and themes has been streamlined with all of the rigor and efficiency available to modern industrial and marketing techniques. In this context, the principle of cultural recycling is both conserva-tionist and conservative; the industry wants to maximize its gain on tried and true resources — formulae proven to be profitable — but the result runs directly counter to the spirit of encouraging image *diversity*. The result resembles what might be called an image monoculture. The ever greater, and, some would say, wasteful sums of capital devoted to recycling the old in pursuit of the transnational megahit has the net effect of drastically reducing the chance of cultural diversity in mainstream film production.

The increasingly crucial role of special effects in the megahit business is geared to the industrial principle of obsolescence. The 'look' of films made only a few years before is outdated by the technologically advanced effects of today's computerized cameras and postproduction image processing. It is only in the realm of cult taste, where camp nostalgia for the shlocky, low-tech, low-budget look (like early stop-motion model effects) of past futures runs high, that this industrial principle is displaced if not directly challenged. Yet, with the increasing monopolization of first-run houses by media giants, and the extinction of revival houses and avant-garde film venues, the channeling of this marginal taste culture into the video rental business has itself become a lucrative subsidiary market that does not cut into the mass-release first-run circuit and therefore supports its mainstream economy. In this regard, one of my favorite comments on the ecology of image production comes from the princely parodist of the bad-taste circuit, John Waters, ever ready to turn a popular cliché to good use: 'At least I've never done anything really decadent, like waste millions of dollars of other people's money, and come up with a movie as dumb as *The Deep* or *1941*. The budgets of my movies could hardly feed the starving children of India.'[13]

A more exhaustive account of these tendencies is obviously required if we are to have anything like an ecological analysis of image production. It's my hunch, however, that we are likely to find many economic and technological processes in the image industry that call out for the kind of ecological critiques that have been brought to bear upon other industrial processes. We are just as likely to find differences, however, for which the application of ecological principles to the field of culture do not have quite the same meaning as they do in a more material economy. The wasteful exploitation of finite resources to manage and control the production of scarcity among material consumer products is an industrial principle that cannot be entirely carried over into an analysis of image production and consumption. Image consumption is not subject to the same quantifiable processes as those that govern the consumption of other industrial products. If it makes any sense at all to talk about the image 'waste stream,' then our own position as consumers within this stream is quite different from our position in the material, consumer product waste stream. Images can be used, and reused, in ways that most consumer goods cannot, not even containers and packaging.

So, too, complaints about the 'visual pollution' of billboards invite the same kind of second-level critique. In the months before the Rio Earth Summit, George Bush was fooling around with one of the ideas that passed for environmental policy in the Reagan—Bush years. The proposal — to ban new billboards along rural highways — was intended to beef up the Highway Beautification Act of 1965, when drivers of automobiles averaging twelve miles to the lead-filled gallon considered billboards to be a major source of 'visual pollution.' One frustrated response to the slow rate of removal came from the executive director of Scenic America, Sally Oldham: 'trying to clean up visual pollution at the rate of 226 billboards a year is like trying to clean up the Exxon Valdez oil spill with a teaspoon.' As bagheaded in its own way as Bush's environmentalism, this analogy is testimony to the way in which such false metaphors are used to mobilize consciousness. That billboard space can be used as a medium for pro-ecological messages is only one of the ways in which the metaphor deserves to be confounded.

Elsewhere, the use of ecological language to describe cultural processes is quite widespread, whether among media critics who describe the transnational media industries as if they were discharging pollutant messages into the mediasphere, or else among government lackeys of those same companies, like Mark Fowler, Reagan's deregulation czar at the Federal Communications Commission, here balancing his remorse over environmental degradation with sunny McLuhanite optimism about the ecology of free information flows: 'As the ecological system deteriorated, I think the man-made information ecology — the ebb and flow of words, voice, data — has vastly improved, so that we now live in a world more tightly bound, more in touch one part with another, than at any moment in history.'

It's when nature writers comment on culture that one sees how far things can go in this direction. In *The Age of Missing Information*, Bill McKibben, a modern, Adirondack-dwelling Thoreau and author of the much-cited *The End of Nature*, describes two days spent in 1990.[14] The first day was passed in camping, hiking, swimming, and solitary meditation in the mountains. On the second, which, through assiduous use of VCRs, lasted well over a thousand hours, McKibben watched all of the TV that the cable company of Fairfax, Virginia (an 'edge city' claiming the largest cable system in the country), broadcast over its ninety-three channels in a single 24-hour stretch. McKibben's aim in this book is to find out how much 'information' can be garnered from each of the two days. But his search rests on vague, shifting criteria, mostly linked to something called 'fundamental knowledge' or 'rightness,' which can only be acquired by hanging out among trees, rivers, and mountains. The odds, you guessed it, are pretty much stacked against the couch potato, tawdry symptom of the recline of Western Civ., and in favor of the nature nerd, groping for wisdoms all but lost to denizens of the info glut. As sympathetic readers, we are invited to embrace the sanity of the hiker, far from the madding crowd of televangelists speaking in tongues, of hucksters dealing-a-meal to the obese or hawking bottles of cleaning powder to home shoppers, while sleek men in Rollses politely lust after Grey Poupon.

Too bad that in his literary passion for the green world, McKibben is no John McPhee. Living in a mountain-rimmed valley without TV, most evenings Bill and his wife 'tune in to *All Things Considered* on the radio,' trusting that 'its familiar theme music helps order the day.' Yikes! For a 32-year-old, McKibben often sounds like Gramps on lithium. This is a man who prefers the mating dance of cranes to semi-naked club kids shaking their Lycra-clad booties on MTV. McKibben understands that learning about nature from *Wild Kingdom* is as unlikely as learning about life from *Dynasty*, but it's no surprise that he can't see where the pleasure of these shows lies, given that his idea of good television is restricted to the lean diet of *60 Minutes*, *Nightline*, and Ken Burns' *Civil War*.

What's of interest in McKibben's commentary is the way he utilizes the current popular wisdom of environmentalism. First, there's the straight choice between the natural world and the manmade world of information. For McKibben, to choose the former is to get back to authentic knowledge, to rediscover human scale, community, and nonanthropocentric time, and to understand that the world has limits. No need to grow crops, however, or revert to hunting-gathering mode: all you need do is take more trips to the countryside — it's 'subversive' — which is exactly what the well heeled urban or suburban readers of his books are likely to do anyway. Less easy to shrug off are McKibben's analogies between ecosystems and information systems. He uses these analogies to indict the loss of species diversity in TV programming, and to argue that the recycling of shows and genres does indeed produce a monoculture. Unlike critics of the media monopolies who use the same metaphors, however, McKibben 'doesn't much care if television is manipulated by giant corporations, the military-industrial complex,' or the 'pressure of ratings.' He doesn't want to combat censorship or involve communities in cultural policy-making, doesn't want to democratize the media. It's enough that his readers leave their TVs and invade what's left of the Adirondacks.

Whatever you think of McKibben and like-minded souls, there are clearly physical components to the image industry that have a large bearing on environmental issues. Filmmakers less arch than John Waters have devoted themselves to low-impact filmmaking.[15] *E Magazine* (June 1993) reports that Hollywood uses, for its film sets, 250,000 sheets per year of luan plywood cut from the rainforests of Southeast Asia. The EPA has estimated that 40 to 60 per cent of all toxic chemical pollution relates to photographic processes. Cine-philes, archivists, and media critics have long been horrified by the scandalous lack of conservationism within the film and TV industry: the studios' throwaway attitude toward film prints (the meltdown of

Erich von Stroheim's *Greed* for thirty cents of silver nitrate is the archetypal horror story), the instant obsolescence of TV film, and the cavalier decisions about use of capital and resources that are made in pursuit of the final cut. Exhaustive analyses of the history of the photochemical and photographic industry would expose worse stories about the chemical underpinnings of the film economy. You do not need to have lived in Rochester, New York, as I have, to know something about the life-threatening history of the image industry's major supplier, Eastman Kodak, consistently among the worst polluters of major US corporations. (Of course, much the same could be said of 'life-saving' industries like medicine and pharmacology.) The common use of materials like nitrocellulose in film stock and in explosives production has long been an element in film historians' accounts of the image industry, whose film technologies invariably were and still are a direct spinoff from military research and development.

In his book *War and Cinema* (1984), an especially prescient text for the Gulf War, Paul Virilio offered a historical analysis of the importance of film technology to military-industrial interests. In his account of the transformation of the modern battlefield from a Cartesian arena of warring objects to a simulated arena of pictures and sounds, Virilio examines the crucial role of camera technology in what he calls the 'logistics of military perception.'[16] This history runs from the emergence of military photography in the American Civil War, through the military use of propaganda film units and Nuremberg-like staged spectacles, to the advent of planetary war vision with spy satellites and advanced simulation technologies. It is a history in which film technologies are fully and materially embedded in the logic of destruction; in which the video-equipped warheads and electro-optically lit battlefields that we saw in the Persian Gulf are continuous with earlier strategic uses of aerial photography in World War I, a war during which D.W. Griffith, the only civilian filmmaker authorized to make propaganda films at the front, said that he was 'very disappointed with the reality of the battlefield' (because soldiers seldom, if ever, actually *saw* the enemy).[17]

The camera's contribution to what Virilio calls the 'demateriali-zation of reality' on the battlefield seems to me a more telling story about the destructive potential of image-making technology than that offered by Sontag. Here, the logic of photography — the dematerialization of reality — goes hand in hand with the apparatus of war, devoted to the *destruction* of reality. This is a materialist epistemology, as distinct from Sontag's idealist epistemology, in which images figure as the means of *depleting* reality. In Virilio's history, the camera is a material participant in the apparatus of destruction. Sontag insists that the world today exists only to be mined and ransacked for images, but there is no urgency at stake in this knowledge because there is no finite limit to the quarrying.

Although I believe that there is an important difference between these kinds of analyses — Virilio's and Sontag's — I am not comfortable with the opposition, nor do I think we can simply appeal to the final superiority of the materialist over the idealist critique. Ideas and images are also constitutive of the world in ways that can counter their role as technological recruits in wars against environmental reality. That is why a discussion of the ecology of images — the ecology of image production and image consumption — of the sort I have briefly pursued here must make room for some understanding of the role played by images of ecology. Neither Sontag's nor Virilio's critique takes into account those instances when images (of destruction and/or ecology) are used to debate, or even to contest, the consequences that both critics lament — the material disappearance of reality. In short, images of ecology today are also produced, consumed, and used in ways that can help to counteract the destruction of the natural world.

Images of Ecology

In turning back, then, to the question of 'images of ecology,' we must recognize that any proper account covers a broad spectrum. At the most visible, activist end are agitprop images that are directly employed within and by the ecology movement to mobilize sympathy, support, and action for environmental causes; what we could call images of ecology *for* ecology. At the other, more sublimated end of the spectrum are images that have some kind of ecological content and which are incorporated into the daily fabric of public and popular culture: images of ecology that are not necessarily *about* ecology. This spectrum is not, of course, a flat political one — it does not simply run from left to right. I shall try to show how and why this is so.

181

Although sectors of the ecology movement (Greenpeace, the Sierra Club, and Earth First! most famously) have made very good use of images of environmental degradation and repair alike, there is no naive faith in their political power. Even though such images speak about the bankruptcy of ideas that have bolstered unsustainable growth and development in the West, the ex-communist bloc, and, increasingly, the Third World, the images themselves cannot, of course, say much about such ideas. Rather, the story is told by the narrative context in which they occur, a problem that is aptly demonstrated by the coverage of the oil spill and burning wells in the Gulf, or by the widespread use of 'images of ecology' in advertising by the most environmentally destructive of the major industrial corporations. A poster of Spaceship Earth is just as likely to adorn the wall of a nuclear weapons designer as that of a soft-energy technician. For these and other reasons, environmentalists tend to be suspicious of the use of images in themselves as a medium of information. In this respect, we can say that discussion of the images of ecology has already moved beyond the assumption that in themselves images have a fixed political meaning for audiences as either 'positive' or 'negative,' or 'good' or 'bad.' It is not yet clear, however, whether the discussion of this issue has fully addressed the means by which forms of representation — narrative logic and point of view — can bring political meanings to bear upon the nature of the information provided about ecological matters. In the examples that follow, I shall show how a focus on narrative logic and point of view can link critiques of the ecology of images with images of ecology.

My first example is from the more activist end of the image spectrum. The ecology movement may be exceptional among new social and political movements in making an overriding appeal to scientific information for proof of the justice of its claims. One of the favored visual forms of organizing eco-statistical information is the cartographic format — maps and graphs are science's favored image genres — and one of the most commercially successful genres of ecology publications is the state-of-the-world atlas. Such atlases capitalize on the fact that the global image is the most stable form of information about a highly unstable environment. Joni Seager's *Atlas Survey of the State of the Earth* (1990) is a typical example. It breaks down, from page to page, the degradation of the world's resources: the state of the rainforests, population increase, energy budgets, acid rain, drinking water, food supplies, sewage, air quality, firewood, petrochemical pollution, coastal erosion, the wildlife trade, genetic diversity, toxic waste, the timber trade, and so on.[18] For the most part, atlases like Seager's, or the *World Wildlife Fund Atlas of the Environment*, or Michael Kidron and Ronald Segal's *New State of the World Atlas*, recognize the current organization of global territory according to the sovereignty of nation states, and their statistics are broken down into the share accorded to national economies (Kidron and Segal's book, at least, seems to be assembled as a cumulative statement against the 'injustices, dangers and irrelevancies of our state-ridden system').[19] These atlases seldom organize the field of representation by biome or bioregion.[20] Because of this focus on nation states, their maps fail entirely to represent the influence and power of transnational corporations; nor does the form of the per capita statistics help to differentiate the average citizen's share from the disproportionately destructive contribution of the military, government bureaucracy, or industry within any given nation state, each citizen in that state sharing differently according to region, color, and class.

Although these images are produced for activist purposes, can their form be described as an activist one if it does not imagine a world organized differently? By accepting the current political and economic organization of the world by the state system, they acknowledge a powerful reality but forego the transnational nature of a large part of ecological and economic life on the planet. A different perspective entirely is provided in the series of atlases that embody the one-worldism of Gaia philosophy and science: *Gaia: An Atlas of Planet Management*, *Gaia State of the Ark Atlas*, and *Gaia Peace Atlas*.[21] Presented under the aegis of the Gaia hypothesis – that the planet is a single, living biosphere with its own global life-support systems and feedback mechanisms – these atlases rarely mention nation states, focusing regionally, if at all, on continents, in their explicit attempts to avoid the 'gloom and doom' ethos that pervades the eco-atlas genre. In the spirit of Buckminster Fuller's Dymaxion Air-Ocean Map of the World (a one-world island in a one-world ocean, with no breaks between the continents), the Gaia maps are either based on Gall's cylindrical projection – to counter the traditionally Eurocentric cartographic perspective – or the Peters projection, which claim to represent more accurately the land mass of the continents. But the maps are only one of an impressive array of creative visual images (tree diagrams, larder diagrams, 3-D globes, and creative low-tech depictions of ecosystems) designed to illustrate statistical information. The polemical overview of the survey is that of planetary management — responsible stewardship of global resources — and therefore meets the gaze of the World Bank, as well as other global economic institutions. The substantial accompanying commentary is suffused with the Gaian view of the human species as a damaging blight upon the landscape, if not an 'evolutionary blind alley' that does not deserve to survive. The species is therefore addressed as a collective 'we,' or, at best, as 'divisions of the human family.' Consequently, there is little room for exposés of the agencies — corporations, governments, large landowners — primarily responsible for the ecological crisis.[22] Nonetheless, the innovative use of graphics, charts, photography, and commentary provide an inspiring feel to the survey that is conspicuously lacking in those primarily dystopian versions of the genre discussed earlier. In all of these atlases, then, we find an instance of how the representational form of the image is a major component of the political meaning conveyed by it.[23]

A similar kind of argument could be made about the form of eco-statistics themselves, the basic ammunition for environmentalists' arguments made in the public arena. Like the eco-atlas, which inherits and often accepts the neoimperialist aerial perspective of military logistics, the persuasive citation of eco-statistics borrows its shock appeal from the rhetoric of military statistics. The arsenal of statistics about eco-atrocities in the global environment is often used to create a climate of fear in the same way as the merchants of war have profited from the statistics of nuclear kilotonnage, projected megadeaths, and strategic firepower. The result of this dystopian climate of shock and terror is not necessarily empowering; it feeds into survivalism, the lowest form of ecological consciousness, especially when these statistics are simply projected into the darkest of doomsday futures. Military science might be fought with science, and that often involves using statistics to counter official figures cooked up for cosmetic purposes by authorities. But when it comes to statistics, you live or die by their sword, and so the most apocalyptic prognoses, like some of those issued at the onset of the Gulf War, weaken the environmentalist cause in the long run when they prove to be off the mark. Even less useful is the apples-and-oranges comparison which is common in environmentalist polemic.

What does it really accomplish to point out that a fleet, say, of F-111 fighters uses as much fuel in an hour as it would take to run the Boston mass transit system for a year? The comparison (even if it is true) makes little sense. So too, we are deceived by the psychology of comparison when each new ecological disaster hits the news. This or that new oil spill, we are told, is twice as much or only half as much as the oil spilled by the *Exxon Valdez*. Bhopal, Chernobyl, Hiroshima, and Prince William Sound have become standards of acceptability that each new ecological disaster must now outdo in statistical dimensions in order to qualify as 'noteworthy' — this is ecological politics waged on the model of baseball statistics, where people are reduced to fruit flies, and all sense of everyday human scale is lost.

Among the genre of images of ecology, perhaps the most familiar and popular is the narrative documentary, with its roots in nature and wildlife film. The noncable context for this genre in the USA is almost exclusively public television, with its demographic appeal to the concerns of a predominantly white, neoliberal, middle-class audience. (On cable, the Discovery Channel in particular presents a host of nature and ecological features.) In the wake of Earthday 1990, the fall schedule of PBS programming was almost entirely devoted to environmental documentaries, culminating in the lavish, ten-hour miniseries, *Race to Save the Planet*, an attempt to narrate the entire ecological history of the human world in a form akin to that middlebrow classic of public television programming, Kenneth Clark's BBC series, *Civilization*. Contextualized by liberal, 'quality' Hollywood performers (introduced by Meryl Streep, and narrated by Roy Scheider) and dominated by laboriously pious narratives and a monotonously conscientious tone, *Race to Save the Planet* was advertised in slots for PBS's annual fundraising fall campaign as exemplary 'television that lets you take action.' The rhetoric of this appeal to a PBS audience was canny: not activist TV, nor TV about activism, but TV that reaffirms its audience's identity as liberal-minded people who are accustomed to taking for granted their social identity and position — middle-class and predominantly pro-fessional — as already 'active' (rather than 'activist') in the world.

In considering the use of images about ecology drawn from the more articulate, or even activist end of my spectrum, I have pointed, all too briefly, to the political importance of representa-tional forms and narratives, heavily contextualized by their appeal to particular histories and audiences. Similar considerations are no less evident if we turn to more popular genres.

With the recent emergence of public ecological consciousness, narratives about environmental repair have begun to surface in popular genres. The Environmental Media Association gives annual awards to TV and film productions that send eco-friendly messages. Hollywood studios and TV networks have been flooded with scripts and proposals for ecologically minded films and series. Movies from diverse genres like *Medicine Man*, *Arachnophobia*, *The Applegates*, *At Play in the Fields of the Lord*, and *Fern Gully* fed off public interest in rainforest politics, and Stephen Seagal's first movie as a director, *On Deadly Ground* (1994), provided an exemplary backdrop for his newfound tough-guy environmentalism among the native peoples of Alaska. Children's programming in particular is heavy with environmental themes. A host of children's features — *Widget*, *Dark Water*, *The Toxic Crusaders* — briefly aired or underwent trial runs for syndication at the start of the decade. The 1990 fall TV season saw the fleeting appearance of two eco-cop shows, *E.A.R.T.H. Police* and *Super Force*, while *Voice of the Planet*, TBS's ten-hour Gaia-inspired New Age adventure series, made a shortlived appearance in February 1991. However, the only eco-shows to have survived from that early glut have been TBS's *Network Earth*, and Ted Turner's personal brainchild, the cartoon show *Captain Planet and the Planeteers* (a superhero and his racially diverse crew battle eco-villains).

Science fiction remains the genre that has elevated ecological commentary to the level of stock conventionality, so much so that films like the recent *Demolition Man* (1993) assume their eco-tyrannical future backdrops as if they were wallpaper, or, at least, like sets left over from the last SF movie on the lot. In the last twenty years of popular SF, the ecological 'look' of the future has been governed by a dark dystopian imagination, feeding off the imagery of global degradation. The cultural power of this imagination has long transcended the vestigial influence of images and narratives of progressive futurism that were the standard diet of early science fiction films like *The Shape of Things to Come*. The historical role of SF film, with its power to 'colonize' the temporality and spatiality of the future, is paramount in any discussion of the ecology of film images. From the slew of 1970s SF dystopias — *Colossus: The Forbin Project, The Andromeda Strain, THX 1138, Silent Running, Westworld, Soylent*

Green, Dark Star, A Boy and His Dog, Logan's Run, The Late Great Planet Earth — which increasingly absorbed the urgency of ecological concerns about overpopulation and pollution in the wake of the energy crisis, to the more recent cyberpunk genre — *Escape from New York*, the *Mad Max* trilogy, *Blade Runner, The Running Man, The Terminator, Robocop, Cherry 2000, Max Headroom, Millennium, Brazil, Cyborg, Fortress* — the degraded bio-future has become a dominant landscape in our cultural imagination. For example, the first cyberpunk film of the 1990—91 season, Richard Stanley's low-budget *Hardware*, featured a grisly futuristic narrative about overpopulation: 'Welcome to the 21st century. Guess what's become the planet's most endangered species? Man.' The real answer to the question, revealed in the film, was fertile women, who are hunted by military cyborgs to keep down population levels.

One might balk at the irony of the film industry's persistently devoting vast sums of money to producing images of futureless futures. In most of the cyberpunk films, this dark future is merely a generic backdrop, a convention whose profitability is tried and tested, just as the genre recycles stunts and scenarios from earlier classics. Different contradictions arise, however, when the genre aims at producing a utopian future. In its action-adventure version of the 'race to save the planet' and liberate its population, Paul Verhoeven's 1990 summer SF film, *Total Recall*, offered a good example of a blockbuster that attempts to include a utopian eco-narrative. It would be wrong to think of it as an eco-friendly film, however. The planet in question is Mars, and the population is a federal worker colony, physically mutated by radiation as a result of inadequate working facilities and organized into underground rebel cadres fighting against labor enslavement by a primitive capitalist exploiter. Air is a commodity whose price is controlled by the mogul, while the colony's mining production, ruthlessly protected by the imposition of martial law, is used to fund an eco-war on Earth between northern and southern blocs.

While the film is dictated by the promotional requirements of its being a Schwarzenegger vehicle, the ecological components of the narrative are everywhere in the forefront. On Earth, pristine environmental spaces — assumed now to be extinct — are simulated for the purposes of tourism and domestic therapy, while advanced mind technologies, freely used for entertainment and politics alike, are used to manufacture human memories in pursuit of the perfect artificial ecology of the mind. In every respect, *Total Recall* tells a plausibly and explicitly Marxist tale about the destructive, alienating conditions of primitive capitalist production. Again, one might stop to speculate about the irony of such a film, since its very existence tells an otherwise astonishing story about the domestic absorption of Marxist critiques of capitalism within mainstream Hollywood film. But this is not my intention here. What concerns me is how the Marxist critique is employed to resolve the film's narrative in a way that works against the proto-ecological critique.

With the aid of the resistance forces on Mars, the Schwarzenegger figure succeeds in utilizing ancient Alien technologies to create an Earth-friendly atmosphere for the colony. The capitalist's power is broken, and the shlocky appearance of blue skies at the end of the film heralds a brave new world for the liberated workers. Here, the Alien technologies are also explicitly Marxist; they are 'alien' to the monopoly-regulated system of capitalist production because they are employed in the service of all — everyone gets air, and it is free. As technologies, however, they are finally 'alien' to the planet's ecology. The process of terraforming the planet is achieved through macroengineering and macroproduction; the vast Alien reactor is employed to melt down the planet's ice core and generate an oxygen-rich atmosphere. In the final sequence of the film, then, the planet's core resources are almost entirely exhausted in three minutes flat in order to create friendly conditions for its liberated human population. Nothing could be more explicitly Marxist than this fantasy about using macrotechnology to free humankind from servitude to both Capital and Nature. Nor could anything be more explicitly antiecological.[24]

At a time when these once-progressive narratives about emancipation through maximized technological production have been challenged to the point of exhaustion, here is a Hollywood film that is at last comfortable with such narratives and which poses them as solutions to an ecological predicament. I present it here as an example of the ways in which ecological concerns are being presented as images of ecology in popular entertainment — not in any ideal form, but in the impure context of other popular or generic narratives (even Marxist ones) that have meanings, often counter-ecological meanings, of their own. In the final analysis, we have to consider, of course, that the dramatic narrative of films like *Total Recall*, favoring the spectacle of ecological reparation, is itself a product of the eco-logic of industrial cost efficiency, balancing massive and wasteful expenditures against the promise of box-office profit.

The Owls Are Not What They Seem

A less direct example of images of ecology, this time from quality TV, is a show that monopolized much of the conversation of film-literate audiences in the USA during its brief run from spring 1990 to spring 1991. Almost from the first time I saw the opening credits of *Twin Peaks*, I watched this show about a Northwest logging town as a commentary about environmental issues. If *Twin Peaks* was one of our first examples of ecological camp (*Green Acres* was a weak, but likely, earlier candidate), as I think it was, it surely will not be the last.[25] One of the enduring effects of *Twin Peaks* was its influential reshaping and reimagining of the Pacific Northwest at a time when urgent ecological questions were being asked about the region's timber economy. At the time, political debate about these issues centered on the protection of the northern spotted owl (even though it is only one of the many animal and fish species threatened by the clearcutting of old-growth forests). It is this owl that increasingly got a bad press in *Twin Peaks* since Bob, the mystery killer entity, seems to be associated with the owls in some way, and since, according to Laura Palmer's diary (the commercially available version), Laura's own psychosexual history was haunted by attacks by owls, imaginary or otherwise. In light of the current ecological challenge to the timber industry, it is hardly surprising that *Twin Peaks* takes place in a lumber town where the surrounding environment is depicted as harboring threatening, evil forces, likely aliens, for whom the owls may indeed be serving as telepathic communicants, perhaps even the Log Lady's log as well. The owls, we are repeatedly told, 'are not what they seem,' and may in fact turn out to be benign agents in the narrative. Nonetheless, the *mise en scène* is one in which natural environment, as in Lynch's work generally, is seen as hostile and complicit with other threats to human life in a small town. This is evocatively suggested by the shots slung together by the opening credit sequence — the foreboding links there are between the images of the birds, and those of the brute facticity of industry and its pollution, the inexorable sharpening of the teeth in the sawmill, the small town besieged by the mist-shrouded mountains, the sublime violence of the waterfall, and the ominous undertows concealed in the river eddies, all reinforced by Badalamenti's theme music where the strings on top are a familiar referent from film melodrama and the bass melody is a sinister undertone.

In view of this demonizing of the environment, no sequence was more crucial in the show than the scene in the April 1990 pilot in which the sawmill is shut down for the day by its female owner Josie against protests by its female manager Catherine. Here we saw the spectacle of a labor conflict between two women who, it is significant, are the two people seemingly in charge of primary economic production. In this scene both women commit transgressive acts. Josie shuts down the mill, and Catherine gratuitously fires a worker — the first and only mill worker, as far as I am aware, to appear in the entire series (you wonder where all these workers are — it's a big mill in a small town, after all). Neither Josie nor Catherine will be forgiven for such transgressions. Alongside the firing — the first intimation that all of these workers will lose their jobs, after the mill is torched — the halt in production is the first public sign that there will be a crisis in the community. This crisis is generated by the death of a woman, Laura Palmer, and was publicized in the pilot by the transgressive acts of these two women. One did not need to be a feminist film theorist to recognize that these were very bad signs indeed, and did not augur well for the future of women in the series.

In the context of the ecology movement's 'threat' to the male workforce of the Northwest logging industry, it is perhaps no surprise to come across this story about a small town whose lumber economy is thrown into crisis by actions involving women, both alive and dead, and by mysterious environmental forces generated by owls and aliens. Toward the end of the series run, the environmental subtext became an overt focus of *Twin Peaks* life, when Benjamin Horne launched a campaign to save the pine weasel as part of his scheme to thwart Catherine's property development ambitions. Perhaps it is also fitting that it is Josie, an Asian woman, who has power over the economy, and who halts the mill, since the Northwest timber industry has recently been dependent on Asia as its prime export market since the 1970s. It is Josie's face, staring into a mirror as she applies her lipstick, that composes the very first shot in the pilot — a completely gratuitous shot but one that suggests an origin for many of the resulting crises in the show: femininity, foreignness, and dreamy narcissism (the latter being the mold for many of the other female characters in the show, especially Donna, the willful romantic, and Audrey, the village vixen). With a figure like Josie at the heart of so many of the show's determinants, small wonder that masculine revenge in the show would be slow but sure, and perhaps only fully apparent after the fact, rather like Hegel's Owl of Minerva which spreads its wings only at dusk.

How To Occupy Your Own Country

My last example of images of ecology brings us back to the toxic landscapes of the militarized zones. Far from the scarred deserts and cities of the Persian Gulf, the US military is facing its domestic irresponsibilities in its own backyard: those vast Western states that have served for over four decades as testing grounds for the Cold War's nuclear armada. With large sectors of the war budget hastily being converted into a makeshift decontamination operation, the full extent of the devastation caused by the Pentagon in the Western deserts is slowly coming into view. The race to dispose of the military's toxic wastes and its geriatric arsenal of death may well trigger a new round of contamination that will make the above-ground testing of the 1950s and 1960s seem like child's play. Over the last decade, artists and photographers have played a significant role in surveying the geography of contamination. The rich cultural history of images of the Western landscapes has provided a highly resonant backdrop for commentary on the new toxic wastelands of Homo Pentagonicus. Modern classics already include *Nuclear Landscapes*, Peter Goin's numbingly mundane photographs of sites in the West and the Pacific ('I am actually photographing something invisible: radiation'); *America Ground Zero*, Carole Gallagher's documentary portraits of Downwinder civilians and servicemen; and Richard Misrach's *Desert Cantos* series.[26] Images of ecology from this region present a precarious lesson in the aesthetics of ugliness.

Early in the decade, eco-artists Helen and Newton Harrison outlined a plan to protect a canyon corridor that runs between the slopes of San Diego County's landfills. Their proposal involved massive earth sculpting and hill creation, and, in the case of some sprawling, adjacent acreage of garbage fill, it also entailed the alteration of perimeter drainage channels to outline on the ground some familiar species shapes — a bird, a snake, and a tortoise — so

191

large that they would be visible from satellites. The most likely spectators, however, were the Top Gun pilots who bend the air above the neighboring Miramar Naval Air Station and whose flight path lies over these lands. The Navy, uninterested in the ecological message being directed skyward, is more concerned about the safety of their aircraft, supposedly endangered by stray civilian pilots eager to view the big earth animals. Since the Navy actually owns all of the landfill areas, they stipulated the removal of the beaks, heads, and tails from this wry menagerie in order to render the animals indistinct from the air.

As always, the Harrisons' project was a smart, critical, and playful solution to a set of environmental problems. In this instance, it also underscored the problems that civilians face these days simply in communicating with the military. Taking the people's case to the elected powers is arduous enough, but nothing compares to the inaccessibility and unaccountability enjoyed by the US armed services at the very heart of this country's vaunted democratic system. Indeed, the military's fabled capacity to procure congressional funding, increasingly for the task of decontamination, will survive the end of the Cold War during which it assumed immunity before the environmental laws. If the public ever does regain portions of the military's vast land holdings, then the much-heralded peace dividend will be dwarfed by the cost of decontaminating these environmental disaster zones.

To move inland from the Harrisons' coastal bioregion to the Great Basin of Nevada and Utah is to enter what is essentially occupied territory, divided among the fiefdoms of the Air Force, the Navy, and the Army. Once American Indian territory, then occupied by white settlers, great swathes of these lands have long been systematically 'withdrawn' from public use and reoccupied by the military's extensive network of bases, shooting ranges, nuclear test sites, bioweapons labs, and training camps.

Historically a proving ground for the heroism of red and white souls, this region has served as a test site for every form of weapon, chemical, or aggressive substance known to Homo Pentagonicus. For indigenous people of the region, it has been one more round of atrocities against their bodies and their cultural and religious contract with these lands; the contested land of the Newe (Western Shoshone) Nation has been home since the late 1940s to the long-used atomic range of the Nevada Test Site, making Newe Segobia, in Ward Churchill's words, 'the most bombed country in the world.'[27] As for the white citizenry, renowned for their libertarian spirit, they too have found themselves living in a state of siege ever since the National Emergency War Powers Act of 1944 opened up the West to the second great land-grab in little under a century, much of it appropriated during the 1980s when Ronald Reagan treated the military to the ultimate free lunch. It is airspace, however, that has been most thoroughly commandeered. While half of the airspace in the continental USA is reserved for military use, the percentage in the West is much greater, and of all the Western states, Nevada boasts the highest level of military occupation and has paid the highest price in terms of poisoning the earth.

Richard Misrach's photographs in *Bravo 20: The Bombing of the American West* document one such site near Fallon, Nevada.[28] In a 45-page introductory text, Myriam Weisang Misrach tells the story of how a coalition of Nevadans (including MAMA, or Mothers Against Military Arrogance) resisted the military over a chunk of land that had been a sacred site for the Northern Paiute Indians and had been illegally appropriated by the US Navy for use as a bombing range in the postwar period. The tripartite book project ends with Richard Misrach's proposal to turn the 64-square-mile bombing range into a national park – the 'nation's first environmental memorial' – when, in the year 2001, Congress has the option to end the Navy's use of the site and return the land to the public domain. The proposed park will convey several macabre themes through its exhibits: the local history of the Navy's high-handed, illegal activities; its sordid environmental record (the military is habitually commissioned to do its own environmental impact studies before its requests for withdrawals are approved by Congress); and its violations of civilians' rights. In addition, more general exhibits regarding nuclear contamination, toxic waste disposal, chemical weapons storage, and the history of radioactive experimentation on US troops and indigenous peoples such as the Marshall Islanders are proposed. Along with a film and video archive, a library, and a conference facility, the park's gift store will purvey a range of equally gruesome artifacts: maps of radioactive landfills, military land, and airspace; topographical trajectories of nuclear clouds; and transportation routes of nuclear materials, alongside Mattel-like models for the kids, based on the very latest, top-secret military designs. Instead of Ansel Adams prints, the fine arts section of the gift shop will be devoted to picture posters of bombing ranges.

This latter aspect will undoubtedly alert art critics of *Bravo 20* to what is 'problematic,' as they say, about a project like Misrach's. Critics like Deborah Bright have long challenged the logophobia of landscape photographers such as Misrach who draw upon the New Topographics doctrine of naive formalism in their approach to subjects.[29] However divorced from the aestheticist tradition of Ansel Adams, Edward Weston, Eliot Porter, and Minor White, the New Topographics school (identified as such in a 1975 show curated by William Jenkins which included the works of Robert Adams, Lewis Baltz, the Bechers, Joe Deal, Frank Gohike, Nicholas Nixon, John Schott, Stephen Shore, and Henry Wessel, Jr.) is associated with photographic studies that are equally stripped of any textual commentary that would expand their social meaning. The intention is to eschew any preemptive ideological or aesthetic positioning on the part of the artist. The medium is a style-neutral image with an 'objective' caption (place, date, taxonomy of the subject), and the effect is a reading that is quarantined off from any explanatory social text about the landscapes. 'Art,' the ever endangered species, is thereby saved from its documentary fate as a mere information medium.

How does *Bravo 20* face up to critiques of this aesthetic? Given the balkanization of the book into three parts — 'The Story,' 'The Photographs,' and 'Bravo 20 National Park: A Proposal' — the obvious answer is that Misrach tries to have his cake and eat it too. The art, in this case, is prophylactically sandwiched between two textual sections that nonetheless provide an extensive social context. One moment that cuts across this textual division of labor, only to reaffirm it in the end, occurs in Misrach's prefatory description of his first encounter with the bombing range. Struck by what would otherwise have been a 'classic beauty' of a desert landscape — 'the sky, the colors, the atmosphere, were cool and brilliant' (*B*, p. xiv) — Misrach is confronted with the traditionally heroic test of the artist's ability to make beautiful art out of an aesthetically devastated subject:

> It was also the most graphically ravaged environment I had ever seen. I found myself at the epicenter, the heart of the apocalypse. Alone, no sounds, no movement. No buildings, no roads. No indication of life, no

promise of civilization. Only the smell of rusted metal. Bombs and lifeless holes. Side by side were great beauty and great horror. (*B*, p.xiv)

Although we are not in the presence of gorges, sunsets, forests, cliffs, and desert valleys, anyone familiar with the history of Western landscape studies will recognize the presence of that tradition's sublime vision in Misrach's description, with its characteristic summoning up of fear and awe in the beholder. Similarly, it is difficult to see Misrach's photographs of Bravo 20 and disregard the legacy of religiosity that suffuses all such views of the desert West.

On the other hand, the bombs, burned-out targets, craters, abandoned tank treads and convoys that litter the landscape belong to a genre of war photography that has no traditional place in the North American West, where the battlefields of the Indian wars have a decidedly preindustrial resonance. Indeed, with the exception of Matthew Brady's Civil War shots of ruined cities like Charleston, modern images of North American terrain ravaged by war scarcely exist; their surrogate is the genre of environmental atrocity, or the bombed-out landscapes of inner cities, or weather-induced disasters. And while for the purposes of his national park proposal Misrach presents Bravo 20 as 'a contemporary version of a Civil War battleground' (*B*, p.95), these photographs are more likely to remind readers of the Iraqi 'highway of death' in Kuwait than the aftermath of Bull Run.[30] The bombs that sprout at surreal angles from Misrach's desert floor like lone, leaping porpoises at sea are the same bombs that fell in Korea, Southeast Asia, Lebanon, Grenada, and the Persian Gulf. So, too, Bravo 20's burned-out targets, like the iconic yellow school bus, are metonyms for the civilian victims of US bombs the world over. Of course, there are no human figures in these pictures, and so readers have a broad set of interpretive choices to make. Do the photographs align themselves with the conventionally unoccupied spaces of the Western landscape genre? Or do they remind us more of the capacity of military press censors to suppress images of the victims of war? Does the spectacle of displaced debris violate that sense of national wilderness morality which solemnly preaches the 'necessity of uninhabited places'? Or does the air of abandonment in these depopulated moonscapes speak more to the emergent reality of the fully automated battlefield?

If we take our cue from Myriam Weisang Misrach's exhaustive account of the contested history of the site, we might expect to place

Bravo 20 within the subgenre of the photography of occupation, perhaps even the photography of resistance. Strictly speaking, what we have here is the photography of ceasefire, however, since the photographs were shot during a sixteen-month legal stay of bombing won by the activist coalition. In any case, there is no ostensible human activity on the ground, and the photographer's point of view is that of an isolated visitor to an isolated spot where, in the absence of humans, some kind of war is being waged against the environment. The war victim is quite literally the desert, while the frame of landscape photography functions as the aesthetically violated medium for telling a story about ecocide. No one needs to know what the targets are standing in for, or to speculate about the variety of battlefield conditions that might require such a training in aerial bombardment. All we need to recognize (and question) is the impunity with which these and other areas of desert land are chosen to be systematically pounded, despoiled, and contaminated, simply because desert lands (and their low-density populations) are considered 'expendable.' Who gives permission for this? One limited response points to the nexus of interests that binds the Department of Defense, the Bureau of Land Management, the Environmental Protection Agency, and a clutch of congressmen in the pockets of the Joint Chiefs of Staff. But the source of cultural authority lies elsewhere, deeply inscribed in a long history of social values that can sanction such aggression towards the natural environment. On the one hand, Misrach's photographs confront these values with a scientific rather than dogmatic disrespect: he is collecting evidence from the scene of a crime. On the other hand, the photographs cautiously engage the symbolic power of the Western landscape genre: acts of violence against nature are thereby accorded the status of un-American activities. In either case the jury is the mythical 'American people' (red, white, brown, yellow, and black) in whose name the mythical Western landscape is inalienably pledged.

For all their evocative power, Misrach's photographs in themselves bear no particular reminder that the book project as a whole intends to indict certain institutions. In fact it is elsewhere, in the book's textual sections, that the scariest images can be found: two US Navy photographs obtained under the Freedom of Information Act and reproduced in all of their grainy, black-and-white facticity (in contrast to Misrach's luminescent color plates). The first is a large-scale aerial view of the bombing range with two minuscule protesters in the middle foreground; one can only imagine how many times these and other activists served as dummy targets in the gunsights of the hotdogging pilots. The second is a surveillance photograph taken in mid-flight from the aircraft of Dick Holmes, an elderly TV repairman who was one of the leading Bravo 20 activists. Well known as a cautious pilot, Holmes died along with his seasoned co-pilot when in 1987 their plane inexplicably crashed during perfect flying conditions in the desert not far from the Fallon Naval Air Station.

These documentary photographs support the more sinister story told by Myriam Weisang Misrach about the power, technology, and political influence directed by the military against its own citizenry. Her conclusion is a Capra-esque complaint about the rapid growth of the military's institutional autonomy in the Cold War period:

> The events at Bravo 20 bring to light an alarming attitude that permeates the military — the 'us against them' syndrome, to put it in the most basic terms. Somewhere between the intrepid GI's storming the beaches of Normandy and the hot-dog pilots buzzing schoolchildren in rural America, something has gone awry. Today the military world is almost completely cut off from the civilian. It has become out of touch, suspicious of outsiders, and it shows ... Whatever the logic behind it may be, today's military is acting as though training done in the name of national security overrides both human rights and the laws of the United States. That has to stop. National security does not entail buzzing schoolbuses filled with schoolchildren, scaring ranchers half to death, dumping fuel in wildlife refuges, or bombing historic vestiges. It does not place the military above the nation's environmental legislation, nor does it excuse toxic pollution and radiation contamination. The defense of this country does not warrant using rural residents as guinea pigs or forcing them out of their homes (or forcing them but refusing to pay adequate compensation). No one should be subjected to 100 sonic booms a day. The end does not justify the means. (B, p.47)

The tone, rhetoric, and address in this passage are manifestly those of the concerned, mainstream citizen. The Misrachs' intent is not to expose the logic that lies behind these activities any more than it is to disperse the smokescreen for economic and political interests maintained in the name of 'national security.' Their purpose, rather, is to capture the credible faith of the small-time homesteader who believes in the 'dream of America' and its laws, who holds out for the promise of a 'good' army, and who might think of a reclaimed Bravo 20 'as a shining symbol for democracy, as it was once intended, burning bright and lighting up the way' (*B*, p.48).

To represent the credible citizens' complaint, it is necessary at times to distinguish the Bravo 20 project from other, more radical responses. At the end of the book, for example, Misrach makes a point of describing the project as one of 'monkey reclamation,' as opposed to Earth First!'s 'monkey wrenching,' which, he argues, many consider to be 'an inappropriate way to regain our beleaguered landscapes' (*B*, p.98). Earlier on, it is pointed out that the camp-in staged by the coalition of Concerned Rural Nevadans (CRN) was an action 'more commonly associated with 1960s radicals than with conservative law abiding Nevadans.' Even so, this perception hardly protected the CRN activists from the wrath of local pro-Navy groups who torched the camp (*B*, p.33).

Above all, it is the proposal to convert Bravo 20 into a national park that resonates most with the appearance of mainstream, reformist credentials. In this respect, there are many famous precedents for the association of an influential body of photography with a government decision to set aside lands for a national park: Carleton Watkins' photographs of Yosemite, Ansel Adams at King's Canyon, William Henry Jackson at Yellowstone, even Robert Ketchum's work at the Tongass, Alaska's rainforest. But Yellowstone is one thing; an antimilitarist, eco-dystopian national park with a walking tour called 'Boardwalk of the Bombs' and a driving tour called 'Devastation Drive' is another. Despite Misrach's very careful attempts to rationalize the history, location, budget, and theme, it is difficult not to wince at the thought of the US Congress debating this plan.

It is equally difficult to imagine visitors incorporating Bravo 20 into the tourist circuit of the West which includes the likes of Yosemite, King's Canyon, Lake Mead, the Grand Canyon, Grand Teton, Yellowstone, and the great national parks of Utah. But that is not to say that the Nevada park, if established, will be neglected. It has long been known that tourists will visit anything, short of their own homes, provided some sufficiently diverting spectacle is offered to them. Indeed, there are genres of tourism that cover almost every kind of restorative experience, physical, emotional, and intellectual. For the arch or ironic postmodern tourist, for example, affirmation comes in the kind of tour that delights in the inauthenticity of kitsch,

THE ECOLOGY OF IMAGES

middlebrow, and *folie de grandeur*, and which heartily eschews the sacred monument for the profane mall. So, too, trips to sites of ecological catastrophe (the burning Kuwaiti oil wells, Prince William Sound, Love Canal) have been added to the tourist itinerary of the morbid, who habitually visit places where people have died, often in great numbers. This latter genre still lingers in the realm of bad taste but could play host in the near future to an emergent genre devoted to the education, rather than the exploitation, of sentiment. Since it stands little chance of courting participants in the more orthodox eco-tourist industry, presently concentrated in remote and 'pristine' destination areas, this perhaps is the tourist genre that Bravo 20 anticipates. Pioneer destinations in this genre already include the Trinity Site, a national historic landmark near White Sands, New Mexico, where the first nuclear device was exploded. Indeed, when the Nevada Test Site opened in the 1950s, the Las Vegas Chamber of Commerce provided advice to tourists on the best locations for viewing a nuclear blast.[31] Perhaps soon the Bikini and Enewetok atolls will be added to the South Pacific tourist circuit.

Although the motives of Bravo 20's likely tourist visitors would not be so far removed from those that helped to consecrate Wounded Knee or even the *USS Arizona* as sightseer locations, the mantle of political acceptability will not grace this site quite so easily. The reasons owe less to the undoubted resistance mobilized by the Pentagon than to the currently undeveloped public recognition of environmentalism as a product of social, as much as of natural, history. The recent inclusion of wetlands and urban recreation areas under the criteria for the creation of state and national parks is hardly at odds with the official parks doctrine of conservation. These areas are easily preserved because they are held to lie outside the realm of social memory. A monument to the environmental aggression of military, government, and corporate institutions invokes a different order of memory, more akin, as Misrach acknowledges, to the Vietnam Memorial and yet arguably more radical if its version of naming names includes the institutional aggressors as well as their victims, human or otherwise. All the same, in the absence of a central commodity spectacle like a visible disaster or a statistically impressive massacre, the Bravo 20 proposal risks being viewed more as an example of conceptual art than as a 'national acknowledgement of a complex and disturbing period in our history' (*B*, p.95). This would be unfortunate, since it promises to be an entirely novel way of presenting an environmental critique: rather than celebrate the preservation of an environment, Bravo 20 would be a park whose purpose is to preserve a record of environmental destruction.

The political integrity of the Bravo 20 National Park proposal lies above all in its tributes to the coalition of Nevadans (city dwellers and rural homesteaders, alongside reservation Shoshone, Paiute, and Washo) who organized and took action to reclaim the land in ways similar to the activist campaigns and legal battles against the Pentagon that have been won by the Downwinder coalition in the Salt Lake City region. It is unlikely, however, that this particular appeal will be decisive in any official debate about the implementation of the proposal. Misrach's best shot probably lies in the more pragmatic appeal to economics in the post-Cold War period. Since the park would be designed for limited access, Bravo 20 would not require site decontamination to the tune of $324 million as estimated by the Navy. Over the years, it has been bombarded with everything from air-to-ground rockets to 2,000 lb bombs, while the plague of toxic materials carried by the bombs — napalm, phosphorus, cadmium, technetium — has spread well beyond the site of Bravo 20 into the Carson Sink and adjacent lands that include two wilderness refuges and some major waterfowl flyways.

If Bravo 20 National Park ever gets official approval, it may be because it offers a bizarre solution to the massive task of environmental cleanups faced by the US military. Pragmatism has long been a dirty word in the mouths of ecologists. Far from posing solutions, the history of environmentalism has shown pragmatism to be part of the problem; but there is no iron law to disqualify its candidacy as a friend of the earth, and Misrach's proposal does a good job of petitioning the powers that be to wear the shoe that fits. Yet the ultimate stakes of this decision lie in some improbable future to which the past is an equally improbable prologue. I am speaking of a day when the ritual activities of US military culture will be viewed with the same kind of camp affect (but with less nostalgia) generated out of historical redundancy that has come to irradiate memories of the Red Army's place in the former Soviet Union and its dominions. It is perhaps impossible for us to imagine that Bravo 20 could ever be an official showcase for both patriotic *and* antimilitarist values, however safely relegated to history. But why not imagine that it could tell stories that would be a cultural counterpart to the Paiute Indian stories about Lone Rock, the 160-foot volcanic plug that forms the focal point of the bombing range? In Paiute mythology, Lone Rock is the Wolf's Head, the decapitated vestige of an epic battle between the people and the Wolf, and henceforth a ceremonial place sanctioned by the Paiute victory over the predator. Ever since the end of the Cold War, the Pentagon has been finding it less easy to keep the wolf inside the door. Would that the task of decontamination were as simple and pleasurable as decapitation.

4

Wet, Dark, and Low, Eco-Man
Evolves From Eco-Woman

Does anyone really want to listen to stories about the victimization of men? This was one of the questions coursing through the culture at large in the early 1990s. The ostensible topic may well have been the mid-life crisis of the white male boomer, whose generational experience seems to have become the dominant media narrative of North American culture. But the underlying conditions may have just as much to do with the mid-life crises of the women's movement and the ecology movement, all too apparent in the emergence of fundamentalist strains of eco-feminism, whose Earth Goddess is now being courted by its male consort, the Green Man, or the Wild Man of the media-struck 'men's movement.'

Lampooned from its first stirrings (the publication of a Robert Bly spoof entitled 'Fire in the John: The Manly Man in the Age of Sissification' was a typical example) the men's movement did a morphing job on the social contours of masculinity — one moment softening, the next hardening the outline in its bid for men to be kings without being tyrants, warriors without being killers. Whatever its enduring effect, the movement helped to confer legitimacy upon a new public style of masculinity, evident even in the White House. Two years after the first heady sighting of well-heeled, white men in mid-life, trekking off in semi-tribal formation to sweat lodges, vision quests, and recovery weekends, the USA had elected a president whose public mode of presentation was frequently organized around the kind of emotional empathy — 'I feel your pain' went the immortal *Saturday Night Live* spoof — that was a requisite part of the masculine profile urged upon middle-aged corporate man by the men's movement. No one really doubted Bill Clinton's emotional sincerity; rather they worried when his own 'feelings' appeared to be the chief fulcrum of his decision-making about matters of state. To have a president who felt for everyone was a questionable improvement over his two predecessors who had selectively practised upwardly mobile empathy. His commitment to jogging was more sincere than that of Bush or Carter, and much more earnest than Reagan's log-chopping on the ranch, but folks worried when his unwillingness to alienate the powerful resulted in a lack of commitment to policymaking or anything else for that matter (after all, this was the man who 'did not inhale,' although the respiratory complaint that prevented this indulgence did not stand in the way, allegedly, of his student-era taste for hash brownies).

As it happened, Clinton's presidency was fundamentally marked from the outset by questions about 'what kind of man' he was; questions fuelled by his own youthful renunciation of military service, by his professed support for gays in the military, and by the assertively visible role in affairs of state claimed by Hillary Rodham Clinton. Some of this concern about the exact tailoring of Clinton's masculinity was a result of generational style; some of it was determined by a shift in the identity of the corporate state. Unlike the wimpy patrician George Herbert Walker Bush, Clinton didn't feel obliged to go to war to prove that he could kick ass. So, too, Clinton's indeterminate style was tied in some representative way to confusion about the redefinition of the national security state in the messy aftermath of the Cold War. But the spectacle of a president who would produce tears at press conferences owed just as much to the confluence of subterranean cultural currents that would allow a man so fully in the public eye to adopt such a high emotional demeanor. Surely this had something to do with the cultural impact of over two decades of feminism, and with the more limited but significant cultural acceptance of gay redefinitions of masculinity. The realignment of style was significant although nowhere near as powerful and policy bound, say, as Theodore Roosevelt's muscular Bull Moose crusade had been when it set the public standard for rugged male endeavor before World War I. By contrast, Al Gore had to have his pulse regularly checked for signs of life. Looking for all the world like Data, the android from *Star Trek: The Next Generation*, his lack of affect had helped inspire George Bush to caricature him as 'the ozone man,' a moniker that partially captured the passionless spirit of the technocrat environmentalist that haunted Gore. Gore was not a deep forest type. In fact, the men's movement was more likely to honor the spirit of Ollie North, a wild-eyed privateer who publicized the pain of his commitments, than that of a wussy Beltway penpusher like Gore, who would eventually find his niche online as the Virtual VP.

The chapter that follows speculates about some of the circumstances that identify the moment of the men's movement. As is often the case, the most symptomatic place to begin is with the summer movies, and, in particular, the two boys' movies that played in theaters during the emergence of the movement in 1991 — *Robin Hood* and *Boyz N the Hood*.

Lincoln Green

Perhaps it was too much to expect a truly 'green' Robin Hood, his Merrie Men in bioregional sync with Sherwood Forest. But Kevin Costner had been well groomed as Hollywood's ambassador of nationalist myths of environmental romanticism. Hamming his way from one pastoral field of dreams to another, he had survived Madonna's most public put-down in *Truth or Dare* and had graduated to the big league of environmental hype with his production of *Dances with Wolves*. His film rhapsodized the subsistence contract between tribe and herd on the buffalo-busy plains (subsequently catalyzing public interest in a vast wildlife sanctuary proposal for a Buffalo Commons that would restore the the Great Plains to the bison),[1] while its friendliness to the Lakota Sioux stroked Hollywood's conscience about its appalling record on Native American docudrama. Most of all, Costner's persona was perfectly tailored to the cut of modern liberal masculinity, harmlessly heroic in spite of its best testosterone-induced intentions. With a little heat, however, this new breed is reduced to old-school Hollywood stock: the white man, now with clean hands and dirty laundry, and the red man, with humor this time, not to mention native authenticity, mouthing, 'We, who are about to die, salute you.'

Environmental kitsch plays a co-starring role in all of this, for the film proved that the untilled plains remain a pivotal location for stories about the national identity of North America's postcolonial societies. The appearance of the unfenced plains always records the last moment of the indigenous hunter-gatherer economy before the new Euro-American ecological revolution engenders stories centered on the white settler's ranch and farm. The transformation of the 'wilderness,' which was once so crucial to Euro-American expansionist destiny in the West, has, in the course of this century, become the very antithesis of white national identity, now so ideologically dependent upon the conservation of that same wilderness, whether on celluloid, on the Native American reservation, or in the strictly policed territories of the national parks.

When Costner donned the Lincoln green and planted himself in Sherwood Forest, Hollywood used his transnational celebrity value to energize another country's mythic geography, similarly laden with historical and ecological symbolism. The history of the loss, and subsequently, the desperate try at preservation, of England's forests occupies a somewhat different place in the national ecological romances from the US example of the Great Plains. In England, the forest is the leafy location of all that has been resistant to the laws and decrees of the official political and religious powers: the outlawed home, respectively, of the pagan spirit traditions feared by the Church's legislators, of masterless men feared by their would-be landed masters, of lost arcadian sentiment feared by Victorian industrialists, and, most recently, of nondeveloped nature feared by would-be developers. Not that these two locations, the ecological and the ideological, are easily separable. The profitable clearing of forests, for example, had long been sanctioned by Christian theology in the name of its holy war against the 'sacred groves' of pagan worship. So, too, in the twelfth- and thirteenth-century England of Robin Hood, early capitalist modes of production in the metal industry had combined with rapid increases in population to reduce drastically the extensive woodland ecosystem, hitherto the preserve of the king and the nobility, now given over to arable land reclamation.[2] The result was a terrain that hosted economic and cultural forces in sharp conflict with each other: the domain of the king's laws of the vert and the monasteries' privileges, each suppressing the peasantry's demand to supplement its subsistence farming with hunting; the site of industrial exploitation of natural resources, contested by the old organic religion's interdiction against such practises as profane; and the location of the gentry's nightmares about social banditry in an unregulated territory, matched by the countercultural fantasy of a sylvan homeland for freed serfs. No wonder that the medieval tales about Sherwood Forest came to provide such an enduring myth for the national culture, or that the Robin Hood ethic of redistributing wealth would come to exert such international significance as a political allegory (the high, or low, point was the banning of Robin Hood stories from US public libraries in the heyday of McCarthyism).

Such historical meanings may seem remote from a contemporary audience's response to the Costner vehicle of 1991, but they are hardly irrelevant to the cumulative associations of the Robin Hood figure as it has survived through centuries of different media: the medieval ballads, the saturnalian rituals of the May Games, mummers plays, Renaissance printed broadsides and garlands, the historical romance, the Victorian penny weekly, and the Hollywood blockbuster. Never a static legend, not even in medieval minstrelsy, it is only in the most recent Hollywood phase that the picture of Robin as a self-outlawed aristocrat has become an established convention, although even this suggestion, which runs against the grain of the plebeian legend, goes back to the Scottish chroniclers of the mid-fifteenth century, and was influentially revived by the most Jacobin of the tale's editors, Joseph Ritson, in the wake of the French Revolution. That aristocratic profile was at last fully incorporated into popular consciousness in Michael Curtiz's lavishly produced 1938 film, where Errol Flynn's noble Robin is posed as a self-outlawed Saxon freedom fighter resisting the Norman yoke. The 1991 version preserved the aristocratic convention and added an actual Middle Eastern location to the Crusader story, which may say just as much about US foreign policy in the 1990s as the Curtiz film's Saxon patriotism said about antifascist sympathies in Hollywood's Popular Front years.

Kevin Reynolds' film missed a golden opportunity to 'green' Costner further; it barely dwells on the eco-communal yeoman order of the Merrie Men, and it deals the pagan hand to the townsman villain, Alan Rickman's deliciously sadistic Sheriff of Nottingham, whose actions are enthusiastically guided by a haggish prophetess. Instead, the film explains Robin's motives with a plot involving baronial treachery against his patriot father and the subsequent dispossession of the son's patrimonial inheritance. Robin fights, then, in the name of an absent father, as part of an initiation rite to reclaim his noble title rather than to liberate the

Saxon masses. The rottenness of the state produces his 'dysfunctional' family, and Robin takes to male company in the wilderness (including a Moor substitute father) in order to regain his legitimate place in society.

In this respect, the film's filial adventure story can be set alongside a different kind of summer movie playing in 1991, John Singleton's *Boyz N the Hood*, a black, urban version of filial initiation. Where white Hollywood renditions of this patriarchal narrative rework mythical figures from comics or superhero history — the urban Batman or the rural Robin Hood — African-American versions from the new black film renaissance, with the exception of Robert Townsend spoofs, have drawn upon a contemporary realist, usually inner-city, setting.[3] Just as *Batman* had played against *Do the Right Thing* in theaters all through the summer of 1989, a mythical Anglo-Saxon outlaw proved Hollywood's match for the young black gangstas who were the focus of the year's spate of black-directed films, from *New Jack City* to *Boyz N the Hood*. Singleton's film was an earnest attempt to address the issue of paternal abandonment that underpins so much of the reality and the discourse about male youth in black America. The ''hood' is a South-Central Los Angeles neighborhood which is boobytrapped everywhere by the corporate police state for the 'self-destruction' of its inhabitants — gun shops and liquor stores on every street corner, the omnipresence of searchlights from LAPD helicopters constantly circling overhead, army recruiters soaking up young surplus labor, and real-estate developers forcing rents up through the downward spiral of neighborhood impoverishment. The film is a story about an experiment in the social ecology of this kind of late twentieth-century urban environment. The son in question, Tre Styles, is delivered by his buppie mother into the care of her estranged but politically savvy husband to do a proper father's job of saving him from the gangsta life on the street. To set up this experiment — which meets with mixed results — the film accepts the standard bromide that responsibility for the dysfunctional black family lies with its flawed matriarchal structure. Consequently, a strong, nurturing father — son relationship is posed as the only shield against a wayward life; the mother is generally written off, and the environment of the 'hood is presented as naturally Hobbesian.

In both *Robin Hood* and *Boyz N the Hood*, the sons survive their initiation adventures through the mediations, respectively, of an absent father and a present father. What the films share is the exclusion of mothers, mythically erased in *Robin Hood*, sociologically expunged in *Boyz*. As such, these films are welcome fuel for Hollywood's obsessive endeavor to find workable narratives of patriarchy for its filial protagonists, extended, in the case of the new black cinema, to embrace narrative 'solutions' for the black family.[4] Let's not forget that the summer's megahit film, *Terminator 2*, whose hardbody Sarah Connor (played by Linda Hamilton) responded to the longstanding feminist demand for nongendered dramatic roles, would also showcase the initial stage of Arnold Schwarzenegger's transformation from mean cyborg motherfucker to ideal father/just warrior. The erstwhile Terminator shared his metamorphosis with the leading men of the summer's cluster of male conversion movies, *Regarding Henry*, *The Doctor*, and *City Slickers*, all focusing on the traumas of male mid-life crisis. Three summers later, in Mike Nichols' *Wolf*, Jack Nicholson showed how easily this genre had incorporated the Wild Man of the men's movement.

Hairy Green

The loudest proclamations of male mid-life crisis and anxieties about filial initiation in the early 1990s were to be found untrammeled in the men's movement, a hybrid outcropping of the exploratory culture of personal growth, New Age psychology, and the social ritual of the recovery program. A number of different branches have emerged from the movement's ostensibly single trunk. Christopher Harding, editor of a central magazine, *Wingspan*, isolates four: (a) the mythopoetic branch, exploring male spirituality and mostly Jungian male psychology; (b) a pro-feminist, gay-affirmative branch, committed to political change; (c) a men's rights or fathers' rights branch, focused on specific family laws detrimental to men; and (d) addiction/recovery groups, in search of the 'inner child.'[5] In the public eye, the movement was primarily associated with the bestseller middlebrow literature of Robert Bly (*Iron John*), Sam Keen (*Fire in the Belly*), John Lee (*The Flying Boy*), Robert Moore and Douglas Gillette (*King Warrior Magician Lover*), the writings and teachings of James Hillman, Shepherd Bliss and Michael Meade, and with the men's seminars, support groups, Wild Man rustic gatherings, and New Warrior training adventure weekends — replete with drum rituals, talking staff councils, medicine wheels and sweat lodges — which became the movement's experiential workshops.[6] Men's support groups and councils had existed for over a decade in many cities before Bly's media prominence brought a new level of visibility to the phenomenon.

Subscribing to the belief that all men share a deep, atavistic masculinity that must be plumbed in order to heal the wounds of an upbringing at the hands of overwhelming mothers and distant or absent fathers, advocates of the long view of this new male emotion therapy present it as a response to a social crisis of masculinity evolving in the West since the Industrial Revolution. The short view is more directly responsive to feminist perspectives. Dismissive of the ruthless, exploitative codes of dominant, competitive masculinity, these men — heterosexual, white, middle-class professionals for the most part — are also seeking an assertive alternative to the softer or 'feminine' personality types favored by sensitive men over the last two decades' responsiveness to the women's movement. The goal is to restore honor and respect to the denigrated name of masculinity. The vehicle is inner work rather than collectively motivated reform of social structures.

A number of common themes sound throughout the literature: the pathology of the modern family has produced a 'father-hunger' in men; the lessons of the women's movement have all been absorbed, and need to be transcended, rather than answered, in the pursuit of authentic, deep masculinity; modern corporate life is only the latest industrial organization of labor that has increasingly distanced fathers from their sons; the work of healing involves initiatory and mentoring relationships with older father figures, and a studied immersion in men's perennial philosophy of fairy tales, myths, and pre-Christian rituals in search of the Great Father archetype.

If this is a social movement on the part of men-in-crisis, then it is not exactly one with a radical lineage or with ends that resonate with anything like familiar radical aims. Fifteen years ago, pro-feminist men's groups sprang up in most cities in North America and Britain in response to the ideas and practises of the women's movement. Groups like Men Against Sexism and Men's Libe-ration flourished in uneasy alliance with feminists and with gay and lesbian liberationists (the response from women and gays ranged from damning with faint praise, to fearing cooptation, to outright condemning of homophobia), generating a steady flow of critical literature which constitutes a significant addition to the body of work produced in women's studies and gay and lesbian studies.[7]

Nowhere in the literature of or about the men's movement is there any mention of these earlier activities or texts. One reason for this omission is that Bly and his fellow travelers are not engaged in a primarily pro-feminist project, and their concerns harbor even less of an appeal to sexual minorities. The broader reason for the lack of dialogue, however, lies in the difference of community. Popular or middlebrow psychology literature like Bly's *Iron John* is addressed to a 'general audience,' a publisher's fantasy that is often used to keep radical books out of the trade market. *Iron John* speaks primarily to men who are alienated from work, romance, family, mainstream politics, and in search of some 'truth' about themselves. Harry Brod has speculated that the ideas appeal in particular to professionals who have psychically disowned their own working-class family origins.[8] The anxieties and guilt of these upwardly mobile sons are the central commodity of the author-therapists who write the books and conduct the workshops. This audience is hardly concerned with responding to the shortcomings of masculinist left thought or to the criticisms of radical feminism; it is an audience that may have had little direct contact with the arguments and debates about masculinity that have engaged these other communities of intellectuals and activists. This is not to say, however, that the discussion about masculinity found in the pages of these new books is untouched by such arguments, or that the desire for a movement of this sort does not have something fundamentally to do with the more radical social, economic, and cultural criticism of the last twenty years. Indeed, at least one attempt has been made to 'politicize' the movement in Andrew Kimbrell's plans for a Men's Action Network which would coordinate the various groups nationwide in the name of a 'Male Manifesto,' a 'political agenda intended to re-establish [men's] ties with one another, their families, communities and the earth' and to resist the degradation of their gender by the 'patriarchal production system.'[9]

For the most part, it has been a cultural and not a social movement, and in this respect was fortunate to have an elderly poet at its visible center, especially one steeped in the ancient art of oral recitation. The oral performance, accompanied by acoustic instrument, is still publicly associated with bardic authenticity (witness MTV's 'Unplugged,' designed to revive the musical authority of ageing rockers like Eric Clapton, Neil Young, and Rod Stewart). Bly the showman has always been regarded as something of a snake oil salesman within the poetry community, or at best — with his cheesy, performative blend of Eastern mysticism, Jungian metaphysics, and folk storytelling soaked in perennial wisdom — as an ersatz version of the truly holy Ginsberg. Aside from his visibility as a peacenik during the Vietnam War years, he was once well known for his Great Mother seminars, an espousal of matriarchalism that underwent a flip reversal in the 1980s when a rapprochement with his father plunged him into a mythopoetic quest to reinstate the patriarch and devalue the matriarch. Having devoted a lifetime's attention to feminine and masculine archetypes, and having so brazenly switched his loyalties from the former to the latter, Bly nonetheless acknowledges that these abstract Jungian categories have little to do with gender itself: 'I've worked with poetry all my life, and I never thought about gender things really, in the intense way that's necessary if you're going to really think it through.'[10]

Bly's career as a poet with shamanic trappings lends philosophical authority to his position today as the paterfamilias of the emergent tribe of newly mature men. *Iron John*'s cultural homeland lies beyond the realm of commercial popular culture, which, Bly believes, ritually degrades men and systematically excludes representations of men prepared to accept the legitimate authority of what he calls 'positive leadership energy' for the sake of the community. Politically speaking, Bly positions himself beyond the twenty-year-old critiques offered by the women's movement, the radical wing of which 'in a justified fear of brutality,' he writes, 'has labored to breed fierceness out of men.'[11] *Iron John* rejects the model of 'soft' masculinity that evolved in response to feminism — that of the nondomineering, receptive, cooperative, supportive, nonaggressive man — just as it rejects the polarizing, red-meat alternative represented by John Wayne. Above all, the book attacks the whole premise of a 'youth culture' which serves, Bly claims, to defer boys' initiatory entry into adulthood. *Iron John* echoes with the revenge of patriarchy, and is quite open about the reprisal of the elders whose gerontocratic power over the young was challenged by the generational disrespect of the 1960s ('never trust anyone over 30'), and whose authority Bly seems most interested in reinstating. Saturated with what Philomena Mariani refers to as 'the bitterness of the patriarch,'[12] *Iron John* may be yet another book originating in some authorial trauma experienced in the course of that turbulent decade. Youths, Bly concludes, need to go to finishing school with older male initiators, not with their own peers. And grown men must give up trying to hold onto their youth. Thus, while his book takes the fairy tale of Iron John as a parable for its advocacy of youthful male initiation, the real winner in the tale is not so much the prince as the much older Wild Man, who is freed from captivity and restored to his social position as a powerful monarch.

In place of the bland, domesticated men of today — 'the sanitized, hairless, shallow man' of the Judeo-Christian corporate world — Bly invokes the pre-Greek myths of the Wild Man as the source of deep masculinity available to men who want to reclaim an energy that has been sapped by popular culture, feminism, and youth culture:

> When a contemporary man looks down into his psyche, he may, if conditions are right, find under the water of his soul, lying in an area no one has visited for a long time, an ancient hairy man . . . Welcoming the Hairy Man *is* scary and risky, and it requires a different sort of courage. Contact with Iron John requires a willingness to descend into the male psyche and accept what's dark down there, including the *nourishing* dark. (*IJ*, p.6)

But who knows where this auto(homo)-erotic look downward and this 'different sort of courage' will lead? While Bly is persuaded that the engagement with this repressed Hairy Man is a highly sexualized encounter, and while the fairy tale he relates about Iron John has a heterosexual-marital denouement, the outcome of this libidinal rendezvous is difficult to place in the world of actual sexual relations. My assumption is that the meeting with the Wild Man trades on the fantasy of a same-sex encounter that dare not speak its name. Too much of this stuff mimics standard, exotic gay male narratives and fantasy sexual types to pass itself off as hetero male bonding, no matter how deep or courageous.

If Bly is diffident about the question of sexuality, he is slightly more open about the racial lineage of this deep male atavism: the Iron John fairy tale which structures his book 'retains memories of initiation ceremonies for men that go back ten or twenty thousand years in northern Europe' (*IJ*, p. 55). This, however, has nothing to do with simple Aryan race worship. Bly is an effortless name-dropper in the realm of comparative religion and world mythology. The Wild Man, as it turns out, is universally present in

Mediterranean, African, Indian, Greek, Celtic, Siberian, Sumerian, Chinese, and Native American myths. If the same atavistic male sexual energy is represented in each culture, then there is no need to worry about cultural difference. By choosing to focus on the suppressed Wild Men of only one (Western) culture — Pan, Dionysus, Hermes — Bly may be stealing a march on the PC-bashers. The barbarians do not lie outside the Eurocentric tradition; they are *within* it, and, what's more, they are life-affirming. With friends like Iron John, the monoculturalist has no need for multiculturalist enemies.

As the men's movement carried over into 1992, the year of the Columbian quincentenary, it was appropriate to recall that the Wild Man of European myth has already had at least one bloody career in the New World. The accounts of indigenous life written by explorers and historians from the Columbian period and from the subsequent century of exploitation are heavily populated by types that divide the 'good' Indian, who resembled the Noble Savage, from the 'bad' Indian, who resembled the Wild Man of European medieval life (for Columbus, the operative distinction was between the 'gentle' Tainos and the 'warlike' Caribs). Portable features of the nature-fearing Wild Man legend provided much of the justification for the violent subjugation and near extermination of the native peoples of Mesoamerica and North America. Despite the protestations that ancient Nordic and Celtic peoples had had their share of drums, animal symbolism, and nature spirituality, any white American acting out the Wild Man role in 1992 was playing in full redface, complete with the offensive minstrelsy of loincloths, drums, war paint, sweat lodges, tribal masks, and hoarse-making New Warrior chants. Renouncing the secret Euro-American male rituals of fraternal orders like the Freemasons, the Kiwanis, Knights of Columbus, the Elks, and whatever it is that really goes on among the power elites at the Bohemian Grove, the New Warriors gave the spiritual huckstering of Amerindian culture its biggest boost since Sun Bear and Wallace Black Elk started reaping the New Age harvest in the 1970s.

While Bly has publicly distanced himself from some of the movement's more theatrical aspects, and while other movement leaders have taken pains to downplay his cult of personality, he is still recognized everywhere as a master-thinker behind such activities. Two other bestselling books in the movement attest to his influence in different ways. In contrast to the analytical temper of *Iron John*, Austin therapist John Lee's *The Flying Boy* is written as a confessional narrative, describing the progress of the author's exercise in self-healing achieved by following Bly's teachings.[13] It outlines the various stages of grieving and releasing anger through which an initial refugee from the world of men, who is unable to make commitments in his life, comes into his true, mature, masculine inheritance. Lee's story is especially revealing in its awestruck veneration of Bly himself, whose poetry he studies as a doctoral candidate for many years, and whose role as a father figure Lee uses to resolve problems with his own father. In the final analysis, this treatment of Bly may say more about the personality cult of the guru than it does about the general role of male initiators in the art of grieving.

While Sam Keen's *Fire in the Belly* does not owe quite the same debt to a master, it does share the tone of Bly's own middlebrow reverence for great artists, writers, 'deep' thinkers, and 'meaning' junkies, especially radical theologians who eat away at the paradoxical heart of religious experience. Anyone, moreover, who enthusiastically cites Norman O. Brown's opinion that 'the loins are the place of judgment' needs to be hit upside his head. In general, Keen is more attentive to the social and the economic contexts of the masculinity crisis than is Bly. His attacks on the theology of work, on the spiritual killing fields of corporate culture, and on the military's claim on young male lives are sound enough, except, perhaps, when he reaches for the transhistorical metaphor: 'The credit card is for the modern male what killing prey was to the hunter'; or 'Most men are shackled to the mercantile society in much the same way medieval serfs were imprisoned in the feudal system.'[14] It isn't long before men *as a gender* are cast as victims, of corporate state violence or whatever. Knowing a thing or two about being a victim, they end up practising victimization themselves. For the most part, Keen does not pursue this shaky thesis about the origins of domination and focuses instead on the emotional injuries incurred by men who cannot live up to the expectations set by dominant models of masculinity in our culture. Keen's solutions, however, do not involve contesting or reshaping these expectations; rather, they lie in withdrawal (especially from a world that includes women), in the discovery of wildness, and in reestablishing a spiritual reconnection to fatherhood. It is from the vantage point of the good father, for example, that Keen cites the gay male community, where arguably the strongest and most admirable forms of emotional solidarity among men exist today, as a *bad* example of unsocialized masculinity:

> It strikes me that the lack of substantial manliness one finds in some gay communities is a result not of a homoerotic expression of sexuality, but the lack of a relationship of nurturance to the young. To be involved in creating a wholesome future, men, gay or straight, need an active, caring relationship to children. A man who takes no care of and is not involved in the process of caring for and initiating the young remains a boy no matter what his achievements. This generation of men knows by its longing for fathers who were absent that nothing fills the void that is created when men abandon their families out of selfishness, dedication to work, or devotion to 'important' causes.[15]

This is not quite the way that Jesse Helms would put it, but Keen's sentiments were nonetheless in basic alignment with the neanderthal 'family values' wielded by the cultural right and unofficially sanctioned by the corporate Judeo-Christian state in the twilight years of the Reagan–Bush years. The significance of the stories told by Keen, Bly and others may lie, ultimately, in their reinstatement of the eroded authority of patriarchal familialism. The worked-up sincerity of a Keen or a Bly received much more serious attention outside Christian fundamentalist circles than did the rabid pronouncements of morality hacks like Helms, but there was little to choose between them when it came to family life. There was no doubt, moreover, that the 'dysfunctional' family model – characterized by an overattentive mother and an indifferent father – that Bly and Keen used to describe the plight of the modern male is more or less the one traditionally used by homophobic pathologists to *explain* the 'plight of the homosexual.'

It was with a good dose of irony that the fundamental question of this men's movement (*Newsweek* described it as a 'postmodern social movement,' because its founding moment was a media event – the 1990 airing of the Bill Moyers PBS special on Bly, called 'A Gathering of Men') was increasingly posed as: 'What do men want?' This question means something quite different from 'What do women want?' or 'What do Chicanos want?' In fact, it can be asked only after questions like these others have already been addressed. Masculinity, in other words, became a salient concept only after the arguments of feminism had made some inroads; the ethnicity of whiteness becomes a nonnormative concept only after the claims of people of color have been established in public consciousness; likewise for heterosexuality and the visibility of gay and lesbian rights. If masculinity today is seen as a 'problem,' it is largely because feminism has focused some of its attention on men in the last decade and a half. After devoting themselves to the task of claiming control over their own lives, women have turned to the 'problem' of masculinity in areas that cover a broad spectrum, from domestic violence, to the appropriation by men of spheres and activities in the home that had traditionally been considered female domain, to rape, and to militarism.[16] If men today, straight and gay, are almost as wary about conventional codes of 'masculinity' as women are about standards of 'femininity,' then it is as much a result of the social pressure exacted by the women's movement and by the alternative models of self-expression and emotional solidarity offered by gay men than it is a result of the changing economic circumstances of men as 'breadwinners,' in or out of the workplace.[17]

But how many men actually share this uneasiness? How broadly, across the spectra of class, race, and sexuality, say, are these anxieties felt? And how can we differentiate these worries from the way men used to feel about their masculinity? For sure, it is important to consider differences of class, education, race, and sexual preference, but these differences may determine only the degree to which male anxiety is experienced from the position of oppressor rather than victim. So, too, the inadequacy of historical perspective poses a real obstacle to estimating comparative shifts in social identity. In discussing the fraught question of the historical relationship between patriarchy and capitalism, Arthur Brittan notes:

> One of the problems here is that it is difficult to reconstruct masculinity before the modern era. We can talk about the role of the father in peasant communities in Medieval Europe, but we find it difficult to dig out the subjective dimension of this role . . . Because some of us are fathers, we may remember our own fathers and grandfathers; we have biographies which intersect with the biographies of parents and children. As men, we also may believe that there is some continuity between our

experiences and those who lived before us. Although the large majority of men in industrial society do not hunt and do not fight wars, they still find it conceivable that this is what they did in the past ... In other words, we see the past as some kind of validation of who and what we are now. The image of economic man, the rational calculator who takes a risk in order to maximize his profits and advantages, is so much taken for granted that it is not surprising that we read all history in these terms.[18]

It is precisely because this illusion of continuity persists that the sense of a crisis can be generated in the present, and it is in this context that I believe we ought to view the current crisis of masculinity with the kind of skepticism that all manufactured crises merit. As Brittan himself points out, the persuasive appeal of this rhetoric depends upon the assumption that men, in the past, knew who and what they were and that the secure sense of identity they once enjoyed has been only recently undermined. We used to live our masculinity as naturally as breathing air, now we are alienated from true consciousness of our gender, from what we once knew about ourselves. Time to come home.

It is this postromantic thesis about the estrangement of men from their true selves that is fully exploited in the pithy wisdoms offered by Bly and his circle. What lies behind this appeal to nostalgic fullness? On the one hand, it has to be assumed that men who actually do speak about heterosexual masculinity in this disingenuous way — manipulating men's uncertainty about their identity — are, in some sense, always involved in a process of reasserting their own authority. The larger, more conspiratorial version of this process is one in which patriarchy seeks to modernize and reconstitute itself through the resolution of a perceived and widely heralded 'crisis.' All ruling groups use the rhetoric of crisis to reconsolidate their power in this way. This is not to say that the conditions of such crises are themselves illusory. The latest crisis of masculinity is a case in point. In many instances, the state's increasingly repressive regulation of the body, linked to changes in the economy, labor market, and social policy, and fomented by a conservative fear of sexuality, poses clear physical obstacles to the rights and freedoms of certain groups of men — in particular, gay men, and young black males — specifically on account of demonized qualities and activities associated with their masculinity. Such groups are used to living with crisis-like conditions of persecution; it is a normative part of the history that has shaped their identity politics. So, too, deindustrialization and class polarization over the last two decades have brought about a precipitous decline in wages for almost all men (African-Americans and Latinos, in particular) who now belong to the secondary layer of today's two-tier economy. Although they are not subject to institutional racism, white working-class male youth can no longer look to a secure economic future of the sort achieved by their fathers through stable, union-wage manufacturing jobs.

The crippling effects of this economic landslide make it quite clear that these crisis conditions are unevenly shared. Increasingly, however, in and around the men's movement, we hear speculation about a crisis of the gender itself, a set of debilitating circumstances that affect men as a class unto themselves. When a crisis is presented as a general condition for all men, this is a sure sign that the process of redefining hegemonic masculinity has gone onto its overtime work schedule, distilling the old truths, compensating for the discards, incorporating this and that trace of hipness from the various countercultures, and generally shifting its contours to camouflage the jagged edges of class and race. This is the often hectic labor of refashioning and repositioning dominant masculine codes, leaning heavily on the narrative of evolutionary adaptation to justify the rejection or the revival of older traits in the name of survival. And this is where Bly's Wild Man, for all the talk about finding his inner child, begins to merge with the weekend grunt in jungle camouflage, nursing an M-16. Healing the psychically wounded foot soldiers in the gender wars might just produce a stronger, more dominant breed of man. What rough beast, in the guise of Iron John, slouches toward the Pentagon? And how will he react to the boys showering together in boot camp?

There is no more reason to trust a narrative of evolution than to swallow the rhetoric of crisis. One of the historical tales told about masculine survivalism in an embattled environment is that the advent of Darwinism provided the stamp of scientific objectivity to the dominant Victorian masculine ideal of stoical discipline. The peak years of strenuous Anglo-American masculinity, from the 1870s to the early 1920s, coincided with the high point of colonialist subjugation of peoples around the world, bolstered by the cultural and scientific vindication offered by neo-Darwinian themes of survival through strength and fitness. Underpinning each revival of social Darwinist masculinity are appeals to Hobbes's picture of brute competitiveness, itself harking back to a primal image of man the hunter-warrior, of men struggling, as they always have, for survival in a hostile environment of rivals. Indeed, the most recent revival was heralded by the kind of 1970s sociobiology, analyzed by Donna Haraway, that sought explicitly to normalize Man the Hunter: in books like Desmond Morris's *The Naked Ape*, *The Territorial Imperative*, *The Social Contract*, *The Imperial Animal*, and *On Aggression*.[19]

You do not have to subscribe to alternative narratives, often quite romantic, about the cooperative ethic of preindustrial or precapitalist times to see how the story of Man the Hunter agrees with the life of competition and the gendered division of labor in a market economy, and how it therefore elevates local capitalist principles to the level of general, transhistorical laws about masculine nature. Nature's laws are thereby understood to embody principles that are primarily social and economic in origin. Men are no more innately competitive or domineering than women are innately cooperative or compliant. Masculinity, defined from context to context as a set of cultural standards to be observed and emulated, is shaped by social institutions, each with a long history and a potentially changeable future, predominantly shaped by the interests and desires of elite groups. All men find it difficult to measure up to those standards. Some men can afford to ignore them. But most actually do suffer to varying degrees in their attempts to emulate these norms, and fall back upon compensatory fantasies. This does not make them losers, nor does it make them victims, both terms drawn from the noxious rhetoric of competition and domination. It does, however, place the studied mark of difference upon their masculinities and their psychosexual lives, differences that are often but not always related to race, class, and sexual preference. To disregard these differences and to view masculinity as a single collective property is just bad social theory. Alternatively, to see men as a universally exploitative class, to see male sexuality as a uniformly violent force, is to accept at face value only our most reactionary fantasies of power (as men), and to reduce the prospects of change to the occasional glimpse of chinks in a vast and formidable armor of toned flesh and social steel.

Neolithic Green

Whatever its current function and eventual destiny, the ideas of the 'men's movement' I have been discussing are primarily a response to feminist arguments that have linked male power to a history of systematic, hierarchical domination. The most full-blown critique of this sort has materialized within sectors of the emergent eco-feminist movement, in their description of the wholesale masculine domination of a natural world that is closely associated with the experience of women. It is no surprise, then, that the philosophy of the Wild Man takes its cue from, and presents itself as, a cognate of the eco-feminist poetics of nature. Just as women have been exploring the Great Goddess, so men can now find a spiritual personification of nature that would correspond to what Bly calls our 'psychic twin' (*IJ*, p. 53), or what William Anderson designates as the Green Man in his recent study of this vegetative figure, long suppressed in the Christian West but consistently surfacing in Europe's art and architecture, folktales, and vestigial pagan rituals.[20] Indeed, this Green Man is likely to become the neo-Jungian complement to the Earth Mother in coming years, as the search for an appropriate (Western) deity rooted in the soil displaces the much-maligned tradition of worshipping patriarchal sky-gods like Zeus, Allah, and Yahweh.

Among the so-called new social movements, the ecology movement has been exceptional in ceding a leading role, in theory and in practical activism, to heterosexual white men. It has been one of the few spaces in post-New Left politics where such men have felt that they can breathe freely and easily, while indulging in varying degrees in the wilderness cults traditionally associated with the making of heroic white male identities: the frontiersman, the cowboy, the Romantic poet, the explorer, the engineer, the colonizer, the anthropologist, the pioneer settler, and so on. In this tradition, the mark of a real man is to have direct and untrammeled contact with the wilderness. At times, the consequences of this legacy to the ecology movement have been atavistic, not only in the deep ecology wing, where a form of macho, redneck bonhomie came to inform Earth First!'s activist ethic, but also in the social ecology wing, which carried some of the weaponry of Old Left sectarianism into its battles with the deep ecologists.[21] For the most part, however, the commitment to the movement by heterosexual white men has been charged with the kind of passion that they have been unable to lend so easily and righteously to movements for women's liberation, gay and lesbian liberation, and civil rights for people of color.

Male visibility notwithstanding, women have played a prominent and leading role at various stages of the history of environmentalism: the women's clubs of the Progressive era which laid the ground for the conservation movement; the animal welfare and wildlife protection groups which pioneered animal rights; the women's camps (like Greenham Common and Seneca) and antimilitarist protests (the Women's Pentagon Action) which sustained the peace movement; and the leadership of women in developing and underdeveloped countries in resisting a whole range of environmental hazards — from the dumping of Western waste to the devastation wrought upon indigenous economies and cultures by the logic of industrial development.[22] In the face of intimidation from male professional scientists and activists, women have made striking interventions in every sphere of the ecology movement, whether as intellectuals, like Rachel Carson, Helen Caldicott, Petra Kelly, Elizabeth Dodson Gray, Carolyn Merchant, Vandana Shiva, Susan Griffin, and Ynestra King, or as activists in community and national struggles.

Increasingly, however, some proponents of eco-feminism claim more than an equal share of responsibility for protecting the natural world. In fact, the arguments of many cultural eco-feminists rest upon the claim that women are the rightful bearers of environmentalist ethics because of their historical role as protectors and intimates of the natural world. This claim does not arise out of the unprivileged locations that women share in relation to environmental threats, although it is certainly reinforced by the extremity of those threats. Women, for example, are often the front-line victims of ecological illness, especially in matters of reproductive health, where contamination by biohazards is responsible for a whole range of birth defects. Indeed, the powerful public impact of Rachel Carson's *Silent Spring* stemmed from her linkage of chemical damage to the reproductive life of animals with the dangers posed by toxic pesticides and radiation to women's reproductive cycles and children's health. Scientifically speaking, it could be proven that chemicals moved up the food chain to humans, but the point had to be made in a culturally effective way. As Vera Norwood has argued, the linkage Carson made between chemical threats to animals and humans was possible largely because of a cultural tradition in which women saw themselves as protectors of the home and hence responsible for matters of environmental health. This role of domestic guardian could thus be extended to the natural environment and vice versa, as if to underline the provenance of the term 'ecology' in the idea of a 'household economy.' In this way were middle-class women mobilized to a degree that neither science nor activism on their own might have done.[23] So, too, in developing countries where the gendered division of labor more often positions women, not in the home, but in the role of providing food, fuel and water, women who work in the fields or even in factories are front-line victims of deforestation and biohazardous labor; their situation has steadily deteriorated as a result of the commercial logic of development, especially the theoretically benign development policies shaped by former colonial powers and exploited by national elites to further their own interests.[24] In this respect, Third World women share this front-line position with First World people of color and the poor who live in inner-city or in rural areas where hazardous industrial activities are located. In none of these places do women have an overriding moral claim in the politics of combating environmental dangers, although they are often among the foremost activists in the threatened communities. On the other hand, there is little doubt that women have been in the front ranks of green consumerism, a position that, Joni Seager argues, has led them 'from the kitchen into the streets,' where they account for over 80 per cent of the membership of grassroots environmental organizing.[25]

The special claim of cultural eco-feminism for women's proprietary rights over environmental politics lies with the long historical association, warranted or not, of women with nature. Second-wave feminism sought to demystify this association and to disconnect the link, insistently placing women on the culture, or social-constructionist, side of the nature/culture divide. The cogency of ecological critiques, however, gave rise to concerns that the feminist repudiation of nature was itself potentially complicit with nature's degradation. In particular, the scholarly and inspirational work of Rosemary Radford Reuther, Carolyn Merchant, Mary Daly, and Susan Griffin underlined the commonality, within the modern mechanistic culture of the capitalist West, of women's oppression and environmental degradation. Consequently, radical feminists sought to rethink the women—nature connection, embracing and strengthening the link to reinvent the claim that women are the instinctual caretakers and custodians of nature. One of the results of this realignment was the transformation of the ecological critique of anthropocentrism into a critique of androcentrism, and the overriding perception that women's liberation was unlikely without the liberation of nature.

Invariably, there was a spiritual dimension to this critique, for eco-feminism was not only a political philosophy, it also had to be a religion of nature. While the male land ethic, in the tradition of Henry David Thoreau, John Muir, and Aldo Leopold, had always been infused with a deep naturalist religiosity, and while environmental activism was ever distinguished by its evangelical zeal, eco-feminism brought a supernatural element to this spirituality in the form of the earth-based Goddess religions. The inspirational basis for what is essentially a liberation theology lay in the myths, symbols, and ritual practises of pagan traditions of nature-worship, Wiccan, pre-Christian creation-centered cults, or in Native American religions, all of which rest upon some principle of immanent spirituality and subscribe to the interconnectedness of human and nonhuman nature. In this respect, eco-feminist spirituality shares in the broad New Age response, over the last two decades, of holistic alternative cultures to the materialist civil religion of scientific and technological rationality. It appropriates the religions of other cultures to generate an alternative to the status quo.

One result of this strong infusion of neomysticism has been the born-again animism of much of eco-feminist thought and literature. The heady combination of poetry, political analysis, experiential confession, inspirational philosophy, and chutzpah magic to be found in the work of Starhawk, for example, has become one of the more influential house styles of the movement, a distinctive strategy of personal empowerment which she describes as 'power-from-within,' as opposed to the destructive patriarchal tradition of 'power-over.'[26] A modern urban witch's invocation of the power of Great Goddess can be a useful, humorous political strategy for 'bending and shaping reality,'[27] as she puts it, and thus for defamiliarizing the given daily truths of a culture ideologically saturated with militaristic values.

Interest in the Great Goddess has been more than inspirational, however, for it has given rise to a full-blown eco-feminist philosophy of history which often threatens to mire debates about the social origins of ecological domination. It is often unclear how seriously the imperative of reclaiming the values of prepatriarchal, earth-worshipping tribal cultures is to be taken. Andrée Collard's sentiments are a case in point. In the introduction to her well-known book *Rape of the Wild* (1988), she asserts that she does not 'believe in trying to reverse time, and 'go primitive,' but it is important to broaden our understanding of the past and learn from other cultures and other times the way of universal kinship.'[28] Despite this concession, the spirit of the book's polemic is more in line with Anne Cameron's atavistic suggestion, cited with approval by Collard, that 'there is a better way of doing things. Some of us remember that way.'[29] By the end of the book, she has prepared the way for a grand historical judgment:

> Historically our destiny as women and the destiny of nature are inseparable. It began within earth/goddess worshipping societies which celebrated the life-giving and life-sustaining powers of women and nature, and it remains despite our brutal negation and violation in the present. Women must re-member and re-claim our biophilic power. Drawing upon it we must make the choices that will affirm and foster life, directing the future away from the nowhere of the fathers to the somewhere that is ours — on this planet — now.[30]

There are a number of leaps condensed in this move, from an initial waiver, to an assertion of female privilege, to the final declaration of historical truths. It goes something like this: we do not want to return to the past, but we ought to seek to reclaim what we have lost even though we have always had it and always will.

To understand what lies behind these rhetorical somersaults is to consider a philosophy of history that draws heavily upon the evidence of archaeologists and scholars of religion in the Neolithic period of 'Old Europe,' from 7000 to 3500 BC, when egalitarian, peace-loving, nature-worshipping societies are held to have flourished in Southeastern Europe in advance of the patriarchal, warrior tribes from Eurasia that destroyed the rule of the Great Goddess religions and introduced the ways of male domination to Western culture.[31] While the goddess religions subsisted, in some part, elsewhere — Isis in Egypt, Ishtar in Canaan, Demeter in Greece,

Magna Mater in Rome, and the Virgin Mary in global Catholicism — the authentic, prelapsarian culture of Old Europe survived only in Minoan Crete, and thereafter in scattered, suppressed folk rituals and heretic pagan traditions. In search of vestiges of continuity with Old Europe, Charlene Spretnak, for example, notes that 'the peasant rituals persisted in parts of Europe even up to World War I, where women would encircle the fields by torchlight and symbolically transfer their fertility to the land they touched.'[32]

Whether Neolithic society really did flourish in the form of a matricentric paradise, or even in a partnership culture, as Riane Eisler argues, has been disputed long and hard.[33] It has often been pointed out that there exists no correlation between societies wherein God was a woman, honored by female priestesses, and the social status of women or the political freedoms of the citizenry; slavery and forced labor were the order of the day in Egypt, and human sacrifices were practised in Minoan Crete. So, too, no clear evidence suggests that the fabled Neolithic egalitarianism immediately dissolved with the introduction of animal husbandry in the transition from hunter-gatherer to agricultural societies. Most social theorists trace the origin of status hierarchy in tribal societies to internal tensions resulting from the ascendancy of elders; in other words, men and women dominated other men and women through gerontocratic privilege before men dominated women through the sexual division of labor. What does seem clear, however, is the structural, or mythical, need for a golden age of organic cooperative harmony between equal peoples which no longer exists. For eco-feminism, this Edenic society flourished in the peaceful, unfortified settlements that fell to an invader culture ruled by a spiritually inferior gender, just as, for classical Marxism, say, the lapsarian break occurred with the rise of class society and the emergence of private property.

In *The Death of Nature*, Carolyn Merchant's more socialistic version of eco-feminist history, the break is located much later, during the scientific revolution, between 1500 and 1700, when a mechanistic rationalism, with its world view of nature as passive and dead, replaced an organicist cosmology with a living female earth at its center. The dominant metaphor of social consciousness of the natural world changed from organism to machine.[34] In her subsequent book, *Ecological Revolutions*, Merchant describes the transformations wrought on indigenous ecologies in New England by, first, the colonial revolution — with its transplantation of European animals, plants, pathogens, and peoples — and then by the capitalist revolution, beholden to a dynamic market economy which extinguished the subsistence farming of the colonial farmer and the indigenous trader alike. In quick succession, then, indigenous hunting and trading economies were displaced by rival settler agricultures and then drawn into a system of worldwide mercantile exchange that soon came to profitably exploit the link between enslaved African labor, American natural resources, and European capital.[35] The ethic of market production for long-term profit displaced production for short-term subsistence. Males replaced females in the fields, plows replaced hoes, maps replaced an animistic sense of space and place. Merchant's account gives a clearcut picture of what was lost: the mimetic consciousness of a hunter-gatherer economy in which humans, animals, and plants coexist as reciprocal face-to-face subjects — 'an active spiritual world of maternal ancestry regulated through participatory consciousness,' where 'the natural and spiritual were not distinct nor were people denigrated by association with the wild.'[36] And what was won? A nature/culture dichotomy, a transcendental god, and the fetishism of commodities. Merchant does not give us much of a choice here. The good organic life, of course, is irretrievably lost, as it must be for all origin stories, especially ecological ones that separate us from paradise at the same time as they blissfully deliver us from the messiness of history.

The lapsarian myth notwithstanding, Merchant's concept of 'ecological revolutions' is a useful one. Such revolutions, she writes, 'arise from changes, tensions, and contradictions that develop between a society's mode of production and its ecology, and between its modes of production and reproduction. These dynamics in turn support the acceptance of new forms of consciousness, ideas, images, and world views.'[37] Her aim is to emphasize the historical agency of the natural world (as opposed to underlining mechanism's inert nature) and to reintroduce nonhuman nature as an actor that either acquiesces to human interventions or resists them by evolving. The ecological, then, becomes a determining factor in historical analysis, alongside the economic, the political, the cultural, the demographic, and so on. While Merchant is careful to insist on the socially constructed character of the conceptions of nature that she discusses, the binary value system employed to divide her organic paradise from our fallen, rationalist world feeds into the nature/culture dualism affirmed by more essentialist eco-feminists, for whom biological reproduction, and not social reproduction, is the ground of all political value. Merchant has little, if anything, to say about the social ecology of the rationalist culture that succeeded her golden age: the contradictions of patriarchal capitalism, both libertarian and repressive, the radical democratic legacies of individual rights and freedoms, the long, checkered career of the Enlightenment's public sphere, the formation of the centralized nation state, the emancipatory potential of science, to name only a few. However mechanistic, instrumental, and utilitar-ian, rationalism has also thrown up evolved institutions which are not necessarily linked to capitalism's grow-or-die ethic and which are the immediate social context and imaginative horizon of most people's lives in a technologically advanced society. This complex of circumstances and traditions cannot be wholly dismissed as male property, whether in the modern or in the post-Neolithic period, without shutting out from history altogether the experience of too many people, especially women, and without forgetting all of the long struggles against hierarchical domination and injustice that must be sustained and developed if the domination of nature is now to be opposed.

Social ecologists have long insisted that the roots of today's global ecological crisis are as much social as they are 'natural.' If the domination of nature evolved out of forms of social domination related to gender, race, class, and age, then it must be combated in the context of these other inequalities. Among the prominent eco-feminists sympathetic to this position, Ynestra King has suggested that the domination of man over woman is nonetheless the *prototype* of these different kinds of social domination and thus worthy of particular attention.[38] Janet Biehl, author of *Rethinking Ecofeminist Politics*, the most resounding critique to date of atavistic nature worship within eco-feminism, is more skeptical of claims that the position of women, whether as victim or as heiress of spiritual intuition, marks them as uniquely ecological beings. To reason that women's relationship with nature is intrinsically bound up with the ecological crisis, or that women are privileged hierophants of nature's mysteries, is to accept the patriarchal conception of what women ought to be. Biehl finds the irrationalism of eco-feminism to be an 'embarrassing' and 'regressive' tendency which has muddied the once clear waters of radical feminism's commitment to claiming for women the equality afforded by Enlightenment thought:

> As a woman and a feminist, I deeply value my power of rationality and seek to expand the full range of women's faculties. I do not want to reject the valuable achievements of Western culture on the claim that they have been produced primarily by men ... We cannot dispense with millennia of that culture's complex social, philosophical, and political developments — including democracy and reason — because of the many abuses intertwined with that culture.[39]

Biehl's commitment to rational humanism is steadfast throughout her book-long 'witch-hunt' for rationalist heresies. Accordingly, she holds to a rather ascetic position against the gynocentric cosmologies, is scandalized by their playful supernaturalism, and is sleuth-like in tracking down argumentative inconsistencies around the women/nature question. For example, she seizes on Ynestra King's suggestion that eco-feminists can

> *consciously choose* not to sever the women-nature connection by joining male society. Rather, we can use it as a vantage point for creating a different kind of culture and politics that would integrate intuitive, spiritual, and rational forms of knowledge, embracing both science and magic insofar as they enable us to transform the nature-culture distinction and to envision and create a free, ecological society'.[40]

Interpreting these comments as a betrayal of King's own commitment to socialist feminism, Biehl takes issue with the pragmatic use of a 'connection' that King has elsewhere asserted is 'not true': 'How can this ecofeminist, who has long criticized instrumental reason, justify an instrumental "use" of something she believes is not true? ... An ethics cannot be based on something that is factually wrong.'[41] Biehl's riposte seems to reflect adequately the position of the rational humanist in response to what is basically the doctrine of strategic essentialism, here invoked in the context of eco-feminism. King, after all, is advocating the strategic use of the essentialist women/nature connection as one of the options open to women, who need to use all the tools available to them. If this strategy helps to confound male adversaries who also have to deal with women's rationalist side, then all the better. In Biehl's political world of fixed identities and crystal-clear reasoning, such strategies are dishonest: committed politics depends on cleaving to truths and should not stoop to the pragmatic exploitation of myths or beliefs; you cannot have your cake and eat it, too. For Biehl, the admission of a different logic is clearly an 'error' and in her view has irrevocably 'tainted' the once 'promising project' of eco-feminism.[42]

To many eco-feminists, Biehl's critique will seem dogmatic, puritanical, and, yes, politically correct, redolent of all of the bad attitudes of the sectarian left. Murray Bookchin's swingeing attack on deep ecology met with a similar response. The new social movements, after all, are supposed to be the home of diversity, where politics is infused with more experimental forms of pleasure and personality than the older, more austere left was wont to recognize. For an Emma Goldman, it was all about being allowed to dance. For a Starhawk, it may be about being allowed to cast a spell or two. Some see this as innocuous enough, others see it as the beginning of the end that Péguy once prophesied: *tout commence en politique, et finit par mystique.* Still others see it as a way of transforming the style of being political.

Biehl is more literal-minded than most. In her view, magic '*never* works — unless sheer coincidences come into play.'[43] One wonders, then, about her attitude toward ideology, which presents itself as orthodox, up-to-date knowledge about eternal wisdoms and yet hovers somewhere between those categories of knowledge that we designate as belief, mythology, truth, disinformation, propaganda, and common sense. Magic surely presents itself as the converse: unorthodox, ancient knowledge about the latest truths. As proscribed knowledge, its symbolic power appeals to those in needy pursuit of autonomy. Look, for example, at the strategic use of black magic and satanism by teenage metalheads in the wilds of suburbia. The point is surely to confirm parents' worst fears about their own loss of authority and influence over their children. As a strategy, it leads more often to parental hysteria than to understanding or self-criticism, but it is one of the few modes of empowerment available to kids whose lives are highly regulated by authorities and institutions. As Donna Gaines puts it in her book on suburban teenagers: 'If you are so bad that you are going to hell anyway, you might as well get in good with the guy in charge.'[44] Feminists practising witchcraft play a similar sort of game with patriarchy. Indeed, it has become a conventional strategy of identity politics for all sorts of groups to reclaim stereotypes of themselves, including derogatory labels ('queer,' or 'nigger,' or even 'girl') from the dominant culture, in a bid to establish control over their own social and cultural identities. Since they feed into longstanding sexist characterizations of 'feminine irrationality,' the pagan rituals of wicca, the Old Religion, and the nature spirituality espoused by eco-feminism can be seen as part of the same response. At best, they are embraced with a sense of humor and in the name of utopian creativity. At worst, they are enforced with a fundamentalist's fervor, whose utopias lie in prehistory, in a world now lost, with little persuasive hold upon a modern social environment.

The progressive ideologies of the post-Enlightenment period have promised us that our utopias lie inevitably in the future, not in the past. With the technoscientific narrative of progress everywhere impeded by the toxic clouds of the ecological crisis, other nondystopian mythologies are clearly needed. If these mythologies are to be elements of a survivalist philosophy, then they must make sense of the lived, daily experience of people in advanced technological societies. If they are to move people beyond their short-term interests, then they must appeal to our social memory of past communal desires and to the creative imagination of disparate futures, without collapsing back into either millennial or year-one mythologies. If they are to avoid the abstraction of universalizing about human (or gendered) experience of nature, then they must recognize the diversity of people's histories with the land: the ancient claims of the indigenous; the dispossessive legacy of slavery; the limited access of immigrant groups; the haughty entitlement of the plantation owner and the rancher; the uneven stakes of the homesteader, sharecropper, and the migrant worker; the insolent propriety of agribusinesspeople, realtors, and developers; the wistful appreciations of the day tripper and the nature lover; and the ironic contempt of the urbanist. And if such mythologies are to improve relations with nonhuman animals, then they cannot be choosy about which members of the biotic world are to enjoy natural rights.

Cyborg Green

One of the most widely discussed efforts at drafting such a mythology remains Donna Haraway's 'Manifesto for Cyborgs,'

230

which repays being read in the context of eco-feminist supernatural-ism, for it presents itself as a blasphemous, heretical tract which regards the cyborg myths it propagates with deep, irreverent irony. Disloyal even to its own convictions, Haraway's postindustrial mythology deviates from each and every principle of eco-feminist spirituality. In contrast to the atavism of the goddess myths, the cyborg, the 'illegitimate offspring of militarism and patriarchal capitalism' is so unfaithful to origins that it 'would not recognize the Garden of Eden.'[45] For the cyborg, there are no ancestral homes to dream back to, no egalitarian matriarchies or phallic mothers, no prelapsarian havens of unalienated labor or pre-Oedipal sexuality; the cyborg is 'completely without innocence'[46] and is a stranger to institutional promises of redemption and salvation. Cyborgism is hardly immanent in the Earth, but its hybrid spirit is manifest everywhere in today's postindustrialist economies, where the boundaries between human and machine, human and animal, are daily crossed. As such, it is a myth for workers within the new information and surveillance networks, a myth for bodies in the grip of medical technologies; a myth for all those who have to face daily life in late capitalist militarism's 'belly of the beast.' It is from the hybrid raw materials of the New World Order, and not from Old Europe, that the cyborg emerges as a useable vehicle for utopian stories about the future.

Elsewhere, Haraway looks for ways of describing human—non-human relations by extending to the natural world the quixotic persona of a 'coding trickster with whom we must learn to converse.'[47] Again, this description speaks profanely to eco-feminism's close linkage of animal rights and women's liberation. Cognizant of the historical connection between the subjugation of animals and women, many eco-feminists reject male formulations of animal rights because they draw upon a dualism between reason and emotion which has played its own historical role in the degradation of nature. Natural rights theory, which extends moral consideration to all self-conscious animals (but only to them) as bearers of inherent value, is based upon moral rationality, exclusive of human sympathy or emotion. More utilitarian theory takes as its moral criterion for equal consideration the capacity of animals to feel pain or pleasure.[48] Such arguments make the case for animal rights by appealing to political abstractions in order to avoid the anthropocen-tric tradition that attributes human characteristics and quirks to the physical properties and nonhuman inhabitants of the natural world. More often than not, this tradition has been androcentric insofar as it has feminized nature in a subordinate fashion, and has projected patriarchal conceptions of production and reproduction onto the patterns of animal life. Many eco-feminists who accept the association of women with nature endow the natural world with a logic, most often spiritual, that transcends the rapacious interests of its male dominators. In this respect, they share with deep ecology the impulse to put the interests of the 'Earth first,' while reasoning that the male gender, and not deep ecology's undifferentiated human species, is the main threat to the welfare of the natural world — a category that is marked as 'female' even if it does not strictly include women alongside animals, plants, rocks, and rivers.

Andrée Collard's *parti pris* is representative:

> I am first of all always on the side of nature. Her innocence (in the etymological sense of 'not noxious') may derive from the fact that she acts not from choice but from inherent need. Whatever nature does that seems cruel and evil to anthropomorphizing eyes is done without intent to harm.[49]

Collard's position here is decidedly antihumanist. Survivalist 'needs' of nature are strictly opposed to the realm of human 'choice.' Rather than seeing these as claims in conflict (i.e. should feminists be allowed to eat meat to demonstrate diversity and pluralism?), Collard demands that we choose to subordinate our freedom of choice to some relation of solidarity with nature's ways. For Collard and other eco-feminists, women's special relationship with nature affords them an intuitive understanding of nature's otherwise 'cruel' ways; they too can feel the 'call of the wild,' or 'the roaring within,' to use Susan Griffin's phrase. In some respects, this is the flipside of the disembodied (male) point of view of science, unclouded by essentially human concerns, which alone purports to understand the rationality of biospheric 'needs.'

Haraway offers a more socialized conception of our relation to the natural world when she describes it as a 'witty agent,' with an 'independent sense of humor.' Like Ursula LeGuin in her novella 'Buffalo Gals, Won't You Come Out Tonight,' Haraway personifies this agency, not as the primal mother, but as the trickster figure of the coyote from Southwest Native American myth. Dealing with the world as coyote is a way of acknowledging that 'we are not in charge of the world' but that we are still 'searching for fidelity, knowing all the while we will be hoodwinked.'[50] The resulting dialogue is respectful, but not innocently reverent. It acknowledges our maturity, as an evolved species, and also the necessity of our connections with an equally evolved nonhuman nature, which is capable of getting the better of us. The coyote personification itself is highly ambiguous: '"Our" relations with "nature" might be imagined as a social engagement with a being who is neither "it," "you," "he," "she," nor "they" in relation to "us."'[51] From a humanist/anthropocentric point of view, such a relationship is entirely corrupt and incomplete, since it promises no end in self-discovery. And yet it is a socially intelligible relationship, which encourages an affinity that ought to make sense to anyone who has felt the incompleteness of his or her connection to the world and yet who refuses to explain this feeling by recourse to some expression of defeat before the 'mysteries' of nature. Avoiding the subordination of the human to the 'needs' of nature, it expresses some of the canny spontaneity of the animal world without romanticizing its 'wildness.'

Allowing the trickster to do some coding of its own is one thing; cyborg coding is something else. While Haraway's cyborg myth points in its own utopian way toward a 'monstrous world without gender,' its current manifestations continue to be hardwired as either male or female. Who could forget the motel room scene in *Terminator* that gave Arnold Schwarzenegger his most famous line but one, the cyborg-eye point-of-view shot which produced the screen readout 'Fuck you, asshole'? Here, surely, was the homophobic embodiment of masculine cyborg vision, guided and programmed by a military-industrial logic that needed no translation into the Hobbesian language of competitive human relations. One might think that seeing the world in this way, or through the perspective of virtual reality, is as 'natural' in an advanced technological society as seeing the world from the point of view of a plant or a beaver had been in predominantly agricultural or hunter-gatherer societies. Film audiences, at least, instantly appreciated this perspective as cyborgism-with-attitude, the dominant bad boy cyborg's world view, but they also recognized its counterpoint in Sarah Connor's parting line to the Terminator: 'You're terminated, fucker.' The sequel, as I noted earlier, contains Connor's remarkable fantasy about the Schwarzenegger cyborg as 'a perfect father,' who has no role in or control over the reproductive process but who is programmed nonetheless to protect her son, come hell or high water. One could say that this fantasy contains prepatriarchal elements (i.e. before men's consciousness of paternity set in, before they discovered their role in biological reproduction and moved to appropriate and control the process). But its debt to technological dependence makes it finally postpatriarchal, a fantasy about the 'good' welfare state of the future, which sends an agent into the present as protector. This time around, the Terminator is no warrior invader, programmed to erase any human threat to the machine-dominated future. Does that make him an evolved, reformed species of eco-man, programmed to learn from a son who adopts him in the name of saving the planet, or is he the latest ruse of patriarchy, who looks good only because the new Terminator — the real, protean cop machine — makes Freddie Krueger look like child's play? For the same reason that movie sequels do not instill our trust in reformed characters, especially in figures so terrifying in the original, Schwarzenegger's Terminator barely persuades us of his capacity for co-evolution. Whatever fantasies are woven around them, terminators are a technofix, attitudinally kin to the dysfunctional nerd sensibility of their creators which is so prevalent in the AI and robotics communities.

Male cyborgs are still very much sexually different. For the men who can afford it, the cyborg myth is a narrative of domination in a world where they are fully empowered to inhabit the firmest ground of masculinity. For those who cannot afford it, cyborgism is a familiar tale of survivalism in a world where forms of social ecology that would promote co-evolution in the name of sexual politics are still very much a luxury. With these kinds of historical lineage, the humanist fantasy of self-discovery cannot help but be destructive. Male cyborgs, whatever their constitution, won't recognize Bly's Wild Man and are more likely to 'find' themselves in the cyberspace of virtual reality than in the wilderness or on a dude ranch. What is more important for men right now? Withdrawal from the social fray in search of some late-breaking rite of passage lifted from the Plains Indians? Or the self-conscious reinhabitation of the world of social reproduction — a world different from but not unrelated to the world of the food chain and the water cycle — in order to champion change, with humor, with passion, and with politics?

Many of the cyborg alternatives are to be found elsewhere, in youth cultures, for example, where the most advanced technologies are creatively spliced into vibrant forms of style tribalism. In the hip-hop nation, and in the trance world of rave, 'low' and 'deep' — the calling cards of Wild Man poetics — can refer at one and the same time to bass levels ('How Low Can You Go?') and to emotional intensities ('Deeper and Deeper'). From the electric boogie style of early breakdancing to the braindraining energy worship of hardcore techno, hybrid species of high technology have been a material presence in recent popular music, comfortably coexisting with ancient oral traditions in rap, and with neopagan forms of tribal communing among ravers. NASA meets Stonehenge; the Roland 808 lays it down for the African griot.

In the age of the drum machine, the Wild Man looks for self-discovery in beating on authentic skins, inviting bemusement and scorn from American Indian voices, like that of Sherman Alexie:

> Last year on the local television news, I watched a short feature on a meeting of the Confused White Men chapter in Spokane, Wash. They were all wearing war bonnets and beating drums, more or less. A few of the drums looked as if they might have come from K-Mart, and one or two men just beat their chests. 'It's not just the drum,' the leader of the group said, 'It's the idea of the drum.' I was amazed at the lack of rhythm and laughed, even though I knew I supported a stereotype. But it's true: White men can't drum. They fail to understand that a drum is more than a heartbeat. Sometimes it is the sound of thunder, and many times it just means some Indians want to dance. As a Native American, I find it ironic that even the most ordinary moments of our lives take on ceremonial importance when adopted by the men's movement ... Native Americans can be lousy fathers and sons, too.[52]

Like the Wild Man in the mythic forest, the raver headed to the countryside for perspiration, percussion, and serious cultural therapy. For tourists of the soul like the Wild Man and the goddess-worshipper, the forest is a place of white flight, a traditional location for regrouping and for recharging spiritual batteries with the exotica of Amerindian and ancient European myths. For their sons and daughters, the all-night sweatfests of the rave were semi-outlawed events, throwing up retrofitted memories of their parents' pastoral hippie gatherings, once the creative social crucible for new forms of sexual and familial behavior. Far from the madding crowd of the patriarchs, what these youth inherited is the result of a quarter-century of splendid individualism (or what is often referred to as

THE CHICAGO GANGSTER THEORY OF LIFE

identity politics), promising the most radical reshaping of individualism in the West since Renaissance humanism. What has been begotten? Animals humans machines girls boys. Just expect the best.

5

Superbiology

Hardly a week goes by without some heady news announcement that scientists have isolated the gene responsible for this or that life-threatening disease, or have 'linked' it with said disease. Nature has offered up another secret to the intrepid seeker of knowledge. When all other science is called into doubt, progress is surely reliable and unsullied in this sector of human endeavor. Things are on the right track after all. Genetics is the stable groove to the future. And yet, it is reported, there are still naysayers, who opine, 'We can put men and women on the moon, but we can't feed our own . . .' or 'We can restructure human DNA but we can't provide minimal medical care . . .' There are also those who, for some reason of ethical faith, are philosophically opposed to genetic engineering: nature wasn't meant to be tampered with. Worst of all, there are even some (the modern equivalent of flat earthers) who dispute the entire world view associated with genetics, and which is rapidly becoming second nature in the public media where the gene is science's new box-office star.

Readers of this book are likely to fall into any of these three categories. The thesis of this final chapter leans toward the latter. It argues that the resurgent biologism that has accompanied the gene boom in recent years is a major feature of the new politics of nature which will consume our oppositional energies well into the next century. In tracing the economic rise of biotechnology, the checkered career of sociobiology, and the influence of neo-Darwinism on environmentalist ideas, I will summarize some of the historical and philosophical components of this new politics. Many of these components are rooted in older social/scientific movements like eugenics, others have been fostered and supported by ideas associated with the New Right, and still others appeal to emergent ecological truisms about natural scarcity. This powerful combination has helped to boost the serviceable power of biological explanations of the world. In each case, I argue the need to resist and challenge the growing reliance upon the authority of 'nature' to deal with problems that are primarily social both in their origin and in their solution. The alternative is to accept a world in which the status quo is taken to be a state of nature, or else to allow human affairs to be governed by limits decreed by experts to govern nature.

Gene-Analogies

The secrets of DNA, as science's heroic narrative would put it, began to unravel in 1953, only five years after the discovery of the semiconductor. The economic consequences of the latter are all too apparent today, in the widespread technological infrastructure of the information society, fuelled by relentless consumer marketing of successive generations of high technology. By contrast, the much-vaunted genetic revolution still has little to show in the way of material product. If you take the later discoveries of the microprocessor (1971) and gene splicing (1973) as critical milestones, the comparison in fortunes is still worth some speculation; only a few biotech companies are in the black, and their products are viewed with widespread public suspicion, while the electronics giants rule the world and fill the imagination of its populations. Considerable differences separate the respective sciences and the economic profiles that underpin these technological revolutions. Beneath all of the public hullabaloo about the ethics of biotechnologies and the heady, Promethean hype associated with the commercial evangelizing of biological engineering lies a story about the early and continuing career of the genetic revolution as a product of the checkered fortunes of venture capitalism in the 1980s.[1]

The first biotech companies were exemplary economic specimens of their times, borne along on the inflated balloon of a speculator's market, soaring and dipping with the growth and collapse of each pressure zone of confidence in the ultimate appearance of the monoclonal magic bullets promised to investors. Conceived from the outset as an entrepreneurial science (the term biotechnology was coined on Wall Street), funded by venture capitalists often to avoid the demanding peer-review system of federally funded science, the research and development of biologicals was supposed to create an economic harvest as profitable as the microelectronics industry had done, while producing the drugs needed for everything up to and including a comprehensive cancer cure. Aside from providing a much-needed stimulant to a stock market still trailing in the wake of the energy crises of the 1970s, the discoveries of gene splicing and recombinant DNA technology were supposed to lead to miracle bioweaponry in the new immunological wars, and, eventually, realize millennarian dreams of eliminating genetic disease, feeding the world, and saving the planet. Hosannas of praise for the gene fed off the same rhetoric of technological utopianism as selling the atom had done in the postwar years. Projections of vast profits from the gene boom were underpinned by public assurances that the vehicles for this biorevolution were environmentally friendly technologies, at least by the fickle standards of the chemical industry. Consequently, the initial levels of investment in the wave of new biomedical companies like Genentech were unprecedented on Wall Street; a chorus of investors, executives, and industry boosters in the early 1980s feverishly intoned the mantras of molecular biology as if it were some new kind of alchemy. Publicity releases about often premature breakthroughs in research were expediently tied to stock values in the new investment field. The media circus often featured top scientists from academic departments drawn into newly intimate relationships with corporations by federal policies explicitly designed to bridge industry and academy.

Within a few years this wild first boom was over, having produced meager profits and little more in the way of biomedical product than a set of monoclonal diagnostics and a few limited antibody therapy treatments. Investors cut their losses and retreated to the blue-chip stocks, while the 1987 crash took its toll on the smaller venture capitalist outfits, leaving the older biochemical drug empires intact and in a position to control the market through their own biotech departments. Speculative creatures, ill-equipped for life outside the rarefied air of the speculators' markets, the biotechnology companies recovered however, and in 1991, sold $17.7b in new stocks — a remarkable performance, as the *Wall Street Journal* might have put it, even in the bull market of that year. The successful marketing of a few high performance drugs, like Amgen's Epogen and Genentech's

Protropin, helped to reinflate the balloon of confidence. By 1992, the industry was also exerting enough collective political pressure to ensure that President Bush refused to sign the biodiversity treaty at the Rio Earth Summit. Among other things, the treaty (subsequently signed by Clinton) would have required American biotech companies in the gene-hunting business of patenting seeds and plants to share profits with countries that host the flora and fauna that are the biological capital of the global industry. But that same year, a loss of investor confidence virtually closed public markets to biotechs from February to November. Anxiety about the Clinton administration's plans for health-care reform, heralded by advance criticism of high drug prices, triggered a repeat performance in 1993, when 33 per cent of the biotech industry's value was eliminated in the first three months. Public offerings of stocks in the last two months in 1993 only barely recovered some of the $10 billion lost over the course of the year. Each new clinical trial of a drug, each new approval by the FDA, is a critical test of survival for the entire biotech group — one thousand companies chasing winner-take-all drugs in an industry that more and more resembles the market logic of Hollywood's search for blockbuster films.

What is there to learn from this fledgling history of the genetic revolution? Take your pick. Either the investors are periodically losing their nerve, or the cold reality of science keeps colliding fatefully with the hot air of the hype. In the case of biotechnology, at least, there is no easy way of distinguishing between the two explanations; the possible economics of the science feeds off the economic science of possibility on the stock exchange. Accounts of the rise of biotechnology that see the industry simply as the outcome of a technological revolution are obviously not the whole story. Sheldon Krimsky, for example, gives an exhaustive account of the stockmarket boosterism associated with the industry only to argue that, finally, the behavior of markets is irrelevant to the inevitable success of biotechnology:

The primary techniques that spawned the new industry — rDNA and cell fusion — were considered so revolutionary that it can be argued the industry was predestined to succeed. Early investments were in the techniques and the scientists who had control over them, not the products per se. Viewing the emergence of the industry from this point of view, it was irrelevant which products succeeded, failed, or met a social need. This was truly a technological revolution. The failure of biotechnology was out of the question whether or not there were existing needs or favorable markets. The techniques would be used over and over again until successful products emerged.[2]

This point of view, however, glosses over the reality that access to and monopoly control of R&D in basic science is the primary motor of corporate investment today. Biotech's short-term cycles of boom and bust tell an exemplary story about how science is increasingly defined, funded, and practised. Biotechnology, after all, was the first major new field in applied science to emerge after the monetarists' transformation of basic science from public knowledge to corporate commodity, a private status hitherto applied only to marketable technology. Under the new university-industry partnerships established in the 1980s, private companies reaped the commercial benefits of basic research performed at universities with massive Department of Defence (DOD) and National Institutes of Health (NIH) funding. Biotechnology's volatile existence stands, then, as a clear warning about the risks of technologically developing a new science wholly within the fickle milieu of corporate culture, notwithstanding the biotechs' parasitical relationship with universities receptive to R&D cash flow and all too ready themselves to invest in the patent game.

As if to respond to the caveat, the North American branch of the Human Genome Project, the large-scale undertaking to map and sequence all of the genes in human DNA, has been almost entirely funded by federal grants and appropriations, and, for the field of biology, at unprecented levels. The interests of national chauvinism aside, a flood of paper boosterism, in the form of popular and semi-popular books about the project, has been accompanied by intense lobbying for funding by big-name biologists. The result of the latter is a massive conflict of interest for major scientists with substantial stock holdings or interests in biotech companies like Genentech, Genzyme, Repligen, and ImClone. Richard Lewontin avers that 'no prominent molecular biologist of [his] acquaintance is without a financial stake in the biotechnology business.'[3] *Genewatch*, the newsletter of the Council for Responsible Genetics, regularly reports on the ties between commercial biotech firms and biomedical faculty at US universities: one-third of the biology faculty at MIT, one-fifth at Harvard, are stockholders, consultants, or directors of such

companies.⁴ James Watson, the bearer of biology's most unim-
peachable pedigree was pressured to resign from the directorship of
the Human Genome office at the NIH partly as a result of
investigations into his financial holdings in biotech companies. Also
at issue in his resignation was a disagreement with the NIH's desire
to copyright and patent DNA sequences (they are not held to be
'natural' even if they come from a natural organism). Like all large,
federally funded science projects, whether at the Pentagon, NASA
or elsewhere, the investment of public monies is used to subsidize
the private profit drawn from spinoff products that emerge from
R&D. The patenting of DNA sequences from the Human Genome
Project (HGP) (encouraged by the NIH and resisted in the courts)
would take this logic one step further.

Critics who question the worth of the HGP point, among other
things, to its astronomical cost, the low probability of its producing
any useable scientific knowledge, and its potential for commercial
abuse. In addition, because the project is mapping the sequence of
only one set of genes − a composite male of American, European
and Japanese origin − there are serious problems with what many
perceive to be its violation of codes of evolutionary variation in the
species. In addition, 3 per cent of its monstrous NIH budget has
been set aside for studying the ethical implications of the project by
the Ethical, Legal and Social Limitations research group. The result
of this unprecedented allocation, in the form of grants to outside
scholars for research and symposia, has been some serious criticism
of the social problems associated with the project. All the same, the
work of ELSL has helped to establish, for the project and its
contractors, a kind of immunity to further scrutiny and interro-
gation from external critics; the ELSL critics have no input,
moreover, into the business of the science itself. On the other hand,
the allocation is a measure of the extent to which its advocates are
now seeking safe passage for the career of biotechnology, after initial
excursions along the rocky road of venture capitalism.

However relevant and important, a strictly economic account of
the first biotechnology boom is not the whole story. Technologies are
no more the blue-sky fantasies of financial speculators than they are
the single determining source of economic revolutions, as is often
supposed in the case of the semiconductor or microprocessor or gene
splicing. Technologies are as much the results of significant changes
in social and cultural values as they are ingenious responses to

physical conditions, industrial demands, or environmental problems. Biomedical technologies, in particular, can be seen as the integrated products of vast phases or regimes (after Aglietta) of environmental life. These regimes can be labor-related, like the Industrial Revolution with its affiliated bodily contagions, and the postindustrial revolution with its stress-related or immunological disorders, or lifestyle related, like the so-called sexual revolution, with its associated infectious diseases and microbiological conditions, or the fitness revolution, with its sporty catalog of complaints and disorders.

But it is equally reductive to think about such regimes without also considering how they are associated historically, with ideologies of the body itself. For example, the recent appearance of the concept of the 'genetic disease' (diseases attributed to a single recessive gene, or a set of genes), and thus of the new hereditarian definitions of the body encouraged by molecular biologists, is indissociable from the explosive growth of genetic biomedicine. Without this conceptual picture of the body as genetically determined, we would not have the dire situation that exists today in biomedicine, where the providers of technological fixes in the form of gene therapies are desperately *searching* for problems — genetic diseases — in the hope of boosting their stocks. Here, science chases its own tail in hot pursuit of profit. The logic is much the same as it was for Thomas Alva Edison, but the stakes are arguably much higher, given what genetic technologies are capable of introducing into the open environment.

This most recent example of science's longstanding inverted priorities — the solution looking for a problem — is primarily a consequence of a conceptual shift from a germ theory to a gene theory of disease. The new theory is as culturally and socially determined as the old, and is having an equally pervasive effect upon the way in which people think of their bodies. Such ideologies of the body are an essential part of the process by which persuasive consent is solicited for the development of any new technology. In this respect, one is tempted to speculate that the initial commercial rise and fall of biotechnology had something to do with its being culturally premature, and that the high level of public anxiety about the ethics of 'going against nature,' as it is often articulated, is a sign that the decisive winning of consent for such technologies still lies somewhere in the future. This opposition persists despite the efforts by industry spin doctors to alleviate such concerns. The industry makes a distinction, for example, between somatic cell therapy for local medical purposes and germline therapy which is passed on to future generations and can therefore be harnessed to political agendas like eugenics. Regardless of the distinction, people still want to think of their bodies as organically inviolate or inalienable, and seem to be resistant, whether on religious or secular grounds, to the idea that their DNA can or ought to be genetically manipulated. The recent fuss about the representation of biotechnologists in Steven Spielberg's 1993 summer film *Jurassic Park* demonstrated the acute sensitivity surrounding this issue. With biotech stocks more jittery than usual, the film drew a slew of responses from industry representatives and boosters complaining about the 'antiscience' bias of the film. There was a lot of nonsense talked about how the film would put youngsters off the idea of studying science. The underlying industry worry, however, was that viewers would find the manipulation of human, and not dinosaur, DNA to be the truly scary idea. Even more recent was the widely antagonistic public response to the appearance in stores of the first milk from cows treated with the Bovine Growth Hormone to increase their milk production.

On the other hand, the popular appeal of a simple technological fix — one gene for each disease — tends to override public skepticism about the 'monstrous' potentialities of genetic engineering, not to mention the much messier political commitment to a welfare system that might guarantee each individual's social right to health. The gene theory of disease may be on the verge of displacing the germ theory, but the mechanistic paradigm of causality will remain intact and unchallenged, both in the industry and in the public mind. Indeed, one of the prerequisites for the acceptance of genetic medicine has been that it could embrace the institutional structure favored by Western medicine — a specific cause for a specific disease, with symptoms relating directly and unambiguously, in this instance, to a hereditary condition.[5] This paradigm persists, despite the evidence that gene causation is rather complex, even in the cases of the very small group of genetically simple diseases like Huntingdon's chorea or muscular dystrophy which are most associated with a 'single gene.' Nothing could be more antithetical to a postmodern paradigm of medicine which seeks to incorporate the social and environmental life of the patient into its purview.

As for the scientific community itself, fears about the hazards of biotechnology were at one time more widely shared among professionals than they are today. As early as 1975, a meeting of 200 leading researchers was convened in Asilomar, California, in order to consider the biohazards of recombinant DNA, and to lift an unofficial moratorium on gene manipulation experiments called for by a committee the year before. The underlying purpose of the conference was to contain the PR damage and to head off restrictive regulation of rDNA by Congress by drawing up self-regulating guidelines, later adopted by the NIH. Despite the noninclusion of public voices in the meeting or in the subsequent trajectory of the industry, Asilomar is ritually cited by industry boosters as proof that geneticists have, from the beginning, been responsive to the public's safety concerns about rDNA research. The more persistent voice of public opposition, epitomized by the efforts of Jeremy Rifkin, has been isolated as an example of personal, even eccentric, opinion.

In spite of the widespread ambivalence toward biotechnology, I don't intend to downplay the power of capital investment to outweigh public or professional skepticism. Increasingly, all eyes are on the patent, and government agencies like the FDA routinely bend to pressure from a cash-hungry industry by relaxing standards of review and easing regulation of biotech products. In the case of the gene boom, however, one could conjecture that the economic model for the research and development of biologicals followed too closely the example of industrial precedents, especially that of microelectronics. The ground rhythm of the biomedical industry is conceivably much slower and much broader in its effects than can easily be encompassed by the short-term forecasting framework of the venture capitalist, who has to accept daily the 'burn rate' of basic research as a loss against marketable returns in the near future. Only the speculative stock market of the last two decades could have floated such an industry on hope and high expectation with so little to show in the way of product. But the disparity may also be related to a more fundamental difference between these two industrial revolutions. The microelectronic revolution was based on industrially rationalizing the control and distribution of information in the service of a surveillance society. The genetic revolution is based on controlling nature and manipulating biological material in the more radical service of the industrialization of life itself.

In addition, while both revolutions were forged in a militarist culture (basic research for each came out of wartime programs, and in the case of Watson's DNA research, some of it funded by the Atomic Energy Commission), and while both bear the mark of their status as militarist offspring, official and popular disapproval of bioweaponry for explicitly military purposes is still widely observed. While populations seem all too willing to accept the logic of using nuclear weaponry, environmental warfare, and all manner of electronically smart armaments, by contrast, nerve toxins, chemical, or biological instruments of war are considered to lie outside the rules of the game. This remains the case, even after over fifty years of expensive research and testing of such weapons, often on civilian populations in peacetime. The battle for the morally legitimate use of such weapons in war has yet to be won by the generals and the bankers, not least because it faces a level of public opposition to biotechnologies that was notably absent, say, from the initial phases of the atomic age. None of this has stopped the DOD from paying the piper by progressively increasing its funding of biotechnology research.[6]

Biologism is Back

In general, the bullish development of the biotech industry is somewhat out of synch with its sticky reception in the culture at large. There are good reasons for this discrepancy. Given the recent rise of popular skepticism regarding technological overdevelopment, fuelled largely by environmental consciousness, today's criteria for public acceptance of new technology are more varied. They appeal to a higher level of public information than in the days of 'better living through chemistry.' In intellectual debate, social questions about biology increasingly are at the dead center of disagreements over the relationship of science to the advancement of the nonphysical aspects of human life. The intellectual struggles that were fought, in the first decades of the century, against the creeds of hereditarianism, eugenics, and social Darwinism have resurfaced in different forms in the last twenty-five years. After a long ruling spell by the schools of culturalism, environmentalism, and social constructionism, the revival of biological determinism from the slough of eugenical disrepute has been brisk, if not mercurial, and has followed closely on the heels of the gene boom and the claim to centrality of geneticist thought within the life sciences. Shifts in the political climate have encouraged this revival: the reemergence of ethnic chauvinism and nativism with their trumped-up appeals to ancient and not-so-ancient racial roots; the ascendancy of an economics that forbids government to intervene against the 'natural' workings of the free market; the backlash against egalitarian gains by women and people of color; the return of social Darwinism.

This powerful resurgence of biologism has fed into some of the great philosophical controversies of the day; from debates among cultural theorists and political activists about essentialism and identity politics, to debates about biocentrism between social ecologists and deep ecologists/eco-feminists. In matters of public policy, the use of biologistic scholarship has been a central player in the struggles over reproductive rights. It is omnipresent in the crusades against sexual minorities, and is openly employed in the racist campaigns against affirmative action and civil rights. So, too, potential abuse of the already routine genetic screening of target populations covers many areas of discrimination. Screening provides employers and insurers with reasons in advance to prejudice the 'genetically susceptible,' and offers parents the opportunity, through fetal screening of birth defects, to make eugenic choices about which children to bear.[7] Crucial issues of global ecology are directly addressed by the development of genetically engineered food and plants through 'barnyard biotechnology': plans for population control (tacitly implemented all over the Third World with the help of institutions like the Rockefeller Foundation), violations of animal welfare, the continuing disaster of monocultural food production, the spectacular loss of biodiversity through hybrid agriculture, and the supercorporatization of health care through gene patenting and the like.[8]

Behind all of these developments lurks the disreputable history of genetics itself, with its unsavory roots in the eugenics movements of the first few decades of this century. Mengele and other Nazi eugenicists have so dominated the public memory that it is often forgotten that the USA was a leader in the international eugenics movement aimed at staving off the 'racial degeneration' of national populations. Eugenics was the active principle behind the Immigration Restriction Act of 1924. Based on quotas tied to the 1890 census that predated the massive immigration of Jews, and Eastern and Southern Europeans, the Act was calculated to restrict immigration to 'superior' Northern European races. In the same spirit, the 1926 Supreme Court decision of *Buck v. Bell* affirmed the constitutionality of sterilization laws framed by more than two dozen states (some of them still on the books) to deal with the 'feebleminded' — a category that could be stretched to include virtually anyone considered to be 'socially defective.' In his judgment, Oliver Wendell Holmes put it this way: 'Three generations of imbeciles are enough.' There is a direct line of descent that leads back from the diagnostic labelling today of single-cause genetic diseases to early pseudo-scientific labelling of diseases like *drapetomania*, a hereditary mental illness held to be prevalent among slaves in the South and manifest in the unreformable desire to run away from their masters.[9] As Troy Duster and others have argued, modern gene therapy and genetic screening offers a 'back door to eugenics,' rechannelling the old prejudices about bad genetic stock at the bottom of society into new forms of social control based on the genetic susceptibility of individuals and groups.[10]

In intellectual circles, the eugenics idea, with its powerful influence over instinctivist thought, was on the decline by the 1920s, challenged most decisively by cultural anthropologists and sociologists.[11] In the three decades following European fascism, culture was most definitely on the winning side in the nature-versus-nurture debates. Biology was not considered destiny, and the civil freedoms, cultural permissions, and political rights achieved in the postwar period have been sustained against attacks by fundamentalists arguing in the universalist name of 'human nature.' Generally speaking, it has not been difficult to demonstrate how spurious such arguments from human nature are, although the persistence of popular belief in its existence has proved a more formidable and enduring obstacle to claims that all appeals to this concept are fashioned out of nothing more than ideology favoring the status quo. In the wake of collapsing ideologies like state socialism which served to underpin and explain an entire social system, ideas about human nature are quick to fill the vacuum, exploited by demagogues in the name of this or that turn to fundamentalist movements.

What is new about the spate of recent arguments from nature is their appeal to the authority of developments in genetic science. Accordingly, the terms of the culture/biology debate *appear* to have changed. Biology's new capacity to synthesize and alter molecules has threatened to shatter the conceptual picture of nature as immutable and degenerate. As Evelyn Fox Keller has pointed out, the new picture of nature as more malleable, less fixed, is one in which nature can be presented as a realm of freedom and improvement where before it was defined as a state of necessity and imperfection.[12] As a result, the nature—nurture debate no longer looks quite the same; the ground on either side seems less sure. Not that it was at all clear why freedom and necessity should have been so opposed in the first place. Necessity ought to include some conception of human needs, but who will decide whether any of these needs are socially created or whether they respond to conditions of survival tied to 'natural' scarcity? Conversely, there are many who view freedom as a direct *consequence* of the potential of human biology, rather than as a bonus achieved by resisting the limits imposed by human biology.

In seeking firmer ground beyond the the quicksands of philosophical debate, culturalists have challenged the claims to objectivity of genetic science itself, uncovering the social and ideological assumptions that saturate its purportedly neutral, positivist principles, while reminding us of its debt not only to the eugenics movements of the past but also to the ascendant values of recent neoconservatism. They have also sought to describe the emergence of the new eugenics, achieved this time not through direct social control, but through technology, and aimed at bringing everyone up to genetic par rather than sterilizing those who bring down the quality of the gene pool.

In the midst of this wrangling, however, a more sophisticated 'politics of nature' has emerged, and in a timely fashion, too, as we speed through what both apocalyptics and reformists have termed the decade of the environment. Is the new politics to be one in which biology limits or liberates human potential? This question covers a wide spectrum of issues and contexts, some addressed in earlier chapters of this book under the general rubric of how to respond to the new arguments made from nature when they are applied directly to our social, cultural and political lives. Surely we cannot continue to dismiss such reasoning as the work of *false metaphor*, and least of all if we still want to think of ourselves as materialists, or as something other than stomach-pump constructionists when it comes to addressing the ecological crisis. The question here is not simply how to resolve the recent face-off between devotees of rhetoric and the lovers of materialism. It is more important to understand how such terribly limited choices come to be posed as the only ones. To do so involves first examining the specific histories of thought associated with particular metaphors and concepts of materiality (for example, Darwin's metaphor of selection and anthromorphic ideas of nature, or the un-Darwinian equation of social Darwinism that binds organic variation to social progress).[13] The second step is to suggest alternative legacies and alternative frameworks for rescuing the use of natural science from its role as legislator or legitimator of bad thought. One important case history to review in this regard is the checkered career of sociobiology.

Sociobiology's Legacy

There may be no easy way of reconciling what conservation biologists mean by 'nature,' what sociobiologists or economists mean by 'nature,' and what poets or politicians mean by 'nature,' but one way of gauging the significance of these differences is to look at the disciplinary wars involving disputes over this terrain. Consider the opening lines of the infamous last chapter of Edward O. Wilson's 1975 book *Sociobiology*, the *locus classicus* of sociobiology where Wilson moves from analysis of animal societies to addressing the features of human societies:

> Let us now consider man in the free spirit of natural history, as though we were zoologists from another planet completing a catalog of social species on Earth. In this macroscopic view the humanities and the social sciences shrink to specialized branches of biology; history, biography, and fiction are the protocols of human ethology; and anthropology and sociology together constitute the sociobiology of a single primate species.[14]

If the consequences of such remarks by Wilson and his disciples had not been so serious and far-reaching, one might be excused for reading this passage as a tasteless parody of some university administrator's attempts, under the pressure of shrinking budgets, to collapse and merge departments and disciplines, rearranging the campus map into the bargain. That university departments, for the most part, still inhabit the same buildings as they did two decades ago has more to do with institutional inertia than with resistance to the colonizing impulse of biology in the life sciences, or the corresponding desire of social scientists to put their discipline on a wholly scientific basis. Of course, there is much more to this than parody. Wilson's proposal to collapse the disciplines in this manner stems from his own reductionism, specifically from his picture of the pyramid of knowledge, with social sciences at the top and physics at the bottom; sociology could thus be derived from biology, from chemistry, and ultimately, from the fundamental physical laws. The whole pyramid resonates in a single chain of causation in the same way as sociobiology's explanation of human behavior reduces itself to the smallest genetic component of the constituent cell.

Wilson's own work had proceeded from his lifelong fascination as an entomologist with the highly organized structure of insect 'societies' which appear to resemble one single superorganism made up of selfless individuals. Such societies, with deeply programmed 'altruism,' did not appear to make sense in the conventional terms of natural selection until William Hamilton advanced the theory of kin selection in 1964. According to sociobiology's version of this theory, the unit of natural selection is not the individual but the gene itself, and so individual sacrifices among social insects for the sake of siblings who share the altruistic gene aids in the gene's survival. Animal behavior evolves in such a way as to encourage kin selection, since the survival of the gene is all. This view is taken to its extreme in the 'gene's eye view of life' popularized by Richard Dawkins, for whom all organisms 'are survival machines — robot vehicles blindly programmed to preserve the selfish molecules known as genes.'[15]

Kin selection, which supports the principle of inclusive rather than individual fitness, allowed sociobiology to reopen the case for arguing the ultimately hereditary basis of social behavior. The way was then clear for Wilson to reduce the ethical systems of human society to biological causes and locations:

> Morality evolved as instinct. If that perception is correct, science may soon be in a position to investigate the very origin and meaning of human values, from which all ethical pronouncements and much of political practice flow ... [Morality] resides in the deep emotional centers of the brain, most probably within the limbic system, a complex array of neurons and hormone-secreting cells located just beneath the 'thinking' portion of the cerebral cortex.[16]

The resulting view of genetic determination is as far removed as can be from the culturalists' picture of humans socialized by their environments. What are the stakes of the argument, advanced by Wilson and others, that traits like militarism, social competition, sexual dominance, territorialism, xenophobia, and the like are genetically encoded in humans? To begin with, general theories that 'biology is destiny' bear the odious stigma of their enduring historical use as justifications for imperialism, genocide, and patriarchal domination. The most recent revival of biological determinism has fed directly into the social Darwinist climate created by the New Right's sanctification of possessive individualism. The revival of theories based on the heritability of differences has marched in tune with the neoconservative faith about the permanence of social inequalities. Biological determinism, which defines individuals as the consequence of the biochemical properties of their constituent cells, seems to be a scientific correlate of the New Right dogma that society, far from being an organic community whose members hold rights and responsibilities, is simply a Hobbesian collection of naturally competitive individuals with no reciprocal obligations.[17] No one really needed an article like 'A Genetic Defense of the Free Market,' which almost inevitably appeared in the wake of the sociobiology brouhaha (in *Business Week*, April 10, 1978) to recognize the degree to which sociobiology was very much an idea of its times.

Subsequently, the genetic paradigm has been used to naturalize ideas about differences of race (the IQ debates and anti-immigrationism), gender (in the campaign against the Equal Rights Amendment), morality ('criminal' chromosomes — the XYY genotype), sexuality (homosexuality both as a genetic error and, more recently, in the debate about the 'gay gene,' as a genetically determined condition), and class (concentration of 'good' genes at the uppermost socioeconomic levels). A direct correspondence is suggested between genetic diversity, such as it exists, and social diversity, thereby considered to be predetermined. Consequently, it is assumed in general that there are 'natural' levels of social attainment for people just as there are 'natural' limits to their social capacity. More visibly, victims of social discrimination are once again blamed, this time for their presumed biological inferiority. Twenty years after the emergence of sociobiology, its explanations can be found institutionalized in every corner of the public health and welfare apparatus, encouraged and funded by pharmaceutical empires looking for new drug opportunities. Federal policy at the

National Institute of Mental Health (NIMH), for example, is partially governed by ideas about the genetic causality of violence. Fred Goodwin, the current director of the NIMH, is associated with a Violence Initiative that would identify innercity kids as young as 5 as biologically prone to violence and in need of advanced pharmaceutical treatment. Such ideas, while they can easily be dismissed as the idiosyncrasies of a powerful individual, are typical of the sociobiological philosophy pursued at government agencies like the NIMH, backed up by extensive NIH-funded studies of animals, especially primates, for clues to human behavior.[18]

Despite the normalization of these ideas, almost every tenet of sociobiology has been strongly rebutted from many quarters.[19] In response, sociobiologists have resented the public criticism of the adoption of their theories to justify the continued inequalities of patriarchal capitalism. Science, and the pure logic of its internal developments, is their domain, they say, and they regret the 'contamination' of their work by the external discourse of social advocates. There is no easy separation of these discourses, however, least of all in the case of sociobiology. The science, from the beginning, is heavily contaminated. What is the 'free spirit of natural history' invoked by Wilson when it can only be imagined as the perspective of a 'zoologist from another planet'? The result, in the case of human perspectives, is a vicious circle of hypothesis and conclusion. Social institutions based on aggression, territoriality, competition, tribalism, militarism, and sexual and social domination are assumed to be universal human traits, for which a genetic cause is sought and then offered as a scientific explanation of the universality of these traits. The most common intermediate move in this 'proof' is to apply these traits to nonhuman societies, where, as Lewontin, Kamin and Rose argue, patterns derivative of human social institutions are projected onto animal societies and then 'human behavior is rederived from the animals as if it were a special case of a general phenomenon that had been independently discovered in other species.'[20] The general tendency to anthropomorphize the 'animal kingdom' with social hierarchies and structures of domination and submission — like caste, royalty, and slavery — is a problem that is hardly confined to Disney nature films: it is a fundamental principle of sociobiological discourse. The language of sociobiology implies relations of identity between human and animal societies and an underlying structure of genetic causality. At best, however, there are only analogies to be found between these different types of species organization, and most agree that such analogies should only be used sparingly as rules of thumb for talking about the social behavior of organisms.

Given the spirit of projection involved in the sociobiologists' reasoning, it is no surprise to find the gene itself being proposed as a bearer of human attributes. One well-known example is Richard Dawkins' description of the 'selfish gene:'

> If we were told that a man had lived a long and prosperous life in the world of Chicago gangsters, we would be entitled to make some guesses as to what sort of man he was. We might expect that he would have qualities such as toughness, a quick trigger finger, and an ability to attract loyal friends. These would not be infallible deductions, but you can make some inferences about a man's character if you know something about the conditions in which he has survived and prospered. The argument of this book is that we, and all other animals, are machines created by our genes. Like successful Chicago gangsters, our genes have survived, in some cases, for millions of years, in a highly competitive world. This entitles us to expect certain qualities in our genes. I argue that a predominant quality to be expected in a successful gene is ruthless selfishness. This gene selfishness will usually give rise to selfishness in individual behavior.[21]

How does one respond to this description? In the spirit of generosity, I immediately think of more appropriate types for this comparison: naked capitalist apologists for social Darwinism like the nineteenth-century robber barons, or junk-bond monsters from the 1980s. Then I stop to consider the historical pertinence of the actual type selected by Dawkins, for whom the type of the Chicago gangster is no doubt as exotic to his own type — the Oxford don — as a Polynesian navigator, an Inuit fisher, or a pygmy hunter from Zaire might be.

The historical heyday of the type was indeed in the high competitive moment of the 1920s when the metaphor of 'the jungle,' (Upton Sinclair's description of another invidious Chicago institution — the meat-packing house) was extended to the pell-mell urbanization of the period. Perhaps this is more or less the kind of Hobbesian environment Dawkins has in mind when he appeals to the 'conditions' in which said type 'has survived and prospered.' But even if we were to follow up on Dawkins' coy invocation of environmental determinism, there might be a different story to tell about those social institutions usually associated with urban gangsterism, and which gained notoriety during Prohibition, itself a eugenicist-style backlash by WASPs against immigrants who controlled the booze trade, and whose social mores were a challenge to the high, ruling Protestant sensibility. The Irish, Jewish, and especially the Italian gangster, to cite the historical order of ethnic succession in organized crime, often functioned as fantasy figures for ghetto communities dreaming of rapid social mobility. Far from being the epitome of the selfish, atomized individual, the gangster was positioned more like the 'big man' of community and kinship-based orders that were being eroded by modern, urban capitalist culture, and which were preserved most famously, like some kind of premodern anachronism, in the traditional extended family organization of the Mafia, with its mutual obligations, its rights of kindred, and its conservative moral stability. The clannish loyalties that held sway in gangland represented, even if they rarely extended, guarantees of community protection against the rapacious ways of the business elite. In the absence, or the corrupt semi-presence, of official institutions like the welfare state in the domestic economy, law enforcement on the streets, and trade union protection in the labor economy, gangster protectionism presented itself as a medium of parallel government for ethnic, working-class communities.

The gangster was no social bandit engaged in the redistribution of wealth, but the underworld society epitomized by the term 'Chicago gangster' had some role, romanticized or not, to play in a period before the state apparatus of the social welfare contract was put in place in the immediate prewar and postwar years. To abstract the selfish, atomistic figure suggested by Dawkins' Chicago gangster from the social and quasi-institutional environments in which the gangster functioned is dishonest, but not unusual if one is trading in types. Dawkins himself makes no effort to flesh out a social profile for his Chicago gangster.

Writing in the mid-1970s, however, in the so-called 'winters of discontent' produced by labor disputes in Britain, he does make a number of asides to the example of industrial action as a test case of the debate about group altruism and selfishness. In Dawkins' discussion, the labor movement is an exemplary case for demonstrating how selfish individuals always seem to be able to prosper under conditions ostensibly dedicated to the principle of mutual aid:

255

> We may frequently behave selfishly as individuals, but in our more idealistic moments we honour and admire those who put the welfare of others first. We get a bit muddled over how widely we want to interpret the word 'others,' though. Often altruism within a group goes with selfishness between groups. This is a basis of trade unionism.[22]

There are many other bases of trade unionism, however, which fall outside of the perilous passage between the Scylla and Charybdis of altruism and selfishness. These other bases are related, on the one hand, to the liberal tradition of claiming social rights and civil protections independent of local circumstances of gain and loss, and, on the other hand, to a more radical tradition that seeks to create a society where equality and cooperation are more normative governors of social behavior than prejudice and competition. These traditions historically evolved out of subaltern views of the world, whereas the limited dyad of altruism/ selfishness belongs to the world view of those who already hold most of the cards in the pack, and whose idea of evolutionist wit today is to see trade unions as a mutant species doomed to extinction due to their lack of survival skills in the postmodern market economies.

For Dawkins, however, there are only two apparently legitimate modes of action and motivation – altruism that appears to increase the welfare of others at the expense of the altruist, or selfish behavior that advances the welfare of the self. As it happens, the first option is a false one, since it 'often turns out on closer inspection that acts of apparent altruism are really selfishness in disguise.'[23] Try as we might to act toward others in the spirit of mutual interest, there does not seem to be any way of outfoxing our selfish genes. For, according to Dawkins' view of natural selection, altruism operates at the level of the gene alone, not the individual, family, group, race, nation, or species. Nothing could be more atomistic than this picture of social behavior, and yet many sociobiologists consider it to be in a direct line of descent from Darwin's original assault on human arrogance. Despite Dawkins' admonition that, through 'free will,' we 'at least have the chance to upset [the] designs' of our selfish genes – 'something that no other species has ever aspired to' – it is difficult to imagine a theory that is less useful as a contribution to human decency or social change. Indeed it is a remarkably impoverished version of the theory of evolution that allows a single, limited choice between altruism and selfishness to dominate the field of play.[24]

Why have I dwelled so long on this analogy with the Chicago gangster? Not to prove that better sociology could have produced a better analogy (it could, but that is not the point), nor yet to show that the analogy is already full of sociology (it is, but that does not get us any farther down the road). Rather, my purpose is to remind us that while there are other, less dismal, orders of social thought than the one that generated Dawkins' 'Chicago gangster' comparison, this should not be taken as an invitation to endorse a revised, reformed, or improved version of sociobiology. In other words, there is no point, finally, in saying that the Chicago gangster is not a good metaphor for the selfish gene. To do so one would first have to accept the hokey idea that genes can be selfish. Alternately, one falls into a different kind of trap if one compares genetic traits with more favorable role models like the Chicago blues musician, or the Chicago activist-preacher, or (a longer shot) the Chicago architect. Perhaps the only really sensible thing to do is to try to eschew this kind of attribution altogether, and look elsewhere, to local and culturally specific explanations, for the existence of selfish or altruistic behaviors. Nor is there any obligation to restrict such inquiries to what are, in essence, very limited descriptions of social activity. For all of the relentless attention afforded them by sociobiologists, altruism and selfishness account for a mere fraction of the range of human behavior. As culturally specific descriptions of behavior, they barely make sense outside of the economic picture of competitive, individual advantage favored by modern liberal societies in the West.

In addition, as Stephen Jay Gould has argued, one can accept the sociobiologists' principle of kin selection without accepting the notion of genetic control of behavior. In Gould's view, the more important and creative aspect of natural selection lies in the biological potential developed by organisms. In the case of mammals, that potential is usually held to lie in the growth of large brains that give humans the capacity to learn and choose from a whole range of behaviors (including creating dumb theories) without being instructed or programmed in these choices by their genetic makeup.[25] Ultimately, then, we ought to be looking hard at the example of alternative social environments (other than, say, the battlefield or the marketplace) for Darwin's legacy. Of course, this does not guarantee that we will get rid of bad metaphors, but at least

257

we ought to know where our metaphors are coming from and where they are going. Robert Young has analyzed at some length the process by which Darwin developed the metaphor of natural selection while drawing analogically upon observations about pigeon breeding. The model of conscious selection on the part of human breeders structurally influenced Darwinism's attribution of agency to 'Nature,' anthropomorphically exercising choices over the survival of this or that species while scrutinizing the whole social spectrum of biological activity. Young also points out that Alfred Russell Wallace, co-author of the theory of natural selection, persistently warned Darwin about the misconceptions that would be drawn from the metaphor of natural selection, arguing that no inferences should be legitimately drawn from the analogy between artificial selection as exercised by domestic breeders of animals and plants, and natural selection as exercised by a nonhuman agency. Such an inference would either preserve the creationist structure of belief in the divine architecture of things, or secularize the voluntarist agency of Nature, personified as a cruel, but ultimately wise, judge of the laws pertaining to evolution.[26] Notwithstanding the alternatives (Darwin considered 'natural preservation'), natural selection survived as the fittest metaphor, and, according to Young, ceased to be a metaphor soon thereafter when it took on the character of a law of nature. A similar history applied to Newton's law of gravity, another metaphor that drew initially upon a human attribute — *gravitas* — and ended up literalized as a description of the mutual attraction between physical bodies.[27]

Accounts of the metaphorical constitution of such fundamental scientific theories are crucial if we want to welcome natural science as an ally, rather than as a silent legislator, in the advancement of social and cultural life. The hope is that we can establish this new relationship while avoiding both the fundamentalism of the old school of empiricism and the rhetorical fetishism espoused by the newer schools of poststructuralist theory. The upsurge of rhetoric as a problem of knowledge in the last twenty years does not have to be viewed as a simple symptom or cause of the crisis of materialism; if anything, it ought to be seen as a complex expansion of materialism. It does not depreciate the value of material life to accept that our knowledge of it also (rather than only) describes the relationship of our culture to nature at one time. We should not have to be obliged, then, to choose between metaphor and materiality. On the other hand, the excesses of sociobiology stand as a clear warning to those who would simply gloss over the problems raised by the metaphorical treatment of matter.

Other Darwins?

To alter the landscape chosen by sociobiologists as the natural habitat for selfish genes, we must consider the significant distinctions in the cultural history of Darwin's legacy. My task here, as elsewhere in this book, is to trace the general influence of these legacies upon the current ecological crisis.

It has often been acknowledged that Darwin's thought about evolution drew primarily upon two conflicting theories of natural life.[28] On the one hand, there was Malthus's dismal picture of a natural economy defined and willed by God as an unequal ratio between population and perpetually scarce resources. What passed from Malthus into popular ideology was the given wisdom that life for most people was fated to be a miserable struggle for existence in a world where there simply isn't enough to go around. Consequently, the backdrop to Darwin's theory of natural selection was a ceaseless war of organic species in competition over limited resources like food and space. Violence, competition, conquest, and scarcity seemed destined, then, to govern the economic struggle over the occupation of nature's finite system of niches. When proponents of social Darwinism like Herbert Spencer and William Graham Sumner took succor from Darwin's naturalist version of the survival of the fittest, they completed the circular logic diagnosed in my earlier discussion of sociobiology. The ideology of classical economics had been absorbed into nature through the Malthus—Darwin connexion, and then projected back onto human society to provide classical economics with an assumed basis in nature.

On the other hand, Darwinism is also indebted to the more Romantic view that nature is imperfect and unfinished, creatively evolving as a realm where species can create new roles and niches for themselves at the expense of no other competing species. According to this view, the key to natural selection lies in the creation of complexity, variation and divergence in a world where co-dependence and diversity, rather than warfare and limitation, are the rule.

Despite the tension between these two theories of nature, it is clear that competition and scarcity held sway as the dominant Darwinian principles, and that they have left their dismal mark on the subsequent path of the life sciences. While Darwinism was also claimed by the left (Marx himself proposed to dedicate the second volume of *Capital* to Darwin, an honor the naturalist declined; Kropotkin sought to ground the social instincts of cooperation in biology), it most visibly served the immediate needs of Victorian entrepreneurialism. In the USA, Herbert Spencer's own *laissez-faire* version of social Darwinism was particularly well received in the ruthless, individualistic milieu of the Gilded Age, and in ways that appealed directly to captains of industry like Carnegie and Rockefeller who seized for themselves the mantle of the fittest survivors as if it were indeed biologically ordained.[29] Spencer, who saw competition amid scarcity as a healthy, progressive environment for the social evolution of humans, preached optimism to the strongest and most powerful, and sought consent from the less fortunate for their natural subordination. The social Darwinist climate had eroded by the turn of the century and was in intellectual disrepute by the 1920s, thanks to challenges by Socialists, Progressives, and the pragmatist school of James and Dewey, all of whom, to some degree, supported the principle that cooperation, as much as competition, was in accord with evolutionary biology. While popular wisdom has never quite shaken off social Darwinist beliefs, a healthy suspicion set in among social thinkers about the extension of biological analogies to society, especially the application of natural selection to economics. At the same time, however, eugenics was according the same ideas a degree of scientific legitimacy that would provide a basis for future revivals of social Darwinism, even after Nazi race credos had rendered it temporarily *persona non grata*.

As a result, the vestigial influence exercised over biological thought by the doctrines of Victorian *laissez-faire* economics has been quite tenacious. While the law of competition and the condition of scarcity have ceded in part to the functionalist paradigm of nature as a 'system' or set of systems (itself another example of circular logic, since functionalism drew upon physiology for its model of social systems, now projected back onto the natural world), they continue to play a role akin to that of default settings within the life sciences. So, too, the identification of evolution with 'progress' has lent the organic process a highly moral coloring that Darwin himself was eager to avoid: for Darwin, nature had no teleology, apart from the better adaptation of species to their environments.

In certain environmentalist circles, you do not have to look far to see the principle of scarcity being regarded as a rudimentary circumstance of nature. This applies as much to resource-minded environmentalists (heirs of the conservationism of the Progressive era), whose apocalyptic prognoses about 'limits to growth' are pragmatically addressed to the managers of industry, as to biocentric nature activists (heirs of preservationism), morally moved to conserve and redeem sacrosanct areas of wilderness from human contamination. On the one hand, the appeal of the reform environmentalists is to an empiricist model of nature as a limited economy of resources: overuse threatens the survival of all species (and ecosystems) but primarily humans. On the other hand, biocentric fundamentalists view nature as a powerful, if fragile, moral economy which zoologically punishes the human species for its cosmic arrogance. In the first model, there is no account of power, while, in the deep ecologists' model, human domination of nature is simply turned upside down – domination is still dominant. Just as in sociobiology, both of these perspectives project particular social prejudices, whether empirical or moral, into ideas about the natural world. Nature only appears to be 'limited' or 'scarce' if it is conceived as a finite quantity of economic resources that can be renewed or exhausted. So, too, nature only appears to be judgmental if it is endowed with a moral sensibility that defines human activity as competitive and transgressive. Both models are regulated by relatively fixed laws, to which we are asked to subordinate our actions and thoughts.

Whether one believes in the existence of 'laws of nature,' or whether one believes that laws (which are made, and can be changed, by men and women) really only exist in human society, I would argue: (a) that both of these views of nature are full of social theory; and (b) that in so subordinating ourselves, we risk forfeiting any independent or alternative response to perhaps the most consequential debates of our times. To accept (a) and (b) is not to deny that there is an ecological crisis, nor to suggest that our response to that crisis should ignore its empirical and its moral components. It is, rather, to recognize that the way we talk about this crisis and the way we imagine our place within the natural world will determine the (often draconian) social prescriptions advocated in the name of resolving the crisis. This is why, for example, it may be better to think of it as an emergency, from which new ideas 'emerge' as a basis for social change, rather than as a crisis, for which one finds a 'solution' which is more likely to be expediently exploited in the name of the status quo.

To the environmentalist and the biocentrist alike (still accepted in public consciousness as if they were noncontradictory sides of the same coin) we may want to respond in Darwinian ways, not because Darwin holds the truth, but because the contradictions that troubled Darwinism are, in some part, vestigially responsible for these divergent models of nature. To resource-minded environmentalists, we can preach the fundamental historical lesson of evolution – the continuity between humans and nature, and the absence of any special privileges that justify human domination over nature. To the biocentrist or deep ecologist, we can preach Darwin's other lesson – evolution has no directed moral purpose, progressive or otherwise, and the survival of organic species is more a matter of sociable intercourse than it is a result of purposive physical laws. One lesson asks us to acknowledge the similarity between nature and society; the other asks us to acknowledge their differences.

Those who distrust such neat symmetrical analyses, who object in principle to preaching, and who favor a more inclusive and dynamic picture of nature and society, will feel more comfortable with a properly social ecology, by which I mean a social theory of nature that presents itself as such, rather than masquerading as zoological theory (sociobiology), economic theory (environmentalism), or moral theory (deep ecology). First and foremost, a social ecology recognizes the *similarity and the differences* of humans from other species in the natural world. In this respect, we might qualify a few myths that continue to circulate in the lifeblood of popular environmentalist consciousness. It is just not true, for example, that humans are unique in transforming their environment while other species merely adapt to theirs. All organisms enjoy an alloplastic, rather than a simply autoplastic relation to their environments. Whether they are bacteria working on host or neighboring cells, plants changing the composition of the soil where they grow, or birds and beavers building nests and dams, all organisms are a cause as well as an effect of their environments, from which they (and their genes) are indissociable. Humans alone, however, have the intellectual and technological capacity to radically reshape environments in self-consciously purposive ways, and that is what differentiates them from, say, 'social insects.' Nor is it true that pre-humanist, or non-EuroAmerican societies uniquely enjoy a harmonious, nondestructive relation with their environments, many of which they exhausted through deforestation and overuse, or with other species, many of which they hunted to extinction. There is no doubt, however, that the scale of destruction has become nigh catastrophic in modern societies, where special dispensation to devastate the natural world arose out of a combination of the ideologies of humanism and rationalism with the intensive development of industrialism.

Similar myths circulate around the topic of scarcity. Human societies are not governed by natural Malthusian 'laws' of overpopulation and scarcity, *if only because humans alone have the capacity to create societies where such 'laws' are not the primary determinants of survival.* At present, since everywhere in the world scarcity is induced and manipulated in the interest of maintaining power hierarchies, all such 'laws' are used as instruments of social subjugation. They cannot therefore be taken to correspond to actual conditions of physical limitation. It is virtually impossible for us to conceive of conditions of scarcity that would be purely physical in constitution, unaffected, that is, by social decisions about the distribution and consumption of resources. Economically speaking, scarcity figures as a measure of limitation primarily with respect to economic systems of growth and development, and only inasmuch as the calculus of such systems does not incorporate ecological costs except as 'externalities.' (This was as true of the ex-socialist societies which inherited wholesale the religion of growth and development from economic liberalism, and which continued to measure their economic health against the global standards set by Western liberal societies.) The key to resolving the ecological crisis does not lie in the ratios of some zoological/economic calculus that will impose mathematical limits on population and consumption levels any more than it lies in the golden codes of natural morality that will prohibit human intervention while delegating supreme authority to Mother Nature. It lies in the radical reorganization of social life on the planet. An ecological code of ethics that does not incorporate that lesson will not be evolutionary at all.

Most people tend to accept that 'limits,' whether they are socially imposed or socially chosen, are a necessary feature of any ecologically minded reorganization of social life, and indeed that limitation is the cardinal principle of ecological thought. It is assumed that in the West, above all, economists, industrialists and politicians will have to be persuaded to limit growth, while citizens will have to be weaned from the exponentially increasing consumer gratifications that underpin the custom of steady economic growth. It is difficult to argue with the intention of these assumptions, but there are reasons to be cautious about the widespread popular deference to this criterion of limitation, especially when it is advanced as a reason for regulation of social and cultural life. In the first place, we should be wary of any discourse of limits that equates an 'excess' of rights and freedoms with the excesses of material growth and development generally held responsible for the ecological crisis. Material scarcity has long been employed as a justification for imposing punitive and repressive measures upon populations. In the global context today, scarcity is increasingly cited as a basis for imposing drastic policies upon developing countries, where dire population measures are 'introduced' — starvation, disease, forced sterilization — which are seen to be consonant with the sustainability, for some, of a Western way of life.

Many of the classical liberties and rights that are a constitutional part of Western modernity today were won on the back of an expansionist liberal economy. The liberal political institutions of the West were achieved in tandem with the growth of imperialism: classical economics often assumed an abundance in nature that could only have been realized by plundering the resources of the New World and the rest of Europe's colonies. It does not follow, however, that these institutions, liberties, and rights are directly tied to the fortunes of an economic system based on unlimited growth. Indeed, it is precisely *because* of the existence of public freedoms that limits on growth can be democratically chosen and agreed upon. And yet, not only are these principles often considered to be a premature luxury in developing countries, they are also threatened with limitation wherever they exist in the developed world, by the manipulation of material scarcity, by the invocation of national security, or by the strategy of economic recessionism (i.e. a pro-scarcity economic strategy and not an economic consequence of scarcity). The 1993 UN Conference on Human Rights highlighted this situation when representatives of a number of Third World member states argued that, in their societies, human rights ought to be considered secondary to the right to economic development. While this was perceived as a challenge to Western hegemony, it demonstrated how the maintenance of political liberties is directly bound up with perceptions of scarcity and underdevelopment. In times of socially induced crisis, even the most 'universal' rights and liberties are subject to more than the usual limitations.

In recent decades, we have seen the partial achievement of nonuniversalist rights — those pertaining to women, people of color, and sexual minorities — that were tied in part to the economic surplus of the long postwar boom, and consequently to the creation of new consumer identities for the bearers of such rights. In the current recessionary mood, where consent for a step-up in regulation can be more directly elicited, the cry to limit these rights is often heard alongside the call to tighten our belts. The dominant metaphor here is one of paying for the excesses of the past. For conservatives, the excesses are the libertarian permissions of the 1960s and 1970s, while for liberals they are related to the yuppie greed of the 1980s. In either case, the call for frugality, austerity, and rollback sounds across the whole spectrum of civil society, and is consecrated in the 'budget cult' of the postmodern fiscal state. In this milieu of reduced expectations, the mission of 'saving the planet' often serves as a compensatory ideology for a generation of eco-kids perceived to be suffering from the prospect of an ever-shrinking future. The heavily Christianized language of sacrifice and redemption recalls a long history in the West of justifying poverty and social inequality by making promises about the kingdom to come. Every recessionary moment, and the present one is no exception, sees the revival of this language in the form of demands for concessions and forfeits, usually from those with the least wealth and power.

When US-led forces occupied famine-struck Somalia in the name of humanitarianism in the winter of 1993, foreign policy provided its own morality play about the sharing of sacrifice. In contrast to a war in the Gulf fought explicitly over control of natural resources, Somalia was supposed to be the kinder, gentler face of New World Order politics. Humanitarianism (not human rights) was the new interventionist ideology. The international relief NGOs attached to the UN acted as the new political agents. Food aid was the new geopolitical commodity. Never mind that the strife in Somalia was primarily the consequence of over a decade of Cold War client-state manipulation or that the famine was partly the result of the USA's political exploitation, through its own grain surplus, of the international hunger industry. Never mind that. There was something environmentalist about what the troops were doing. Smells like eco-spirit, so give peace a chance.

Operation Restore Hope was as much a public relations exercise in demonstrating the West's capacity for self-sacrifice as a way of securing a new ideological basis for interventionism. These days, the meaning of the spectacle of famine in an African country lies somewhat closer to home than it used to do. Indeed, it is almost a commonplace that the North American economy is increasingly creating conditions of underdevelopment more akin to those of Third World societies. With 35 million North Americans living below the poverty line, and 100,000 children homeless, famine in some distant 'famine-prone' sector of the globe can no longer be talked about in the neo-Darwinian rhetoric of the survival of the fittest — at least not when the fittest are no longer North Americans. With the drastic erosion of a domestic culture of abundance (in the USA, six out of ten incomes fell between 1977 and 1990) it is no longer so easy to obscure the common economic forces that sustain the extreme disparity between affluence and poverty in the First and Third World. The rise of environmentalism has further underscored the structural links between these respective conditions. Everything, we are asked to consider, is globally connected.

But environmental consciousness has not only helped to reinforce the current recessionary messages about self-sacrifice and deprivation in our daily lives. It has also provided some backing for the call to limit freedoms, because it offers an argument about 'natural limits,' based upon empirical projections, which (as in the case of sociobiology) can be used to support discourses of social limits. In the social realm, these discourses have taken the primary form of a conservative backlash against women's and minority rights, but they have been echoed in neoliberals' clarion call to exclude 'special interests,' and also in the hard left's complaint about the 'fragmentation' of old class-based alliances resulting from the growth of the new social movements. In the cultural realm, we have seen the holy war against sex-positive expression in art and popular culture, the moral injunction to 'just say no' to certain forms of cultural experience and experimentation, and the redrawing of social norms around the nebulous quotient of 'family values.' In the latter realm especially, the green ideology of the natural body in a natural environment can very easily translate into drastic prescriptions about social behavior, especially when it appeals to traditional or antimodern values, common to conservatives and greens alike.

While it may be necessary to rebut the call for limits — sounding across a whole spectrum from the economics of corporate environmentalism to the cultural politics of traditional values — it would be historically naive to suggest that cultural freedoms can be uncoupled from the social conditions in which they were won and are maintained today. On the one hand, popular consciousness tenaciously insists that people are less free when they have less to consume even though many consumers recognize that higher levels of consumption involve them in socially constraining networks of dependency and debt that are not always visible or economically quantifiable. But it is rank First World arrogance to suggest that people in nonconsumer societies are somehow more free in their less commodified ways, or more healthy in their freedom from diseases associated with life in high-consumption societies. On the other hand, new forms of cultural expression often find their most fertile soil in the pockets of permissibility created as a marginal offshoot of a free-market economy. Countercultures, alternative cultures, and underground cultures feed off this kind of surplus. Such forms of expression in an 'open' democratic society are as vital to the dynamics of social change as those created out of resistance to more oppressive circumstances in a 'closed' nondemocratic society. Neither enjoys the luxury of conditions of its own making. Not only may it be impossible, it is probably undesirable to abstract cultural freedoms and political rights, even natural rights deemed inalienable, from the social milieu in which they are exercised.

A larger problem, however, lies with our conceptual understanding of 'limits' themselves. Limits, whenever they are invoked, call to mind either a mechanical system with a restricted capacity for production or distribution, or some finite quantity of material resources. Yet neither of these is an adequate representation of the dynamic interplay between human societies and the natural world. More constraining yet is the suggestion of encountering limits or confines on a linear path, along which route we are then obliged to withdraw. This conceptual model, in particular, helps to support atavistic calls for a return to preindustrial infrastructures, or else punitive demands to scale back along the road of consumerist gratification and/or civil rights. The linear model of advance and retreat (there is nowhere else to go) is an equally inadequate way of representing the life of civil rights movements, which diversify their 'gains' almost immediately, each step forward being a step sideways (what Viktor Shklovsky in another context called the 'knight's move') into an alternate world where new and often unforeseen relations of power come into play, and where what had been seen as 'advances' at the previous stage now take on a different and less straightforward appearance. The sexual revolution is a case in point, where the sexuality of bodies has undergone a radical change in social meaning in the age of AIDS. So, too, fighting the battle over reproductive rights in the political landscape of the 1980s and 1990s means something different from the struggles that achieved legal protection of abortion in the 1970s. The clock is never turned back.

Above all, the discourse of limits is best eschewed wherever it implies that our lives and actions are to be reckoned according to some irrefutable calculus or moral cipher of nature. The kind of action needed to address the ecological crisis is not best served by coercive messages about restraint in the face of immutable outcomes. People respond better to a call for social fulfillment than to a summons to physical deprivation, and that is why any social movement that uses self-denial as a vehicle for inducing change is as pathetic as one that uses apocalyptic threats or appeals to Mother Nature's vengeance. A common conception of green politics in general is that the ecology movement aims to make people satisfied with less, and that the green code of voluntary simplicity is a democratic ideal, especially when it can be supported by apocalyptic predictions of material scarcity. The same perception used to apply in crude conceptions about communism, which Marx himself reviled: to wit, that since luxuries and privileges and 'bourgeois' desires were exclusive by definition, they ought to be scaled back and levelled down. Big Bill Haywood, the famous labor organizer, had a better response. When asked by a would-be leveller why he always smoked large cigars, he deadpanned: 'Son, nothing's too good for the proletariat.'

Unlike the other new social movements, ecology is commonly perceived as the one that says no, the antipleasure voice that says you're never gonna get it, so get used to going without. Theoretical support for this message can always be found elsewhere. Psycho-analysis is wheeled in as an explanation for psychic craving. Desire is always incomplete, it's founded on an impossible gap between the human drives and whatever reality they are perceived to correspond to – therefore, you're never gonna get it, so get used to going without. Hunting and gathering societies are cited as examples of the original affluent society, proving that the satisfaction of human needs and wants is really quite effortless – why work harder when you're never gonna get it, so get used to going without. The 'false needs' of consumer capitalism are cited as the reason for the inauthentic economy of our desires – no matter what the ads tell us, you're never gonna get it, so get used to going without.

So what are we left with? A dog's breakfast of self-denial, self-restraint, guilt, and disavowal – hardly promising instruments of liberation. Or else, we are barraged with persuasion by threat. Thus, a magazine ad I saw recently for New Cycle Menstrual Lingerie proclaims:

> Mother Earth won't swallow this for much longer! 11 billion disposable, chlorine-bleached menstrual pads buried or burned each year. Use cloth for Menstrual Flow! Confront the Inconvenience! Overcome the Taboo! Beautiful, soft, washable cloth menstrual pads & accessories in organic knit or cotton flannel. Next Time: Tampons as sexual harassment & earth abuse. Stay tuned. Don't stuff it! Reuse it! CALL 1-800-845-FLOW

Don't get me wrong about this ad. I am an advocate of reuse, and share the reservations of many environmentalists about the preference of big business for recycling practices.[30] I submit, however, that people for the most part do not respond favorably to coercive messages of this sort that invoke guilt and self-denial. No more productive is a frontal assault on consumer gratifications. The problem lies deeper. Consumerism has shallow historical roots (only two or three generations in the West), but the concept of perpetual scarcity is deeply entrenched in our minds and cultural memories – there simply isn't enough to go around, sounds the ominous refrain. The history of liberal political economy that runs from Adam Smith and David Hume to Malthus, Ricardo, Marx, Mill and thence onto Keynes, Galbraith, and Marcuse is, from a certain angle, little more than a long debate about the exact ratio between natural scarcity and social scarcity.[31] For those who reject the postulates of classical economics about the permanance of scarcity, it is a debate about whether the postscarcity future of abundance comes about (a) through the market creation of wealth, (b) through some grand postcapitalist transition in social development, (c) through a reversion to premodernist production, or (d) through a simple transcendence of the present structure of inequalities. In recent years, we have seen economic rationalism reinstitutionalize scarcity as a universal condition, rendered tolerable only by the profitable manipulation of markets designed to address the imbalance between supply and demand. The result? The kind of cost-benefit analysis that can accommodate, if it does not serve as an actual blueprint for, corporate environmentalism. Alternately, the ecological crisis has raised the specter of new forms of scarcity not envisaged by any of the thinkers in the classical tradition of liberal politics. The result? Calls to scale back our hard-won liberties, now equated with the excesses of Western privilege and abundance upon which our liberal political institutions were founded.

In this respect, it is easy to see how the practice of wielding the threat of eco-collapse is an activist sword that cuts both ways. It has prompted action in many quarters — communities, institutions, governments — but, like any other political movement partially pursued through coercive, and not liberatory, means, it has also laid the basis for a draconian politics that is not always friendly to civil rights and social freedoms. The eco-apocalypse, however useful as an activist tool, is sometimes only another means of exploiting the category of scarcity — it cannot in itself help us create a politics of liberation. Much better to abolish the concept of scarcity altogether. But doesn't that mean doing away with abundance as well? If scarcity is an invention of modernity, then surely the concept of plenty is equally a myth of modernity's ideas about the future, not to mention the lost golden age? Those of us who still want to retain the idea of a postscarcity future may have to reexamine the content of the 'better world' traditionally promised as a haven of abundance in the tradition of utopian thought. Postscarcity describes a moment when scarcity is no longer an operative concept; it does not necessarily describe an economy where distribution is just and equal, and where scarcity has been temporarily staved off. Getting rid of scarcity is not the same as getting rid of hunger and poverty, although it may coincide with or lead to that happy state of affairs. Getting rid of the concept of scarcity is part of the cultural work that is necessary in order to make a world in which hunger and poverty

270

no longer prevail. In that very different world, scarcity no longer exists conceptually as a default condition, and an ecological society has developed a more democratic way of ordering its priorities. Such a world lies in the future, not in a mythical past to be recreated by simply scaling back current levels of production and consumption.

For a critique so focused on the natural world, it may seem ironic that I should be advocating an ecology that looks first and foremost to the task of social reorganization and cultural innovation for its cardinal principles. It has been a good part of my argument in this book, however, that nature does not always know best, nor does it always harbor the most beneficial solutions. Technologies, for example, that are based upon natural elements, or that imitate natural processes (Lewis Mumford, after Patrick Geddes, called them biotechnics) are no guarantee of health, sustainability, or even biodiversity. Substances extracted from the Brazilian rainforest can be used to make toxic chemical compounds; in fact, many of the most toxic chemicals are naturally occurring elements, not industrial products. Principles of animal physiology are habitually used to construct weapons of destruction; the dreaded heatseeking missile, for example, was modelled upon the heat-sensitive snout of the rattlesnake. Biomorphic houses designed according to the principles of botanical architecture — the growth rate of bamboo shoots, the structure of a rose — are just as likely to be instruments of social apartheid as housing modelled on industrial factories.[32] As for biotech's more advanced industrialization of life forms, recombinant DNA — the results of technologies considered nontoxic and environmentally friendly by past industrial standards — is capable of introducing catastrophic strains into the open environment. Genetic engineering was sold as an eco-conscious technology that might fix the ecological damage wrought by earlier energy-intensive technologies, and eventually restore the balance between human industry and nature. Such promises could not shake off their vile associations with racist ideologies about the social perfection of nature, while their hungry reception by the corporate welfare state raised alarm signals among those who feared a new round of social control through biomedecine. Besides, for the sociobiologists and neo-Malthusians, who do not see nature as a harmonious theater of activity, restoring equilibrium would necessarily involve the kind of competitive violence and extinction of the unfit that they see as natural components of all forms of social life. Just as people have different ideas about what nature's balance might be, so too, their versions of abundance and scarcity are often at odds: poor people, for example, have little patience with the voluntarist bohemian philosophy of 'in poverty, abundance.'

At this point in the debates about ecological politics, it is imperative to have some arguments against conceiving nature as a model of behavior, let alone a moral authority, magistrate, or lord high executioner. Judgments, models, and arguments from nature are usually always derived from society. This is something that does not go without saying. The idea, never exhausted and ever more current today, that nature's way is going to free us is a cruel inversion of the idea that liberation from nature is what frees us — the very idea that helped get us into this mess in the first place. Neither nature nor economics are conscious agents; consequently, our best future lies with an anti-Malthusian belief in the power of human needs and abilities to reorganize the social order of the natural and economic world.

Even more important, however, is the task of imagining what lies beyond scarcity, and to do so in ways that account for the very different character of people's desires. Here, we surely bump up against the conceptual limits of our own political imagination. Much of environmental literature is full of practical blueprints for, and statistical projections of, an ecological society. This book, by contrast, has offered no such programmatic agendas, subscribing to the belief that a radically different future only comes about through hard critique of the present, including a critique of our conceptual frames for imagining the future. Utopias do not come about without struggle; everything must be called into doubt if everything is to be declared possible. Statistics just don't do the trick when what is required is a transformation of our own political consciousness. With these caveats in mind, what kind of admittedly abstract eco-utopian aims am I prepared to describe at this point?

A world of common prosperity, for sure, where social fulfillment is experienced individually as well as collectively, but not as a feat of private gratification enjoyed and prized because others are not in a position to do so. This would be a world where public goods are no longer considered to be in short supply or in lavish excess, neither indigent nor affluent, if only because they would now be taken for granted and assumed to be a normative part of our daily, social environment. A world where individual gratification is intensified, and not determined, by concerns for common environmental well-being: where transnationalism is a promoter and not a saboteur of local self-sufficiency; where hedonism has replaced asceticism as the dominant mode of green conduct; where forms of cross-species justice have replaced misanthropic 'laws' of nature as ecological rules of thumb; and where nature itself is a participant in our social plans, and not an authority locking us privately and publicly into some incontrovertible fate.

As with scarcity, abundance is usually only perceived as plenitude when it is thrust upon us or at us. The boosterism currently associated with the Information Age is a case in point; who really needs to be in the constant state of bounteous hypercommunication promised by all the ads? The blissed-out invitations to venture into cyberspace carry an undertow of retribution for those rash or obstinate enough to decline the Info Love Boat. Refuse this abundance and you will be perceived as obsolete: a citizen with no information access. (This is the true face of *1984*-style domination in a consumer society; oppression does not come in the form of 24-hour online surveillance, it consists of being excluded, by individual choice, from the Net.) Leaving aside the many radical uses that can be made of the new communications technology, it would be foolish to ignore the logic that links these heady promises of cybernetic profusion with the austerity regime of resource scarcity enforced elsewhere. Here, surely, is a dual condition that is vital to the exercise of power in a consumer economy, systematically regulating the barometric highs and lows of citizen desire. The corporate and state institutions that introduce these forms of coercive scarcity and abundance into our lives are the same institutions primarily responsible for the ecological crisis. But central tendencies in mainstream environmentalist thought, as I have tried to show, have also helped to perpetuate the conceptual grip of scarcity/abundance upon our social imagination.

Enough of these cycles of binge and purge. Let us get on with the task, crucially deepened by the ecology movement, of challenging and transforming those institutions which profit from such cycles and which are even now wearing their newfound environmentalism like some bad-taste badge of honor.

Notes

Introduction

1. As Anita Roddick, founder of the Body Shop, puts it: 'a socially responsible business operates in a manner consistent with principles of sustainable development, respects human rights, and minimizes the environmental impact of its operations at all times.' 'The Business of Business,' *Utne Reader*, 59 (September/October 1993), p. 67.

2. See Michael Redclift's early account, in *Sustainable Development: Exploring the Contradictions* (London: Routledge 1987); and Tom Athanasiou's report on the Earth Summit in Rio, 'After the Summit,' *Socialist Review*, 92, 4 (October/December 1992), pp. 57–92. In his recent article, 'Political Ecology: Expertocracy versus Self-Limitation,' *New Left Review*, 202 (November–December 1993), pp. 55–68, André Gorz argues that the sustainability so esteemed by MBAs may be little more than a codeword for the elite management of a hitherto unregulated process — the plundering of nature by everyone.

3. Robert Stavins and Thomas Grumbly, 'The Greening of the Market: Making the Polluter Pay,' in Will Marshall and Martin Schram (eds), *Mandate for Change* (New York: Berkley Books, 1993), pp. 197–216. See also Al Gore, *Earth in the Balance: Ecology and the Human Spirit* (New York: Houghton Mifflin, 1992).

4. This condition has been debated at some length in the journal *Capitalism, Nature, Socialism* under the editorial direction of James O'Connor.

5. The Natural Resources Defense Council, the Enviornmental Defense Fund, the World Wildlife Fund for Nature, the National Audubon Society, and Conservation International supported NAFTA. Opposing the pact were Greenpeace, the Sierra Club, Friends of the Earth, Earth Island Institute, Public Interest Research Group, Rainforest Action Network, Public Citizen, and the American Society for the Prevention of Cruelty to Animals. There was much less of a split over the Uruguay Round agreement of GATT, with almost all of these organizations in opposition to a set of rules that could serve to gut existing global protocols for environmental regulation in the name of eliminating trade sanctions.

6. In *Blood and Soil: R. Walther Darre and Hitler's 'Green Party'* (Bourne End, Bucks.: Kensal Press, 1985), and *Ecology in the 20th Century: A History* (New Haven: Yale University Press, 1989), Anna Bramwell has examined the relationship of green ideology to the Third Reich, and to reactionary back-to-nature movements in Germany, Britain, and North America.

7. For a polemical account of the whole spectrum of tendencies, see Carolyn Merchant, *Radical Ecology: The Search for a Livable World* (New York: Routledge, 1992).

8. See Roderick Nash, 'Do Rocks Have Rights?' *Center Magazine,* 10 (December 1977), pp. 2–12; and *The Rights of Nature: A History of Environmental Ethics* (Madison: University of Wisconsin Press, 1989); Christopher Stone, *Should Trees Have Standing? Toward Legal Rights for Natural Objects* (Los Altos, Ca.: W. Kauffman, 1974).

9. Susanna Hecht and Alexander Cockburn give a comprehensive history of these alliances in *The Fate of the Forest: Developers, Destroyers and Defenders of the Amazon* (New York: Harper, 1990).

10. See Susan Meeker-Lowry, 'Killing Them Softly: The 'Rainforest Harvest,'' *Z Magazine,* 6, 7/8 (July–August 1993) pp. 41–7; and the exchanges between Stephen Corry, of Survival International, and Alexander Cockburn, in *The Nation* (November 30, 1992).

11. Ted Benton, *Natural Relations: Ecology, Animal Rights and Social Justice* (London: Verso, 1993), p. 176.

12. See Robert Bullard, *Dumping in Dixie: Race, Class, and Environmental Quality* (Boulder, Co.: Westview Press, 1990); and Bullard (ed.), *Confronting Environmental Racism: Voices From the Grassroots* (Boston: South End Press, 1993).

13. See Kirkpatrick Sale, *Dwellers in the Land: The Bioregional Vision* (Philadelphia: New Society Publishers, 1991).

14. Shelby Steele. *The Content of our Character: A New Vision of Race in America* (New York: St. Martin's Press, 1991).

15. See Garret Hardin, *The Limits to Altruism: An Ecologist's View of Survival* (Bloomington: Indiana University Press, 1977); *Living Within Limits: Ecology, Economics, and Population Taboos* (New York: Oxford University Press, 1993); Donald Worster, *The Wealth of Nature: Environmental History and the Ecological Imagination* (New York: Oxford University Press, 1993); William Catton, *Overshoot: The Ecological Basis of Revolutionary Change* (Urbana: University of Illinois Press, 1980); Paul and Anne Ehrlich, *The Population Explosion* (New York: Simon & Schuster, 1990); William Ophuls, *Ecology and the Politics of Scarcity: Prologue to a Political Theory of the Steady State* (San Francisco: W.H. Freeman and Co., 1977); Norman Myers, *The Sinking Ark* (Oxford: Pergamon, 1979).

16. It is almost redundant to cite sources, since these sentiments are so pervasive. The exception, among major ecological thinkers, is Murray Bookchin, who has argued consistently for a postscarcity society, in a series of books, from *Post-Scarcity Anarchism* (Berkeley: Ramparts Press, 1971) to *Remaking Society: Pathways Toward a Green Future* (Boston: South End, 1990). *The Ecology of Freedom* (Palo Alto: Chesire Books, 1982) is perhaps the most exhaustive presentation of his thought.

17. See James Lovelock, *Gaia: A New Look at Life on Earth* (Oxford: Oxford University Press, 1979); and *The Ages of Gaia: A Biography of our Living Earth* (New York: Norton, 1988); Lawrence Joseph, *Gaia: The Growth of an Idea* (New York: St. Martin's Press, 1990); Lynn Margulis and Dorion Sagan, *Microcosmos: Four Billion Years of Microbial Evolution* (New York: Summit Books, 1986); William Irwin Thompson (ed.), *Gaia: A Way of Knowing: Political Implications of the New Biology* (Great Barrington, Mass.: Lindisfarne Press, 1987); Elisabet Sahtouris, *Gaia: The Human Journey from Chaos to Cosmos* (New York: Pocket Books, 1989); Michael Allaby, *Guide to Gaia* (London: Macdonald, 1990).

18. See Michael Watts, *Silent Violence: Food, Famine, and Peasantry in Northern Nigeria* (Berkeley: University of California Press, 1983); and David Goodman and Michael Redclift, *Refashioning Nature: Food, Ecology, and Culture* (London: Rout-

ledge, 1991).

19. David Pepper, *Eco-Socialism: From Deep Ecology to Social Justice* (New York: Routledge, 1993), p. 5.

20. Mark Lewis has written a sharp critique of these antiprogressive tendencies and others, in *Green Delusions: An Environmentalist Critique of Radical Environmentalism* (Durham: Duke University Press, 1992).

21. John Young, *Sustaining the Earth* (Cambridge, Mass.: Harvard University Press, 1990), p. 36.

22. Peter Kropotkin, *Mutual Aid: A Factor of Evolution* (London: William Heinemann, 1902), p. 74–75.

1. Cultural Preservation in the Polynesia of the Latter-Day Saints

1. For an account of the recent political developments, see Victor Lal's *Fiji, Coups in Paradise: Race, Politics, and Military Intervention* (London: Zed Books, 1990). Commentators differ as to whether race or class was the decisive factor in the Taukei movement that led to the coup. In *Fiji: Race and Politics in an Island State*, Michael Howard argues that the chiefly elite of the Eastern-dominated establishment had been challenged by the assertive interests of the Western provinces in the Labour Party. Taukei was merely an ideological cover. A. Ravuvu presents the case for race in *The Facade of Democracy: Fijian Struggle for Political Control* (Suva: University of South Pacific, 1991). See also the Fijian special issue of *The Contemporary Pacific*, 2, 1 (Spring 1991) edited by Brij Lal, entitled 'As The Dust Settles;' and David Robie, *Blood on the Banner: Nationalist Struggles in the South Pacific* (London: Zed Books, 1989).

2. Evidence for direct US involvement, rather than mere moral support, is spotty, but some hold to this view: 'Noor Dean, Deputy Speaker of the now-deposed Bavadra government, said he was positive that the so-called Fijian soldiers who invaded his parliament were in fact US Marines.' Lenora Foerstel (ed.), *Women's Voices on the Pacific*, the proceedings of The International Pacific Policy Congress organized by Women for Mutual Security (Washington, DC: Mainsonneuve Press, 1991), p. 37.

3. Quoted by Bengt Danielsson and Marie-Thérèse Danielsson, *Poisoned Reign: French Nuclear Colonialism in the Pacific* (Harmondsworth: Penguin, 1977), p. 29.

4. Quoted in Scott L. Malcolmson, *Tuturani: A Political Journey in the Pacific Islands* (London: Hamish Hamilton, 1991), pp. 76–7.

5. This has been the legacy of the school of historiography pioneered by J.W. Davidson at the Australian National University. One of the most persuasive recent attempts to think beyond the 'fatal impact' thesis is Nicholas Thomas's *Entangled Objects: Exchange, Material Culture, and Colonialism in the Pacific* (Cambridge, Mass.: Harvard University Press, 1991).

6. See Arif Dirlik (ed.), *What is in a Rim? Critical Perspectives on the Asia-Pacific Idea* (Boulder, Co.: Westview Press, 1993); 'Asia/Pacific as Space of Cultural Production' special issue edited by Rob Wilson and Arif Dirlik, *boundary 2*, 21, 1 (Spring 1994); Albert Robillard (ed.), *Social Change in the Pacific Islands* (London: Routledge, 1992).

7. Scott L. Malcolmson, *Tuturani*, p. 152. Malcolmson's politically self-conscious odysseys in the Pacific are worth comparing with the rude self-indulgence of Paul Theroux's *The Happy Isles of Oceania: Paddling the Pacific* (New York: Putnam, 1992).

8. Clive Ponting, *A Green History of the World* (London: Penguin, 1992).

9. See William C. Clarke's account of these traditional environmentalist practices, in 'Learning from the Past: Traditional Knowledge and Sustainable Development,' *The Contemporary Pacific*, 2, 2 (Fall 1990), pp. 233−53; and G.A. Klee (ed.), *World Systems of Traditional Resource Management* (London: Edward Arnold, 1980).

10. See Roy Rappaport's classic *Pigs for the Ancestors: Ritual in the Ecology of a New Guinea People* (New Haven: Yale University Press, 1967), for a study of how rituals control environmental management in the Madang district of the New Guinea Highlands.

11. Marshall Sahlins gives a comprehensive account of this process in *Islands of History* (University of Chicago Press, 1985).

12. K.R. Howe makes this point in *Where the Waves Fall: A New South Seas Islands History, from First Settlement to Colonial Rule* (Honolulu: University of Hawaii Press, 1984), pp.164−8.

13. See Lilikala Kame'eleihiwa's account of the ambivalent response of *ali'i* to the privatization of land in Hawaii. Kame'eleihiwa argues that, in agreeing to Western demands for privatization, the chiefs believed they were further sharing, rather than 'dividing' the land. *Native Land and Foreign Desires: Pehea la e Pono ai (How Shall We Live in Harmony?) A History of Land Tenure Changes in Hawaii from Traditional Time until the 1848 Mahele* (Honolulu: Bishop Museum Press, 1992).

14. Despite these fantasies of abundance in nature, Kirkpatrick Sale argues that the European replacement of the multicrop *conuco* system on Española − a highly productive and self-sustaining system with a continuous harvest − with imported European crops led to recurrent famines. The row-style plantation system and the red-meat *ranchero* system that were introduced by Columbus made little sense in tropical ecosystems; soils were eroded, rivers silted over and dried up, and deforestation was rampant. Scarcity (from the point of view of a European diet) was thereby introduced to a region where it had been alien. *The Conquest of Paradise: Christopher Columbus and the Columbian Legacy* (New York: Knopf, 1990), pp. 162−6.

15. Howe, *Where the Waves Fall*, p. 88.

16. Sahlins, *Islands of History*, pp. 1−31.

17. Caroline Ralston, 'Changes in the Lives of Ordinary Women in Early Post-Contact Hawaii,' in Margaret Jolly and Martha MacIntyre (eds), *Family and Gender in the Pacific: Domestic Contradictions and the Colonial Impact* (Cambridge University Press, 1989), pp. 45−64.

18. Perhaps we can never know or say how much Western fantasy, for example, is bound up in Douglas Oliver's relatively recent observation that the sexual habits of traditional Pacific Islanders varied from the extreme of Tahiti, 'most of whose sexually potent members copulated frequently, pleasurably, and almost openly,' to that of the Mae Enga of the New Guinea Highlands, for whom 'sexual intercourse was generally considered to be debilitating and magically dangerous, especially for males, whose fear of the pollution effects of menstrual blood approached paranoia.' *Native Cultures of the Pacific Islands* (Honolulu: University of Hawaii Press, 1989), p. 53. Doubtless, there is some continuity, however, with the eighteenth-century idealization of Polynesia, on the one hand, as a lost preindustrial state of nature, and the denigration of Melanesia, on the other, as an ugly caricature of industrial capitalism.

19. Bernard Smith, *European Vision and the South Pacific*, 2nd edn (New Haven: Yale University Press, 1985).

20. Bernard Smith, 'Style, Information and Image in the Art of Cook's Voyages,' in *Imagining the Pacific: In the Wake of the Cook Voyages* (New Haven: Yale University Press, 1992) pp. 173−91.

21. Margaret Mead, Preface to *Coming of Age in Samoa* (New York: William Morrow, 1961, 1928).

22. Ibid.

23. James Clifford has named this kind of narrative 'salvage ethnography,' where the Other is lost at the very moment it becomes the object of ethnographic study, and can only be saved in the text: 'the persistent and repetitious "disappearance" of social forms at the moment of their ethnographic representation demands analysis as a narrative structure.' 'On Ethnographic Allegory,' in James Clifford and George Marcus (eds), *Writing Culture: The Poetics and Politics of Ethnography* (Berkeley, Ca.: University of California Press, 1986), p. 112. In *Equatoria* (New York: Routledge, 1992), Richard and Sally Price have also written about their ambivalent attempts to respond to an invitation to help institute a museum of traditional and popular art in Guyane and thereby 'save' traditional culture from oblivion.

24. H.R. 4739, 6/3/88, Foreign Affairs Committee. Reprinted in *Cultural Survival Quarterly* 12, 2 (1988), pp. 67−8. The bill did not pass.

25. Derek Freeman, *Margaret Mead and Samoa: The Making and Unmaking of an Anthropological Myth* (Cambridge, Mass.: Harvard University Press, 1983).

26. See Lenora Foerstel and Angela Gilliam (eds), *Confronting the Margaret Mead Legacy: Scholarship, Empire, and the South Pacific* (Philadelphia: Temple University Press, 1992).

27. Thor Heyerdahl, *Fatu-Hiva: Back to Nature* (London: Allen & Unwin, 1974) (hereafter *FH*).

28. See Alan Howard's comprehensive history of this obsession, 'Polynesian Origins and Migrations: A Review of Two Centuries of Speculation and Theory,' in Genevieve A. Highland (ed.), *Polynesian Culture History* (Honolulu: Bishop Museum Special Publications, 56), pp. 45−101.

29. Malcolm Crick, 'Tracing the Anthropological Self: Quizzical Reflections on Field Work, Tourism, and the Ludic,' *Social Analysis*, 17 (August 1985), pp. 71−92.

30. In his iconoclastic book, *The Apotheosis of Captain Cook: European Mythmaking in the Pacific* (Princeton University Press, 1992), Gananath Obeyesekere suggests that the thesis of Cook's deification was largely a European myth (drawing upon prior myths about Columbus and Cortes) accepted by or imposed upon Hawaiians in the interregnum between the old and the new religion. Cook was installed, and dismembered, as a Hawaiian chief (and therefore treated 'like' a deity), but no one took him for a Hawaiian, least of all a Hawaiian deity. Obeyesekere argues that the Makahiki festival to honor Lono, with which Cook's arrival coincided, was a minor festival until it was glorified by Kamehameha as 'the main national ritual of integration.'

31. See Valene Smith's introduction to *Hosts and Guests: The Anthropology of Tourism*, 2nd edn (Philadelphia: University of Pennsylvania Press, 1989).

32. Dean McCannell, 'Cannibalism Today,' in *Empty Meeting Grounds: The Tourist Papers* (New York: Routledge, 1992), pp. 17−73.

33. See Paul Greenhalgh, *Ephemeral Vistas: The Expositions Universelles, Great Exhibitions and World's Fairs, 1851−1939* (Manchester University Press, 1988). As far as American imperial display goes, the Buffalo Pan American World's Fair in 1901 was the first to include native exhibits from Cuba, Puerto Rico, Alaska, the Hawaiian Islands, and the Philippines.

34. T.D. Webb, 'Profit and Prophecy: The Polynesian Cultural Center and Laie's Recurrent Colonialism,' forthcoming in the *Hawaiian Historical Journal*.

35. The nearest thing to an objective history of the PCC is a doctoral dissertation

completed by Craig Ferre in 1988 in Theater and Film at BYU, Hawaii: 'A History of the Polynesian Cultural Center's Night Show', 1963–1983.' Of less interest is the PCC's official celebration of itself, Robert O'Brien's *Hands Across The Water* (Laie, 1983). Other scholarly accounts of the PCC include Max Stanton's articles, 'The Polynesian Cultural Center: A Multi-Ethnic Model of Seven Pacific Cultures,' in Valene Smith (ed.), *Hosts and Guests*, pp. 247–62, and 'The Polynesian Cultural Center: Presenting Polynesia to the World or the World to Polynesia,' in Ben Finney and Karen Ann Watson (eds), *A New Kind of Sugar: Tourism in the Pacific* (Santa Cruz, Ca.: Center for South Pacific Studies, 1977), pp. 229–33; James Whitehurst, 'Mormons and the Hula: The Polynesian Cultural Center in Hawaii,' *Journal of American Culture*, 12, 1, (Spring 1989), pp. 1–5; and Rubina Forrester, 'The Polynesian Cultural Center: The Realization Gone Far Beyond the Dream,' paper presented to Mormon Pacific Historical Society, 1986; also Anne-Marie Robinson, 'The Polynesian Cultural Center: A Study in Authenticity,' *Chico Anthropology Society Papers*, 13 (1991).

36. Terry Webb, 'Highly Structured Tourist Art: Form and Meaning of the Polynesian Cultural Center,' *The Contemporary Pacific* (January 1994). As Webb points out, the Marquesan presentation has been revised after the PCC's 'discovery that Marquesan society really isn't dead after all, but has actually flourished in its home islands.'

37. See William Mitchell (ed.), *Clowning as Critical Practice: Performance Humor in the South Pacific* (University of Pittsburgh Press, 1992), especially Caroline Sinavaiana, 'Where the Spirits Laugh Last: Comic Theater in Samoa,' pp. 192–218; and Vilsoni Tausie Hereniko, 'Polynesian Clowns and Satirical Comedies,' PhD thesis, University of South Pacific, Suva.

38. Max Stanton, 'Mormons and Matais: Status and Change among Samoans in Laie, Hawaii,' paper presented at American Anthropological Association, 1972 (in Pacific Collection, University of Hawaii, Manoa).

39. Craig Ferre suggests that a decisive factor in including the Fijian village was the architectural attraction of the tall slender towers of the heathen temples (*bure kalou*). 'A History of the Night Show,' p. 33.

40. R. Lanier Britsch, *Unto the Islands of the Sea* (Salt Lake City: Deseret, 1986), p. 502. After 1979, when the Church's 'negro problem' was resolved, many more missionaries moved into Melanesia.

41. Raymond Firth, *We, The Tikopia: A Sociological Study of Kinship in Primitive Polynesia* (London: Allen & Unwin, 1936).

42. Epeli Hauofa, 'Anthropology and Pacific Islanders,' Institute of Papua New Guinea Studies, Discussion Paper No. 8 (Port Moresby, PNG, 1975), p. 3.

43. See Jocelyn Linnekin and Lin Poyer (eds), *Cultural Identity and Ethnicity in the Pacific* (Honolulu: University of Hawaii Press, 1990).

44. In *Tourism as Cultural Learning: Two Controversial Case Studies in Educational Anthropology* (Washington, DC: University Press of America, 1977), the most extensive study of the PCC, Theodore Brameid and Midori Matsuyama criticized those features of the park that prevent greater intercultural awareness, and recommend more authenticity of detail in the presentations. This includes their suggestion that the women wear dresses above the knee, and bare their breasts. PCC administrators responded to the study by lamenting the 'continuous supercilious insinuation' of the authors' assumption of moral superiority over the Mormon community (p. 52).

45. Alexander Wilson, *The Culture of Nature: North American Landscape from Disney to the Exxon Valdez* (Oxford: Basil Blackwell, 1992).

46. Nonetheless, longstanding complaints about the heritage industry's sanitized

narratives have led to a good deal of rethinking among curators about the ethics of historical reconstructions. This has resulted in postmodern attempts to preserve some of the history of reconstructing history — what a 1930s version of the colonial USA looked like, for example. See Wilson, *The Culture of Nature*, pp. 217–19.

47. Michael Sorkin (ed.), *Variations on a Theme Park: The New American City and the End of Public Space* (New York: Hill & Wang, 1992).

48. See Bruce Robbins' critique of this narrative in 'The Public as Phantom,' his introduction to *The Phantom Public Sphere* (Minneapolis: University of Minnesota Press, 1993).

49. See John Urry, *The Tourist Gaze: Leisure and Travel in Contemporary Societies* (London: Sage, 1990).

50. I was told that the University of the South Pacific, in Suva, is currently considering a PCC-type complex to help fund students' education.

51. John L. Culliney, *Islands in a Far Sea: Nature and Man in Hawaii* (San Francisco: Sierra Club Books, 1988), p. 177.

52. Patrick Vinton Kirch, *Feathered Gods and Fishhooks: An Introduction to Hawaiian Archaeology and Prehistory* (Honolulu: University of Hawaii Press, 1985). To explain this divergence, Kirch leans, lightly, on sociobiology, by referring to the 'founder effect' in biological evolution, which occurs 'when a new island or environment is colonized by one or a few individuals of a species who do not carry the full genetic complement of the larger mother population. Thus as natural selection begins to operate on this restricted 'sample' of the genetic complement of the original species population, the descendants will begin to diverge — often significantly — from the ancestral form. An analogous process occurred with the settlement of remote islands by small groups of Polynesians' (p. 285).

53. For a detailed, local study of postcontact developments, see the collaborative study by Marshall Sahlins and Patrick Kirch of the mediation of the 'world capitalist system' by local cultural forces in a Hawaiian river valley community, *Anahulu: The Anthropology of History in the Kingdom of Hawaii*, 2 volumes (University of Chicago Press, 1992). Kirch seems to have changed his mind about his thesis (advanced in the earlier *Feathered Gods and Fishhooks*) of declining population in the immediate precontact period. In *Anahulu*, he suggests that population was still increasing at the time of Cook's first visit (vol. 2, p. 170).

54. David Stannard, *Before the Horror: The Population of Hawaii on the Eve of Western Contact* (Honolulu: Social Science Research Institute, University of Hawaii, 1989); Haunani-Kay Trask, introduction to *From a Native Daughter: Colonialism and Sovereignty in Hawaii* (Monroe, Maine: Common Courage Press, 1993) pp. 4–7.

55. Harold Lloyd Lyon, 'Ten Years in Hawaiian Forestry,' *Hawaiian Planters' Record*, XXXIII (January 1, 1929), p. 58.

56. Culliney, *Islands*, pp. 210–12.

57. See Werner Sollers, *Beyond Ethnicity: Consent and Descent in American Culture* (New York: Oxford University Press, 1986), pp. 102–30.

58. David Stannard gives this estimate in *Before the Horror*.

59. The classic account, according to dependency theory, is Noel J. Kent, *Hawaii: Islands under the Influence* (New York: Monthly Review Press, 1983).

60. See, for example, Jonathan Friedman, 'Cook, Culture and the World System,' in *Journal of Pacific History*, 20 (1985), pp. 191–201; and Marshall Sahlins' response in 'Deserted Islands of History,' *Critique of Anthropology*, 8, 3 (1988), pp. 41–51.

61. Sahlins, *Islands of History*, p. 30.

62. See Davianna Pomaika'i McGregor, *'Kupa'a I Ka 'Aina*: Persistence on the Land,' PhD dissertation, University of Hawaii, 1989; and Jocelyn Linnekin's

study of exchange-in-kind economies in Keanae, *Children of the Land: Exchange of Status in a Hawaiian Community* (New Brunswick: Rutgers University Press, 1985).

63. See Davianna McGregor-Alegado, 'Hawaiian Resistance, 1887–1889,' MA thesis in Pacific Island Studies, University of Hawaii.

64. The renaissance is chronicled in texts from Albert Wendt's 'Towards a New Oceania,' in Guy Amirthanayagam (ed.), *Writers in East-West Encounter: New Cultural Bearings* (London: Macmillan, 1982), to Subramani's *South Pacific Literature: From Myth to Fabulation* (Suva: University of South Pacific Press, 1985), to Rob Wilson, *Re-Imagining the American Pacific: Local Culture, National Identity, Transnational Space* (Durham: Duke University Press, forthcoming).

65. Kame'eleihiwa, *Native Land*, pp. 22–3.

66. See Haunani-Kay Trask, '*Kupa'a 'Aina*: Native Hawaiian Nationalism in Hawaii,' in Zachary A. Smith and Richard C. Pratt (eds), *Politics and Public Policy in Hawaii* (Buffalo: SUNY Press, 1992), pp. 243–60.

67. Haunani-Kay Trask, 'Hawaiian Nationalism,' *Ka Huliau* (April–May 1983) (MS in Hawaiian Collection, University of Hawaii library), p. 8.

68. See George Kanahele, *Ku Kanaka, Stand Tall: A Search for Hawaiian Values* (Honolulu: Project Waiaha, 1982); and George Lewis, 'Don' Go Down Waikiki: Social Protest and Popular Music in Hawaii,' in Reebee Garofalo (ed.), *Rockin' the Boat* (Boston: South End Press, 1992), pp. 171–83.

69. *Aloha 'Aina* (Molokai, PKO Fund, Summer 1979), p. 9.

70. See Roger Keesing and R. Tonkinson (eds), 'Reinventing Traditional Culture: The Politics of Kastom in Island Melanesia,' special issue of *Mankind*, 13, 4 (August 1982): Margaret Jolly, 'Specters of Inauthenticity,' *The Contemporary Pacific*, 4, 1 (1992); Jocelyn Linnekin, 'Defining Tradition: Variations of Hawaiian Identity,' *American Ethnologist* 70, 1 (1983), pp. 241–52; Roger Keesing, 'Creating the Past: Custom and Identity in the Contemporary Pacific,' *The Contemporary Pacific*, 1/2 (Spring and Fall 1989), pp. 19–42.

71. See Allan Hanson's controversial essay, 'The Making of the Maori: Culture Invention and its Logic,' *American Anthropologist* 91 (1989), pp. 890–902; and commentaries by Robert Langdon, H.B. Levine, and Jocelyn Linnekin, in *American Anthropologist*, 93 (1991), pp. 440–50.

72. See Haunani-Kay Trask, 'What Do You Mean "We," White Man?' *From a Native Daughter*, pp. 161–78; and the exchanges in *The Contemporary Pacific* between Roger Keesing, 'Creating the Past'; Haunani-Kay Trask, 'Natives and Anthropologists: The Colonial Struggle'; Keesing's 'Reply to Trask'; and Jocelyn Linnekin, 'Text Bites and the R-Word: The Politics of Representing,' all in 3, 1 (Spring 1991).

For other texts relevant to, and illustrative of, the invention of tradition school, see Klaus Neumann, *Not the Way It Really Was: Constructing the Tolai Past* (Honolulu: University of Hawaii Press, 1992); Roy Wagner, *The Invention of Culture* (Englewood Cliffs: Prentice Hall, 1975); Adam Kuper, *The Invention of Primitive Society* (London: Routledge, 1988); Jocelyn Linnekin, 'On the Theory and Politics of Cultural Construction in the Pacific,' *Oceania*, 62 (1992), pp., 249–63; Jocelyn Linnekin and Richard Handler, 'Tradition, Genuine or Spurious,' *Journal of American Folklore* 97, 385 (1984), pp. 273–90; and Allan Hanson, 'The Making of the Maori.'

73. Hugh Trevor-Roper, 'The Invention of Tradition: The Highland Tradition of Scotland,' in Eric Hobsbawm and Terence Ranger (eds), *The Invention of Tradition* (Cambridge University Press, 1983), pp. 15–41.

74. In Fiji, Governor Arthur Hamilton Gordon held a *kava* ceremony every night in Government House, where he furnished rooms, as in an ethnological museum, with displays of spears and clubs. Thomas, *Entangled Objects*, pp. 170–5.

75. See Geoffrey White, 'The Discourse of Chiefs: Notes on a Melanesian Society,' *The Contemporary Pacific* 4, 1. (Spring 1992), pp. 73–108.

76. Epeli Hauofa, 'The Future of Our Past,' in Robert Kiste and Richard Herr (eds), *The Pacific Islands in the Year 2000* (University of Hawaii at Manoa, Working Papers, Pacific Islands Studies Program, 1985), p. 152.

77. Epeli Hauofa, 'The New South Pacific Society: Integration and Independence,' in Anthony Hooper (ed.), *Class and Culture in the South Pacific* (Suva: University of South Pacific Press, 1987), p. 12.

78. In 1913, LDS missionaries reckoned that 22 per cent of Hawaiians were Mormons. R. Lanier Britsch, *Moramona: The Mormons in Hawaii* (Laie, Hawaii: Institute for Polynesian Studies), p. 119.

79. James Boutilier, Daniel Hughes, and Sharon Tiffany (eds), *Mission, Church, and Sect in Oceania* (Lanham, Md.: University Press of America, 1978); *Messengers of Grace: Evangelical Missionaries in the South Seas, 1797–1860* (Oxford University Press, 1978).

80. Harold Bloom has written quite brilliantly about the imaginative feat of Smith's invention of a new religion, in *The American Religion: The Emergence of the Post-Christian Nation* (New York: Simon & Schuster, 1992), pp. 77–128.

81. See Samuel George Ellsworth, *Zion in Paradise: Early Mormons in the South Seas* (Logan: Utah State University, 1959).

82. William A. Cole and Elwin W. Jensen, *Israel in the Pacific: A Genealogical Text for Polynesia* (Salt Lake City: Utah Genealogical Society, 1961), p. 40. Some Polynesians can trace their genealogy back for over 70 generations. Mormon genealogists reckon that 144 generations will get you to Adam. The longest in Hawaii is 27 generations short.

83. See Milton Hunter and Thomas Stuart Ferguson, *Ancient America and the Book of Mormon* (Oakland: Kolob Book Co., 1950).

84. R. Lanier Britsch, *Unto the Islands*, preface, p. xv.

85. Letter from 1819, *The Letters and Journals of Samuel Marsden*, ed. J.R. Elder (Dunedin: Coulls Somerville Wilkie, 1932), p. 219.

86. Josiah Priest, *American Antiquities and Discoveries in the West* (Albany: Hoffman and White, 1833).

87. Jacob Adler and Gwynn Barrett (eds), *The Diaries of Walter Murray Gibson 1886, 1887* (Honolulu: University of Hawaii Press, 1973), p. xiii.

88. Ibid., p. xiv.

89. Robert Kamins, *The Fantastic Life of Walter Murray Gibson: Hawaii's Minister of Everything* (Honolulu: University of Hawaii Press, 1986), pp. 69–72.

90. Edwin Burrows interprets these 'reversions' as a form of withdrawal rather than a form of resistance, *Hawaiian Americans: An Account of the Mingling of Japanese, Chinese, Polynesian and American Cultures* (New Haven: Yale University Press, 1947) p. 149. They were most pronounced in the 1820s and 1830s, when the Christian missions were at the height of their power and when foreigners were establishing political power, and again in the 1880s when the monarchy was tottering (pp. 148–55). Caroline Ralston describes the Hapu cult in southern Hawaii in relation to similar syncretic formations, like Mamaia in Tahiti, Sio Vili in Samoa, and Papahurihia in New Zealand, in 'Early Nineteenth Century Polynesian Millennial Cults and the Case of Hawai'i,' *Journal of the Polynesian Society*, 94, 4 (December 1985), pp. 307–31.

91. Kamins, *The Fantastic Life*, pp. 54–5.

92. Ibid., p. 52.

93. Tamar Gordon, 'Inventing Mormon Identity in Tonga' (PhD dissertation, University of California, Berkeley, 1988).

94. See Donna Haraway's account of the role of photography in the history of the American Museum of Natural History, 'Teddy Bear Patriarchy: Taxidermy in the Garden of Eden, New York City, 1908–1936,' in *Primate Visions: Gender, Race, and Nature in the World of Modern Science* (New York: Routledge, 1989).

95. For the history of Mormon involvement in science fiction see Constance Penley, *Popular Science* (London: Verso, forthcoming).

96. Ben Finney, *Hokule'a: The Way to Tahiti* (New York: Dodd, Mead, 1979): 'Myth, Experiment, and the Reinvention of Polynesian Voyaging,' *American Anthropologist*, 93 (1991), pp. 383–404: and *From Sea to Space* (Palmerston North: Massey University, 1992).

97. Brigham Young, *Discourses of Brigham Young*, selected and arranged by John A. Widstoe (Salt Lake City: Deseret Book Co. 1925) p. 616.

98. Quoted in Morris Fox, 'The Social Impact of Tourism,' in B.R. Finney and K.A. Watson (eds), *A New Kind of Sugar*, p. 30.

99. Ibid., p. 29.

100. George S, Kanahele, 'Tourism: Keeper of the Culture,' in John E. Hay (ed.), *Ecotourism: Business in the Pacific – Promoting a Sustainable Experience* (Conference Proceedings, University of Auckland and East-West Center, Honolulu, 1992), pp. 30–4.

101. See Valene Smith, 'Eskimo Tourism: Micro-Models and Marginal Men,' and Margaret Byrne Swain, 'Gender Roles in Indigenous Tourism: Kuna Mola, Kuna Yala, and Cultural Survival,' in Smith (ed.), *Host and Guests*, pp. 55–82, 83–104.

102. Kathleen Adams, 'Come to Tana Toraja, 'Land of the Heavenly Kings': Travel Agents as Brokers in Ethnicity,' *Annals of Tourism Research*, 11, 3 (1984), pp. 469–86.

103. Ward Churchill, 'Nobody's Pet Poodle,' *Z Magazine*, 5, 2 (February 1992), pp. 68–72.

104. Dean McCannell, 'Reconstructed Ethnicity: Tourism and Cultural Identity in Third World Communities,' in *Empty Meeting Grounds*, pp. 158–71.

105. See Barbara Kirshenblatt-Gimblett, 'The Objects of Ethnography,' in Ivan Karp and Steven D. Lavine (eds), *Exhibiting Cultures: The Poetics and Politics of Museum Display* (Washington, DC: Smithsonian Institute, 1991), p. 402.

106. For only one text from a vast literature on the subject, see Stephen Britton, 'The Political Economy of Tourism in Third World,' *Annals of Tourism Research*, 9, (1982), pp. 331–58.

107. Philip Frick McKean makes this argument in 'Towards a Theoretical Analysis of Tourism: Economic Dualism and Cultural Involution in Bali,' in Smith (ed.), *Hosts and Guests*, pp. 119–38.

108. See Elizabeth Buck's accounts of *hula* culture, in *Paradise Remade: The Politics of Culture and History in Hawaii* (Philadelphia: Temple University Press, 1993).

109. Nelson Graburn makes this analogy in 'The Evolution of Tourist Arts,' *Annals of Tourism Research*, 11, 3 (1984), pp. 393–420.

110. Stephen Greenblatt, *Marvellous Possessions: The Wonder of the New World* (University of Chicago Press, 1991), pp. 90–1.

111. R.J. Scott, quoted in John Samy, 'Crumbs from the Table: The Workers' Share in Tourism,' in Ron Crocombe and Freda Rajotte (eds), *Pacific Tourism: As Islanders See It* (Suva: Institute for Pacific Studies, 1980), p. 80.

112. *New York Times* (February 21, 1993), sec. 5, p. 15.

113. Marguerite Young, 'Ecotourism: Profitable Conservation,' in John Hay (ed), *Ecotourism Business in the Pacific: Promoting a Sustainable Experience* (Honolulu: East-West Center, 1992), p. 55. See, also, 'The New Ecotourism' issue of *Cultural*

Survival Quarterly (1990); Elizabeth Boo, *Ecotourism: The Potentials and Pitfalls* (Washington DC: World Wildlife Fund, 1990); Dwight Holing, *Earthtrips: A Guide to Nature Travel on a Fragile Planet* (Los Angeles: Living Planet Press, 1991); Andrew Mitchell, *The Fragile South Pacific: An Ecological Odyssey* (Austin: University of Texas Press, 1990).

114. Konai Helu-Thaman, 'Ecocultural Tourism: A Personal View For Maintaining Cultural Integrity in Ecotourism Development,' in Hay (ed.), *Ecotourism Business*, pp. 24−9.

115. See Patrick West and Steven Brechin (eds), *Resident Peoples and National Parks: Social Dilemmas and Strategies in International Conservation* (Tucson: University of Arizona Press, 1991).

116. K.R. Howe gives a detailed account of the rise of each of these dynasties in *Where the Waves Fall*, pp. 125−200.

117. Two of the most contested sites have been the geothermal developments at Kilauea volcano on the Big Island of Hawaii, and the Kalaupapa leper colony on Moloka'i. The successful opposition to the geothermal wells in the Puna district has involved ecologists and other natural scientists but has mostly been channelled through appeals to traditional Hawaiian religion and rights of access to the rainforests in the district; above all, the campaign has invoked the religious significance of the region as the home of the Goddess Pele.

At Kalaupapa, the former, mostly native Hawaiian, patients petitioned successfully for Congress to designate the colony a National Historic Park, which it did in 1980: it has since become a burgeoning tourist destination. In an ongoing study, Christine Harrington of NYU and Barbara Yngvesson of the University of New Hampshire show how this exercise in 'alternative tourism' has placed competing claims (from the National Park Service, the Hawaiian Home Lands Commission and the patients themselves) upon the discourse of *preservation*. The question of what should be preserved is indissociable from the question of entitlement claims to the land at Kalaupapa.

2. Bombing the Big Apple

1. See, for a variety of perspectives, David Gordon (ed.), *Green Cities: Ecologically Sound Approaches to Urban Space* (Montreal: Black Rose, 1990); Brenda and Robert Vale, *Green Architecture: Design for a Sustainable Future* (London: Thames & Hudson, 1991); David Nicholson-Lord, *The Greening of the Cities* (New York: Routledge, 1987); Anne Whiston Spirn, *The Granite Garden: Urban Nature and Human Design* (New York: Basic Books, 1984); David Engwicht, *Reclaiming Our Cities and Towns: Better Living with Less Traffic* (Philadelphia: New Society Publishers, 1993): Bob Walter, Lois Arkin, and Richard Grenshaw, (eds), *Sustainable Cities: Concepts and Strategies for Eco-City Development* (Los Angeles: Eco-Home Media, 1992): and Mark Francis, Lisa Cashdan, and Lynn Paxson, *Community Open Spaces: Greening Neighborhoods Through Community Action and Land Conservation* (Washington, DC: Island Press, 1984).

2. This deficiency in standard accounts of the history of environmentalism is discussed in Marcy Darnovsky, 'Stories Less Told: Histories of US Enviornmentalism,' *Socialist Review* 22, 4 (October−December, 1992), pp. 11−54.

3. David Goode, in Gordon (ed.), *Green Cities*, p. 7.

4. See Robert E. Foglesong, *Planning the Capitalist City: The Colonial Era to the 1920s* (Princeton University Press, 1986), pp. 89−123.

5. Edward O. Wilson and Stephen Kellert (eds), *The Biophilia Hypothesis* (Covelo, Cal.: Island Press, 1993).

6. Christine Boyer provides an admirable history of the transition from the age of the voluntary improver to the professional planner, in *Dreaming the Rational City: The Myth of American City Planning* (Cambridge, Mass.: MIT Press, 1983).

7. Rosalyn Deutsche's work on this topic has been exemplary, in articles like 'The Fine Art of Gentrification' (with Cara Ryan), *October*, 31 (Winter 1984), pp. 91–111: 'Krzysztof Wodiczko's *Homeless Projection* and the Site of Urban 'Revitalization,'' *October*, 38 (Fall 1986), pp. 63–98; 'Alternative Space,' in Brian Wallis (ed), *If You Lived Here: The City in Art, Theory and Social Activism* (a project by Martha Rosler), (Seattle: Bay Press, 1991); and 'Uneven Development: Public Art in New York City,' in Diane Ghirardo (ed), *Out of Site: A Social Criticism of Architecture* (Seattle: Bay Press, 1991), pp. 157–219, which includes a discussion of the Battery Park City site. The latest example of developers' exploitation of public art was the siting of avant-garde installations in storefronts, theaters, and on marquees on 42nd Street in the summer of 1993, a project supported and sponsored by the 42nd Street Development Project partly to ease the transition between the eviction of hundreds of small businesses and the planned gentrification of the Times Square area.

8. Quoted in Josh Barbanel, 'Explosion at the Twin Towers: Tougher Code May Not Have Helped,' *New York Times*, (February 27, 1993) sec. 1, p. 24.

9. Ada Louise Huxtable, 'Big But Not So Bold,' *New York Times* (April 5, 1973), sec. 1, p. 34.

10. Leonard Ruchelman, *The World Trade Center: The Politics and Policies of Skyscraper Development* (Syracuse University Press, 1977), p. 20: Downtown Lower Manhattan Association, *Planning for Lower Manhattan* (New York, 1969), p. 6.

11. Ralph Nader's Study Group on the First National City Bank called for an IRS investigation into this loan-syndicate's activities. See David Leinsdorf and Donald Etra, *Citibank* (New York: Grossman, 1973), pp. 141–9.

12. 'Analysis of World Trade Center Occupancy and Rentals,' Audit Report, New York Authority Division of Audits and Accounts, State of New York, February 6, 1981.

13. Quoted in Huxtable, 'Big But Not So Bold.'

14. Theodore Kheel, 'How the WTC is Strangling New York City,' *New York Magazine* (May 1969).

15. Jewel Bellush and Murray Hausknecht, *Urban Renewal: People, Politics and Planning* (Garden City, NY: Anchor Books, 1967); and William Tabb and Larry Sawyer, *Marxism and the Metropolis: New Perspectives in Urban Political Economy* (New York: Oxford University Press, 1978).

16. Michael Sorkin, *Exquisite Corpse: Writing on Buildings* (London: Verso, 1991), p. 299.

17. The Port Authority had replied to such a charge in the 1980 audit report by insisting that WTC tenants 'represent a comprehensive cross-section of world trade activity' and that a survey of tenants revealed rising profits in seven out of ten cases on account of the proximity to firms involved in world trade facilitated by the centralized community of the WTC. See Audit Report, Appendix B.

18. Saskia Sassen, *The Global City: New York, London, Tokyo* (Princeton University Press, 1992).

19. See Robert Fitch's exhaustive account of the impact of a FIRE (finance, insurance, and real estate) economy on the city, in *The Assassination of New York* (London: Verso, 1993).

20. Joel Garreau, *Edge City: Life on the New Frontier* (New York: Anchor, 1988),

pp. 9, 14.

21. Mike Davis, 'Urban Control: The Ecology of Fear' (Westfield, New Jersey: Open Magazine Pamphlet #23, 1992), p. 20.

22. Castells argues that environmentalism is the most complete expression of what he calls 'the urban ideology.' See *The Urban Question: A Marxist Approach*, trans. Alan Sheridan (Cambridge, Mass.: MIT Press, 1980), pp. 184—91, and also pp. 73—112.

23. Peter Hall, *Cities of Tomorrow* (Oxford: Basil Blackwell, 1988), p. 35.

24. Patrick Geddes, *Cities in Evolution* (1915 rpt; New York: Howard Fertig, 1968), p. 26.

25. Ibid., p. 97.

26. Robert E. Park, Ernest W. Burgess, and Roderick McKenzie, *The City* (University of Chicago Press, 1925), pp. 73—6.

27. Park, 'Suggestions for the Investigation of Human Behavior in the Urban Environment,' in Ibid., p. 45.

28. Rodrick McKenzie, 'The Growth of the City: An Introduction to a Research Project,' in Park *et al.*, *The City*, pp. 56—7.

29. Park *et al.*, *The City*, pp. 53—9.

30. Rodrick Wallace, 'A Synergism of Plagues: 'Planned Shrinkage,' Contagious Housing Destruction, and AIDS in the Bronx,' *Enviornmental Research* 47 (1988), pp. 1—33.

31. In an earlier article, Wallace discusses the 'incubation' period of fire contagion in the South Bronx and Bushwick, Brooklyn. 'Contagion and Incubation in New York City Structural Fires 1964—1976,' *Human Ecology*, 6, 4 (1978), pp. 423—38.

32. Rodrick Wallace and Deborah Wallace, 'Origins of Public Health Collapse in New York City,' *Bulletin of the New York Academy of Medicine*, 66, 5 (September/October, 1990), pp. 427—8.

33. Peter Salins, *The Ecology of Housing Destruction* (New York University Press, 1980), p. 2.

34. Salins, *Ecology*, p. 13.

35. Peter Salins and Gerard Mildner, *Scarcity by Design: The Legacy of New York City's Housing Policies* (Cambridge, Mass.: Harvard University Press, 1992).

36. For a typical example of this approach to urban analysis, see *The Urban Ecosystem: A Holistic Approach*, the report of a 1973 Institute of Ecology workshop, edited by Forest Stearns and Tom Montag (Stroudsburg, Pennsylvania: Dowden, Hutchinson & Ross, 1974). For a case study, see Stephen Boyden, Sheelagh Millar, Ken Newcombe, and Beverley O'Neill, *The Ecology of a City and its People: The Case of Hong Kong* (Canberra: Australian National University, 1981).

37. Boyer, *Dreaming*, p. 217.

38. James O'Connor, *The Fiscal Crisis of the State* (New York: St. Martin's Press, 1973).

39. Eric Lichten, *Class, Power and Austerity: The New York City Fiscal Crisis* (South Hadley, Mass.: Bergin & Harvey, 1986).

40. Ibid., p. 177.

41. William Tabb, *The Long Default: New York City and the Urban Fiscal Crisis* (New York: Monthly Review Press, 1982), pp. 15—20.

42. Alberta Sbragia, 'Finance Capital and the City,' in Mark Gottdiener (ed.), *Cities in Stress: A New Look at the Urban Crisis* (Beverly Hills: Sage, 1986), pp. 199—220.

43. Eric Goldstein and Mark Izeman, *The New York Environment Book* Natural Resources Defense Council (Washington, DC: Island Press, 1990).

44. Murray Bookchin takes Marx's formulation in *Capital* — 'the whole of economical history is summed up in the . . . antithesis' between 'town and country' — as the origin of his own history of urbanization in *The Limits of the City* (1974 rpt; Montreal: Black Rose, 1986).

45. Murray Bookchin, *Urbanization Without Cities: The Rise and Decline of Citizenship* (Montreal: Black Rose, 1992), pp. ix—x; see also *The Limits of the City*.

46. See my discussion of 'black invisibility' in the film in 'Ballots, Bullets and Batmen: Can Cultural Studies do the Right Thing?' *Screen* 31, 1 (Spring 1990).

47. Fitch, *The Assassination of New York*, p. xvii. See especially 'The Deal of a Dynasty,' pp. 185—205.

48. Ever since the Wagner Report of the Commission on the Year 2000 reaffirmed the RPA's 1929 designs by recommending the development of New York's waterfront (*New York Ascendant: Report of the Commission on the Year 2000* [New York: Harper & Row, 1987], pp. 47—50), a myriad of plans have entered the public arena. The most extensive is for the riverfront development of Manhattan's West Side, from Battery Park City to 59th Street, to include parks, recreational facilities, an expressway, and residential and corporate buildings. The project, entrusted to a subsidiary of the state's Urban Development Corporation called the Hudson River Park Conservancy, has been fought at every step by the Clean Air Campaign, the New York Public Interest Research Group and other civic organizations who filed suit to halt any implementation of the plan until environmental impact statements had been prepared.

49. Mike Davis, 'Urban Control: The Ecology of Fear.'

50. Neil Smith, 'New City, New Frontier: The Lower East Side as Wild, Wild West,' in Michael Sorkin (ed.), *Variations on a Theme Park: The New American City and the End of Public Space* (New York: Hill & Wang, 1992), pp. 61—93: and 'Gentrification, the Frontier and the Restructuring of Urban Space,' in Neil Smith and P. Williams (eds), *Gentrification of the City* (London: Allen & Unwin, 1986), pp. 15—34.

51. Louis Wirth, 'Urbanism as a Way of Life,' in Paul Hatt and Albert Reiss (eds), *Cities and Society* (Glencoe, Ill.: Free Press, 1957), p. 56.

52. Jim Stratton, *Pioneers in the Urban Wilderness* (New York: Urizen Press, 1977), p. 7.

53. This is the story told in James R. Hudson, *The Unanticipated City: Loft Conversions in Lower Manhattan* (Amherst: University of Massachusetts Press, 1987).

54. Sharon Zukin argues that the recycling of old buildings in areas where values were destined, eventually, to rise filled an important investment niche in the period between real-estate booms in the early 1970s. The full impact of the loft-living movement may have been unplanned, but it was hardly spontaneous: 'in the grand scheme of things, loft living gave the *coup de grâce* to the old manufacturing base of cities like New York and brought on the final stage of their transformation in service-sector capitals,' *Loft Living: Culture and Capital in Urban Change* (Baltimore: Johns Hopkins University Press, 1982), pp. 191—2.

55. For an 'invasion-succession' analysis of SoHo, see James Hudson, 'SoHo: A Study of Residential Invasion of a Commercial and Industrial Area,' *Urban Affairs Quarterly*, 20, 1 (September 1984), pp. 46—63.

56. Saskia Sassen, *The Global City*; Manuel Castells, *The Informational City* (Cambridge, Mass.: MIT Press, 1989).

57. 'The Seekers,' *The Nation* (July 26, 1993), p. 124.

58. Quoted in Alison Mitchell, 'The Two Towers: Sifting Through Mideast Politics in Ashes of World Trade Center,' *New York Times*, (March 14, 1993), sec. 1, p. 1.

59. Robert I. Friedman, 'The Four Questions,' *Village Voice* (March 8, 1994), p. 23.

60. Robert Stone, 'The New Barbarians,' *New York Times*, (March 4, 1993), sec. A, p. 25.

3. The Ecology of Images

1. For example, see Paul Virilio, *L'Ecran du désert: Chroniques de guerre* (Paris: Galilée, 1991); and James Der Derian, *Antidiplomacy: Spies, Terror, Speed and War* (Oxford: Blackwell, 1992).

2. Noam Chomsky, 'The "Gulf War" in Retrospect,' in Nancy Peters (ed.), *War After War* (San Francisco: City Lights Books, 1992), pp. 13−16.

3. George Gerbner, 'Persian Gulf War: The Movie,' in Hamid Mowlana, George Gerbner, and Herbert Schiller (eds), *Triumph of the Image: The Media's War in the Persian Gulf: A Global Perspective* (Boulder, Co.: Westview Press, 1992), pp. 243−65. Douglas Kellner generally supports this view in *The Persian Gulf TV War* (Boulder, Co.: Westview Press, 1992).

4. A study of TV viewers conducted by Sut Jhally, Justin Lewis, and Michael Morgan concluded that the more people watched the TV Gulf War the less they knew about US policy and the Middle Eastern situation. 'More Viewing, less Knowledge,' in Mowlana et al (eds), *Triumph of the Image*, pp. 216−33.

5. William Arkin, Damian Durrant, and Marianne Cherni, *On Impact, Modern Warfare and the Environment: A Case Study of the Gulf War* (London: Greenpeace, 1991), p. 1.

6. Individual journalists and the alternative press launched the lawsuits and provided the criticism. For a sample of views on this issue, see John MacArthur, *Second Front Censorship: Propaganda in the Gulf War* (New York: Hill & Wang, 1992); Hedrick Smith (ed.), *The Media and the Gulf War: The Press and Democracy in Wartime* (Washington DC: Seven Locks Press, 1992); The Gannett Foundation Report, *The Media at War: The Press and the Persian Gulf Conflict* (New York: Gannett Foundation/ Freedom Forum, 1991).

7. Meadows' comments are reported by Grace Paley in 'Something About the Peace Movement,' in Victoria Brittain (ed.), *The Gulf Between Us: The Gulf War and Beyond* (London: Virago, 1991), pp. 75−6.

8. T.M. Hawley, *Against the Fires of Hell: The Environmental Disaster of the Gulf War* (New York: Harcourt Brace Jovanovich, 1992), p. 46−7. Hawley reports that Kuwaiti Oil Company employees prevented a much greater spill by switching valves on the storage tanks while the Iraqi occupiers had temporarily abandoned the facility.

9. Jassim Mohammad al-Hassan, *The Iraqi Invasion of Kuwait: An Environmental Catastrophe* (Kuwait City: Department of Biochemistry, Kuwait University, 1992).

10. These estimates are from the Greenpeace report, *On Impact*. An Iraqi Health Ministry report from January 1994 claimed that 400,000 civilians, a third of them under the age of 5, had died as a result of sanctions imposed in 1990. Two million others were currently suffering from malnutrition.

11. Susan Sontag, *On Photography* (New York: Dell, 1977); page references are cited hereafter as *OP*.

12. On the other hand, Sontag's remarks about 'credible forms of lust' may remind many of us of the debate within film theory about psychoanalytical descriptions of the role of sexuality in visual pleasure. As it happens, I don't think this is a productive path to pursue − for the following reason. For Sontag, the

visual – the field of vision – is not an element in the *construction* of reality, as it is for most film theorists. Images, for her, are fundamentally a *substitute* for reality. In her model, image addiction ultimately determines our diet – our need to 'consume' more and more images reduces our tolerance for more nutritious encounters with reality. The result à la Balzac (a man of considerable girth, it should be remembered) is a thinner body of attention to the real world. The operative model of health in this analogy is strictly biological; there is no room for psychosexual, or even biocultural determinants. In this respect, there seems to be little common ground between feminist film theory's assumption that 'perversions' are a normative aspect of our relation to images, and Sontag's view that our addiction to images is a fundamentally unhealthy, even immoral perversion.

13. John Waters, *Shock Value* (New York: Delta, 1981), p. 272.

14. Bill McKibben, *The Age of Missing Information* (New York: Random House, 1992).

15. Larry Fessenden (with Michael Ellenbogen), *Low Impact Filmmaking* (New York: Glass Eye Pix, 1993).

16. Paul Virilio, *War and Cinema: The Logistics of Perception* (London: Verso, 1989). Less interesting, and more conventional, are his comments about the linkage between ecology and the global media explosion: 'this planetary shrinkage will have fatal consequences for social and moral life. It is time to create an ecology of the media' (*L'Ecran du désert*, p. 71). Throughout this book, he invokes the 'media pollution' of the Gulf War as one more element to add to the ecological damage caused by the hostilities.

17. Virilio, *War and Cinema*, p. 15. Griffith's comment reminds us of so many discussions about the lack of any visible enemy sightings in the Gulf War, not only for TV audiences, but for combatants themselves. Saudi gravedigging teams were delegated to each Allied unit in order to dig the mass graves for the Iraqi dead. While this action was officially taken for religious reasons, the result was that Western soldiers were prohibited from seeing the people they had killed.

18. Joni Seager, *Atlas Survey of the State of the Earth* (New York: Simon & Schuster, 1990).

19. Geoffrey Lean, Don Hinrichsen, and Adam Markham, *World Wildlife Fund Atlas of the Environment* (New York: Prentice Hall, 1990); and Michael Kidron and Ronald Segal, *The New State of the World Atlas* (New York: Simon & Schuster, 1987).

20. For a bioregional map of the world, see Miklos D.F. Udvardy, *World Biogeographical Provinces Map* (Sausalito, Ca.: Co-Evolution Quarterly, 1975).

21. Norman Myers (ed.), *Gaia: An Atlas of Planet Management*, (London: Gaia Books, 1984); Lee Durrell, *Gaia State of the Ark Atlas* (London: Gaia Books, 1986); Frank Barnaby (ed.), *Gaia Peace Atlas* (London: Gaia Books, 1988).

22. The remote-sensing, earth-imaging technologies developed through LandSat and NASA have encouraged a similar kind of one-worldism. Crucial to displaying the changes wrought by land development, their 'god's-eye' view of earth nonetheless helps to desocialize – 'there is nowhere else to go' – any further analysis of the material causes and effects of environmental deterioration on the ground. For a good example, see Payson Stevens and Kevin Kelley, *Embracing Earth: New Views of our Changing Planet* (San Francisco: Chronicle Books, 1992).

23. For studies of the politics of cartographic representation, see Denis Wood, *The Power of Maps* (New York: Guildford Press, 1992): Mark Monmonier, *How to Lie with Maps* (University of Chicago Press, 1991).

24. Those who know the film will remember that the plot itself doesn't seem to 'work,' since the Alien reactor can only be activated by a three-fingered Martian fingerprint, and not by the human hand of Quaid that Verhoeven utilizes to do

the job. Dan O'Bannon, the original scriptwriter, has argued that this inaccuracy is symptomatic of the film's overall failure. In O'Bannon's script, Quaid, who discovers that he is the resurrection of a Martian race in a synthetic human body, uses the Alien technology to totally recall his own identity. The ending chosen by Verhoeven, in spite of its diegetic flaws, seems to be more faithful to the film's social ambition. Carl Brandon, 'Total Recall: Dan O'Bannon on Why It Doesn't Work,' Cinefantastique 21, 5 (April 1991), pp. 36—7.

25. By the time of the fall 1991 season, a 900 number, called the Twin Peaks Sheriff's Office Hotline, was being operated by Lynch-Frost Productions. The phoneline recapped the previous night's episode and included new clues and information. A portion of the revenue was to be set aside for 'environmental causes.' The environmental questions raised by the show cannot, of course, be divorced from the historical psychopathologies of David Lynch himself; for example, his history as an Eagle Scout from Montana, who fondly recalls camping trips in the Northwestern forests with his father, a research scientist with the US Forestry Service who wrote his doctoral dissertation on the Ponderosa Pine.

26. Carole Gallagher, *America Ground Zero: The Secret Nuclear War* (Boston, 1993); Peter Goin, *Nuclear Landscapes* (Baltimore: Johns Hopkins University Press, 1991); Richard Misrach, *Desert Cantos* (Albuquerque, 1987), and *Violent Cantos: Three Cantos* (New York, 1992). See Mike Davis's commentary on these books and the activist backdrop to the work of the Atomic Photographer's Guild in 'Ecocide in Marlboro County,' *New Left Review*, 200 (July/August 1993), pp. 49—74.

27. Ward Churchill, 'The Struggle for Newe Segobia,' *Z Magazine*, 5, 7/8 (July/ August 1992), pp. 92—6. See also Churchill's 'Radioactive Colonization: Hidden Holocaust in Native North America,' *Struggle for the Land: Indigenous Resistance to Genocide, Ecocide and Expropriation in Contemporary North America* (Monroe, Maine: Common Courage Press, 1993), pp. 261—328.

28. Richard Misrach (with Myriam Weisang Misrach), *Bravo 20: The Bombing of the American West* (Baltimore: Johns Hopkins University Press, 1990) (hereafter cited as *B*).

29. Deborah Bright, 'Of Mother Nature and Marlboro Men: An Inquiry into the Cultural Meanings of Landscape Photography,' in Richard Bolton (ed.), *The Contest of Meaning: Critical Histories of Photography* (Cambridge, Mass.: MIT Press, 1989), pp. 125—44.

30. See Kenneth Jarecke's desert photographs from the Gulf War in *Just Another War*, with text by Exene Cervenka (Joliet, Mont.: Bedrock Press, 1992).

31. Peter Goin, *Nuclear Landscapes*, p. 18.

4. Wet, Dark, and Low, Eco-Man Evolves from Eco-Woman

1. Anne Matthews, *Where the Buffalo Roam: The Storm Over the Revolutionary Plan to Restore America's Great Plains* (New York: Grove Weidenfeld, 1992). Ward Churchill suggests that the proposal be taken one step further, by restoring the lands to Indian peoples as the basis for a much larger North American Union of Indigenous Nations. 'I Am An Indigenist,' in *Struggle for the Land* (Monroe, Maine: Common Courage Press, 1993), pp. 425—31.

2. Carolyn Merchant notes the effects of diminished forestland in *The Death of Nature: Women, Ecology and the Scientific Revolution* (San Francisco: Harper & Row, 1980): 'By the late thirteenth century in London, it was becoming necessary to

import sea coal from Newcastle, a soft coal with a high sulfur content which when burned polluted the air with black soot and irritating, choking smoke' (p. 62). In Merchant's account, the demographic collapse of the fourteenth century helped the forests recover until the sixteenth century, when a more advanced ecological crisis, caused by the destruction of forests for naval construction, helped generate the first movement for conservation and a new managerial approach to nature, exemplified by John Evelyn's *Discourse on Forest Trees* (1662).

3. See my discussion of *Batman* and *Do the Right Thing* in 'Ballots, Bullets and Batmen: Can Cultural Studies do the Right Thing?,' *Screen*, 31, 1 (Spring 1990).

4. See Vivien Sobchak, 'Child/Alien/Father: Patriarchal Crisis and Generic Exchange,' *Camera Obscura*, 15 (1986), pp. 7–34.

5. Christopher Harding (ed.), *Wingspan: Inside the Men's Movement* (New York: St, Martins Press, 1992).

6. Other movement literature includes: Marvin Allen, *In the Company of Men: Freeing the Masculine Heart* (New York: Random House, 1993); Herb Goldberg, *The Inner Male: Overcoming Roadblocks to Intimacy* (New York: New American Library, 1987); James Wyly, *The Phallic Quest: Priapus and Masculine Inflation* (Toronto: Inner City Books, 1989); Samuel Osherson, *Finding Our Fathers: The Unfinished Business of Manhood* (New York: Free Press, 1986); Michael Meade, *Men and the Water of Life: Initiation and the Tempering of Men* (San Francisco: HarperSanFrancisco, 1993): Robert Moore and Douglas Gillette, *The Lover Within: Accessing the Male Lover in the Male Psyche* (New York: Morrow, 1993); Michael Sky, *Sexual Peace: Beyond the Dominator Virus* (New York: Bear and Co., 1993); Guy Corneau, *Absent Fathers, Lost Sons: The Search for Masculine Identity* (Boston: Shambala, 1991); Stuart Miller, *Men and Friendship* (Los Angeles: J.P. Tarcher, 1992); John Lee, *At My Father's Wedding* (New York: Bantam, 1991); Gregory Max Vogt, *Return to Father: Archetypal Dimensions of the Patriarch* (Dallas, Tex.: Spring Publications, 1991); Richard Rohr and Joseph Martos, *The Wild Man's Journey: Reflections on Male Spirituality* (Cincinnati: St. Anthony Messenger, 1992); and Patrick Arnold, *Wildmen, Warriors and Kings: Masculine Spirituality and the Bible* (New York: Crossroad, 1991). Aside from *Wingspan*, periodicals include *Inroads, Journeymen, Man!, Men's Council Journal* and *MENTOR*.

Bibliographies are to be found in *Men's Issues* (American Association of Counselling and Development Committee on Men, 1987).

7. Some of the more prominent titles in this basically heterosexual literature include: Jon Snodgrass (ed.), *For Men Against Sexism: A Book of Readings* (Albion, Cal.: Times Change Press, 1977); Harry Brod (ed.), *The Making of Masculinities: The New Men's Studies* (Boston: Allen & Unwin, 1987) and *Men's Lives* (New York: Macmillan, 1990); Warren Farrell, *The Disposable Sex: The Myth of Male Power* (New York: Simon & Schuster, 1993); Jeff Hearn, *The Gender of Oppression: Men, Masculinity and the Critique of Marxism* (Brighton: Harvester, 1987) and *Men in the Public Eye* (New York: Routledge, 1992); Arthur Brittan, *Masculinity and Power* (Oxford: Basil Blackwell, 1989); J. Nichols, *Men's Liberation* (New York, Penguin, 1975); Robert Connell, *Gender and Power: Society, the Person, and Sexual Politics* (Cambridge: Polity Press, 1987); Michael Kaufman (ed), *Beyond Patriarchy: Essays by Men on Pleasure, Power and Change* (London: Oxford University Press, 1987); Paul Hoch, *White Hero, Black Beast: Racism, Sexism, and the Mask of Masculinity* (London: Pluto, 1979): Joseph Pleck, *The Myth of Masculinity* (Cambridge: MIT Press, 1981); Andrew Tolson, *The Limits of Masculinity* (London: Tavistock, 1977); Emmanuel Reynaud, *Holy Virility: The Social Construction of Masculinity* (London: Pluto, 1983); Andy Metcalfe and Martin Humphries (eds), *The Sexuality of Men* (London: Pluto, 1985); Brian Eslea, *Science and Sexual Oppression: Patriarchy's Confrontation with Women*

and Nature (London: Weidenfeld & Nicolson, 1981) and *Fathering the Unthinkable* (London: Pluto, 1983); Anthony Easthope, *What a Man's Gotta Do: The Masculine Myth in Popular Culture* (London: Paladin, 1986); Alice Jardine and Paul Smith (eds), *Men in Feminism* (New York: Methuen, 1987); Joseph Boone and Michael Cadden, *Engendering Men: The Question of Male Feminist Criticism* (New York: Routledge, 1990); Vic Seidler, *Rediscovering Masculinity: Reason, Language and Sexuality* (New York: Routledge, 1989) and *Recreating Sexual Politics* (New York: Routledge, 1991).

Journals include *Changing Men* (originally *M: Gentle Men for Gentle Justice*), *Journal of Men's Studies, NetWork, Transitions*, and *RFD* (United States) and *Achilles Heel* (Britain). In addition, Vic Seidler has edited a selection of essays from *Achilles Heel* entitled *The Achilles Heel Reader: Men, Sexual Politics, and Socialism* (London: Routledge, 1991). Bibliographies include *Men's Studies* (Littleton, Co.: Eugene August Libraries Unlimited, 1985, second edn, 1993).

8. Harry Brod, 'The Mythopoetic Men's Movement: A Political Critique,' in Christopher Harding (ed.), *Wingspan*, pp. 232–7.

9. Andrew Kimbrell, 'The Male Manifesto,' *New York Times* (June 4, 1991), sec A, p. 27.

10. Interview with Mim Udovitch, *Mirabella* (October 1992), p. 36.

11. Robert Bly, *Iron John: A Book About Men* (Reading, Mass.: Addison-Wesley, 1990), p. 46; hereafter cited as *IJ*.

12. Philomena Mariani, in 'God Is A Man,' an introduction to Mariani (ed.), *Critical Fictions: The Politics of Imaginative Writing* (Seattle: Bay Press, 1991), p. 6.

13. John Lee, *The Flying Boy: Healing the Wounded Man* (Deerfield Beach, Fla.: Health Communications, Inc., 1989).

14. Sam Keen, *Fire in the Belly: On Being a Man* (New York: Bantam, 1991), pp. 52, 55.

15. Ibid., p. 227.

16. Lynne Segal, *Slow Motion: Changing Masculinities, Changing Men* (New Brunswick: Rutgers University Press, 1990), pp. 294–7. Segal also addresses the concomitant shift of focus within the women's movement, from the concept of *equality* to that of *difference*. By the late 1970s, it was clear that only a minority of well-educated, professional, white women were benefiting directly from two decades of feminist thought and action. Overall, the situation for women had worsened in the course of the 1970s and was still stymied by the basic contradiction that compelled capitalism to exploit the cheap labor of those whose primary work was reproduction and childcare. Equality was considered unachievable in the current conditions (i.e. with capitalism as it was, and with men as they were, unwilling to eradicate their own relative power). At that point, difference became the favored concept of analysis across the whole spectrum of feminism, from cultural criticism to legal inquiry. Men's difference became a 'problem' subject to examination.

17. For a discussion of men's economic conditions, see Kathleen Gerson, *No Man's Land: Men's Changing Commitment to Family and Work* (New York: Basic Books, 1993).

18. Brittan, *Masculinity and Power*, pp. 99–100.

19. See Donna Haraway's discussion of Man the Hunter in these books and others as an outcropping of postwar militarism, in *Primate Visions: Gender, Race, and Nature in the World of Modern Science* (New York: Routledge, 1989), especially pp. 126–29, 187–88.

20. William Anderson, *Green Man: The Archetype of Our Oneness with the Earth* (New York: HarperCollins, 1990).

21. See the dialogues between Murray Bookchin and Dave Foreman representing the positions of social ecology and deep ecology, respectively, in Steve Chase (ed.), *Defending the Earth* (Boston: South End Press, 1991). From the perspective of sexual politics, some of the insults traded between the antagonists speak for themselves: Foreman is branded by Bookchin as a 'macho mountain man,' Bookchin is dismissed by Ed Abbey as a 'fat old lady' (p. 11).

22. For a global overview of the political initiatives led by women, see Rosi Braidotti et al, *Women, the Environment and Sustainable Development: Towards a Theoretical Synthesis* (London: Zed Books, 1994). Vera Norwood charts the American side of this history in *Made From This Earth: American Women and Nature* (Chapel Hill: University of North Carolina Press, 1993). Her history also includes early illustrators of flora and fauna, pioneers of nature study and nature appreciation, creators of community gardens, and proponents, like Lady Bird Johnson, of the City Beautification movement, along with female ornithologists, botanists, zoologists, and biologists. These areas are not normally associated with activism, but are crucial to the tradition of women working on an amateur or professional basis in ecology.

23. Norwood, *Made From the Earth*, pp. 154−9.

24. Vandana Shiva and Maria Mies, *Ecofeminism* (London: Zed Books, 1993); Vandana Shiva, *Staying Alive: Women, Ecology and Development* (London: Zed Press, 1988); Esther Boserup, *Women's Role in Economic Development* (London: Allen & Unwin, 1970); Rosi Braidotti, Ewa Charkiewicz, Sabine Hausler, and Sakia Wieringa, *Women, the Environment and Sustainable Development: Towards a Theoretical Synthesis* (London: Zed Books, 1994). A survey of 'women in development' literature can be found in Brinda Rao's useful *Capitalism, Nature, Socialism* pamphlet 'Dominant Constructions of Women and Nature in Social Science Literature' (published by the Center for Ecological Socialism, Santa Cruz).

25. Joni Seager, *Earth Follies: Coming to Feminist Terms with the Global Environmental Crisis* (New York: Routledge, 1993), pp. 253−79.

26. Starhawk, *Dreaming the Dark: Magic, Sex and Politics* (Boston: Beacon Press, 1982); *Truth or Dare: Encounters of Power, Authority and Mystery* (San Francisco: Harper & Row, 1988).

27. Starhawk, 'Feminism, Earth-Based Spirituality, and Ecofeminism,' in Judith Plant (ed.), *Healing the Wounds: The Promise of Ecofeminism* (Philadelphia: New Society, 1989), p. 175.

28. Andrée Collard, *Rape of the Wild: Man's Violence against Animals and the Earth* (London: Women's Press, 1988), p. 2.

29. Ibid., p. 8.

30. Ibid., p. 168.

31. See, in particular, the works of the archaeological historian Marija Gimbutas, including *The Goddesses and Gods of Old Europe, 6500−3500 B.C.: Myths and Cult Images*, rev. edn. (Berkeley: University of California Press, 1982). See also Merlin Stone, *When God Was a Woman* (New York: Harcourt Brace Jovanovich, 1976).

32. Charlene Spretnak, 'Ecofeminism: Our Roots and Flowering,' in Irene Diamond and Gloria Orenstein (eds), *Reweaving the World: The Emergence of Ecofeminism* (San Francisco: Sierra Books, 1990), p. 9.

33. Riane Eisler, *The Chalice and the Blade* (San Francisco: Harper & Row, 1988).

34. Carolyn Merchant, *The Death of Nature: Women, Ecology, and the Scientific Revolution* (New York: Harper & Row, 1980).

35. Carolyn Merchant, *Ecological Revolutions: Nature, Gender, and Science in New England* (Chapel Hill: University of North Caroline Press, 1989), p. 55. See also

William Cronon, *Changes in the Land: Indian Colonists and the Ecology of New England* (New York: Hill & Wang, 1983).

36. Merchant, *Death of Nature*, p. 50.

37. Ibid., p. 3.

38. Ynestra King, 'The Ecology of Feminism and the Feminism of Ecology,' in Plant (ed.), *Healing the Wounds*, p. 19.

39. Janet Biehl, *Rethinking Ecofeminist Politics* (Boston: South End Press,. 1991), p. 7.

40. King, 'The Ecology of Feminism,' p. 23 (King's emphasis).

41. Biehl, *Rethinking Ecofeminist Politics*, p. 95.

42. Ibid., p. 5.

43. Ibid., p. 91 (Biehl's emphasis).

44. Donna Gaines, *Teenage Wasteland: Suburbia's Dead End Kids* (New York: Pantheon, 1991), p. 190.

45. Donna Haraway, 'A Cyborg Manifesto: Science, Technology and Socialist-Feminism in the Late Twentieth-Century,' in *Simians, Cyborgs, and Women: The Reinvention of Nature* (New York: Routledge, 1991).

46. Ibid., p. 151.

47. Donna Haraway, 'Situated Knowledges: The Science Question in Feminism and the Privilege of Partial Perspective,' in *Simians, Cyborgs, and Women*, p. 201.

48. Tom Regan puts the natural-rights argument in *The Case For Animal Rights* (Berkeley and Los Angeles: University of California Press, 1983). Peter Singer argues the utilitarian case in *Animal Liberation* (New York: Avon, 1975). For eco-feminist discussion of this debate, see Josephine Donovan, 'Animal Rights and Feminist Theory' (pp. 167—94) and Lori Guen, 'Dismantling Oppression: An Analysis of the Connection Between Women and Animals,' in Greta Gaard (ed.), *Ecofeminism: Women, Animals, Nature* (Philadelphia: Temple University Press, 1993), pp. 60—90.

49. Collard, *Rape of the Wild*, p. 2.

50. Haraway, 'Situated Knowledges,' p. 199; Ursula LeGuin, *Buffalo Gals and Other Animal Presences* (New York: New American Library, 1987).

51. Haraway, 'Introduction,' *Simians, Cyborgs, and Women*, p. 3.

52. Sherman Alexie, 'White Men Can't Drum,' *New York Times*, October 4, 1992, sec. 6, p. 30.

5. Superbiology

1. Robert Teitelbaum gives a detailed account in *Gene Dreams: Wall Street, Academia, and the Rise of Biotechnology* (New York: Basic Books, 1989). See also Sharon McAuliffe and Kathleen McAuliffe, *Life For Sale* (New York: Coward, McCann & Geoghegan, 1981).

2. Sheldon Krimsky, *Biotechnics: The Rise of Industrial Genetics* (New York: Praeger, 1991), pp. 30—1.

3. Richard Lewontin, *Biology as Ideology: The Doctrine of DNA* (New York: HarperCollins, 1991), p. 74.

4. *Genewatch*, 7 (November 1991); also see 'Science and Wall Street,' in Krimsky, *Biotechnics*, pp. 59—82: and Martin Kenney, *Biotechnology: The University-Industrial Complex* (New Haven: Yale University Press, 1986).

5. See E.J. Yoxen, 'Constructing Genetic Diseases,' in Troy Duster and Karen Garret (eds), *Cultural Perspectives on Biological Knowledge* (Norwood, N.J.: Ablex, 1984), pp. 41—62.

6. Charles Piller and Keith Yamamoto, *Gene Wars: Military Control over the New Genetic Technologies* (New York: William Morrow, 1988).

7. Dorothy Nelkin and Laurence Tancredi, *Dangerous Diagnostics: The Social Power of Biological Information* (New York: Basic Books, 1989).

8. See Pat Spallone, *Generation Games: Genetic Engineering and the Future for our Lives* (Philadelphia: Temple University Press, 1992); and Vandana Shiva, *Monocultures of the Mind: Perspectives on Biodiversity and Biotechnology* (London: Zed Books, 1993).

9. Ruth Hubbard and Elijah Wald, *Exploding the Gene Myth* (Boston: Beacon Press, 1993), p. 16.

10. Troy Duster, *Back Door to Eugenics* (New York and London: Routledge, 1990). See also Daniel Kevles, *In the Name of Eugenics* (Berkeley: University of California Press, 1985); and 'Out of Eugenics,' in Kevles and Leroy Hood (eds), *The Code of Codes: Scientific and Social Issues in the Human Genome Project* (Cambridge, Mass.: Harvard University Press, 1992); and Richard Lerner, *Final Solutions: Biology, Prejudice, and Genocide* (College Park, Pennsylvania: Penn State University Press, 1992).

11. Carl Degler, *In Search of Human Nature: The Decline and Revival of Darwinism in American Social Thought* (Oxford University Press, 1991).

12. Evelyn Fox Keller, 'Nature, Nurture, and the Human Genome Project,' in Kevles and Hood (eds), *The Code of Codes*, pp. 288−90.

13. On these respective questions, see Robert M. Young's *Darwin's Metaphor: Nature's Place in Victorian Culture* (Cambridge University Press, 1985), especially, pp. 79−125; and Stephen Jay Gould's 'Darwin's Dilemma: The Odyssey of Evolution,' in *Ever Since Darwin: Reflections in Natural History* (New York: Norton, 1977), pp. 34−8.

14. Edward O. Wilson, *Sociobiology* (Cambridge, Mass.: Harvard University Press, 1980 [abridged edn]) p. 271.

15. Richard Dawkins, *The Selfish Gene* (London: Oxford University Press, 1976), preface.

16. Edward O. Wilson, *On Human Nature* (Cambridge, Mass.: Harvard University Press, 1978), pp. 5−6.

17. R.C. Lewontin, Steven Rose, and Leon Kamin present an exhaustive critique of the link with neoconservatism in *Not in Our Genes: Biology, Ideology and Human Nature* (New York: Pantheon, 1984); see also Martin Barker, *The New Racism: Conservatives and the Ideology of the Tribe* (Fredrick Md.: Aletheia Books, University Publications of America, 1981).

18. See Judith Reitman, 'Jungle Fever: Is Violence in the Genes?' *Village Voice* (August 17, 1993), p. 35.

19. See the collection of critical essays edited by Ashley Montagu, *Sociobiology Examined* (London: Oxford University Press, 1980); also, Marshall Sahlins's anthropological critique in *The Use and Abuse of Biology* (Ann Arbor: University of Michigan Press, 1977); Philip Kitcher, *Vaulting Ambition: Sociobiology and the Quest for Human Nature* (Cambridge, Mass.: MIT Press, 1987); and Richard Lewontin, *Biology as Ideology*.

20. Lewontin, Rose and Kamin, *Not in Our Genes*, p. 249.

21. Richard Dawkins, *The Selfish Gene*, p. 2.

22. Ibid., p. 9.

23. Ibid., p. 4. See, also, Robert Axelrod's elaboration, through game theory, of these issues in *The Evolution of Cooperation* (New York: Basic Books, 1984).

24. Wilson operates on a similar limited choice argument when he projects sociobiology onto the terrain of biodiversity. In an article in *The New York Times Magazine* (May 30, 1993) entitled 'Is Humanity Suicidal?' he extends the obsession

with sacrifice and altruism to the concept of a genetically programmed drive to self-extinction. Cheesily reprising the 'zoologist from another planet' from *Sociobiology*, his article begins: 'Imagine that on an icy moon of Jupiter — say, Ganymede — the space station of an alien civilization is concealed. For millions of years its scientists have closely watched the earth · · ·' waiting for the moment when a carnivorous primate comes to rule the world and destroy its biosphere. 'The human species,' Wilson speculates, is 'an environmental abnormality. It is possible that intelligence in the wrong kind of species was foreordained to be a fatal combination for the biosphere. Perhaps a law of evolution is that intelligence usually extinguishes itself · · · Is humanity suicidal? Is the drive to environmental conquest embedded so deeply in our genes as to be unstoppable?' No, there is still some time remaining, concludes Wilson, but not before he divides the entire spectrum of opinion into two camps — exemptionalist and environmentalist. The first is the 'don't worry, be happy' option; the second proposes that we obey the constraints of our natural environment. Are these our only choices?

25. Stephen Jay Gould, 'Biological Potentiality vs. Biological Determinism,' in *Ever Since Darwin: Reflections in Natural History* (New York: Norton, 1979), pp. 251–60.

26. Robert M. Young, *Darwin's Metaphor: Nature's Place in Victorian Culture* (Cambridge University Press, 1985).

27. Robert M. Young, 'Darwin's Metaphor and the Philosophy of Science,' *Science as Culture* 3, 3 (1993), pp. 375–403.

28. Donald Worster gives a lucid account of these contradictions in *Nature's Economy: A History of Ecological Ideas* (Cambridge University Press, 1985), pp. 113–89.

29. Richard Hofstader tells the story well in *Social Darwinism in American Thought* (1944 rpt; Boston: Beacon Press, 1955).

30. Recycling is probably not the most prudent course for a consumer society to adopt. Unlike the policy of reuse, which facilitates local distribution, the more expensive process of recycling is heavily favored by business interests for its promotion of centralized production, long-distance distribution, and the perpetuation of the consumerist ethics of disposability and obsolescence. See Simon Fairlie, 'Long Distance, Short Life: Why Big Business Favours Recycling,' *The Ecologist*, 22, 6 (November/December 1922), pp. 276–83.

31. See Nicholas Xenos's fine account of this history in *Scarcity and Modernity* (London and New York: Routledge, 1989).

32. Victor Papanek cites these examples as models for green design in *Design for the Real World: Human Ecology and Social Change*, revised edn (London: Thames & Hudson, 1984).

Index